Making Global Norms

Making Global Norms

Politics versus Science in International Organizations

Alexandros Kentikelenis
Leonard Seabrooke

Oxford University Press is a department of the University of Oxford.
It furthers the University's objective of excellence in research, scholarship,
and education by publishing worldwide. Oxford is a registered trade mark of
Oxford University Press in the UK and in certain other countries.

Published in the United States of America by Oxford University Press
198 Madison Avenue, New York, NY 10016, United States of America.

© Oxford University Press 2025

This is an open access publication, available online and distributed under the terms of a Creative
Commons Attribution-Non Commercial-No Derivatives 4.0 International license (CC BY-NC-ND 4.0),
a copy of which is available at https://creativecommons.org/licenses/by-nc-nd/4.0/.
Subject to this license, all rights are reserved.

Inquiries concerning reproduction outside the scope of the above should be sent
to the Rights Department, Oxford University Press, at the address above.

You must not circulate this work in any other form
and you must impose this same condition on any acquirer.

CIP data is on file at the Library of Congress.

ISBN 9780197828625

ISBN 9780197828618 (hbk.)

DOI: 10.1093/9780197828656.001.0001

The manufacturer's authorized representative in the EU for product safety is
Oxford University Press España S.A. of Parque Empresarial San Fernando de Henares,
Avenida de Castilla, 2 – 28830 Madrid (www.oup.es/en or product.safety@oup.com).
OUP España S.A. also acts as importer into Spain of products made by the manufacturer.

Contents

Preface	vi
1. Politics Versus Science in International Organizations	1

PART I. PROCESSES

2. Global Norms as Contestation	25
3. How to Study Policy Scripts in International Organizations	44

PART II. SCRIPTWRITERS

4. The Board	71
5. Technocrats	100

PART III. NEGOTIATIONS

6. Sovereign Debt	127
7. Capital Controls	164
8. Taxation	194

PART IV. EXTENSIONS

9. Politics Versus Science Across Global Organizations	217
List of Archival Documents Cited	235
References	237
Index	267

Preface

This book developed through a decade of intellectual sparring and ever-blossoming friendship. We met in 2014 at a University of Warwick workshop that assembled nerds interested in the International Monetary Fund (IMF). Fundheads. Indeed, there is a vibrant academic cottage industry in Fund-watching. One could reasonably argue that the number of scholars studying the IMF, an organization that employs only 3,000 people, is outsized. But the IMF is an apex organization in the making of global policies that affect billions of people, and it has a coercive toolkit to see these policies through to their implementation the world over. The IMF shapes—sometimes determines—how governments tax people, how they engage with international trade and investment, and how they can deal with their sovereign debt. In short, the Fund is a key actor that defines how countries are integrated into global capitalism: It develops norms for appropriate domestic economic management, operationalizes them in the form of policy scripts, and then diffuses them worldwide through its conditional lending practices and economic advice.

While our empirical setting is the IMF, this is *not* a book only for Fundheads. Our ambition is to provide both a theoretical framework and a methodological toolkit to explain how policy scripts are produced across global organizational settings—a script on how to study scripts, using a multipronged methodological strategy to dissect underlying processes and putting both qualitative and quantitative techniques to work. This book is for those interested in how international organizations, large international non-governmental organizations, and even multinational enterprises and global professional-service firms shape the normative and policy underpinnings of globalization. All these types of organizations rely on the mechanisms we study in this book: a board where politics-versus-science battles are fought, and a technocratic body to provide knowledge and purported best practices.

We wrote this book in a series of bursts and flurries, mainly working together in person because it's more fun. While the lion's share of this time was spent on discussion and writing, there were also fish to grill and parks to run in. These writing meetings took place in Adelaide, Athens, and Copenhagen, reflecting our origin stories and where we light our hearths. Running the final mile to complete this book was, however, a feat we could not have achieved without a small group of scholars who took the time and effort to carefully read the whole manuscript and interrogate our reasoning: Phillip Ayoub, Mette Eilstrup-Sangiovanni, Tine Hanrieder, Mirko Heinzel, Rohan Mukherjee, and Stephanie Rickard. We are grateful for their generous engagement and hope to repay the favor. We also thank the reviewers from Oxford University Press, who provided extensive suggestions on how to improve the manuscript. All remaining errors are our own.

Over the many years of this book's gestation, we presented elements of the argument at the Australian National University, Copenhagen Business School, Geneva Graduate Institute, London School of Economics, McGill University, Norwegian Institute of International Affairs, Sciences Po, University of Amsterdam, University of Copenhagen, University of South Carolina, and University of Sydney. We also gave presentations at our regular haunts in the American Sociological Association, the International Studies Association, and the Society for the Advancement of Socio-Economics. Many thanks to those who gave generous feedback and sharp criticisms at these events. For these barbs of support, we thank Sarah Babb, Grace Ballor, Cornel Ban, André Broome, Martha Finnemore, Timon Forster, Lars Gjesvik, Oddný Helgadóttir, Witold Henisz, Stephanie Hofmann, Anja Jetschke, Stephen Kaplan, George Lawson, Andrea Liese, Annabelle Littoz-Monnet, Grégoire Mallard, Frédéric Mérand, Manuela Moschella, Sienna Maria Nordquist, Susan Park, Scott Robert Patterson, Vincent Pouliot, Ole Jacob Sending, Susan Sell, Laura Shepherd, Jakob Skovgaard, Matthias Thiemann, Liz Thurbon, Eleni Tsingou, Robert Wade, Kate Weaver, Wes Widmaier, Cornelia Woll, and Ole Willers. We are also grateful to Timon Forster, Noya Kohavi, and Emelie Nilsson for providing excellent research assistance at different stages of this project. Last, we thank Quinn Slobodian for alerting us to the treasure trove of old NATO posters, from which we drew the cover image of this book.

On the home front, Len thanks his wonderful children, Ἄρτεμις and Λεξ, for their tolerance and for embracing their father's co-author on this monograph as their ακαδημαϊκό νονό. Len thanks Ελένη for her love and intellectual encouragement.

Alex thanks the friends with whom he has shared the highs and lows of academia: Tarik Abou-Chadi, David Adler, Benjamin Braun, Catherine De Vries, Kristin Fabbe, Stephanie Hofmann, Charlotte Kühlbrand, Giovanni Menegalle, Domna Michailidou, Philipa Mladovsky, Thomas Stubbs, Isabella Weber, and Nathan Wilmers. Without their camaraderie, support, and encouragement, writing this book would have certainly been much less enjoyable.

Open access for this book is supported by the European Commission Research and Innovation Action, Horizon 2020 Framework Program project NAVIGATOR (#101094394), as well as the Norwegian Research Council's TAXLAW project (#3148259). This book contributes to both projects' methodological ambitions of learning how global organizations create policy and how that process very much depends on politics-versus-science contests over the respective issues.

Alexandros Kentikelenis and Leonard Seabrooke

1
Politics Versus Science in International Organizations

Introduction

Actorhood in globalization is notoriously diffuse. States, international organizations (IOs), corporations, civil society, and professional or faith-based communities all shape decisions over what policies are considered desirable and legitimate at the global level. This is a social process, involving hundreds—if not thousands—of individuals working collaboratively or competitively. Witness multilateral negotiations occurring in international fora like the annual COP environmental conferences, trade negotiations, United Nations (UN)-level meetings to set development goals, or Group of 20 summits. Such settings are where key decisions are made about the normative infrastructure of globalization—the behavioral prescriptions that give structure and direction to international cooperation and exchange.

This book traces the microfoundations of how norms emerge, evolve, and change at the global level. We seek to explain normmaking within IOs in two analytical steps. First, we foreground the role of individuals involved: Who does what and why? Answering these questions in a systematic and generalizable way is far from straightforward; it requires information on who these individuals are, detailed evidence on what they do in the course of their duties, and interpretation of why they behave the way they do. Second, with this knowledge at hand, we can then begin to unpack how these individuals relate to each other: How do they negotiate to reach collective decisions? Such unpacking requires in-depth analysis of the interactions between the individuals participating in global normmaking, thus foregrounding relational and dynamic explanations. We answer these core questions by decomposing the underlying complex processes into discrete, empirically traceable steps, then fitting the ensuing empirical account into a comprehensive analytical framework.

In pursuing these objectives, our theoretical starting point is humble in its embrace of complexity. On the one hand, we are ultimately interested in

Making Global Norms. Alexandros Kentikelenis and Leonard Seabrooke, Oxford University Press.
© Oxford University Press (2025). DOI: 10.1093/9780197828656.003.0001

explaining the mechanics of global-level normative change and are wary of monocausal explanations. On the other hand, we are also aware that writing a whole book on how normative change happens only to argue that 'it depends' is likely to be unedifying for most social scientists. To escape this bind—between parsimonious-but-simplistic and complex-but-inconclusive accounts—we take an analytical route that is guided by theory without being deterministic. Our quest is informed by an abductive logic that, as we explain later on, relies on a constant interrogation of emergent findings in relation to theoretical logics, and opens up the possibility of surprise in what is found.[1] To put it another way: We are not so much interested in inferring from a singular model but from social interactions that provide a better approximation of how things actually work.[2]

This book makes two core arguments. The first is that those sitting in the executive organs of IOs are best understood as dual loyalists. They are loyal not only to the constituencies they are mandated to represent but also to the professional identities from which they enter into executive roles (and to which they often return). A German representative will very likely advocate for German interests, but whether they have a background as a Ministry of Finance bureaucrat or as a private banker matters for how they establish their positions on policies relative to other board members. Similarly, the expert bureaucracies that staff IOs do not slavishly obey their scientific and technical training but also have political objectives when proposing particular policies.[3]

Politics versus science within IOs is where these dual loyalties play out, with significant deviation from what we may expect by presuming practitioners have only formal political interests. For example, the conventional thinking is that—in global economic governance—the primary divide is between Global North and Global South countries, or—in global environmental governance—between historical polluters, current polluters, and low-emission countries. Such broad categorizations can indeed be analytically meaningful, but not always. Our point is that these state-derived identities (e.g., representing a Global North country within an IO) are not the sole drivers of individuals' behavior. Members of IO governing bodies are also experts in their own right with extensive professional experience in relevant policy areas—without such a background it is unlikely that they would have been selected to represent their home authorities. In a nutshell, we argue that dual loyalties shape what content executives and policymakers will support.

---

[1] Timmermans and Tavory 2022.
[2] Martin 2022b, 41.
[3] Lang et al. 2024.

Accordingly, the second argument is that diversity in IOs matters. Changing the composition of who is present at the table where decisions are made alters what positions are represented in deliberations, even if the formal representation of official entities is stable. This point has been convincingly made by scholarship exploring decision making in settings marked by gender or racial diversity.[4] Our innovation is to introduce another dimension: the types of professional expertise that executives possess. As has long been established in the corporate governance literature, executives can trump the elite credentials of others in the room by calling on their diverse experience.[5] Why couldn't this be the case for IOs, even when those sitting around a boardroom table are formally representing different official mandates? Thus, we argue professional training and career trajectories matter for how politics and science interact within IOs. To understand how this happens, we should not default to 'flat actorhood' explanations. Rather, we should look for variation in politics-versus-science dynamics, which center around how contested an issue is and to what extent there is a scientific consensus on what to do. These factors are filtered through executives' dual loyalties and the composition of their decision-making body.

In pursuing these arguments, we treat norms as malleable and constantly evolving, rather than reflecting semipermanent equilibria that can only be upended on rare occasions. Our account's point of departure is a seemingly settled global norm. We demonstrate that how relevant actors internalize this norm can vary considerably, then proceed to show how these differently situated and socialized actors go on to modify it. We start our analysis at the end of the norm-diffusion process. Individuals become exposed to variants of dominant global norms during their training and professional socialization, then carry them forward in how they interpret the world and perform their duties. While this marks the endpoint of one cycle of norm diffusion, it also marks the beginning of a cycle of normmaking as these same individuals interact with each other to adjust, adapt, overturn, or stabilize global norms. The reason is that norms, even dominant ones, are continuously shaped by contestation, because they ultimately have distributional implications—they create winners and losers in economic, political, or cultural terms. The evidence of a recent backlash to the liberal international order clearly points to the political–economic aftermath of these distributional consequences.[6]

---

[4] Westphal and Stern 2006; Herring 2009; Miller and Del Carmen Triana 2009; Stern and Westphal 2010; Hafsi and Turgut 2013; Zhu et al. 2014.

[5] Westphal and Stern 2006.

[6] See Frieden 2019; Broz et al. 2021; Walter 2021; Colantone et al. 2022; Nordquist et al. 2024.

We demonstrate the benefits of this theoretical framework and empirical approach through an in-depth examination of one of the world's most powerful IOs: the International Monetary Fund (IMF). The organization executes its core mandate to maintain global financial stability through its two most prominent functions: lending to countries in crisis, and conducting regular economic surveillance of its members' economies. However, given its status as the focal point of the global economic governance architecture, the IMF is also a core site of global normmaking on policy areas covered by its mandate. As we cover throughout this book, key global economic norms—on fiscal and monetary policy, sovereign debt management, capital mobility, and even climate change—are negotiated within the organization, which then has to codify them. Thus, for example, the norm on the superiority of consumption-based taxation becomes operationalized as a model for how countries can introduce a value-added tax (VAT), the norm establishing the principle of debt relief becomes operationalized into a set of prescriptions for what countries need to do to secure it, and so on. In other words, the IMF serves as the key terrain for developing and operationalizing norms, in iterative cycles of negotiations. These are the processes we unpack in this book.

International Organizations as Scriptwriters

IOs structure international affairs and determine the standards of appropriate behavior for transnational actors, including states, individuals, businesses, and civil society.[7] Over time, these organizations have increased greatly in number, size, and scope. As of 2019, the Union of International Associations estimated there are 42,000 active IOs operating in different regions and policy areas.[8] Of this number, approximately 800 have a bureaucracy with administrative capacity and claims on policymaking autonomy.[9] These IOs are funded and governed by member states with distinct views on the appropriate policy priorities and how well organizational policies reflect their interests.[10] High-performing IOs are often given greater autonomy, while those perceived as less adept are kept on a tighter rein.[11]

In the course of their operations, IOs spend considerable time and effort in creating, fine-tuning, and spreading what we term 'scripts.' Scripts carry normative content, but they are not, by themselves, norms. Scripts *reflect* global

---

[7] Dezalay and Garth 2002; Halliday and Carruthers 2009; Block-Lieb and Halliday 2017.
[8] Union of International Associations 2019.
[9] Moloney 2022, 248.
[10] Heinzel et al. 2023.
[11] Hooghe and Marks 2015; Lall 2017.

norms; it is in these scripts that norms are distilled and codified into programs of action. Subsequent script modifications feed normative change. Thus, in the simplest terms, scripts define a policy problem and spell out a plan of action for how to address it.[12] Norms, by contrast, set the parameters for appropriate and legitimate action.[13] As scripts are generally approved through formal decision-making structures where the organizational membership is represented, and because they are seen to reflect the IOs' technocratic prowess, scripts developed by IOs commonly have a high degree of legitimacy and authority.[14] For these reasons they also invite the active engagement of all relevant intra-organizational actors, who collaborate or compete in generating script content. That is, each script is an outcome of an iterative negotiation process and provides a snapshot of what an organization thinks its members should do in order to treat a policy issue. By extension, the study of scripts is necessary to provide insight into the interactions that shape which policies are seen as appropriate and 'diffusable' and how, as well as the multiple power asymmetries in these processes.[15] Indeed, as we eschew monocausal arguments, ours is a search for intra-organizational variation, and we argue that the concept of scripts can empower and propel such a research objective.

Scripts are distinct from more general policy positions: The latter can be abstract preference statements, while the former identify specific (but widely applicable) measures to be taken at the national level to address a policy problem. Consider two contrasting cases. The World Bank has a policy position that tax avoidance is deleterious to economic development[16] but has not developed comprehensive guidelines and recommendations on how countries can curb it with concrete policy measures. In contrast, the Office of the UN High Commissioner for Refugees (UNHCR) both identifies that refugees are entitled to legal protection (a policy position derived from its formal

---

[12] Carruthers and Halliday 2006; Halliday et al. 2010.
[13] Finnemore 1996; Tannenwald 1999; Sending 2002; Chorev 2012a; Carpenter and Montgomery 2020.
[14] Halliday and Carruthers 2007; Boyle et al. 2015.
[15] One counterargument may be that these interactions may be primarily performative (see Ding 2020; Aykut et al. 2021). In this hypothetical line of argument, scriptwriting processes are reducible to power dynamics, so interactions between officials in formal fora are merely song and dance intended to signal to their home authorities and other audiences that appropriate processes are being followed even though the policy outcome is negotiated and known before any formal debate begins. Our view is that even in cases where this can be confirmed, it is wrong to dismiss these processes a priori as carrying little, if any, analytical payoff. At minimum, they provide information of the public positioning of states and the preferences they articulate—similar, for example, to the voluminous scholarship on world leaders' speeches at the General Debate of the UN General Assembly (e.g., Binder and Heupel 2015; Baturo et al. 2017). But even beyond this minimal threshold, scriptwriting processes contain valuable information about where and how negotiations and policy designs vary significantly from assumed state preferences and associated horse trading. As we show in the empirical chapters to follow, these processes pertain to how certain horses can be reined in and how seemingly predetermined outcomes can be changed.
[16] World Bank 2015.

mandate) and spells out how this protection is to be provided.[17] For example, UNHCR publishes detailed analyses to guide countries' decisions over who is eligible for protection and under what terms. In the case of lesbian, gay, bisexual, transgender, and intersex (LGBTI) individuals, UNHCR spells out the evidence of a 'well-founded fear of persecution' that asylum seekers need to present, and then provides procedural guidance to asylum application assessors for what to do and not do in evaluating the credibility of the claims (e.g., requesting 'medical testing' or 'photographic evidence of intimate acts' is prohibited).[18] In the case of victims of organized gangs, UNHCR explains that 'not all individuals who are affected in some way by the activities of organized gangs qualify for international protection' and then elaborates on how to ascertain the veracity of claims, how to examine whether these individuals can relocate internally within their country of origin, and under what conditions they can be excluded from refugee status.[19] These UNHCR guidelines are examples of policy scripts: They clearly define a policy problem and outline how public authorities evaluating asylum claims should operate in order to reach their decision.

Scripts are also distinct from organizational policies that spell out how an IO should treat a particular issue in the course of its own operations. For example, in recent years the IMF has acknowledged that gender inequalities have macroeconomic implications and thus fall under its purview.[20] Consequently, a new Strategy for Mainstreaming Gender in its operations sets out how IMF staff should treat gender issues in their various activities and clarifies the sequencing of this strategy and its monitorable targets.[21] This is not a policy script in our conception, because its ultimate target is changing the internal functioning of the IMF. That is, it is an internal organizational policy that affects staff actions, not a template meant to be diffused around the world. Instead, in our account, policy scripts refer to policy prescriptions that have global origins (i.e., they are products of IO decision-making processes) but target national-level policy changes: They are scripts in the sense that a policymaker can pick them up and implement them in their home country in order to deal with some policy problem.

IOs' policy scripts have a dual life. They are both instruments of the powerful to pursue their interests and tools of rationalization to encourage organizations and peoples to adopt similar conceptions of their self-interest. Those

---

[17] Kennedy 1986.
[18] UNHCR 2012.
[19] UNHCR 2010.
[20] IMF 2018; IMF 2022d; Goyal and Sahay 2023.
[21] IMF 2022d; Weaver et al. 2022. On the World Bank, see Heinzel et al. 2024.

who write scripts combine politics and science to justify their articulation and content, engaging in alliances to advance state interests while drawing on epistemic communities to justify what is appropriate. IOs contain technocracies geared toward producing best practices with scientific principles, as well as the members of their governing bodies, who not only represent state interests but also have been professionally socialized, sometimes within strong scientific cultures. This book focuses on how IOs produce scripts, as it is in these sites where politics and science intertwine.

While our interest here is in IO-produced policy scripts, we do not suggest that IOs are the only producers of scripts or that they necessarily produce scripts that become dominant globally. Many organizations—governmental, intergovernmental, nongovernmental, and private—develop distinct scripts on appropriate policy over a given issue, and these scripts are subsequently taken forward to global-level debates, where they compete with alternative scripts by other actors.[22] The case of LGBTI rights presents a case in point. The growing adoption of liberal policy scripts at the transnational level has been coupled with the rise of organizations—like the UN Family Rights Caucus or the World Congress of Families—that promote a conservative agenda on these issues and lobby both states and IOs for their introduction.[23] In environmental policy, scripts by IOs and other transnational actors spell out a range of policy responses to climate change: The IMF advocates for additional carbon taxes, the World Bank calls for halting investments in fossil fuel, while international NGOs call for banning fossil fuel exploitation altogether.[24] This polyphony points to the political and epistemic challenges involved in these processes. Yet these interorganizational processes of trying to make policy scripts dominant have already received extensive coverage in the relevant literatures and are not treated here—our focus is squarely on *intra*-organizational processes of policy 'scriptwriting.'

As the title of the book suggests, we are ultimately interested in how global *norms* are made or changed, thus begging the question of the relationship between norms and scripts. Scripts operationalize norms and spell out how these general prescriptions of appropriate behavior are to be applied in concrete contexts. Scriptwriting—because it aggregates and crystalizes the various political and scientific inputs—is the contentious codification of norms within organizational settings. Once codified, these norms have clearer application and greater staying power, as their diffusion is facilitated by their wider applicability to deal with concrete policy problems. But precisely

---

[22] Halliday and Carruthers 2007; Boyle et al. 2015.
[23] Ayoub 2014, 2015; Ayoub and Stoeckl 2023; Velasco 2023.
[24] Blondeel et al. 2019; Kentikelenis and Stubbs 2025.

because norms are essentially contested, any normative equilibria are inherently fragile: Changes in the global power distribution, scientific advances, major events, the rise of new political forces and ideologies, and pressures from an organization's external environment can all force a destabilization of the normative status quo, thereby prompting tweaks or overwrites to policy scripts. How this process plays out within IOs—the privileged terrains of global normmaking—is what this book seeks to explain.

In particular, our empirical account focuses on how the IMF develops policy scripts. As a focal organization in global economic governance, its scripts have high status and recognition. This is not to say that they are the only available scripts on macroeconomic management or even necessarily dominant. Multiple scripts circulate at the transnational level, championed by different actors. But not all are created equal; the resources and authority of some organizations accord their scripts privileged status, and IOs commonly expend extensive efforts to make them globally dominant, as this expands organizational relevance, authority, and perceived legitimacy.[25] For instance, the worldwide diffusion of bankruptcy law came from policy scripts designed within IOs and then spread directly through policy implementation and indirectly through consultancies and legal networks.[26] Once dominant, scripts can be rapidly diffused, adapted, and adopted around the world.[27] This is an altogether different process from the one we seek to explain in this book, and we do not treat interorganizational struggles over script dominance and diffusion.

How Politics and Science Shape Global Norms

The question of policy norm emergence and change has long vexed social scientists. Some scholars favor explanations that derive from world cultural systems, tracing the diffusion and institutionalization of norms and how this leads to changed policies and behaviors. Others emphasize high-level politics, as norms often have global-distributional implications and thereby elicit hands-on engagement by potentially affected states. Our view is that we need theorizing on both scientific and political drivers to produce an adequate explanation of how normmaking happens within IOs.

Sociological scholarship has a particular focus on norms as, at base, 'group-level evaluations of behavior.'[28] In the world society tradition, the stress has

---

[25] Halliday and Carruthers 2007; Boyle et al. 2015.
[26] Halliday and Carruthers 2007.
[27] Dobbin et al. 2007.
[28] Horne and Mollborn 2020, 468.

been on how global norms 'make similar behavioral claims on dissimilar actors.'[29] The nuts-and-bolts view of change here is that modern world society fosters norms as institutions, with individuals encouraged to agree on what is proper behavior. These norms diffuse across states and are enacted by individuals and organizations to make practices conform to the norm.[30] Policy scripts are a way to encourage norm compliance. While this scholarship stresses how decoupling of practices from the norm is commonplace and a source of social change,[31] the general model flows from top to bottom: from the macro-level in which norms are institutionalized; to the meso-level of organizations like state bureaucracies, epistemic communities, IOs, NGOs, professional groups, and universities; and ultimately to the micro-level of individuals who are socialized into enacting the locally dominant variant of these norms. For example, the global diffusion of the university has been explained around a norm that knowledge can be singular, universal, truthful, and comprehensible to all humans.[32] An easy criticism here is that the process is too smooth, which is supported by new literature on norm contestation (see chapter 2). We know, to stay on the last presented topic, that the spread of knowledge across universities follows competing notions of scientific truth that are linked to which groups are more socially cohesive and have access to resources to propagate transnationally.[33]

A more recent strand of this literature discusses how expert and professional networks form to control issues and determine the content of global norms. This builds on earlier work on epistemic communities of like-minded professionals and adds teeth.[34] The bite here is that those operating in epistemically oriented networks do not only seek to coordinate best practices and roll them out. Experts and professionals also actively maneuver to control what content is allowed into normmaking,[35] including the creation of in-groups and out-groups.[36] Such networks rely on exclusivity and circularity to support gatekeeping,[37] and manage norm content through corralling national-level elites, expert groups, and IOs.[38] Seeking to control norm content emerges not only from activity within and across IOs but also through the development of shared scientific practices.[39] These shared ways of working

---

[29] Finnemore 1996, 334.
[30] Boli and Thomas 1997; Meyer, Frank, et al. 1997; Drori and Meyer 2006; Meyer et al. 2006.
[31] Meyer 2010.
[32] Frank and Meyer 2020.
[33] Mirowski and Plehwe 2009; Henriksen et al. 2022.
[34] Haas 1990, 40.
[35] Breen and Eilstrup-Sangiovanni 2023.
[36] Tsingou 2015; Henriksen and Seabrooke 2016; Baker 2017; Hearson 2018; Seabrooke and Stenström 2023.
[37] Littoz-Monnet 2022.
[38] Carruthers and Halliday 2006.
[39] Clift 2018; Ban and Patenaude 2019; Thiemann et al. 2021.

are often coordinated both within the formal organization of the IO and in gray areas where new practices are legitimated.[40] This scholarship tends to link micro- and meso-levels of analysis, linking the careers and work teams of IO technocrats and elite policymakers to issue treatments for global normmaking.[41]

Political economy scholarship operates on the meso-level of analysis, identifying transnational conflicts—commonly taking place within IOs and other multilateral fora—where states, elites, and experts interact, with the aim of tracing why one party won over another.[42] Here, the focus is on high-level politics,[43] global horse trading,[44] informal backroom deals,[45] and tilting the governance scales to preserve the power of those already powerful.[46] At base these explanations view global normmaking as a product of bargaining among state representatives, who hold interests in line with the economic and geopolitical priorities of their home authorities.

These accounts may seem to contradict each other: They operate at different levels of analysis and thus illuminate different underlying social processes. It should not be surprising, then, that the respective bodies of scholarship have developed in relative isolation. But, in this book, we propose a theoretical and empirical bridge between theories of norm emergence and change. We propose a syncretic approach that enables opening up the black box of how IOs codify norms into scripts, with lessons for other types of organizations.

We propose that these processes rest on an interplay between political contestation and scientific consensus. Figure 1.1 presents the space for competing explanations of scriptwriting within IOs, locating four possibilities. Moving clockwise, A is where there is a high degree of scientific consensus but little political contestation, allowing technocratic and scientific communities to control scriptwriting. B is where there are high degrees of political contestation (i.e., competing interests by IO member states) and scientific consensus (i.e., authoritative views on what should be done vis-à-vis a given policy problem). This is where battles are likely to occur: between IO technocrats (defending their scientized logic) and their political masters (advancing core state interests), and between these political masters in the governing structures of IOs, who—as we will see—have dual loyalties: to their appointing authorities and to scientized expertise. C is where there is high political

---

[40] Kortendiek 2021; Pouliot 2021b.
[41] Ponte 2014; Coman 2020; Seabrooke and Tsingou 2021.
[42] Chase-Dunn 1998; Halliday and Carruthers 2007; Babb 2009; Babb and Chorev 2016.
[43] Thacker 1999.
[44] Dreher et al. 2015.
[45] Stone 2011, 2013.
[46] Wade 2013; Vestergaard and Wade 2013.

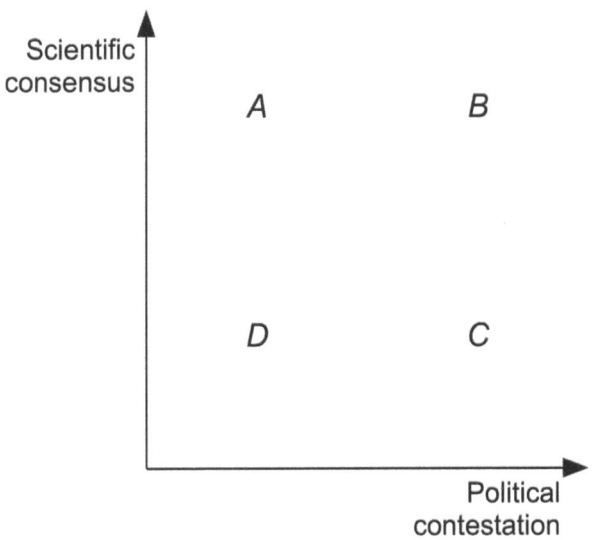

Figure 1.1 Competing explanations for scriptwriting within international organizations

contestation but low scientific consensus, allowing power politics to control scriptwriting. The final possibility, D, is the space of limited scriptwriting (as neither politics nor science can serve as guides),[47] where there is potential for norm entrepreneurship by strategic actors.[48]

Building on past scholarship, we understand scriptwriting by IOs as a process that incorporates scientific advances and power politics. First, we draw on the idea of situated individuals as enactors of global norms.[49] Individuals are socialized through educational training and professional development. They adopt epistemic frames that affirm particular global norms, often creating networks where professional affiliations shape cognitive frames on what is to be included or excluded from consideration in scriptwriting. Thus, these individuals are best understood not as agency-charged 'change agents' that can out-muscle others to forge new norms, but as enactors of dominant norms into which they have been acculturated through education and professionalization. In other words, those engaging in the politics and science of scriptwriting carry a great deal of professional, political, and cultural baggage. While they do have a capacity for action, they act through these identities and experiences.

---

[47] For exceptions, see Seabrooke et al. 2020; Bruzelius 2023.
[48] Finnemore and Sikkink 1998; Sikkink 1998; Stuenkel 2016; Müller and Wunderlich 2018.
[49] Meyer and Jepperson 2000.

Second, from theories of power politics we take the empirical focus on the parallel and mutually informing negotiation processes that underpin the generation or adaptation of global norms. Here the focus is on the bargaining over norm content, where what is to be included and excluded is driven by geopolitical strategic interests. From this view, norms are governance tools that accentuate the political and economic interests of the powerful and are part of a larger game of great-power rivalry.

Together, the joint focus on the micro-level (the educational and professional socialization of individuals) and the meso-level (the negotiations between the differently socialized and situated individuals within organizational settings) allows us to elaborate on the foundations of macro-level normative change. This is where the coalescence or clash between intra-IO scientific and power-political influences becomes crystalized into a new policy norm and its corresponding policy script. But this is not the end of the story: Once an IO reaches a position on a norm, it still has to take it forward to global-level negotiations with other organizations, including states, IOs, NGOs, and epistemic communities.[50] This is an additional process of interorganizational conflict, contestation, and negotiation that has already been covered elsewhere,[51] and is therefore not treated in this book. In short, our ambition is to bring to light the multiple *intra*-organizational processes and their cultural, political, and epistemic underpinnings.

To do this, we advance a methodological toolkit that aims to be dual purpose. The first purpose is to improve theorization on how global normmaking operates at macro-, meso-, and micro-scales. This is the flow (a) from an established norm to its diffusion, (b) to its enactment among individuals, and (c) to its codification in the form of a policy script with both scientific and political inputs. This contentious process includes iterative rounds of exchange between state representatives and the technocrats that help write scripts, as well as the world cultural context in which these scripts are to be diffused. We offer a theoretical toolkit able to cope with case variation while also allowing a conversation across cases. Our second purpose is to produce a methodological toolkit that allows those interested in globalization to investigate how organizations produce scripts, and who and what they rely on to do so. Our dual aim, in short, is to identify theoretical and methodological strategies that can reveal new empirical information on how global norms are shaped and reshaped through actions within the respective leading organizations.

[50] Boyle et al. 2015.
[51] Abbott et al. 2016; Andonova 2017; Grigorescu 2020.

The IMF as a Strategic Research Site

To scrutinize this framework's merits, we focus on the International Monetary Fund as a strategic research site[52] that offers a unique analytical lens for studying globalization. According to Robert Merton, such sites help 'clarify the workings of social and cultural processes,'[53] and rely on the collection of empirical evidence that 'enables the fruitful investigation of previously stubborn problems and the discovery of new problems for further inquiry.'[54] In this understanding, strategic research sites provide fertile grounds for examining the remit of different theories, identifying blind spots and new opportunities, and linking up narrowly focused studies to problems of a much wider scope.[55]

The IMF provides precisely such analytical potential. To begin with, it is a substantively important IO, acting as the lynchpin of the postwar international economic system. Initially, the organization oversaw the Bretton Woods system of stable but adjustable exchange rates, thereby acting as the guarantor of the world order's embedded liberalism.[56] Following the collapse of that system in the 1970s, the IMF survived and thrived as the world's lender of last resort and became the midwife of the world order's neoliberal turn. That is, the IMF's role in the diffusion of market-oriented policies from the 1980s onward marked the ever-greater expansion of the scope of markets within developing countries, often implemented as part of the policy conditions attached to IMF loans.[57]

Today, the IMF remains the focal organization for key aspects of global financial and monetary governance and has been expanding its activities to deal with newly prominent issues like climate change, inequality, or gender policies. In this context, its Executive Board, the main locus of IMF decision making, is a highly consequential body in global economic governance, evidenced by its wide-ranging authority and the persistent debates around its reform.[58] The Fund's Board contains professionals who are dual loyalists in that they represent particular member states and constituencies while possessing a professional identity, be it central banker, financier, academic

---

[52] Merton 1987.
[53] Merton 1973, 373.
[54] Merton 1987, 10–11.
[55] Merton 1959.
[56] Ruggie 1982.
[57] Babb and Kentikelenis 2021.
[58] For example, Buira 2003; Woods 2000, 2004; Van Houtven 2004; Wade 2013; Wade and Vestergaard 2015; Ocampo 2017.

economist, or otherwise. As noted by a historian of the IMF, the Board acts from both political and scientific motivations, with frequent situations in which 'Executive Directors are more likely to exchange views that they have gained from their own professional knowledge and experience and less likely to advance the positions of member governments.'[59]

The IMF's centrality in global governance may raise questions about external validity: How representative can this case be of the broader universe of IOs and how can we generalize on the basis of this case? For our purposes, the IMF's centrality is a strength rather than a weakness of the research design. The merits of such an analytical strategy were long foreseen by French anthropologist Marcel Mauss, who advocated for purposefully studying societies and social phenomena that 'represent the extremes, an excessiveness which allows us better to perceive the facts than in those places where, although no less essential, they still remain small-scale and involuted.'[60] In other words, highly influential cases allow for capturing the richness of underlying social and political processes, in a way that enables us to investigate the utility of our theoretical framework as well as its scope conditions. Such an ambition is consistent with the understanding of scientific progress offered by Hungarian philosopher Imre Lakatos, who saw scientific progress as the outcome of competition between different research traditions.[61] In this approach, the study of highly influential cases is important because they 'become battlegrounds for comparing research traditions and metatheories,'[62] and thus enable theoretical innovation and the advancement of new arguments. The IMF certainly fits this criterion, as the organization has been one of the most studied IOs across the social sciences.

In the organizational case of the IMF, we pursue three comparative issue-area case studies of scriptwriting that underpin norms central to the functioning of contemporary capitalism. The first is the norm of free movement of capital, which undergirds contemporary economic globalization. The second is the norm that sovereign debtors should pay back what they owe to their creditors or face surveillance and/or conditions to reform their economic systems. The third is the norm that tax burdens should fall on a broad consumer base rather than income. Together, these norms permit high capital mobility for financial interests, a system of punishment and rewards for international lending, and fiscal revenue based on consumption. Capital mobility with oversight allows states to support themselves via the consumption of

---

[59] de Vries 1985, 51.
[60] Mauss 1985, 10.
[61] Lakatos 1970; see also Burawoy 1989.
[62] King and Sznajder 2006, 767.

their masses, as 'the more open a country is, the greater the contribution of the VAT to total taxation.'[63] Within these broader norms over the debt repayment, capital mobility, and public revenues, we examine institutionalization attempts of policy scripts related to three issues: sovereign debt management, capital controls, and consumption taxes.

The Structure of the Book

Our aim in this book is to provide a theorization of global normmaking that flows from the micro to the macro, with special attention on meso-level intra-organizational interactions. This is where our concept of an organizational policy script comes in handy: It is a concrete operationalization of a global norm and thus makes the study of underlying script-generation processes very tangible. We provide both theoretical and methodological tools to study how scripts are created in IOs.

In chapter 2 we present a theoretical framework for viewing global norms as products of contestation. We establish that while the diffusion of norms is a common focus, our interest is in the processes of global norm modification. Here actors that enact prior global norms are selected into IOs and negotiate new content through the production of scripts. This is where science-versus-politics struggles come into play. We outline how key scientific drivers can be found in the technocracy, epistemic communities, and professional networks, and how key political drivers are likely to be found in state bargaining. To understand how both drivers lead to the modification of global norms via scripts, we provide a syncretic model that includes variation in preference intensity for scientific consensus and political contestation. These preferences come from the technocrats, who want both academic excellence and a highly attuned political radar; and especially from the IMF Board, who are dual loyalists in representing their respective constituencies while being professionally socialized into different ways of thinking about script content. Tracing interactions between the technocrats and the Board, and within the Board itself, reveals how scriptwriting happens and what mix of science and politics is involved in attempts to modify global norms.

Chapter 3 focuses on how to study scripts. It builds on the theoretical framework and links it to a practical guide to studying IO-based scripts. We advocate for the use of abductive logic, which Martha Finnemore and John Ruggie have promoted as a form of interrogative reasoning that combines

---

[63] Appel 2011, 148.

inductive and deductive thinking to provide compelling evidence.[64] Once we have clarified abductive logic, we walk the reader through a mixed-method approach to scripts. We then delve into the computational toolkit, explaining how to study the actors and texts involved in scriptwriting. This includes the educational and career characteristics of those engaged in scriptwriting, the text used in policy production, the work teams involved in script development, and the verbatim text on script modifications. Our aim is to provide tools to answer the question: How does scriptwriting work? To explain this, we need to know (1) who is doing the work, (2) their preferences and predilections, (3) what terms are used to guide script content, (4) who uses these terms, (5) how these terms are used in context, and (6) how those writing scripts are positioned to act in supporting or rebuffing their peers.

Some of the tools in our methodological arsenal already have been applied to IO policymaking processes. Research on the similarity of educational background of IO professionals has been developing for many years, with prominent examples on the IMF[65] and UN peacebuilding.[66] Content analysis has also received some recent attention in the study of IOs.[67] This includes using semiautomated or fully automated content analysis of text to study, for example, the links among IMF surveillance reporting, working papers, and board minutes to identify different speeds of policy change[68] or ideological criticisms in UN General Assembly General Debate speeches.[69] 'Close-reading' content analysis has also been used, such as tracing the congruency of changes in fiscal policy from the IMF[70] or the absence of mentions of gender, women, and sex in the World Health Organization's COVID-19 policies.[71] On the composition of scriptwriters within IOs, their professional backgrounds have been traced using sequence analysis; this includes cases on international financial surveillance by the IMF and Basel Committee for Banking Supervision,[72] as well as locating those who can improve access to medicines in discussions among the World Health Organization, World Trade Organization, and World Intellectual Property Organization.[73] Last, the development of 'word embeddings' to visualize proximity between

---

[64] Ruggie 1998; Finnemore 2013; see also Friedrichs and Kratochwil 2009.
[65] Chwieroth 2007; Nelson 2014.
[66] Goetze 2017.
[67] For an overview, see Ban 2025.
[68] Kaya and Reay 2019.
[69] Kentikelenis and Voeten 2021.
[70] Broome and Seabrooke 2007; Ban 2015.
[71] Tomsick et al. 2022.
[72] Seabrooke and Nilsson 2015; Seabrooke and Tsingou 2021.
[73] Nilsson 2017.

those using terms in a network is a new development from natural language processing that we exploit in this book.[74]

Chapter 4 unpacks who sits on the IMF Board as a starting point for discussing the types of theorization and rationalization processes that go on in this paramount structure, where states, through their representatives, convey their preferences and priorities to the organizational bureaucracy. As we have described, Board members have a dual role as experts and state representatives, but the precise mix of these two identities can vary by individual, which can have momentous consequences in the aggregate on the types of decisions that the Board makes. To document these processes, we collected the curricula vitae of all 727 IMF Board members of the 1980–2009 period. Initially, we found remarkable homogeneity in terms of education: Nearly everyone was trained in economics or related disciplines, and—more surprisingly—half were educated in Anglo-American universities, despite hailing from nearly 120 nationalities. In particular, Board members from low- and middle-income countries were *more* likely than the average high-income-country official (excluding US and UK representatives) to be educated at US or UK institutions.

But homogeneity stops with educational background; we found more diversity when examining Board members' professional backgrounds. Applying sequence analysis methods on a new dataset we compiled on the basis of the curricula vitae, we revealed evidence of six types of career profiles: central bankers, finance ministry officials, bankers and businesspeople, political appointees, academics, and staff of IOs. The precise mix of these professional backgrounds in the IMF boardroom varies over time; for example, the late-1980s Board composition had almost nobody with a previous career in the private sector, academia, or IOs, whereas in the late 2000s more than one in four Board members had such a background. We posit that variation in the types of backgrounds present during Board deliberations matters, influencing the types of interactions they have with IMF technocratic staff, and ultimately shaping organizational decisions over what scripts to settle on and propagate at the transnational level.

In chapter 5 we explore the role of technocrats in the IMF. The IMF employs around 3,000 people from 150 countries, and the core of this staff are highly trained economists who enter through the Economist Program to become professionalized as IMF technocrats. As conveyed to us in interviews, these professionals view themselves as 'mini-Keyneses'—those who

---

[74] Boy 2020; Lamba and Madhusudhan 2022.

can combine scientific excellence in economics with tarmac-laying policy relevance. Achieving this combination requires academic publications to gain prestige in the broader expert community, an embrace of the IMF's surveillance and training roles, and demonstrations of policy applications to regional and member-state concerns.[75] This identity is steeped in a world culture of academic economics rationalization that they counterpose against the 'bean counters' and 'box tickers' from the private sector.[76] IMF technocrats carry cognitive or intellectual authority over the design of universal policy scripts,[77] and often customize them for member states based on notions of types of economies and peoples.[78] Important internal dynamics are also at play for the technocrats, including the development of subcultures around particular economic ideas, active boundary work to demarcate their policy territory relative to other IOs, and their own awareness of state-based power hierarchies on what is thinkable policy.[79]

While IMF staff are often presented as neoliberal through and through,[80] they actually come in a range of varieties, including the Chicago school–style 'Freshwater' type and, prominently, the more Keynesian 'Saltwater' type.[81] Internal dynamics within the IMF technocracy also allow a capacity for ideational change, especially in some areas like fiscal policy and the inherent stability of financial markets.[82] Chapter 5 traces the characteristics of IMF technocrats and locates their work in surveillance, academic production, policy development, and the fostering of transnational training networks. All of these activities are important in how they replenish their ties to expert communities and a world culture of economic theorization, and for how they provide inputs to the Board.

In chapters 6 to 8 we focus on scriptwriting related to three issues: sovereign debt management, capital controls, and taxation. The IMF is the key organization for all three issues, with a mandate to develop scripts for 'appropriate' policy in these areas. Figure 1.2 locates our cases, showing that the different elements of our theoretical account are not equally important in each case. The significant variation in how these policy scripts were developed within the IMF illustrates the payoff of our analytical framework's openness and flexibility. After systematically examining how the scriptwriting processes

---

[75] Thiemann et al. 2021.
[76] Interview with IMF junior economist, June 2009.
[77] Broome 2010; Clift 2018.
[78] Broome and Seabrooke 2007; Seabrooke 2012; Broome 2015.
[79] Clift 2018, 92; Kranke 2022.
[80] Chwieroth 2007; Nelson 2014.
[81] Lang et al. 2024.
[82] Ban 2015; Henning 2017; Clift 2018.

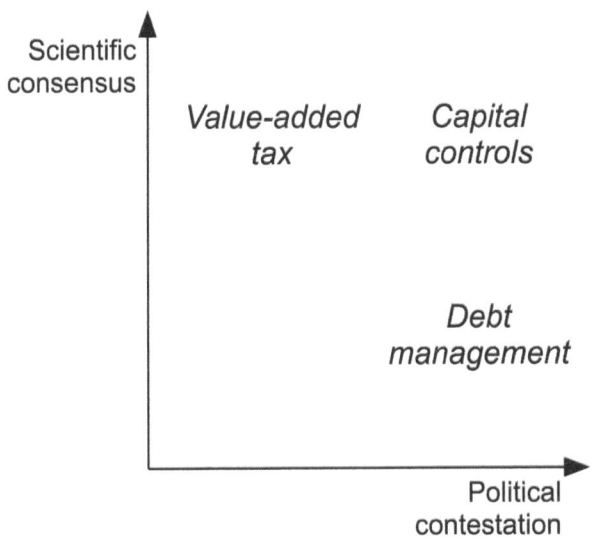

Figure 1.2 Overview of policy case selection to demonstrate politics versus science dynamics

play out in practice, we can then develop comprehensive and comparative accounts of how these processes unfold that eschew monocausal explanations and instead seek to integrate complexity into a more parsimonious framework. As our case studies show, the process of scriptwriting ultimately depends on the outcome of normative struggles within the IMF's Executive Board and between the staff technocrats and the Board.

Chapter 6 examines the debates and divisions over the development of a script on how to manage sovereign over-indebtedness. In the mid-1980s, the dominant script was that debts should be repaid in full, unless the Paris Club—rich-country creditors—agreed to their rescheduling or cancellation. By the mid-1990s, the script was modified to outline how debts could be deferred or even slightly reduced if the debtor country agreed to extensive control and surveillance of its economic policies by the IMF and the World Bank. And in the mid-2000s, this script was further modified to enable cancellation of part of developing countries' debt.

In the development and evolution of this script, the main fault lines were political rather than scientific. A lack of scientific consensus over how to proceed, other than stressing procedural requirements and initial forms of debt sustainability analysis, allowed politics to play out. Importantly for our argument, these processes did not play out solely as rich (creditor) versus poor (debtor) countries. Instead, the policy positioning of Board members in the debates over these scripts was informed not just by their national affiliations (and the implied preferences depending on whether their home authorities were creditors or debtors) but also by their professional socialization. For example, Board members with central banking backgrounds had more in common with each other, regardless of their country of origin, than they did with Board members with more overt political positioning, even if they represented countries at a similar level of development. In turn, the different mix of professional backgrounds on the Board shaped the ultimate decisions that were reached over scripts.

Chapter 7 shows that the technocrats' preferred script on capital account management failed to institutionalize due to normative contention on the Board. The drive to create a clear script on forbidding capital controls came from the technocracy, which was influenced by economic ideas linking the free movement of capital to increased levels of economic development and reduced levels of purportedly deleterious political meddling in the economy. But a move to ban capital controls was contrary to a foundational IMF principle on the right of governments to regulate international capital movements to better steer their economies. A serious change in position thus required thinking through a change to the IMF's Articles of Agreement. Contention over a 'no capital controls' script heightened between the mid-1980s and 1990s, with powerful Board members calling on technocratic support for their arguments. Increasingly the IMF staff advocated for the removal of controls in its surveillance work. While these arguments rested on a strong scientific consensus, the rolling out of logics into policy programs hit the hard wall of power politics in the Board.

By the mid-1990s, developing economies increasingly rejected both the economic logic of capital liberalization and its capacity to help steer their economies. As powerful Board members and Fund technocrats mobilized to institutionalize capital account liberalization, developing-country Board members also organized to counter this move. They drew on a battery of arguments—from political to procedural, and from personal to scientific—to reject capital account liberalization as an institutionalized Fund policy script. Importantly, even though this script was favored by a powerful combination of high-income countries and IMF staff, its institutionalization was successfully blocked by concerted efforts of these weaker actors. That is, even though power asymmetries are crucially important in global normmaking, they do not play out in institutional vacuums; existing rules can be leveraged by coalitions of seemingly weak actors to block the institutionalization of new norms.

Chapter 8 examines a tax script institutionalized as a result of strong normative and scientific consensus among the technocrats, with the Board paying little attention other than seeing the IMF as the best organization to develop these policy scripts. The case is noteworthy in that the biggest policy revolution in international tax policy—and far more significant in revenue raising than changes to corporate taxation[83]—occurred with the IMF Board barely making a sound.

The spread of the VAT is a case where actors drawing on a scientized world culture propelled a script through the IMF. The VAT, which was introduced in some European and South American economies in the 1950s and 1960s, was promoted in the 1980s to help the IMF's Fiscal Affairs Department solve a two-part problem with closer economic integration and, thus, globalization. The first part of this problem was to reduce and remove tariffs to accelerate trade integration. The second part was to have a resilient fiscal base that would allow governments to withstand exogenous shocks and invest in human and physical infrastructure. Key figures from Fiscal Affairs developed the VAT in a clear and coherent policy script and sought to diffuse it among member states, primarily through technical assistance. This script then supported a change in broader taxation norms, where trade tariffs should be removed, corporate and personal income taxes lowered and simplified, and VAT applied with as few exemptions as possible. The IMF technocracy supported these arguments by customizing tax advice according to different types of economies while insisting on a universal scientific answer to the two-part globalization problem. The case of taxation shows that when the technocracy can steel-plate scientific consensus over the best way to proceed, it can get the Board to accept their logics, even on highly distributive issues like taxation.

In Chapter 9 we discuss how our framework travels to other contexts, with an eye on both internal and external validity. We first discuss how our cases on sovereign debt, capital controls, and taxation may have evolved since 2009, noting consistencies and potential changes. We note how the IMF's engagement with climate change has been filtered through variations in scientific consensus and political contestation highlighted in our approach, as well as the adjustment of scripts already developed. On external validity, while recognizing the distinctive characteristics of the IMF that render it an exceptional case among the universe of IOs, we still posit that our analytical approach can be fruitfully applied to other organizations involved in global normmaking, and we argue our framework is encompassing enough to

---

[83] Zucman 2015.

capture the dynamics underpinning these processes in other issue areas. Most proximate to our empirical setup is the board governance model present in most IOs, ranging from other multilateral organizations, like the executive boards of the World Bank, the World Health Organization, or the United Nations Educational, Scientific, and Cultural Organization, to the boards of regional organizations like the Asian Infrastructure Investment Bank.[84] Beyond IOs, boards also have a key role in nongovernmental organizations, standard-setting organizations, and multistakeholder forums,[85] including politics-versus-science struggles that occur in global lawmaking and regulatory networks. Last, boards of global professional service firms and large consultancies also establish scripts that affect global business decisions.[86] We return to these issues and extensions of our model to other empirical cases in chapter 9. We also reflect on how IOs are changing in response to existential threats like climate breakdown. Given that IOs were established primarily to gradually build rather than radically transform,[87] we can expect to see the heightened relevance of struggles over scientific consensus and political contestation as urgency to modify global norms intensifies.

---

[84] Chorev 2012b; Kentikelenis and Babb 2025.
[85] Henriksen and Seabrooke 2016; Stroup and Wong 2017.
[86] Gupta and Wowak 2017.
[87] Paterson 2021.

PART I
PROCESSES

2
Global Norms as Contestation

Introduction

International organizations (IOs) are composed of bureaucracies and executive bodies that are collectively responsible for producing policy scripts that codify and operationalize global norms. The main source of contention between the bureaucracy and governing board of an IO is over the merits and power of scientific and political preferences that determine script content. Our theoretical starting point is that global norms are fundamentally a product of contestation. Apex IOs like the International Monetary Fund (IMF), investigated in these pages on issues like sovereign debt, capital controls, and taxation, have an outsized influence on global norms.

A keystone criticism of the early literature on global norms is that it should avoid the depiction that 'world culture marches effortlessly and facelessly across the globe. Little attention is paid either to contestation or coercion.'[1] Many scholars have heeded this observation, developing theoretical frameworks that view global norms as a product of contestation. This takes earlier literature, which focused on impassioned entrepreneurs working via transnational advocacy networks (TANs) to diffuse norms,[2] and examines how norms are entangled in selection dynamics among gatekeepers and struggles between organizations.[3] Such research points to how global norms are a product of emergent and persistent struggles. For example, Phillip Ayoub and Kristina Stoeckl explain how the transnational mobilization of norms around lesbian, gay, bisexual, transgender, and intersex rights reflects a double helix model in which rival TANs navigate norm promotion in light of what the other is doing.[4] Such investigations are interested not only in how global norms are created and spread but also in how they are contested, localized, violated, and eroded.[5] While we acknowledge the roles of both these interorganizational struggles and the external environment, in this book we

---

[1] Finnemore 1996, 339.
[2] Keck and Sikkink 1998. On identity-switching tactics, see Seabrooke and Wigan 2024.
[3] Carpenter 2011; Eilstrup-Sangiovanni 2023.
[4] Ayoub and Stoeckl 2023.
[5] Ben-Josef Hirsch and Dixon 2021.

Making Global Norms. Alexandros Kentikelenis and Leonard Seabrooke, Oxford University Press.
© Oxford University Press (2025). DOI: 10.1093/9780197828656.003.0002

want to turn analytical attention inward by examining the process of developing policy scripts within IOs as a microcosm of global norm contestation. Not the whole story, but a deep dive into the intra-organizational mechanics propelling global-level change.

Our view is that if we want to understand how global norms are contested, explaining how they are supported or rejected in the context of negotiations within apex organizations is crucial. We break global normmaking as contestation down into a simple opposition: politics versus science. Within this arena of struggle are interactions among Board members who carry dual loyalties as professionals and national representatives, and technocrats who want both academic excellence and policy relevance. What do they struggle over? They are fighting to determine the content of policy scripts that modify global norms.[6] These science-versus-politics struggles are interventions to disrupt what previously has been diffused—to modify and make anew. In contrast to standard accounts, we thus start our investigation of global normmaking at the end of the diffusion process rather than the beginning; not when the dust has settled but when it is kicking off.

The Diffusion of Global Norms

The world society approach details how norms are integral to making a 'world safe for organizing,' especially by disciplining and rationalizing uncertainties into rule systems.[7] At the aggregate level, norms in world society belong to processes of scientization and rationalization—that is, the ordering of logics by how to behave and what should be believed in.[8] Scripts are essential tools in this propagation, offering guiderails for actors to follow toward a norm.[9] In this sense, scripts are not simply functional tools of governance but also sacred objects that belong to the rituals of world society and those who seek ever more organization within it.[10] IOs and other organizations foster and maintain these rituals as a way to legitimate their ways of scriptwriting and to develop best-practice policy scripts that affirm dominant global norms or contribute to efforts to modify them.[11] Diffusing norms is an easier process if there is belief among those in world society in the appropriateness and legitimacy of the rituals through which scripts are brought into action.

---

[6] Pollack and Shaffer 2009.
[7] Drori 2006.
[8] Bromley and Meyer 2015.
[9] Meyer, Frank, et al. 1997; Boyle 2002; Hironaka 2014.
[10] Meyer and Rowan 1977; Durkheim 2001.
[11] Schofer et al. 2012.

The use of scripts and diffusion of norms is underpinned by the enactment of world culture by individuals, instead of understanding them as self-directed actors.[12] In other words, rather than positing that individuals are free-floating and all-powerful actors—an element that is grossly exaggerated in social life[13]—they are instead seen as situated within the world culture of rationalized governance of society that underpins globalization.[14] The centerpiece of this process is the belief in science and the scientific method, which are core inputs into rationalization. Individuals then enact and fine-tune the prevailing rationalities of the macro-structure.[15] They are thus 'enactors' rather than actors with independent agency,[16] deriving their 'identities and interests from some perceived natural order.'[17]

However, individuals do not blindly enact a universal, scientized world culture. This would yield a level of normative consensus absent from global governance.[18] Instead, they act in accordance to vernacularized variants,[19] which are developed as global norms come into contact with—and are influenced by—local institutions.[20] While this yields variation—including the fostering of 'corridors' and 'pockets' of world society in particular locales[21]—the vernacularized versions of norms are still developed in direct correspondence to dominant world cultural frames and thereby bear a level of family resemblance to them, short of complete overlap. This also means that individuals who are involved in transnational normmaking processes and exposed to vernacularized variants of norms held by other participants can lean on their socialization and training, which provide them an identity and the means to discipline and rationalize uncertainty.[22]

Figure 2.1 depicts a simple model through which global norms are diffused down to polities and then enacted by individuals. On the macro-level (the level of institutions), we have the dominant global norm, which provides actionable information on how to implement policies in support of a broader norm. This global norm is then diffused to organizations at the meso-level. Here norms are commonly decoupled from their global form[23] and begin to be vernacularized into a local setting—that is, they are locally adopted with some variation. This process of diffusion followed by modification has

[12] Meyer, Boli, et al. 1997, 150.
[13] Meyer and Jepperson 2000.
[14] Meyer, Boli, et al. 1997; Drori and Meyer 2006; Bromley and Meyer 2015.
[15] Meyer, Boli, et al. 1997; Hironaka 2014.
[16] Broome and Seabrooke 2021.
[17] Boyle and Meyer 1998, 213.
[18] Carruthers and Halliday 2006; Block-Lieb and Halliday 2017.
[19] Levitt and Merry 2009; Velasco 2023.
[20] Guillén 2001; Chorev 2012a.
[21] Ferguson 2022; Sendroiu and Levi 2023.
[22] Meyer 1977; Hwang 2006; Djelic and Quack 2010.
[23] Meyer and Rowan 1977.

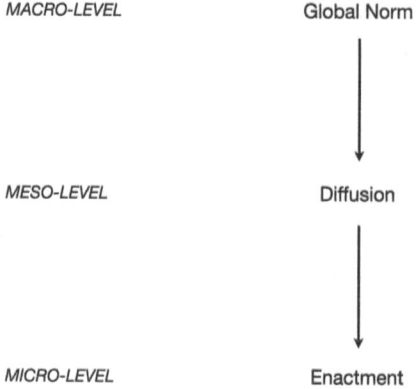

Figure 2.1 The diffusion of global norms

also been described as translation, in which 'domestic actors do not simply cut-and-paste new economic policies' from a global norm but filter them through local institutions.[24] At the bottom of figure 2.1, we have enactment at the micro-level, inhabited by individuals, where vernacularized or translated norms are enacted by individuals around the world, who embody them and carry them forward. For example, Peggy Levitt and Sally Merry show the local uses of global women's rights in different countries, demonstrating how vernacularization shapes their varied institutionalization in Peru, China, India, and the United States.[25]

However, the process described in figure 2.1 lacks contestation, which yields theoretical problems for scholarship on global norms. If norms are vernacularized, there will not be total overlap between the preferences of different actors; moreover, challenger norms may emerge. The World Society literature cannot easily handle questions of conflict over norms because everyone is assumed to live within rationalized modern society and share the same premises over how the world should be run. Additionally, there is the issue of what happens after enactment at the individual level. For example, research on the globalization of professions has shown how the diffusion of global norms generates a form of Schumpeterian creative destruction at the local level. Winners and losers emerge from this process, which leads to socioeconomic reconfigurations that then support norms with greater 'diffusability.'[26] Distributional gains and losses from the diffusion of global norms occur not only in political and economic domains, but also the cultural: For example, there are asymmetries in which cities can qualify as 'creative

---

[24] Bockman and Eyal 2002; Ban 2013.
[25] Levitt and Merry 2009.
[26] Fourcade 2006, 152–55.

cities' in the Global South—and what social engineering is needed for such recognition.[27]

Recent theoretical advances have identified how the diffusion of global norms is likely to foster layers of cultural and institutional complexity at the local level, alongside regional 'polythetic' overlapping institutions, and a multichanneled 'rhizoid' structure for diffusion at the global level.[28] The integration of scholarship on diffusion with the transnational field-theoretic approach has also been useful in identifying the pathways for global norms and their adaptation as they land, as well as how they infuse and contaminate other fields.[29] Yet we still need an appreciation of precisely how science finds its way into meso-level normmaking processes, as well as an elucidation of the (potentially) conflictual nature of normmaking.

Scientific Drivers of Global Normmaking

In our view, 'science' encompasses people with qualified expert and technical authority, which includes both those we would automatically identify as scientists (e.g., physicists, biologists, or other highly trained experts) and those with specialized technical knowledge and higher learning (e.g., accountants, lawyers, or economists). International relations scholarship on global norms focuses on technocratic and scientific actors as scriptwriters within and around IOs. Most prominently, Michael Barnett and Martha Finnemore[30] discuss how IO bureaucracies embody rational-legal authority and expert control over information, which is used to 'spread, inculcate, and enforce global values and norms,' with technocrats acting as the 'missionaries' of our time.[31] Technocratic knowledge over technical issues is strongly informed by technocrats' professional training and socialization, which fosters distinct worldviews that can be amplified when bureaucratic specialization concentrates like-minded professionals together. For Barnett and Finnemore, this process can lead to pathologies that undermine policy success and create frictions with political masters,[32] while allowing technocrats to play favorites with member-state representatives that share similar worldviews and professional socialization.[33] As a consequence, member states may view IO technocrats

---

[27] Molho et al. 2020.
[28] Wimmer 2021.
[29] Ballakrishnen and Dezalay 2020; Lim 2021; Rotem 2022.
[30] Barnett and Finnemore 1999, 2004.
[31] Barnett and Finnemore 1999, 713; more recently, see Liese et al. 2021.
[32] Barnett and Finnemore 1999; Weaver 2008.
[33] Chwieroth 2013, 2015; Nelson 2014.

as less impartial,[34] and IO staff may be less able to include new agendas that shake their fundamental training and socialization.[35]

Along with working in bureaucratic silos, technocrats also belong to networks that coordinate and compete on what knowledge should be included in normmaking. Reaching out from IOs, technocrats can actively seek to propagate how scripts should be treated through policy training networks[36] and epistemic communities.[37] Being embedded in an epistemic community is especially important for professionals, including technocrats, because it affirms their identities and claims to recognized expertise,[38] increases the chance that they may be called upon for advice in uncertain times, and allows them to locate peers (or lock them out).[39]

An important function of epistemic communities and their professional networks is that they not only affirm internally—producing scientific consensus—but also search externally.[40] For IOs, locating sympathetic interlocutors to collaborate on institutionalizing scripts at the national level is especially important.[41] Scripts can be pushed through technocratic networks and affirmed as legitimate, creating lock-in effects for future script development. For example, policy space for countries in the Global South is shaped by these communities as they focus on universalizing solutions created within IOs and shut off alternatives.[42] IO-based technocratic networks affirm what is appropriate input into normmaking and scriptwriting, including what can be measured, who has a mandate to work on the issue, and which IOs accrue status from doing such work.[43] While technocrats primarily operate within IOs, they also externally form what Juliet Johnson calls 'wormholes' of professional self-affirmation that can conflict with politics.[44] This phenomenon is particularly well known among central bankers, who are highly socialized and aware that they need to maintain their reputations.[45] Recursive cycles of normmaking include the mediation of science and politics, with ensuing scripts recognized as governance tools that can replicate power asymmetries.[46]

---

[34] Heinzel et al. 2021.
[35] Clift and Robles 2021.
[36] Broome and Seabrooke 2015.
[37] Haas 1992.
[38] Haas 1992; Djelic and Quack 2010.
[39] Littoz-Monnet 2022.
[40] Seabrooke and Henriksen 2017.
[41] Woods 2006; Berge and St John 2021; Heinzel and Liese 2021.
[42] Wade 2003; Gallagher 2005; DiCaprio and Gallagher 2006; Kentikelenis et al. 2016; Reinsberg et al. 2019; Seabrooke and Sending 2020.
[43] Ban et al. 2016; Kentikelenis and Seabrooke 2021; Aragão and Linsi 2022.
[44] Johnson 2016; James and Quaglia 2022.
[45] Moschella 2024.
[46] Halliday and Carruthers 2009; Broome and Seabrooke 2021.

Those operating in technocratic networks draw on world culture to circulate knowledge but also need to watch out for formal politics, taking into consideration the links between different claims to authority, be they based on a formal mandate or delegation, or on their expertise, moral principles, or demonstrated capacities.[47] Our politics-versus-science framework allows scholars to empirically trace variation in how authority manifests in policy scriptwriting. Many studies have shown how IO technocrats seek to slip from the grasp of their political masters through ambiguity[48] but ultimately remain answerable to formal political authorities. While technocrats sometimes may have more influence on scriptwriting than delegated officials,[49] this does not stop external political forces from presenting a trump card. As such, experts are not free-floating professionals but often are tied to formal political interests.

Political Drivers of Normmaking

Political economy scholarship has also yielded major contributions to our understanding of how policy norms are developed, and the conflicts—involving states, IOs, nongovernmental organizations, professional associations, and epistemic communities—inherent in this process. This strand of work has traditionally emphasized the role of geopolitics,[50] and accounts see IOs as functional instruments that have been rationally designed by states to advance particular preferences.[51] By extension, decision-making structures in IOs are conflict zones for states pursuing their geopolitical strategies and material interests. From this view, global norms and, by extension, the content of IOs' policy scripts are primarily a function of the intensity of interests and salience of issues for the dominant geopolitical player(s) in the system.[52]

Unsurprisingly, the focus of many political economy arguments is the role of the US. A strong assumption here is that US strategic interests will filter through IOs into normmaking and scriptwriting, either through deliberate political action or technocratic staff working under a shadow of hierarchy. For example, there is evidence that Japan and the US routinely intervene in the distribution of funds from the Asian Development Bank, with Japan

---

[47] Avant et al. 2010.
[48] Babb 2003; Best 2012; Van Gunten 2015b.
[49] Seabrooke and Stenström 2023.
[50] Keohane and Nye 1974; Fligstein and Mara-Drita 1996; Chase-Dunn 1998; Waltz 2000.
[51] Koremenos et al. 2001.
[52] Thacker 1999; Momani 2004; Kentikelenis and Babb 2019.

leaning on executive control while the US relies on its geopolitical prowess.[53] Or to take a different case, when World Health Organization (WHO) staff attempted to shift the organization's focus to the social (rather than biomedical) determinants of ill health in the 1970s and 1980s in line with scholarly advances, its powerful member states, particularly the US, blocked the institutionalization of relevant norms, as they contradicted the emerging neoliberal orthodoxy of the time.[54] This has also happened recently with US discouragement of scripts within the WHO to fight obesity linked to high-sugar-content foods.[55]

The main mechanism through which normmaking occurs in IOs is through a process of global horse trading.[56] What is being traded here are favors in one area of global policy in exchange for support of the dominant power in another area. According to a prominent account within this scholarship, such bargaining processes commonly occur in the back corridors of IOs, where member states seek to advance their interests and influence each other and the organizational bureaucracy behind the spotlight and without leaving a paper trail that media, advocates, or scholars can access.[57] Such horse trading reflects both state intervention and corporate intervention. Rabia Malik and Randall Stone find that when American and Japanese multinational corporations are involved in World Bank projects, there are 'disbursements that are unjustified by project performance.'[58] A further argument here is that even when a great power—nearly always the US—does not intervene, there is still a strong perception from IO technocrats that they should appease a hegemon. Richard Clark and Lindsay Dolan show that World Bank staff design programs that suit US preferences, even without US interference, due to a conscious or unconscious desire to 'please the principal.'[59]

In this scholarship, state-appointed individuals involved in global normmaking are seen as just that: embodiments of state power who populate international fora to execute orders and advocate state interests. If scholars know which states participate in a global forum or IO, the resources at their disposal, and the decision-making procedures, then ultimate outputs—like policy scripts—become legible through the lens of interstate relations. This approach assumes a degree of fungibility of state representatives: Their own ideas and expertise become muted or even irrelevant when faced with the task of delivering their country's material interest. For example, research

---

[53] Krasner 1981; Kilby 2006.
[54] Chorev 2012b.
[55] Kentikelenis et al. 2023.
[56] Dreher et al. 2009.
[57] Stone 2008, 2011, 2013.
[58] Malik and Stone 2018.
[59] Clark and Dolan 2021.

on multilateral trade negotiations pursues analysis of outcomes with primary reference to the state-representation role of participants.[60] After all, before sending someone to represent them in international missions, fora, and negotiations, 'nation-states want assurances that their advisors will serve single-mindedly the causes advanced by national policymakers.'[61]

These theories illuminate the organizational-level processes behind the emergence and change of global norms and their associated policy scripts. The mechanism through which scripts are generated is negotiation among the relevant political actors who commonly have different policy preferences, whence conflicts emerge. As we have seen, negotiation can be formalized in on-the-record debates, like in the boardroom of an IO or in a multilateral forum, or informal, like backroom deals reached by participants in the very same processes. But political economists generally assume negotiation takes place between individuals who have relatively flat identities, as extensions of the state they represent. To explain the ultimate content of scripts, the amount of additional knowledge about these individuals a researcher requires is very limited. Background characteristics—like their education and career trajectories—are notably absent as inputs to relevant theorizing, despite extensive evidence of their explanatory significance.[62]

Building Blocks Toward a Syncretic Approach

The strands of scholarship on scientization in world society and the politics of IO policymaking have generally developed without much interaction, as they operate on different levels of analysis and generate competing arguments on the primary explanatory factors behind global normmaking. This theoretical ringfencing is unfortunate because these two lines of thought can collectively contribute to explaining the normative foundations of contemporary globalization and the key role of policy scripts. This scope for convergence opens up a research agenda ripe for theoretical and methodological innovation.

Such innovation can be achieved by blending two key insights. First, we understand individuals as enactors of global norms because of their educational and professional socialization. These spaces of socialization affirm particular norms and shape individuals' views on what is to inform the development of policy scripts. When performing their jobs, these individuals likely will carry the imprint of the 'appropriate' knowledge, legitimized by socialization processes. Second, we consider these individuals not in isolation but

---

[60] Halliday et al. 2013.
[61] Carruthers and Halliday 2006, 531.
[62] Centeno 1994; Adolph 2013; Seabrooke and Henriksen 2017.

relationally.[63] That is, individuals are not taking positions independently from each other or their environment.[64] Rather, they are taking positions on the content of scripts in relation to each other. Those involved are all trying to make positions, which vary in their intensity, to whom they are directed, and how. The directional and quantitative aspects of these 'tryings,' as John Levi Martin has put it, create vectors within a defined space, within a field.[65] As we show in chapters 6 and 7, our text-as-data approaches can help us see how relations produce vectors of position taking.

Global norms and scripts are developed through rounds of negotiations within IOs, and the related bargaining is substantially shaped by geopolitical strategic interests. Combining these insights allows us to develop explanations that jointly focus on the micro-level (individuals and their educational and professional socialization) and the meso-level (the negotiations within IOs over script content) while permitting us to elaborate on the foundations of macro-level change in global norms.

Figure 2.2 presents our syncretic model for how the content of global norms changes over time. The left side integrates the information already presented in figure 2.1 and expands it to illustrate both the central role of negotiations in modifying macro-level norm content and the temporal structure to this process. Together, both sides bind individuals to organizations and structures. Our theoretical argument begins at the endpoint of the diffusion process: with individuals as enactors of global norms. They carry with them vernacularized variants of these norms, the precise content of which depends on individual attributes, like country of origin, educational background, and professional socialization. Yet even though vernacularized norms likely will not fully overlap, they still will have a degree of similarity and family resemblance, as they both stem from the same dominant global norm.

The dynamics of change are introduced in the right side of figure 2.2, as they further spell out the mechanism of norm generation as they apply to intra-IO processes. This process has been undertheorized, as relevant accounts focus primarily on the relative role of political power or epistemic privilege. We suggest that analyses of normmaking should start with unpacking the individual-level attributes of those involved in these processes. Enactment means that these individuals will hold vernacularized versions of global norms—they bring this background with them in their negotiations over the precise content of ensuing policy scripts at the organizational level. The

---

[63] Emirbayer 1997.
[64] Jackson and Nexon 1999; McCourt 2016.
[65] Martin 2011, 251.

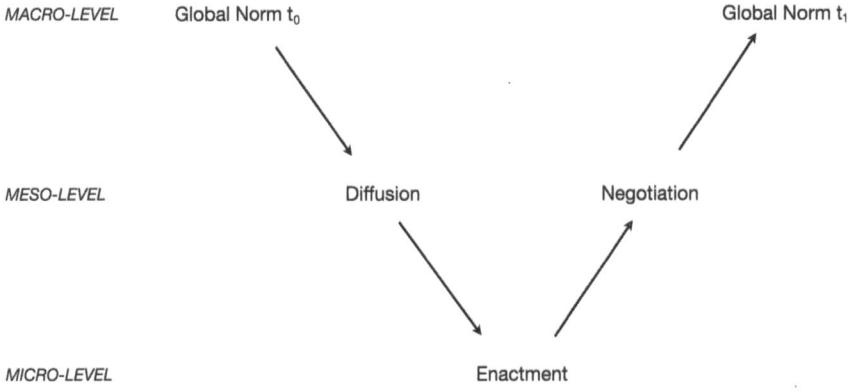

Figure 2.2 A multilevel model of global normmaking

prime venue where this takes place is the organizational governance structure, commonly taking the form of a board, council, executive committee, or conference. These venues are spaces for deliberation and negotiation between representatives. For example, the World Bank has an Executive Board, the World Trade Organization has general councils, the International Energy Agency has a Governing Board, the World Intellectual Property Organization has a system of committees, the International Telecommunications Union has an Administrative Council, and so on. For simplicity, we adopt the terminology of boards, even though our arguments encompass similar processes taking place across operational governance structures (i.e., not the highest-level bodies where ministers of member states are represented, but one level below).

These structures are, de jure, the main loci where negotiations occur. Appointees to such boards are tasked with state representation, but we posit they are also experts in their own right in a way that makes analytically treating them as mere mouthpieces of their home authorities misguided. The deliberative nature of global normmaking—rather than mere up-or-down votes—suggests that professional identities might also nontrivially shape the behavior of state representatives and, consequently, their ultimate script outputs. Indeed, actual voting is rare in global governance. Voting procedures exist but are rarely exercised outside the United Nations General Assembly; instead, most IOs decide on the basis of consensus following extensive deliberations.[66] Their governance structures is where negotiations occur to determine norm and script content, and board members' stances

[66] Martinez-Diaz 2009.

can range from silence to aggressive debate. Extending recent work by Mark Copelovitch and Stephanie Rickard that has pointed to how IO executive leadership can contain partisan technocrats that influence policy design,[67] we argue that board members carry not just their political representation into the negotiation room but also their professional affiliations, which have implications for the treatment of policy scripts.

Unpacking Normmaking in International Organizations

Framing normmaking in the terms just described poses the challenge of how we can jointly consider processes that operate at different levels of analysis. This is where our emphasis on policy scripts helps sharpen the theoretical discussion, as scripts are tangible devices whose development can be empirically decomposed. As we have explained, IOs' policy scripts codify and operationalize global norms—they are policy devices that countries worldwide can pick up and integrate into domestic policy environments. Given scripts' direct correspondence to and affirmation of global norms, we are interested in generating a holistic explanation of the dynamics behind script content by homing in on the role of IOs' boardrooms and technocratic staff.

We argue that we can understand scriptwriting processes within IOs through three analytical steps: (1) unpacking the role of the IO bureaucracy, (2) discussing the role of the IO board, and (3) turning our attention to boardroom interactions. First, we consider the technocracy to be the key repository of scientific knowledge, by virtue of staffers being highly trained in their fields of expertise. Our conception of science is not intended to connote that it either prescribes policies that are objectively right or that it is divorced from politics. Instead, we understand science as the set of theories, worldviews, and empirical methods that are legitimated at a moment in time. For example, Luciana de Souza Leão and Gil Eyal have documented how, in the field of international development, randomized controlled trials have become the gold standard for judging development interventions.[68] In our logic, this theoretical and empirical approach is classified as a science because of its dominance in the field of academic development economics, its valorization by high-status awards (like the Nobel Prize), and its establishment as a standard requirement in many development projects. We in no way imply that it is the only or even best way to establish whether a development intervention

---

[67] Copelovitch and Rickard 2021.
[68] de Souza Leão and Eyal 2019, 2020; de Souza Leão 2020.

was effective. Relatedly, we do not claim that politics are external to legitimating certain versions of science as opposed to competing models. Ample scholarship has documented that science is inherently shaped by politics.[69] However, it is analytically useful to identify what elements of scriptwriting are primarily driven by science or by politics, and how they clash, issue by issue. We return to this question of analytical leverage in chapter 9.

By describing IO bureaucracies as repositories of science, we mean that they are hierarchical organizational structures that rely on scientific expertise to develop official views and strategies on certain policy issues. This scientific expertise has roots both internal (offered by staff) and external (offered by consultants or academics) and is developed in dialogue with globally dominant interpretative frames. For example, in the early 1990s, the World Bank developed policy prescriptions for how developing countries should organize their health systems that promoted marketizing health services and introducing user fees for access. These policy prescriptions drew directly on contemporary leading arguments in academic economics[70] and diffused around the world over the subsequent 15 years, notwithstanding the intense controversies surrounding these measures.[71] While the Bank acknowledged the criticisms and jettisoned the policy in 2004,[72] this experience reveals the staying power that certain dominant scientific frames have within IOs.

These frames are transmitted to IO staff through their professional socialization in their workplace. Conformity is rewarded, dissent is disincentivized.[73] For these reasons, we consider IO bureaucracies as collective actors, rather than decompose them into individual staffers and their predilections or priorities. While staffers certainly have individual views on a range of policy issues, when they work toward developing policy scripts they adhere to the technocratic frames dominant within their organization. The thorough review process behind any policy statements ensures that IO outputs are 'on brand.'[74] In short, science within the IO bureaucracy—in the aggregate—is highly internally coherent. After all, IOs are not academic departments that value and celebrate diversity of views; their legitimacy comes from advancing scientized policies that can be advertised as being the 'right' policies (regardless of their actual track record). As we will see in our cases, staff from different departments within the IMF actively work to develop, and defend, the institutional view through policy scripts.

[69] Eyal 2019.
[70] For example, see Akin et al. 1987.
[71] Abbasi 1999; Buse and Walt 2000; Birn and Dmitrienko 2005; Chorev 2012b; Noy 2017.
[72] Rowden 2013.
[73] Wade 1997, 2009.
[74] Wade 1996.

Second, we turn to board members because they have the final say in what their IO decides. On one hand, these individuals are state representatives who need to take into account the geopolitical or material considerations of their home authorities, whose interests they have been appointed to serve. On the other hand, they are also highly skilled experts in their own right, having honed their expertise through educational and professional socialization—this is where they are exposed to variants of global norms that they then carry forward as interpretative schemas in their professional lives. Unlike IO technocrats, however, the expertise of board members is not bound by the house views of their organization—they are there to set the strategic direction of their IO, not to merely rubberstamp what the bureaucracy proposes. For this reason, diversity of relevant expertise can be an asset in the design of policies and interventions, as it is less amenable to groupthink. This also opens up scope for disagreements on the scientific merits of policy, which we discuss hereafter.

These two characteristics reflect the dual loyalties that IMF Board members have, both to their status as experts and to their political masters.[75] That is, while Board members are performing the role of a state agent when sitting on the Board, their professional allegiances and expertise also inform their positions on particular policy scripts. In this sense, Board members are dual loyalists: As state representatives they must pursue the interests of their appointing authority, but they also belong to a professional group that has preferred treatments of different issues. For example, what a US representative with a background in private finance thinks about norms and scripts on appropriate tax policy may well differ from what a German former finance ministry official thinks, even though they both sit on the same board and represent large high-income countries.

This description is not intended to evoke split personalities à la Dr. Jekyll and Mr. Hyde, whereby a Board member constantly oscillates between representing their home country or acting in correspondence to legitimate expertise in their professional field. Instead, the relative importance of these two identities in shaping their behavior depends on two issues: political contention among Board members' appointing authorities and the degree of technocratic contention in the issue area. These issues can also be conceived of as domains of activity: the politics and the science. One is the political domain of negotiation with distributive effects; the other is the scientific domain of theorization, where epistemic consensus or dissensus drives debate

---

[75] Lewis 2005.

over appropriate solutions to problems. Board members span these two domains and can identity-switch between them;[76] when done successfully, this allows them to project to others that they have the capacity to operate at a high level not only in the political domain of horse trading and negotiation but also in the scientific domain of economic theorization.[77]

Locating preferences in the political domain is reasonably straightforward, with income level often acting as a shorthand for what state representatives will want. For instance, in the global economic realm, rich-country representatives will want to entrench their cumulative advantage, while poor-country representatives will want to expand their policy space and avoid external interference in their domestic political economies.[78] Political contention may also follow status dynamics, with concessions given to provide legitimacy or recognition.[79] Preferences are further informed by well-worn patterns of domination, such as relationship dynamics that reflect imperial networks.[80] Last, the chance of political contestation will be strongly informed by the immediacy of the threat at hand, with short-term crises creating more urgency than longer-term problems seemingly over the horizon.

Variation in the degree of scientific consensus is also important for how Board members project their positions. We especially note that while rationalizations and scientization are strongly associated with the expansion of formal organization,[81] this process does not roll out evenly or uniformly across organizations and societies. While we know that IOs have produced ever more scientific product,[82] there are degrees of contention over how settled the scientific or technocratic consensus is around an issue. Uri Shwed and Peter Bearman have documented how the temporal structure of epistemic rivalry can be differentiated as following three patterns. The first is 'spiral,' in which, over iterations, substantive questions on an issue are revisited and addressed at a high-level, forming consensus around issue treatment. The second is 'cyclical,' in which questions around the issue are revisited without stable closure.[83] The third is 'flat,' in which there is simply not a lot of scientific

---

[76] White 2008; Seabrooke 2014.
[77] McLean 2007.
[78] Wade 2003; Gallagher 2005; Kentikelenis and Babb 2019.
[79] Mukherjee 2022.
[80] Kohli 2020.
[81] Meyer and Bromley 2013.
[82] Zapp 2017.
[83] Abbott 2001b.

Table 2.1 Locating Political and Scientific Preference Intensities

		Political Contestation	
		Low	*High*
Scientific Consensus	Low	Incoherence	Representation function dominant
	High	Expert background dominant	Clash between political instructions and scientific position *or* Congruity between political instructions and scientific position

contestation present.[84] These types of variation in the degree of settled knowledge are useful in helping us understand when Board members will lean on explicit theorization in debates, or when they can let the common sense—or no sense—do the work.

Table 2.1 summarizes the preceding logic into a matrix, locating political contestation along the top, and scientific consensus down the side. Within the matrix, we can see variation, with low political and scientific preference intensities leading to incoherence in what should be included in a script (if one is to exist at all). When scientific consensus is lacking but political contestation is high, we can expect the representation function to be dominant—in short, more politics. Where political contestation is low, but the degree of scientific consensus is high, we can expect expertise to be dominant—in short, more science, which also empowers the technocrats to have a strong hand on script content. Last, where both political contention and scientific consensus are both high, we can expect to see either coherence or a clash. When they cohere, we would expect a script to gain prominence and be accelerated as a priority. When they clash, we would expect to see extensive argumentation around preferences and theorizations on what a script should contain. In short, compromises are to be made between politics and science.

Having covered the two individual-level determinants of board members' behavior and the role of IO bureaucracies as repositories of scientific knowledge, we turn to the relational element of our account. The individual attributes of board members become analytically relevant when seen not as baggage that an individual passively carries with them by virtue of their biography, but as active toolkits that inform the policy positions they take during policy script negotiations. While members of global boards are likely to have some shared common experiences (e.g., elite education), they differ in both

---

[84] Shwed and Bearman 2010, 818.

their home authorities' interests and professional allegiances. The ultimate scripts depend on boardroom-level interactions between these individuals, as well as many rounds of exchanges with the IO bureaucracy, which is there to help and support scriptwriting activities. The boardroom deliberations can take many forms—from collective puzzling to aggressive strong-arming to passive disinterest—in how board members as professionals–cum–state representatives reach decisions over script content. Here, at this global organizational level, participants' dual loyalties take concrete form in the articulation of policy positions and preferences—who is writing matters for what is written.

External Influences on IO Scriptwriting

The processes described thus far almost treat IOs as closed systems: What matters is what happens in their governance structures and inside their technocratic bureaucracies. How does this square with prominent arguments about the opening up of IOs? A strand of scholarship has documented that IOs are increasingly open to civil society actors, facilitating organizational channels for them to voice concerns.[85] Other work points to how global governance work is conducted by technocrats and board members as well as within consultancies.[86] New research on multistakeholder initiatives now locates IOs as important members in deliberative processes,[87] which are thought to be important in legitimating IOs' existence.[88] Our account does not challenge such arguments, and we are conscious of the fact that the processes we focus on do not occur in a vacuum; the IOs' external environment includes challenger actors and their preferred policy scripts, global crises, the emergence of new political forces, and demands by social movements.

In our model, external forces become internalized insofar as they lead intra-organizational actors to adjust their preferences and actions. For example, recently the World Bank has reformed its accountability mechanisms to deal with criticisms by groups its projects have harmed.[89] In another example, since the emergence of the COVID-19 pandemic, the WHO has been thrust into the limelight for its activities—or lack thereof—to prevent a global health emergency. But this was not the first time that a health emergency hit. The absence of a mechanism to transmit external criticisms into the WHO board

[85] Tallberg et al. 2013.
[86] Seabrooke and Sending 2020; Broome 2022; Tsingou 2022.
[87] Reinsberg and Westerwinter 2021.
[88] Hurd 2019.
[89] Park 2022.

arguably left the IO vulnerable to other organizations' taking the scriptwriting initiative and changing the policy narrative. The rise of global health security work from foreign-policy-driven initiatives, like the Global Health Security Index, provides a clear challenge to the WHO's One Health script.[90] In other words, there is no guarantee that external pressures will translate into action on changing IOs' preferred policy scripts, but if they do, they will need to be championed by intra-organizational actors, like a group of board members or a highly esteemed technocratic department, at which point external pressures become the focus of internal negotiation. Our model is designed to capture precisely such instances of organizational change.

A note of caution is needed, however. We posit that for extra-organizational pressures to be relevant for scriptwriting, they will need to be manifested in intra-organizational processes. For example, as Robert Wade shows in the case of environmental reforms at the World Bank, popular protests became relevant insofar as the criticisms were taken seriously by internal actors, who chose to alter organizational practices in response.[91] To be relevant, the external environment needs to affect the preferences and actions of intra-organizational actors; at that point, these pressures cease to be external and become internal to the IO. When this occurs, we can then trace the actors and text involved in scriptwriting, as discussed hereafter and in the next chapter.

A further note of caution relates to the scope conditions of our argument and framework. Politics-versus-science struggles can only take place with some regularity when there is a stable and sufficiently staffed technocracy. Regularity is vital in having sufficient data on the extent to which there is scientific consensus in the technocracy and how much political contestation is present over an issue. Our framework runs into difficulties when international organizations choose to govern via more ad hoc coalitions, as has increasingly been the case in areas like peacekeeping.[92] When the distance between the bureaucracy and the actual expertise on the ground is great, as with asylum and migration issues,[93] poor reporting mechanisms will weaken the credibility of scientific consensus or prevent it from forming. The growth of 'informal' global governance, in which 'rules, norms, and institutional structures and procedures [...] are not enshrined in formally constituted organizations or in their constitution,' also poses a hurdle for our framework, given that the formal means to express political contestation has been removed.[94] In such

---

[90] Kentikelenis and Seabrooke 2021, 2022.
[91] Wade 1997.
[92] Reykers et al. 2023; Brosig and Karlsrud 2024.
[93] Kortendiek 2024.
[94] Westerwinter et al. 2021, 2.

cases, political-versus-science struggles will lack regularity, offering opportunity structures for particular experts and professionals to exert issue control.[95] Still, we know that the best-regarded IOs—in terms of their perceived performance among key member states and their capacity to create their own policies—are those with regularity in formal political representation and a substantive expert technocracy.[96]

---

[95] Henriksen and Seabrooke 2016; Breen and Eilstrup-Sangiovanni 2023.
[96] Lall 2023.

3
How to Study Policy Scripts in International Organizations

Introduction

A policy script provides a 'definition of a reform issue: a diagnosis of problems followed by a set of prescriptions'[1] and is composed by authors who collaborate or compete in generating content. Each script is an outcome of an iterative negotiation process. It provides a snapshot of what an organization declares as its thinking and position on how an issue should be treated. Many organizations may produce policy scripts on an issue, and these scripts will compete for attention in an audience looking for solutions. Globally, a range of organizations produce scripts, including international organizations (IOs), nongovernmental organizations (NGOs),[2] multinational enterprises,[3] think tanks and foundations,[4] esteemed expert groups,[5] consultancies,[6] and various combinations of multistakeholder initiatives. Given that scripts can have powerful effects on the activities of individuals, states, and businesses, we need a methodology to understand how they are composed in organizations. In our case, we are concerned with how they are composed in IOs, particularly the International Monetary Fund (IMF) as an illustrative case of the underlying processes.

This book offers a multilevel model of scriptwriting that moves from the micro through the meso to the macro. The micro-level of enactment is important in imprinting individuals with global norms, transmitted through education and career experiences. They carry these to the meso-level of organizations, where interactions take place to negotiate script content on behalf of political masters and/or expert communities. Once decided, the outcome is projected to the macro-level of global norms. Chapter 2 established that

---

[1] Halliday et al. 2010, 84.
[2] Carpenter 2007.
[3] Bartley 2022.
[4] Plehwe et al. 2018.
[5] Tsingou 2015.
[6] Stone et al. 2021; Seabrooke and Sending 2022.

Making Global Norms. Alexandros Kentikelenis and Leonard Seabrooke, Oxford University Press.
© Oxford University Press (2025). DOI: 10.1093/9780197828656.003.0003

global normmaking can be explained with theories that stress power politics and the world culture of scientization. These theoretical approaches provide different assumptions about actors' motivations, incentives, and behavior during the scriptwriting process.

In this chapter we discuss methods to study scriptwriting in order to understand how they are composed with a range of 'abductively' derived qualitative and quantitative techniques. These techniques systematically treat the ingredients of scriptwriting processes: what toolkits individuals bring with them to the table, how these individuals interact with each other, and what texts emerge from this iterative process. Interrogating scripts in this multimethod manner can identify unique information that may deviate from assumptions carried in the theories from chapter 2—a further rationale for pursuing our abductive approach.

Scripts provide pieces of the puzzle of why globalization took its current form and not a different one, thus yielding explanations that denaturalize dominant global policies. As anticipated in this introduction, we argue that scripts are a product of the interaction between politics and science. 'Politics' is shorthand for how state representatives in IOs act on their preferences to create the art of the possible via scriptwriting. 'Science' is shorthand for the theorization and rationalization of what are best practices and/or appropriate solutions to integrate into script content. Both politics and science are necessary components of scriptwriting. It is difficult to imagine how a script from any IO—all of them charged with solving collective-action problems—might be composed from politics or science alone. Such a script likely would be illegitimate for a broad part of the IO's constituency and audience, seen as violating its mandate of broad representation or projecting an unrealistic view of what can be achieved.[7] We suggest that differences in script content from a singular IO will reflect variations in the balance between politics and science in the crafting of scripts.

We conceive of politics primarily as willingness to engage in political contestation—how committed representatives push forward a particular choice. We know from the extensive literature on IOs that political contestation is composed of material and symbolic elements. The most basic of these is straightforward economic self-interest: wealthy economies being reluctant to support scripts that extend moral hazards for developing economies, or developing economies seeking to lower the chance of interference and conditions imposed by IOs in which wealthy economies dominate.[8] Preference

---

[7] Lall 2017.
[8] Vreeland 2007; Babb and Kentikelenis 2021.

intensity may also follow social status dynamics as representatives seek to demonstrate their allegiances, affinities, and equivalence.[9] Preferences in political contests are likely to follow established historical paths of domination and exploitation, including those trodden by imperialism.[10] The impact of crises is also critical for variations in preference intensity, especially short-term shocks with high economic, environmental, military, and social costs.[11]

We treat science as the degree of epistemic consensus over an issue. While it is common to assert that IOs are propulsion devices for scientization,[12] we suggest that for scriptwriting, the key element is variation in epistemic agreement. Research on the sociology of science suggests that we can view the degree of settled knowledge through the patterning of scientific advancement: Sometimes there is gradual analytical clarification and consensus; other times, constant debates and disagreements without one side clearly dominating.[13] These forms of variation in the degree of settled knowledge—embodied in diverging opinions among the experts in decision-making structures—can be present in IOs' scriptwriting.[14]

Given how political contestation and scientific consensus can vary, this chapter provides a methodological toolkit for how to study global scripts. We begin by discussing the importance of abductive logic for exploring cases in which there is no predetermined outcome and, indeed, an element of surprise. We then discuss our toolkit, which provides the means to study those involved in scriptwriting. This toolkit allows us to investigate who is engaged in scriptwriting, their professional dispositions, and their use of language. The remainder of the chapter walks the reader through the methods employed to study scripts, linking qualitative and quantitative techniques to abductive reasoning.

In Favor of Abduction

Scripts should be studied with abductive logic. Our argument here is that while scholars tend to side with either deductive or inductive approaches, the best course of action is to generate strong guesses and gather empirics, then

[9] Mukherjee 2022.
[10] Stone 2004; Kohli 2020.
[11] Widmaier 2007; Widmaier et al. 2007.
[12] Hironaka 2014; Zapp 2017.
[13] Shwed and Bearman 2010.
[14] Collins 1981a.

revise initial assumptions and repeat until a convincing case is produced. Or, to use John Ruggie's words, abductive approaches use the 'successive adjusting of a conjectured ordering scheme to the available facts, until the conjecture provides as full an account of the facts as possible.'[15] Abduction—an ungainly term from the American pragmatist philosopher Charles Peirce[16]—advocates moving back and forth between data and theory, treating claims to inference as 'a hypothesis on probation.'[17]

An important element of abductive reasoning is that the scholar is literate in a range of theories that can explain the phenomena under investigation. Rather than picking a favored theory or theoretician, the scholar uses their theoretical knowledge to produce good guesses, to 'look for analytical patterns in a corpus of data in light of existing literatures.'[18] This is a process of probing which theoretical explanations stick best against data. As such, abduction is not inductive grounded theory, which does not start from theoretical propositions as a principle;[19] nor is it deductive theory testing, which seeks disconfirmation as a principle. Following a pragmatist stress on learning, abductively reasoned casual explanations should be convincing to a community of inquiry, provided they are not ideologically and theoretically bound to a monocausal explanation.[20] The aim of abduction, then, is knowledge extension rather than knowledge confirmation. A capacity to generate unexpected findings or discover scope conditions for prevailing accounts is crucial to this extension.[21]

Abduction does not remove inductive and deductive forms of reasoning from the table but subsumes them under an iterative process.[22] Inductive reasoning is useful for identifying patterns and outliers, and for providing confidence that we are sufficiently saturated with data to make a confident next step in the iteration. Deductive reasoning is important in identifying expectations from known theories that can generate propositions and hypotheses that lead to a search for more data. This includes negative cases that can help affirm better guesses on the links between theoretical frameworks and the

---

[15] Ruggie 1998, 98.
[16] Peirce 1984, 108. Peirce takes the term from Julius Pacius's term 'abductio,' which means 'to lead away'—see Sytko and Kuzina 2019.
[17] Timmermans and Tavory 2022, 156. As clarified by Ruggie, there is a lot of overlap between Peirce's thinking and Max Weber's ideal types as a means to foster 'successive interrogative reasoning between explanans and explanandum'; Ruggie 1998, 880.
[18] Timmermans and Tavory 2022, 156.
[19] As commented by Stefan Timmermans and Iddo Tavory, quite a lot of grounded theory, especially the extended case study approach, ends up positing theoretically derived structures after the fact, which they refer to as an instance of magical thinking. Timmermans and Tavory 2022, 168n1.
[20] Tavory and Timmermans 2013, 684.
[21] Timmermans and Tavory 2022.
[22] Friedrichs and Kratochwil 2009, 709.

empirics.[23] A recursive back-and-forth between induction and deduction is important for abductive logic because it fosters the selection of better leads to pursue.

With that in mind, abduction proceeds from the identification of theoretically informed good guesses on what drives what within the data, and then locating variation within an identified set of cases. Explaining variation can only be sensibly claimed with a delimited set of cases, lest anything goes.[24] Three forms of variation are particularly important for an abductive approach: 'dataset' variation, where there are different instances of the same thing; 'over time' variation; and 'intersituational' variation, wherein the cast of characters being studied vary in how they interact with others in relation to different phenomena. These three sources of variation—in the object under study, how it changes over time, and how actors interact around it—provide good grounds for specifying what drives change in an argument that can be recognized as plausible by a community of inquiry.[25]

Abductive logic has been applied primarily using qualitative methodologies, including to the study of IOs.[26] Recent developments, which we seek to exploit, marry abductive logic with computational techniques to 'defamiliarize' established theories.[27] These techniques include text-as-data, social network, and sequence-analytical approaches,[28] and are now increasingly being applied to IOs. For example, an inductive study of agenda congruence between the decision-making bodies and administrations of the International Labour Organization, the United Nations (UN) Environment Programme, and the World Health Organization (WHO) found that organizations with limited administrative autonomy tend to align their agendas with those of their political masters.[29] Other studies take a deductive approach. A 2023 study found that in the negotiations for the UN Framework Convention on Climate Change, states from comparable levels of economic development made similar statements.[30] Another 2023 investigation found that the adoption of NGO-derived information by the Office of the United Nations High Commissioner for Human Rights favors NGOs with high status that use neutral language.[31] This work is crucial in furnishing supportive evidence for well-established theories. We suggest that abductive reasoning can

---

[23] Timmermans and Tavory 2022, 156.
[24] Goertz and Mahoney 2012.
[25] Tavory and Timmermans 2013.
[26] Finnemore 2013; Hendriksen 2022.
[27] Karell and Freedman 2019, 729.
[28] Brandt and Timmermans 2021.
[29] Bayerlein et al. 2020.
[30] Genovese et al. 2023.
[31] Nie 2023.

take us one theoretical step further, and—when fused with computational techniques—heighten the chance of novel and surprising findings.

Our approach uses abductive reasoning and mixed methods that offer multiple avenues to understand scriptwriting, each entailing different motivating subquestions, data, and methods of analysis. Some of these approaches are not novel in isolation. For example, analyses of IOs have collected biographical data to examine the similarity of educational backgrounds of IO professionals.[32] Relatedly, studies of how densely connected actors are within social networks in IOs have been gaining prominence, through recent inquiries into the gender and racial composition of elite networks present in IO leadership,[33] and the coordination of economic elites advocating for certain types of reforms.[34] Similarly, studying textual output of IOs is well established using both quantitative and qualitative approaches. For example, semi- or fully automated content analysis is helpful for processing the large amounts of text that IOs produce, including speeches within IO forums,[35] annual reports,[36] working papers,[37] and board minutes.[38] The strength of the methodological toolkit presented here is that it can embed these diverse methods and research foci into a unified framework, then employ them synergistically to yield novel theoretical and empirical insights and adjudicate between competing accounts.

Individual-Level Analyses

The first analytical step in unpacking scriptwriting processes is interrogating the background of the individuals involved. This follows from a long strand of prosopographic scholarship that investigates the 'common background characteristics of a group of actors in history by means of a collective study of their lives.'[39] The aim of prosopographic research is to differentiate group members by distinguishing career pathways,[40] mechanisms of social cohesion,[41] and claims to different identities to erect boundaries of difference.[42] Individuals within the group—typically elites—are located in a social space, which can be

---

[32] Chwieroth 2007; Nelson 2014; Goetze 2017; Weaver et al. 2022; Heinzel et al. 2024; Lang et al. 2024.
[33] Young et al. 2021.
[34] Gautier Morin and Rossier 2021.
[35] Baturo et al. 2017.
[36] Moretti and Pestre 2015; Allen and Easton-Calabria 2022.
[37] Kaya and Reay 2019.
[38] Forster et al. 2025.
[39] Stone 1971, 46. For a review see Hasselbalch and Seabrooke 2021.
[40] Ellersgaard et al. 2019; Rossier et al. 2022; Bühlmann et al. 2023.
[41] Henriksen et al. 2022; Littoz-Monnet 2022.
[42] Ban and Patenaude 2019.

understood as a field,[43] ecology,[44] or network.[45] In line with our expectations, we posit that two key characteristics matter most for the expert community under study here: educational background and professional socialization. To be sure, various other individual-level characteristics also may shape behavior, and their relevance depends on the analytical focus of a country. For example, political preferences, ideological orientation, gender, or race—topics that do not receive in-depth engagement in this book—may affect what IO officials say and do, and these are topics that can be explored in future research.

First, analysis of educational data has long been utilized in the relevant literature and relies on the core insight that one's university and degree subject shape how they approach the world and policy problems within it. This empirical approach relies on such educational backgrounds to infer individuals' worldviews and preferences and is prominent across different strands of scholarship. For example, in his pioneering study of French public administration, Pierre Bourdieu documented how graduates of the prestigious *grandes écoles* are socialized to have a common perception of policy problems and appropriate responses, as well as a strong sense of esprit de corps (i.e., 'homogeneity of mental structures').[46] Following a similar logic to the study of global governance, Stephen Nelson's analysis of similarity of beliefs among economic policymakers relies on a classification of these policymakers 'as neoliberal if they earned a master's degree or above from a highly ranked American economics department.'[47]

Second, and more demanding in terms of data and computation, professional trajectories are also highly relevant in shaping the ideas and toolkits of individuals involved in scriptwriting global policies. The aim of such analyses is to trace patterns of belonging to different types of expert communities. To do this, sequence analysis—a well-established method in biology and demography—provides an important analytical tool for identifying groups from data on sequences of different states, like the career histories of professionals. Doing this relies on optimal matching (OM), an approach that analyzes sequences of information to assess the degree of similarity or difference among them by using pattern-search algorithms.[48] The basic technique OM provides is to identify differences in sequences. Within political science and

---

[43] Lebaron 2008; Mudge and Vauchez 2012.
[44] Seabrooke and Tsingou 2021.
[45] Apeldoorn and Graaff 2016.
[46] Bourdieu 1998, 84.
[47] Nelson 2014, 309.
[48] Abbott and Tsay 2000; Abbott 2001a.

sociology, the method has been applied to a range of cases,[49] including the rise of female executives in finance,[50] the transnational emergence of welfare systems,[51] and revolving doors in international financial governance.[52]

When using sequence analysis and OM, one defines an alphabet and the states within it. These established, the basic method is to compare the sequence of states to distinguish how dissimilar they are. For example, consider the following sequences:

X:	A	A	A	C	C	B	B	B	E	E
Y:	A	B	C	D	E	F	G	G	H	H
Z:	A	A	A	B	B	B	B	E	E	E

Assume these reflect career histories and describe transitions between different 'states,' like an individual's professional position in a given year. Individual Y would appear highly professionally unstable by changing professional fields nearly every year. In contrast, individuals X and Z exhibit much more stable careers as they remain in their professional fields for longer, and these professional fields are similar to each other (note the prevalence of states A, B and E). Via OM analysis, Y would be identified as most dissimilar to X and Z, who have more common states.

The comparison is done through the assignment of costs of transforming one sequence into another. In our context, we assign costs based on the effort and risk of moving from one work role to another. Movement between career stages is costly because it involves several risks (e.g., of failure in the new position, to professional prestige, and to income), and requires a lot of energy to adapt one's knowledge to the new professional environment, including the need to develop professional skills for the work task at hand. Viewing cost this way, we suggest that movement between career states within a professional ecology is less costly than moving outside one's established professional role and into a different professional ecology. For example, a move from working at a major bank to working at a major asset manager would entail cost of energy and risk of 1, a move from being an academic economist to a central bank economist would entail a cost of 2, and a move from being an academic economist to working at an asset manager would entail a cost of 3. The latter career move would entail more risks, such as leaving a tenured job, learning

---

[49] Abbott and Hrycak 1990.
[50] Blair-Loy 1999.
[51] Abbott and DeViney 1992.
[52] Seabrooke and Tsingou 2021.

new skills that are relevant in asset management, potentially underperforming in the new role and becoming redundant, facing the difficulty of returning to academia given job scarcity, or losing social status. The underlying OM algorithm is Euclidian based, meaning that costs are absolute. For example, the cost of moving back to being an academic from being an asset manager is still 3.

These approaches offer an initial building block for the analysis of scriptwriting: interrogating the individual attributes of those who participate in these processes. The next step is using these findings to closely examine how these individuals behave in scriptwriting. Doing this requires matching the findings on educational background and professional trajectories with evidence of what scriptwriting participants do in these processes: what they say and how they position their statements. This requires analysis of text, to which we now turn.

Studying Text

A very common way of studying policy-design processes is by studying text: treaties, reports, meeting minutes, policy announcements, public speeches, and so on. For analyses of circumscribed events or processes, this can be a manageable (if highly ambitious) empirical task, as historically minded social scientists can attest. However, in the study of scriptwriting in global governance, complexity quickly kicks in: The number of actors involved (states and their representatives, as well as international bureaucrats) and of global policies being developed is large, thus making it unrealistic for individual scholars to be able to meaningfully process hundreds of thousands—if not millions—of words on global policy negotiations while considering the diverging interests and priorities of dozens of states and organizations, as well as the individual attributes of those representing them.

For these reasons, the standard analytical step is to make some major assumptions to reduce complexity. For example, a standard assumption in studies of global policy design is that rich-country representatives want more market liberalization, whereas those representing poorer countries resist it.[53] While this matches prior knowledge and is likely true on average, it is possible that some developing-country officials (e.g., those representing right-wing governments) might want to see markets spread more thoroughly and evenly around the world, while some Keynesian officials from rich countries might be skeptical of the promise of such measures. Such nuance may not be necessary for macroscopic work that is bound in a specific period and issue area.

[53] Babb 2009.

In a hypothetical example, if a representative of a smaller rich country—say, Denmark—has views that are not in line with the broader advocacy of market liberalization by other high-income-country officials, this can be down to idiosyncratic factors and be easily dismissed because of the limited power they command. But when using large textual databases that contain information for many issue areas over a longer period, differences between participants in the scriptwriting processes may become more pertinent and analytically relevant. Indeed, such methods allow scholars to process information in a different way than traditional historical methods—a complement, rather than supplement, to more traditional qualitative analyses, as we argue hereafter.

Consequently, the approach adopted in this book is to rely on a mix of quantitative and qualitative methods to elaborate on scriptwriting processes. On the quantitative side, a flurry of recent research has sought to apply a range of approaches to the study of IO texts.[54] A review of all text analysis methods is beyond the scope of this book and available elsewhere.[55] Here, we focus the discussion on two methods—frequency analysis and word embeddings—that jointly can illuminate different aspects of the underlying scriptwriting processes, and that rely on different computational approaches. In both cases automated and supervised approaches to the text reveal different elements for interpretation.

First, frequency analysis is useful for identifying what terms are used often in a given context. Frequency can be revealed via unsupervised or supervised approaches, depending on the extent to which they lean on the researcher's domain knowledge. The main difference is that unsupervised approaches entail a process of discovery, where the researcher does not have specific expectations on the outcome, while supervised approaches rely on a *search* that the researcher bases on their expectations of what should be found. Applying these methods is generally straightforward: Once a corpus of text has been identified, a topic-modeling machine-learning algorithm is used to reveal which words are frequently used within the corpus. The output can then be interpreted by the researcher and linked to power dynamics within the case. For example, Ian Gray and Jean Philippe Cointet applied topic modeling to UN Framework Convention on Climate Change summary reports from 1995 to 2016.[56] Their topic modeling revealed patterns of word usage that reflected how developing countries attempted to 'persuade from the

---

[54] For example, Bunea and Ibenskas 2015; Moretti and Pestre 2015; Baturo et al. 2017; Gurciullo and Mikhaylov 2017; Kaya and Reay 2019; James et al. 2021; Kentikelenis and Voeten 2021; Cormier and Manger 2022; Eckhard et al. 2023; Gray and Cointet 2023.
[55] For example, Wilkerson and Casas 2017; Edelmann et al. 2020; Hovy 2020; Grimmer et al. 2022; Stoltz and Taylor 2024.
[56] Gray and Cointet 2023.

periphery.' A more supervised approach to frequency relies on the creation of a dictionary by researchers, using their knowledge of the case context. For instance, Ayse Kaya and Mike Reay isolated terms they associated with neoliberal or moderate thinking across a range of economic issues and applied them to a large corpus of IMF surveillance documents from the technocracy as well as Board minutes.[57] This revealed whether the Board or the technocracy used particular terms more often.

A common criticism of frequency analysis is that it is a 'bag of words' approach that does not locate the use of words in context.[58] That is, this approach merely counts the occurrence of words in a given text; the ensuing metrics, while indicative, are very hard to interpret on their own. Further, supervised frequency analysis is prone to cherry-picking and limits the element of surprise—the fun aspect of abductive approaches—since the researcher can select preferred terms to be found in the corpus. For these reasons, such an approach is best employed in conjunction with additional quantitative and qualitative analysis approaches that can aid the interpretation of findings.

Second, word-embeddings approaches are derived from structural linguistics, an approach to language that focuses on the relationship of words to each other within the context of a text, rather than investigating the relationship of these words to phenomena in the real world.[59] From this starting point, the intuition behind word embeddings is simple—as pioneering structural linguist John Rupert Firth explained, 'You shall know a word by the company it keeps!'[60] For Firth, the meaning of a word can be understood through its habitual 'collocation'—that is, the words that tend to surround it. The empirical task, then, pertains to how to 'consolidate various kinds of information about a word's contexts into a single representation that characterizes those contexts.'[61]

The main idea behind word embeddings is that the meaning of a word can be derived from its context: Words close to the target word are better to use for understanding the target word's meaning and contribute more to the meaning than words farther away. In a hypothetical analysis of World Bank annual reports, the terms 'health,' 'hospital,' and 'HIV' should be located closer to each other than the terms 'health' and 'value chain,' or 'hospital' and 'trade,' or 'HIV' and 'exchange rate.' This collocation of 'health,' 'hospital,' and 'HIV' thus indicates semantic similarity and can give us a glimpse into how these

---

[57] Kaya and Reay 2019.
[58] Rudkowsky et al. 2018.
[59] Arseniev-Koehler 2022.
[60] Firth 1957, 11.
[61] Miller and Charles 1991, 24.

hypothetical reports discuss health and what 'health' means in the context of the document. These word embeddings need not be stable over time. For example, in a UN context, 'health' in the 1990s would appear close to 'reproductive' and 'maternal,' in the early 2000s close to 'newborn' and 'child,' in the mid- and late 2000s close to 'HIV' and 'AIDS,' and in the early 2010s close to 'malaria.'[62] In short, word embeddings enable researchers to perform comparisons on the company words keep over time, or—as we will do in this book—between different text authors.

In empirical terms, word-embedding analyses start from a text, which—in itself—is uninterpretable by a machine as it does not know the underlying semantic structure.[63] To do this, one must first convert words into vectors. The most commonly used approach—known as Word2Vec—calculates how frequently words co-occur using a shallow neural network, resulting in a multidimensional vector for each word.[64] Words with similar contexts will have similar co-occurrence matrices and thus similar vectors. The distances between these vectors 'are informative about the semantic similarity of the underlying concepts they connote for the corpus on which they were built.'[65]

The key methodological decisions to be taken in word embeddings analyses pertain to two issues.[66] First, the researcher needs to decide how to operationalize the context of each word—that is, how many words on either side of the word of interest are to be selected. Second, the degree of complexity of the model—how many dimensions a word vector should have—needs to be calibrated so that the model neither omits important information (too few dimensions) nor becomes noisy (too many dimensions). The high dimensionality of this data makes visualization difficult, however. For this reason, a technique called t-distributed stochastic neighbor embedding[67] is used to present word embeddings in a 2D plot that shows semantic relationships between words. Contextually similar terms are thus located near each other.

Both empirical approaches discussed thus far yield important insights, but are, at core, static: They compare text without considering interactions between those behind the text. Participants in scriptwriting discuss, negotiate, and engage with one another in order to develop and institutionalize new scripts. This means that we need a way to examine these interactions and how

---

[62] These hypothetical term collocations are drawn from the evolving focus areas in development assistance for health; see Micah et al. 2021, 1326.
[63] For more in-depth explications of the methodology, including applications in the social sciences, see Gurciullo and Mikhaylov 2017; Rudkowsky et al. 2018; Kozlowski et al. 2019; Rheault and Cochrane 2020; Stoltz and Taylor 2021; Arseniev-Koehler 2022; Rodriguez and Spirling 2022; Van Loon and Freese 2023.
[64] Mikolov et al. 2013.
[65] Rodriguez and Spirling 2022, 101.
[66] This discussion draws closely on Rodriguez and Spirling 2022.
[67] Maaten and Hinton 2008.

they affect what they say and do. To this end, 'close-reading' content analysis is the standard method employed, as it allows researchers not only to follow the paper trail of who said what, when, and to whom, but also to use their background knowledge and domain expertise to elaborate on the scriptwriting processes. In this context, nuance in rigid technical, bureaucratic, or diplomatic language can be more easily picked up and the sources of agreement or disagreement dissected.

This discussion of multiple methodologies for the study of scriptwriting in global governance begs a key question: How many methods does one need to study these processes? On one hand, mixed-methods approaches are broadly accepted as appropriate for studying social, political, and economic processes that are not amenable to precise measurement or causal identification techniques. On the other, increasing the number of methods used to tackle a research question also increases the complexity of the argument and places high demands on readers to keep several moving parts in mind when following how the empirical work unfolds and fits together. The approach we advance in this book is pragmatic: We rely on as many methods as necessary to develop comprehensive explanations of the phenomenon under study and triangulate our findings. This triangulation entails attempts to tackle wicked methodological problems by validating the findings of one approach with those of other approaches. If all findings point in the same direction, we can have a high degree of confidence in the veracity and robustness of our findings.[68]

Applying the Methodological Toolkit to the IMF

We apply the range of aforementioned methods to the study of scriptwriting in the IMF, on which we have accumulated a large arsenal of data on actors and text over the 1980–2009 period. Our account focuses on the phase of hyperglobalization,[69] which extends from the 1980s onward and entails the 'deep integration of markets for goods and capital (but not labor), [which] became an end in itself, overshadowing domestic agendas.'[70] The IMF was a crucial organization in this process, acting as a technocratic cheerleader[71] for market-augmenting approaches to policy problems. We end the analysis in

---

[68] On triangulation, see Tarrow 2010, 2019.
[69] Drori 2009; Rodrik 2011.
[70] Rodrik 2011, 76.
[71] United Nations Conference on Trade and Development 2017, v.

2009, the latest year of available data for full Board minutes at the point of data collection.

First, we collected the full curriculum vitae (CV) information for the 727 Executive Board members active during this time. These CVs are transmitted to the organization when each Board member is appointed and have a standardized format throughout the period of study. They report educational credentials and chronological employment background, as shown in figures 3.1–3.3 for three individuals in our dataset. Even a cursory look at these CVs suggests that these Board members are different types of professionals. Hirotake Fujino joined Japan's Ministry of Finance immediately upon graduation from Tokyo University in 1956, shortly thereafter took two years off to study for a master's in public administration at Princeton University, and then returned to the same ministry, where he rose through the ranks to senior roles like assistant vice minister of finance, before being appointed to the IMF in 1984. Lebanon's Samir El-Khouri had a similarly unvaried professional background. After receiving his PhD at Vanderbilt University, he immediately joined the IMF, where he remained over the subsequent three decades before joining the Board in 2006 as a representative of Middle Eastern countries. In contrast, US representative Nancy Jacklin had a more diverse career. She was trained in both economics and law at Georgetown, spent the subsequent 12 years working at the US Treasury and Federal Reserve, then pivoted to the private sector, where she spent nearly two decades working for Citibank and Clifford Chance. This variation across professional backgrounds already hints that these individuals may have different ways of interpreting policy problems, a topic that is of central analytical importance here.

While collecting CVs, we adopted a broad definition of Board members to include all individuals able to participate in Board deliberations. This includes, ex officio, the Executive Director and the Alternate Executive Director for each constituency. These individuals are resident in the IMF for the duration of their appointment: They hold two-year renewable terms, although few individuals hold their post for very long; median tenure is 3.3 years. These officials are aided by advisors, who can also participate in Board deliberations when their superiors are unable or unwilling to attend. Our dataset covers the entire career trajectories of the 727 individuals who held one of the aforementioned ranks.[72] Missing data did not represent a

---

[72] Initially, we collected and coded the career trajectories of 738 individuals, but we removed 11 from our sample because they had pre-Board careers of less than five years (e.g., an individual joined their country's central bank for two years upon university graduation, and then was sent to the IMF Board). Inclusion of these very short careers would have created theoretical quandaries (professional socialization is commonly assumed to occur over the medium run and not immediately upon entering a professional

BIOGRAPHICAL STATEMENT

Hirotake Fujino

Executive Director for:	Japan
Appointed as of:	July 28, 1984
Date of Birth:	June 18, 1933
National of:	Japan
Marital Status:	Married, two children
Education:	1956 – Tokyo University, Faculty of Law
	1960 – Princeton University, Woodrow Wilson School, MPA
Experience:	1956-date – Ministry of Finance:
	1963 – Chief, South Gifu Taxation Office
	1964 – Deputy Director, Coordination Division, International Finance Bureau
	1967 – Second and First Secretary, Japanese Delegation to the OECD
	1971 – Deputy Director, Coordination Division, Securities Bureau
	1973 – Director, Planning Division, Fair Trade Commission
	1975 – Director, Treasury Division, Financial Bureau
	1977 – Counsellor and Minister, Japanese Delegation to the OECD
	1980 – Assistant Vice Minister of Finance
	1982 – Deputy Director-General, Securities Bureau

Figure 3.1 Curriculum vitae of Hirotake Fujino
Source: IMF archives, Circ/84/95

major problem; we could not identify the CVs of only 14 individuals (primarily Board members with tenures starting in the 1970s, and therefore without CVs among the archival material we collected).[73]

environment; see Djelic and Quack 2010) and empirical difficulties (the OM analysis described hereafter performs more reliably when longer sequences—i.e., more data—are provided).
[73] We also do not have data for individuals holding the title of Assistant to Executive Director. These are junior officials who aid the executive directors and, in exceptional cases (when none of the more senior staff

BIOGRAPHICAL STATEMENT

Samir F. El-Khouri

Alternate Executive Director for:	Bahrain, Egypt, Iraq, Jordan, Kuwait, Lebanon, Libyan Arab Jamahiriya, Maldives, Oman, Qatar, Syrian Arab Republic, United Arab Emirates, and Republic of Yemen
Assumed Duties Date:	January 3, 2006
National of:	Lebanon
Marital Status:	Married, two children
Education:	American University of Beirut, B.A. (Economics), 1968; Vanderbilt University, Ph.D. (Economics), 1975
Experience:	1975-2005 - International Monetary Fund:
	1975 - Young Professional Program (YPP)
	1977 - Economist, Middle East Department
	1980 - Economist, IMF Institute
	1981 - Advisor to Executive Director for Saudi Arabia
	1981 - Alternate Executive Director for Saudi Arabia
	1982 - Advisor to Executive Director for Saudi Arabia
	1984 - Senior Economist, IMF Institute
	1985 - Deputy Division Chief, IMF Institute
	1989 - Senior Economist, Middle East Department
	1991 - Deputy Division Chief, Middle East Department
	1992 - Assistant to the Director, Middle East Department
	1994 - Division Chief, IMF Institute
Other Background:	Secondment to the World Bank, 1992

Secretary's Department
January 2006

Figure 3.2 Curriculum vitae of Samir F. El-Khouri
Source: IMF archives, Circ/06/1

Once these archival data were collected, we converted the CVs into a person–year dataset listing each person's employment details by year. Subsequently, we coded the professional positions an individual held in a given year

are available), can attend Board debates. As per IMF procedures, the CVs of these junior officials are not circulated around the organization and—consequently—leave no paper trail among archival documents.

BIOGRAPHICAL STATEMENT

Nancy P. Jacklin

Executive Director for:	United States
Assumed Duties Date:	December 4, 2002
National of:	United States
Marital Status:	Married
Education:	School of Foreign Service, Georgetown University, B.S.F.S.. (Honors)(International Economics), 1969
	Georgetown University Law Center, J.D., 1973
Experience:	1973-1982 - Attorney Advisor, U.S. Department of Treasury
	1982-1985 - Assistant General Counsel, International Banking, Federal Reserve Board of Governors
	1985-1992 - Sector Counsel and Associate General Counsel, Citibank, NA
	1992-2002 - Partner, Clifford Chance
Other Background:	Member, Council on Foreign Relations

Secretary's Department
December 2002

Figure 3.3 Curriculum vitae of Nancy P. Jacklin
Source: IMF archives, Circ/02/112

into distinct states (e.g., central banker or finance ministry official), as anticipated in the methodological discussion in the previous section. This coding exercise yielded the sequences that we analyzed through OM methods to generate clusters of professionals with similar backgrounds. We elaborate in greater detail on the data collected and coding decisions in the appendix of chapter 4.

Our data on IMF staff draw on other scholars' data collection efforts.[74] Unlike Board members, who must report their CVs to the secretary's department upon being appointed, there is no similar obligation for IMF staff, and their CVs are nowhere available in a systematic and comprehensive format. This is partly deliberate: The IMF has rigid hierarchical structures and takes pride in being able to mold individuals to toe the organizational line, thus purportedly reducing the independent agency of any one staffer. The fact that policy output is commonly developed by teams and passes many rounds of internal revisions contributes to deemphasizing the role of individual agency and instead foregrounding the bureaucracy's collective agency. To the extent that detailed evidence on staff professional trajectories is available, these draw on ad hoc research and publicly available information.

In terms of textual data, we collected a battery of archival material on the three case studies that we pursue in this book. As an initial step, we collected the minutes of all 4,449 Executive Board meetings over the 1980–2009 period and extracted information on the topics considered during each meeting, yielding a dataset of 20,120 topics. We then searched this dataset for titles of documents relevant to our case studies, as summarized in each empirical chapter. The Board commonly discusses the same topic several times per year (or even over multiple years), as this is the necessary process to build the consensus on which decision making is premised. The analytical importance of this process is that it offers scholars ample empirical material to trace the evolution of policy thinking within the Board vis-à-vis the same issue areas.

The transcripts provide a list of all those attending the meetings and the verbatim comments of everyone who spoke. Board debate is highly structured. The opening of the meeting specifies which topic the Board is considering, cites background discussion papers and reports prepared by IMF staff, and— where relevant—an introduction by the Managing Director, who chairs the meeting. Subsequently, a range of speakers deliver prepared statements, and free discussion follows. In addition to Board members and the very senior management of the organization, selected IMF staff are also present for technical clarifications and commonly speak only when explicitly asked by a Board member. Figures 3.4–3.6 present sample pages from a single Board discussion to illustrate the structure of the archival data.

Once we collected these documents, we extracted all the individual statements from each meeting and matched them to the Board member

---

[74] Nelson 2014; Broome and Seabrooke 2015; Seabrooke and Nilsson 2015; Heinzel and Liese 2021; Chwieroth 2015.

```
                                                    NOT FOR PUBLIC USE
         MASTER FILES
         ROOM C-130                  0404
                           INTERNATIONAL MONETARY FUND

                        Minutes of Executive Board Meeting 88/53

                              10:00 a.m., March 30, 1988


                              M. Camdessus, Chairman
                         R. D. Erb, Deputy Managing Director

              Executive Directors          Alternate Executive Directors

              A. Abdallah
              F. Cassell
                                           Yang W., Temporary
              C. H. Dallara
              J. de Groote                 J. Prader
              A. Donoso                    E. V. Feldman
                                           A. M. Othman
              G. Grosche
                                           J. Reddy
              A. Kafka                     J. Hospedales
              M. Massé                     D. McCormack
                                           C. V. Santos
                                           I. A. Al-Assaf
              G. Ortiz                     L. Filardo
              J. Ovi
              H. Ploix
              G. A. Posthumus              G. P. J. Hogeweg
              C. R. Rye
                                           M. A. Hammoudi, Temporary
              A. K. Sengupta               L. E. N. Fernando
              K. Yamazaki
                                           S. Rebecchini, Temporary

                     L. Van Houtven, Secretary and Counsellor
                              S. L. Yeager, Assistant


              1.  Debt Situation - Developments, Issues, and
                    Role of Fund ........................... Page 3
              2.  Executive Board Travel ..................... Page 38
```

Figure 3.4 Cover page of IMF Board meeting minutes
Source: IMF Archives, EBM/88/53

articulating them, as well as to background information on their prior education and career trajectory, drawing from the OM analysis. Subsequently, we relied on a range of text-analysis methods to yield inferences. Our data consist of approximately 2.8 million words of structured text from Executive Board meetings and more than 400 IMF staff documents. This corpus exhibits the three forms of anticipated variation we described earlier: *dataset variation* across a range of cases treated by the Board and technocrats (capital controls, sovereign debt management, value-added taxation); *time variation* pertaining to our data coverage from 1980 to 2009; and *intersituational variation*

EBM/88/53 - 3/30/88   - 10 -

Mr. Posthumus made the following statement:

It is a matter of great concern indeed that while substantial external adjustment has taken place in several highly indebted countries since 1981, balance of payments viability is not in sight for many of those countries. The case-by-case approach to the debt problem is the only realistic approach, but it apparently does not work. It is the only realistic approach because it involves as central elements the debtor's policies for macroeconomic and structural adjustment and the debtor's efforts to obtain the required finance in a way which helps to make its debt burden sustainable. The approach does not work because the debt burden in many cases has not become sustainable.

The conclusion is that a way must be found to make the debt strategy work. I do not believe that the strategy should be changed by searching for an international debt facility: the problems of determining the eligibility of debtor countries, of burden sharing between creditors, of the risks to be borne by international institutions, of the costs to be carried by creditor or donor countries, and of the political consequences for governments in both debtor and creditor countries are insurmountable. I would hope that the Interim Committee would once again underline its support for the existing strategy, implicitly or explicitly making clear that nonmarket-based, centralized debt relief operations and general solutions are out of the question. Otherwise, creditors may continue to hope that they will be, partly, bailed out. Consequently, they continue to be reluctant to increase their exposure and to accept the facts of life.

In seeking to make the debt strategy work, the question to be addressed is: can and should the Fund do more? The main staff paper analyzes several elements of the Fund's catalytic role, which is indeed the crucial point.

It is clear that the Fund should stand ready to support adjustment programs in member countries. Adjustment may often be a condition of creditors for providing either new money or for debt restructuring. But it should be clear that adjustment is, first and foremost, in the interest of the debtor country itself. The role of the Fund is essentially to assist the debtor, and it should be perceived as being supportive of the debtor's policies, which implies that the Fund should help the debtor to make an analysis of the various possibilities of adjustment and financing. The best way to do this is to make several medium-term scenarios, analyzing alternatives with respect to growth, the strength of adjustment efforts, and balance of payments developments, including foreign financing. Such scenarios should help to obtain at least an idea of what can be done by debtors and creditors, respectively, to obtain a

Figure 3.5 Transcript of an IMF Board meeting with prepared statements
Source: IMF Archives, EBM/88/53

as interactions over scriptwriting change from technocratic to executive decision-making contexts.

To fully exploit our data arsenal and maximize the prospect of knowledge extension, we applied a mixed-methods approach. In terms of quantitative text analysis, we used word embeddings and supervised frequency analysis to

- 29 -   EBM/88/53 - 3/30/88

> Mr. de Groote observed that it was impossible for the Fund to exercise its responsibilities vis-à-vis member countries unless it became involved to a certain extent in negotiations and discussions with other sources of financing. Because Fund financing alone could not fill a member's financing gap, it would be meaningless for the Fund to contribute its own resources without assurances that others would assume their share of the financing burden. That principle underlay the entire growing-out-of-debt strategy and the Baker initiative. It was extremely difficult to defend the idea that the Fund could forget about other partners in the game and still justify the magnitude of its own contribution to financing members' adjustment efforts.
>
> Mr. Grosche remarked that Mr. Posthumus had identified the issue: in developing programs and determining the financing gap to be filled, the Fund had to consider the role of the banks. In his view, the Fund had only to ask the banks to close the gap, without indicating the way in which it should be done. However, the issue of the banks' role in the debt strategy raised difficult questions to which the Board would have to return in the future. In that regard, the Fund could not avoid confronting the issue of how financing gaps in programs supported by the Fund would be filled.
>
> Mrs. Ploix commented that there seemed to be some confusion between placing pressure on the commercial banks and assisting countries in the gap-filling exercise. The case of Côte d'Ivoire, for example, had been difficult because the Fund was not sufficiently involved and because some new, innovative techniques were attempted that the commercial banks found difficult to implement. If the Fund had been more involved in assisting the participants, or at least monitoring developments, perhaps the technical difficulties which arose could have been avoided.
>
> The Chairman remarked that he welcomed the debate and Directors' tentative comments on the Fund's evolving role in the debt strategy. Indeed, if the Fund had a unique role to play in the debt strategy it was precisely because the Executive Board was one of the few places where such a discussion could take place. It was also true that in recent months, authorities and other participants in the debt strategy had perceived the evolution of the Fund's role, as Mr. Massé had suggested.
>
> There was great appeal in the alternative scenario in which the Fund, as well as the World Bank and other international institutions, would not be involved in assembling financing packages for debtor countries, the Chairman continued. But the history of the debt strategy showed that if the international institutions did not assume an active role in that process, the result would be a standstill in creditor-debtor negotiations and an increase in the number of countries financing their debt through the accumulation of arrears. In 1987, 6 of the 15 most heavily indebted countries had, willingly or otherwise, resorted to that practice. That perverse development had to be dealt with, not only because of the risk of arrears to the Fund, but because no real adjustment could take place in countries while they were pursuing that course.

Figure 3.6 Transcript of an IMF Board meeting with free discussion
Source: IMF Archives, EBM/88/53; underlining added for illustration purposes

scrutinize whether and how these attributes shaped the positions individuals took during Board meetings. To do this, we first matched all comments with the professional clusters identified through the OM algorithm discussed earlier, then employed the quantitative approaches. Yet, these methods are static in how they approach our text corpus, and we were ultimately interested in the dynamic aspect of normmaking processes: interactions between Board members. Thus, we relied on more traditional qualitative analysis methods: We selected a subset of relevant debates, matched speakers to their countries of origin and professional clusters, and closely read the minutes of these meetings. Our focus was on tracing the policy positions that Board members took and whether—in doing so—they expressed agreement or disagreement with other Board members. That is, we delved deeper into the interactions that ultimately shaped the policy scripts that emerged from IMF Board deliberations. Each of the empirical chapters provides additional information on the methodological approach employed there.

Summary of Analytical Strategy

This chapter introduced a mixed-method, multipronged methodological approach to the study of scriptwriting within global governance. This is the essence of the idea of an 'extended computational case study'.[75] The 'case' is the organizational context of the IMF, the 'computation' element refers to reliance on an array of quantitative methods in conjunction with qualitative analysis of a subset of the data, and the 'extended' dimension links to the reliance on several instances of scriptwriting in order for the abductive logic of inference to yield fruit and enable the scope conditions of the theoretical account to be articulated. The obvious drawback of this approach is that it expects the reader to consider many moving parts in the analysis and hope they all come together in a streamlined way. To aid this process, we capture these moving parts in a schematic form in figure 3.7.

The initial analytical step entails measuring the attributes of those with formal authority in scriptwriting—that is, the state-appointed members of the board, council, or committee of interest. We collected the biographical information of the individuals involved in these processes: where are they from, where and what did they study, and their career trajectory before taking on their current role. All these are pertinent questions for understanding the input to their theorization processes and the policy positions they take. With these data in hand, we yield a range of inferences using different methodological approaches. Most crucially, we can use quantitative techniques to group individuals with the most similar backgrounds, thus identifying clusters of people who share many background attributes. We have demonstrated the promise of this approach on IMF Board members in chapter 4.

[75] Pardo-Guerra and Pahwa 2022.

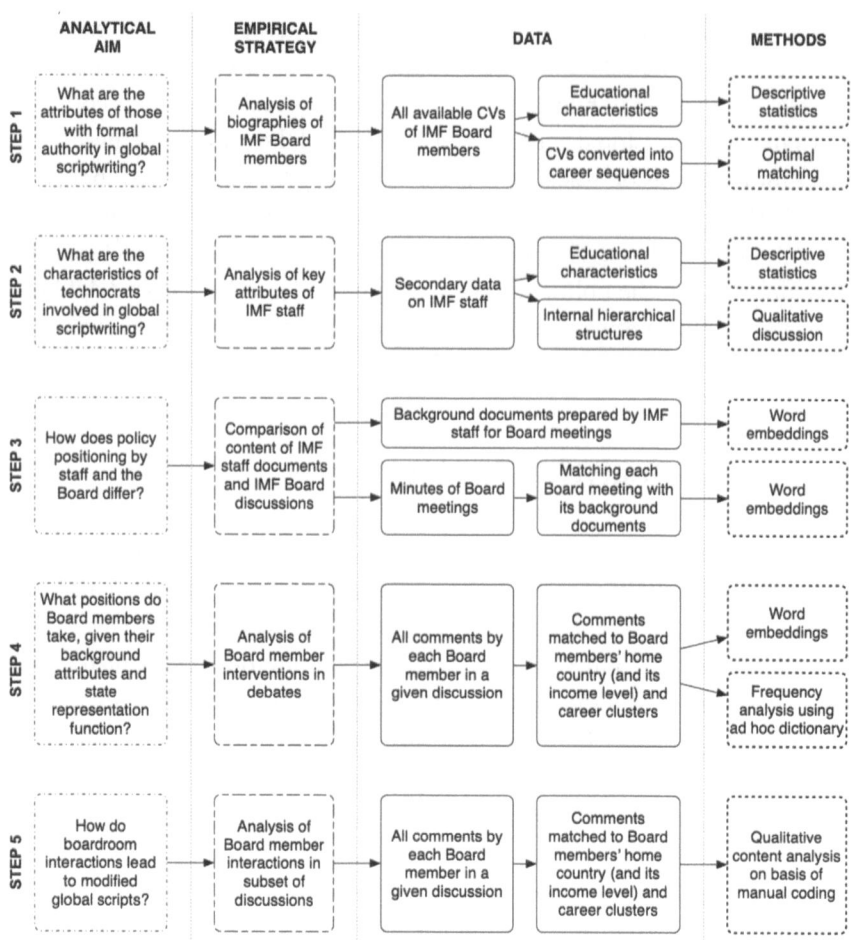

Figure 3.7 Analytical approach to the study of scriptwriting and application to the IMF
Source: Authors

But knowledge of the attributes of state representatives in scriptwriting is not enough. These individuals are supported by the bureaucracy of the IOs in which they operate, and these bureaucrats have analytically relevant attributes of their own. In some cases, they all have similar types of training and a strong sense of esprit de corps, as we show for the case of the IMF in chapter 5. In other cases, they might have varied backgrounds that give them different frames through which to interpret policy problems, like the case of the World Bank or the UN Environment Programme. In yet other instances, organizations may outsource some of their key functions by bringing in consultancies and professional service firms as key advisors or even substitute staff—a growing phenomenon in global governance organizations.[76] Here, scholars need to grapple with the diversity of the professionals involved. Capturing these attributes is important because they feed into the preparatory work for scriptwriting.

This background knowledge offers important clues for the inputs into scriptwriting, but is not revealing in itself of how these processes unfold. To determine this, scholars need to match IO board members and the bureaucracy with what they do on the job. While not everything they do is observable, two aspects of their professional activities leave clear—and often voluminous—paper trails: what they say in formal meetings (for which transcripts are invariably kept) and what they write in organizational reports. Through these texts, we can trace policy preferences and their evolution using quantitative and qualitative methods. Two comparisons are pertinent here. First, how does the textual output of an organization's bureaucracy compare to the policy positioning of the state representatives who have ultimate decision-making power? This yields important knowledge on the degree of congruence between the policy positions of staff and their political masters, while enabling examination of whether staff positions are closer to some state representatives than others. As we saw in chapter 1, a long-standing strand of scholarship would expect staff to be closely aligned with representatives of powerful countries from the Global North.

The second comparison is between state representatives themselves. We have already argued against a flat actorhood perspective on these individuals—that they are there as mere mouthpieces of their appointing states.[77] Instead, they are commonly experts in their own right, with professional trajectories that potentially inform their policy positions. By knowing how these representatives cluster together based on attributes unrelated to their country of origin, we can then start exploring whether they are also similar in how they position themselves in scriptwriting processes. For example, in the case of the IMF, we can investigate whether and how Board members with central banking backgrounds position themselves in comparison to those who were previously employed in political offices, finance ministries, or the private sector. Other empirical settings would offer other types of juxtapositions, such as how those with backgrounds as climate scientists versus as economists position themselves in global environmental-governance negotiations, how those with backgrounds as medical doctors versus as

---

[76] Seabrooke and Sending 2020; Eckl and Hanrieder 2023.
[77] A similar, more ethnographic approach can be found in Block-Lieb and Halliday 2017.

public health professionals position themselves in global health-governance negotiations, and so on.

Thus far, our analyses have focused on individual-level attributes and observed behaviors. Such stage setting is important because it enables the generation of hypotheses (in line with the abductive reasoning set out earlier in this chapter), provides important hints of underlying processes, and allows for the use of computational methods to uncover variation in professional backgrounds or policy positioning. Ultimately, however, scripts are developed through interactions: These individuals, with their different political priorities and distinct knowledge and expertise, come together to make a range of decisions. In doing so, they need to negotiate, convince each other, or occasionally and diplomatically threaten dissenters. All these processes occur at the meso-level in the boardrooms and committee meetings that aggregate and seek to reconcile competing preferences. It is here that scripts are made, and it is these interactions that form the culmination of the analytical scrutiny of scriptwriting. Without analysis of interactions, the individual-level attributes and behaviors remain unwedded from their real-world terrain, and without prior analysis of these individual determinants of scriptwriting, the interactions that yield scripts cannot be fully understood.

Our outline of this approach is not to imply that all steps need to be followed in every empirical instance; this is ultimately a domain-specific decision. For example, we follow each of these steps in chapters 6 and 7, but not in chapter 8 because we found that the IMF's Board had a very limited role in shaping tax policy scripts and thus focused on the role of staff. In other words, this framework offers enough versatility to enable application in different instances of scriptwriting. We return to these issues in the concluding chapter.

PART II
SCRIPTWRITERS

4
The Board

Introduction

Boardroom governance is a commonplace feature of intergovernmental organizations, and the International Monetary Fund (IMF)—as well as its Bretton Woods sibling, the World Bank—have provided a template for how to set up such structures in a range of other organizations. The main decision-making body of the IMF is the Executive Board, a 24-member body housed in the top floors of the IMF's Washington, DC, headquarters. Its members, the Executive Directors and their alternates, are there to formally represent the member states of the organization. For this purpose, they meet approximately three times per week, in sessions that generally last for several hours, to decide on the broad range of the IMF's business: from the norms and policy scripts that underpin the functioning of contemporary economic globalization to selecting or terminating a Managing Director, and from debating country-specific loan agreements to discussing various administrative issues.[1]

While boardroom governance—premised on tight oversight of staff and extensive engagement with day-to-day organizational issues—is now widespread, this model was not predestined to become dominant. John Maynard Keynes, the leading figure behind the Bretton Woods conference of 1944 and chief negotiator for the UK, strongly opposed the idea of having a resident board of directors.[2] In his view, this would unduly politicize the institutions and turn directors into 'politicians [whose] every thought and act shall have an *arrière-pensée* [ulterior motive]' and everything they 'determine shall not be for its own sake or on its own merits but because of something else.'[3] When Keynes arrived at the IMF's first annual meeting in 1946, he was appalled to find out that the Board of Governors—the plenary decision-making body

---

[1] Van Houtven 2002.
[2] Swedberg 1986, 378. The classic study here on Anglo–American rivalry in this context is Gardner 1956. See also Ikenberry 1992 for a more expertise-based argument.
[3] Skidelsky 1986, 465; see also Frieden 2020. As Helleiner makes clear, the structure of Bretton Woods followed on from US financial relations with Latin America, including the US's 'fear of growing Nazi influence in Latin America.' Bretton Woods was designed to reform both North–North and North–South relationships; Helleiner 2014, 31.

Making Global Norms. Alexandros Kentikelenis and Leonard Seabrooke, Oxford University Press.
© Oxford University Press (2025). DOI: 10.1093/9780197828656.003.0004

where all member states are represented by their finance ministers or central bank governors—had selected political Washington, rather than financial New York City, as the seat of the IMF. The Fund's headquarters—initially joint with the World Bank—were only a short walk from the US Treasury, and some Treasury staff were even housed in the same building.[4] Keynes's disappointments intensified upon learning that Executive Directors and their alternates would have full-time positions; he noted they would comprise 'a body of persons who could amount at the maximum to a mob of forty-eight.'[5] This aggravated his concerns that the Fund risked becoming too 'grandmotherly' in its policing powers.[6] These developments represented for Keynes concrete steps toward the impending politicization of an institution he had envisaged as thoroughly technocratic and removed from political influences and the associated bargaining that normally takes place in international affairs.

Ultimately, Keynes lost this struggle, and the IMF's Executive Board acquired extensive decision-making powers. This entire infrastructure rested on the role of Executive Directors, who collectively decided on organizational policies and priorities. Given the IMF's significance as the focal point of global economic governance, most countries—from the early days of the organization—sent individuals with high prestige and expertise to represent them. The initial composition of the Board included towering figures such as Harry Dexter White, assistant secretary at the US Treasury and Keynes's counterpart in the Bretton Woods negotiations; Pierre Mendès-France, the lead French negotiator at Bretton Woods and a former economy minister; George Bolton, a prominent British banker and advisor to the Bank of England; Camile Gutt, the former Belgian finance minister who shortly thereafter became the IMF's first Managing Director; and Yee-Chun Koo, a member of China's negotiating team at Bretton Woods and former general manager of the Farmers' Bank of China.[7] While it is less common in more recent years to find former finance ministers among the ranks of the Executive Board, the individuals that take on Executive Director posts are still commonly of high caliber, as we will see hereafter.

This chapter provides the first comprehensive account of the characteristics of IMF Board members and outlines its implications for organizational decision making. First, we examine the legal arrangements underpinning the

---

[4] World Bank 2021.
[5] Keynes 1980, 225.
[6] Martin 2022a, 228–30.
[7] Following the Chinese Communist revolution of 1949, the Bretton Woods institutions recognized Taiwan as China's representative. China reengaged with the IMF in 1980. See Helleiner 2019, 1121.

Board's functioning: who is represented, how many votes they command, and what the internal decision-making rules and norms are. Second, we discuss how power functions within the Board setting. We review the dominant arguments in global governance scholarship and outline their scope conditions. Subsequently, we present novel evidence on the educational and professional backgrounds of Executive Directors. This evidence reveals a high degree of educational homogeneity (almost every director is an economist, and one in two has studied at an elite Anglo-American university) and extensive professional heterogeneity. Nearly half the Board members were previously employed in central banks, while the rest held roles in varied areas: finance ministries, high politics, the private sector, academia, or international organizations (IOs). Last, we show that the precise professional backgrounds present in the Board change over time, thus eliciting a well-grounded suspicion that the types of expertise present may be related to the Board's policy outputs. Documenting this case is the focus of the rest of this book.

How IMF Governance Works

The IMF's system of governance diverges from the one-country-one-vote processes that can be found in many IOs, particularly in the United Nations system.[8] That model gives precedence to the principle of equality between sovereign states, and means—at least in theory—that well-organized but politically and economically weak countries (i.e., most countries comprising the international system) can win major victories, even against the preferences of the world's most powerful countries. In practice, however, organizations governed by one-country-one-vote decision-making processes are often less consequential, precisely because powerful countries are not keen to invest in organizations where they are likely to find themselves on the losing side on important questions. Instead, various decision-making systems have been developed to ensure that IOs' outputs reflect the underlying balance of power among their member states.

The IMF's model is based on unequal voting shares for its member states, also known as the shareholders of the organization. In this model, what matters most is not sovereign equality but the relative economic significance of a country and the resources it provides to the institution. The important question, then, becomes how financial contributions and voting shares are calculated—a major concern for participants at the Bretton Woods

[8] Martinez-Diaz 2009.

conference.⁹ What emerged was a formula—drafted by the US team—that estimated voting rights by considering a country's gold and dollar holdings, income level, and openness to international trade.¹⁰ But these calculations were merely a fig leaf for their true purpose: to enshrine a predetermined pecking order into formal law. According to Raymond Mikesell, the US Treasury official who drafted the original formula, the ultimate voting shares were designed to reflect the US's political priorities and reward its wartime allies: During the negotiations, Harry Dexter White handed him a list of how major countries should rank in the IMF's pecking order, and Mikesell had to reverse-engineer appropriate weights for the relevant variables to end up with the desired ranking.¹¹

While the calculation of voting shares has evolved considerably over time (the IMF's founding treaty foresees revisions every five years), high-income countries still control the bulk of the votes. The US is the largest shareholder and holds a veto over decisions, and even relatively small rich countries enjoy inflated voting rights. For example, in 2009, Belgium held 2.1% of total votes, considerably more than Türkiye (0.55%) or Indonesia (0.95%)—both populous developing nations and members of the Group of 20. Since then, votes have been rebalanced further,¹² although not substantially enough to reflect a meaningful transfer of power from countries in the Global North to those in the Global South.¹³

The countries with the largest voting shares (the US, Japan, Germany, the UK, France, China, Russia,¹⁴ and Saudi Arabia) simply appoint the officials that represent them and are free to recall them at any time.¹⁵ The US stands out not only for being the largest shareholder of the organization with veto power over organizational decisions (albeit one that is rarely necessary to employ in practice, as most issues that reach the Board in the first place have at least passive US acceptance) but also because its senior representatives are political appointees. Congress needs to approve their nominations, and times of

---

⁹ Helleiner 2014.
¹⁰ Leaver and Seabrooke 2000; Weaver and Moschella 2017.
¹¹ Mikesell 1994.
¹² Extending the same example, as of 2022, Belgium holds 1.3% of total votes, Türkiye holds 0.95%, and Indonesia holds 0.9%.
¹³ Vestergaard and Wade 2015; Wade and Vestergaard 2015.
¹⁴ Since 2019, Russia has formed a constituency with Syria, representing geopolitical alignments, while both the Executive Director and the Alternate Executive Director remain Russian nationals. Prior to this, Syria belonged to the constituency of mostly Middle Eastern countries, like Egypt, Iraq, Jordan, Lebanon, and Libya.
¹⁵ Technically, only the five countries with the largest voting shares can 'appoint' their directors, while all other countries 'elect' their directors through the constituency system. During the period covered in this volume, China, Saudi Arabia, and Russia (since 1993) each formed a single-country constituency that elected its own representation.

political deadlock in Washington, DC, can force the US to temporarily fill the seat with more junior Treasury staff.

The remaining countries voluntarily cluster together to form multicountry constituencies that elect their representatives for fixed but renewable terms of two years. How constituencies organize themselves varies considerably, and different norms underpin this process.[16] In some cases, the principle of equal representation is important. For example, most African countries are clustered together under two constituencies: one for Anglophone countries with 20 members that represent 3% of total votes, and one for Francophone countries with 23 members and 1.35% of the votes (2009 data). Countries that can send officials to the IMF rotate, so that all members can eventually have one of their nationals holding an Executive Director or Alternate Executive Director position. In other cases, constituencies contain a dominant shareholder and several smaller ones, which tilts appointments to favor the larger country. For instance, the constituency that encompasses Albania, Greece, Italy, Malta, Portugal, and San Marino always selects an Italian Executive Director and a Greek alternate. Regardless of how they are selected, directors representing constituencies are expected to advance the interests of all their appointing authorities in their dealings with the IMF.

Table 4.1 presents the IMF's 24 constituencies as of 2009 (the year our data collection ends). As the country groupings reveal, there is no single way to organize a constituency. Often, there is a degree of geographical proximity among constituency members. In some cases, countries with very limited voting shares like Tajikistan and Turkmenistan (0.05% of total votes each) opt to form constituencies with larger high-income countries that command much higher shares, like Switzerland (1.57% of total). While, to our knowledge, there have been no in-depth studies on the internal functioning of constituencies, smaller shareholders likely perceive they can secure stronger representation by banding with a high-voting-share country. As shown in table 4.1, half of the multicountry constituencies are represented by an individual hailing from a high-income country, despite the inclusion of countries with different income levels.

There is a paradox in policy debates over voting in the IMF: Actual votes only very rarely take place, but member states expend considerable energy in regular intervals to renegotiate voting shares.[17] How to explain this? Decision making at the IMF operates on the basis of establishing consensus among Board members, even though these discussions unfold in the shadow of

---

[16] Woods and Lombardi 2006.
[17] As Pauly states, the important element here is not actual voting but a US 'shadow' of power in who controls scriptwriting. See Pauly 1997.

Table 4.1 Representation and Voting Shares at the IMF Executive Board, 2009

Executive and Alternate Directors	Representing (%)	Countries in Constituency	Vote Share (%)[a]
Single-country representatives			
Meg Lundsager / Daniel Health	United States	1	16.77
Daisuke Kotegawa / Hiromi Yamaoka	Japan	1	6.02
Klaus D. Stein / Stephan von Stenglin	Germany	1	5.88
Ambroise Fayolle / Benoît Claveranne	France	1	4.86
Alexander Gibbs / James Talbot	United Kingdom	1	4.86
G. E. Huayong / H. E. Jianxiong	China	1	3.66
Abdallah S. Alazzaz / Ahmed Al Nassar	Saudi Arabia	1	3.16
Aleksei V. Mozhin / Andrei Lushin	Russia	1	2.69
Multicountry-constituency representatives			
Willy Kiekens (Belgium) / Johann Prader (Austria)	Austria (0.86); Belarus (0.19); Belgium (2.09); Czech Republic (0.38); Hungary (0.48); Kazakhstan (0.18); Luxembourg (0.14); Slovak Republic (0.17); Slovenia (0.12); Turkey (0.55)	10	5.16
Age F. P. Bakker (Netherlands) / Yuriy G. Yakusha (Ukraine)	Armenia (0.05); Bosnia & Herzegovina (0.09); Bulgaria (0.3); Croatia (0.18); Cyprus (0.07); Georgia (0.08); Israel (0.43); Macedonia, former Yugoslav Republic of (0.04); Moldova (0.07); Montenegro (0.02); Netherlands (2.34); Romania (0.48); Ukraine (0.63)	13	4.78

Ramón Guzmán Zapater (Spain) Alfonso Guerra (Mexico)	Costa Rica (0.09); El Salvador (0.09); Guatemala (0.11); Honduras (0.07); Mexico (1.43); Nicaragua (0.07); Spain (1.39); Venezuela, República Bolivariana de (1.21)	8	4.45
Arrigo Sadun (Italy) Miranda Xafa (Greece)	Albania (0.03); Greece (0.38); Italy (3.2); Malta (0.06); Portugal (0.4); San Marino (0.02); Timor-Leste (0.01)	7	4.10
Michael Horgan (Canada) Stephen O'Sullivan (Ireland)	Antigua and Barbuda (0.02); Bahamas, the (0.07); Barbados (0.04); Belize (0.02); Canada (2.89); Dominica (0.01); Grenada (0.02); Ireland (0.39); Jamaica (0.13); St. Kitts and Nevis (0.02); St. Lucia (0.02); St. Vincent and the Grenadines (0.02)	12	3.66
Perry Warjiyo (Indonesia) Adrian Chua (Singapore)	Brunei Darussalam (0.11); Cambodia (0.05); Fiji (0.04); Indonesia (0.95); Lao People's Democratic Republic (0.04); Malaysia (0.68); Myanmar (0.13); Nepal (0.04); Philippines (0.41); Singapore (0.4); Thailand (0.5); Tonga (0.01); Vietnam (0.16)	13	3.52
Hi-Su Lee (Korea) Christopher Legg (Australia)	Australia (1.47); Kiribati (0.01); Korea (1.33); Marshall Islands (0.01); Micronesia, Federated States of (0.01); Mongolia (0.03); New Zealand (0.42); Palau (0.01); Papua New Guinea (0.07); Samoa (0.02); Seychelles (0.02); Solomon Islands (0.02); Vanuatu (0.02)	13	3.44
Jens O. Henriksson (Sweden) Jarle Bergo (Norway)	Denmark (0.75); Estonia (0.04); Finland (0.58); Iceland (0.06); Latvia (0.07); Lithuania (0.08); Norway (0.77); Sweden (1.09)	8	3.44
A. Shakour Shaalan (Egypt) Samir El-Khouri (Lebanon)	Bahrain (0.07); Egypt (0.44); Iraq (0.55); Jordan (0.09); Kuwait (0.63); Lebanon (0.1); Libyan Arab Jamahiriya (0.52); Maldives (0.01); Oman (0.1); Qatar (0.13); Syrian Arab Republic (0.14); United Arab Emirates (0.29); Yemen, Republic of (0.12)	13	3.20
Samuel Itam (Sierra Leone) Moeketsi Majoro (Lesotho)	Angola (0.14); Botswana (0.04); Burundi (0.05); Eritrea (0.02); Ethiopia (0.07); Gambia, Republic of the (0.03); Kenya (0.13); Lesotho (0.03); Liberia (0.07); Malawi (0.04); Mozambique (0.06); Namibia (0.07); Nigeria (0.8); Sierra Leone (0.06); South Africa (0.86); Sudan (0.09); Swaziland (0.03); Tanzania (0.1); Uganda (0.09); Zambia (0.23)	20	3.01

Continued

Table 4.1 Continued

Executive and Alternate Directors	Representing (%)	Countries in Constituency	Vote Share (%)[a]
Thomas Moser (Switzerland) Katarzyna Zajdel-Kurowska (Poland)	Azerbaijan (0.08); Kyrgyz Republic (0.05); Poland (0.63); Serbia (0.22); Switzerland (1.57); Tajikistan (0.05); Turkmenistan (0.05); Uzbekistan (0.14)	8	2.79
Mohammad Jafar Mojarrad (Islamic Republic of Iran) Mohammed Daïri (Morocco)	Afghanistan, Islamic Republic of (0.08); Algeria (0.58); Ghana (0.18); Iran, Islamic Republic of (0.69); Morocco (0.28); Pakistan (0.48); Tunisia (0.14)	7	2.42
Paulo Nogueira Batista, Jr. (Brazil) María Inés Agudelo (Colombia)	Brazil (1.38); Colombia (0.36); Dominican Republic (0.11); Ecuador (0.15); Guyana (0.05); Haiti (0.05); Panama (0.1); Suriname (0.05); Trinidad and Tobago (0.16)	9	2.42
Adarsh Kishore (India) K. G. D. Dheerasinghe (Sri Lanka)	Bangladesh (0.25); Bhutan (0.01); India (1.89); Sri Lanka (0.2)	4	2.35
Pablo A. Pereira (Argentina) David Vogel (Uruguay)	Argentina (0.97); Bolivia (0.09); Chile (0.4); Paraguay (0.06); Peru (0.3); Uruguay (0.15)	6	1.96
Laurean W. Rutayisire (Rwanda) Kossi Assimaidou (Togo)	Benin (0.04); Burkina Faso (0.04); Cameroon (0.1); Cape Verde (0.02); Central African Republic (0.04); Chad (0.04); Comoros (0.02); Congo, Democratic Republic of the (0.25); Congo, Republic of (0.05); Cote d'Ivoire (0.16); Djibouti (0.02); Equatorial Guinea (0.03); Gabon (0.08); Guinea (0.06); Guinea-Bissau (0.02); Madagascar (0.07); Mali (0.05); Mauritius (0.06); Niger (0.04); Rwanda (0.05); São Tomé and Principe (0.01); Senegal (0.08); Togo (0.04)	23	1.35

[a]Country's percent of IMF total voting shares.
Note: Voting shares do not total 100% due to rounding.
Source: Adapted from IMF 2009, appendix IV.

unequal voting rights. This approach dates back to the early days of the Fund, and is enshrined in its internal regulations, which specify that the Managing Director[18]—who is the nonvoting chairperson of the Board and by convention a European—'shall ordinarily ascertain the sense of the meeting, in lieu of a formal vote.'[19]

The consensus-building approach was initially based on the premise that the use of IMF resources would have a revolving character, so that there would be no settled division between creditor and debtor countries and therefore everyone would have an incentive to compromise. Indeed, in the first three decades of the IMF's operations, industrialized countries like the UK, France, and Italy borrowed from the IMF several times.[20] By the 1980s, however, high-income countries stopped borrowing and in effect became the core creditor group. This could have led to a situation where power asymmetries were such that there would be no need for consensus building, as industrialized countries with their larger voting shares would not find a reason to compromise if they knew they were unlikely ever to be on the receiving end of IMF lending. According to former IMF Secretary[21] Leo van Houtven, even when it became clear that the IMF's membership would be divided between debtor and creditor members, all countries agreed that 'consensus decision making should continue in order to maintain the cooperative character of the IMF; safeguard the interests of the developing and transition countries who are, de facto, the users of IMF resources; maintain a reasonable balance between the interests of debtors and creditors; and—ultimately—protect the rights and interests of the minority shareholders.'[22]

For these reasons, votes are still shunned in favor of building consensus and the chairperson relying on the 'sense of the meeting' to gauge support for a given policy or activity. While there are elaborate procedures for capturing what this sense is, in practice this is understood to comprise two elements: support by an expanded majority of Executive Directors and the 'absence of explicit, significant and strong dissent.'[23] The IMF's Executive Board Procedures themselves clarify that this approach to decision making is based on the principle that 'the required voting majority would be very comfortably satisfied if there were to be a vote taken and all, or almost all, directors

---

[18] If the managing director cannot attend, then one of the deputy managing directors chairs the Board meeting.
[19] IMF 2011b, rule C-10.
[20] Clift and Tomlinson 2008.
[21] The secretary and head of the secretary's department support the functioning of the Executive Board, and are considered senior officers of the organization.
[22] Van Houtven 2002, 23.
[23] Portugal 2005, 90–91.

can go along with the majority view in the sense that they would not vote against it.'[24]

Such consensus emerges through deliberations based on reports, discussion papers, and research notes submitted by the IMF's bureaucracy, after approval by senior management and rigorous internal review—that is, the internal bureaucratic processes described in detail in Chapter 5. In cases of policy disagreements, the Managing Director is responsible for constructing the widest possible agreement among directors. This process may last between months and years, and commonly includes scheduling multiple Board meetings and instructing IMF staff to draft reports that seek to bridge disagreements, a practice that allows developing countries to exercise influence larger than their voting shares would grant.[25] This practice is needed because vocal opposition by several Executive Directors can derail decision making, even though their aggregate votes may be relatively few.[26]

In short, consensus building can be difficult and time consuming, thereby giving weaker countries opportunities to stall debates or construct alternative coalitions. Even directors commanding limited voting shares have more power within the logic of Board governance than their shares would suggest, and a lot depends on their ability to form alliances, persuade their colleagues, and rely on their technical expertise to compellingly make their case.[27] This means that many of the IMF's policies are generated only after repeated rounds of deliberation and negotiation.[28] Thus, while unequal voting shares lie at the core of IMF governance and are rightly the focus of reform attempts, they do not tell us much about how the Board actually operates day to day. Analyses that tend to foreground such voting issues[29] mistake organizational features for practices; were the IMF Board to actually operate on an iterated voting game, the internal dynamics would be completely different from reality.

In the background of formal Board debates lie preparatory discussions and coalition building. In practice, coordination between constituencies is extensive and aided by institutionalized forums that support these coordination efforts. The Group of 5 (high-income countries), Group of 20 (the world's 20 largest economies), and Group of 24 (developing countries) are the most prominent such examples of coordination of international financial issues (including on IMF topics) at the ministerial level. Even within the IMF, there

---

[24] Cited in Chelsky 2009, 219.
[25] Portugal 2005.
[26] Van Houtven 2002.
[27] Woods and Lombardi 2006.
[28] Stiles 1987.
[29] For example, Rauh and Zürn 2020, 591.

are different groupings of Executive Directors (by region or income level) that facilitate the creation of joint positions to take during Board deliberations.[30] Given the unequal distribution of voting shares, high-income countries can often dominate decision making, prompting Mark Copelovitch to refer to the largest shareholders—the US, UK, Germany, France, and Japan—as the IMF's 'collective principal' that controls the Board.[31]

In performing their duties, directors are expected to be in close communication with their home authorities on IMF issues, although the latter do not always transmit detailed instructions—sometimes none at all—on what positions they are expected to take in Board deliberations. For example, a former Board member reminisced that they only received clear instructions when issues or countries of perceived priority for their home authorities were being discussed, thereby allowing them free rein on many issues debated at the IMF.[32] Even a cursory look at Board meeting attendance records and debate lengths confirms this view: Discussions over the IMF's lending to small states are generally poorly attended and short, while—unsurprisingly—debates over policy on issues like sovereign debt or capital controls (the empirical cases we cover later on) attract high-level attention and span several meetings. Occasionally, however, Board members can even adopt policy positions on the basis of their independent judgment. For instance, Karin Lissakers, US Executive Director in the 1990s, reportedly 'bypassed US national interests for the sake of the Fund's bureaucratic interest' in her positioning vis-à-vis a proposed amendment to the IMF's Articles of Agreement.[33] This hints at the potential for Board members stealthily or openly pursuing agendas that may neglect the priorities of their appointing authorities—an issue we covered in theoretical terms in chapters 1 and 2 and to which we return in light of our empirical evidence.

Power in IMF Governance

Our pragmatic discussion of how the IMF's Board operates opens several avenues for further research and does not always sit comfortably with theories of how IMF governance functions. One strand of discussion in the literature understands the organization as the long arm of the US administration, which can use its institutionalized dominance through its high voting-share

---

[30] Woods and Lombardi 2006; IMF 2022a.
[31] Copelovitch 2010a, 2010b.
[32] Interview with authors, September 30, 2015.
[33] Abdelal 2007, 129–30.

percentage and veto power to steer organizational decision making.[34] For example, scholars have found evidence of direct US meddling in IMF lending operations[35] and policy design.[36] Even so, these arguments can be taken too far. While there is wide agreement that the US looms large in the organization's functioning, this does not mean that the country is always successful at accomplishing its preferences or that the IMF always acts in accordance with US interests.[37]

A second argument still foregrounds the role of the US and other major shareholders but adds agency for developing countries in shaping organizational outputs. In this telling, IOs are where 'global horse-trading' takes place: 'Governments use their influence in one international organization to gain leverage over another.'[38] The best-known empirical case of this process is when developing countries that are elected to hold a temporary seat on the UN Security Council (UNSC) use this newly available power resource as a bargaining chip. UNSC votes matter a lot for its permanent members, and three of these (the US, the UK, and France) are also major shareholders at the IMF, where they can use their status to tilt the scales in favor of the temporary UNSC member to receive more generous or lenient loans by the IMF, provided it votes in accordance with major shareholder interests.[39] While this literature has yielded robust evidence of how individual developing countries can trade or sell their votes to major IMF shareholders in exchange for preferential treatment by the organization, there is little evidence that the same process will be as effective in larger-level negotiations over how scripts should codify global norms. In the latter case, most IMF member states are likely to have intense preferences, and decisions would require construction of consensus among many more countries than are likely available to trade votes between multilateral forums.

A third prominent account traces the functioning of power through informal governance mechanisms: the ability of some countries 'to obtain desirable outcomes within an organization, at some cost, by going outside of normal channels.'[40] This argument traces decision making to the back corridors and private meetings of the IMF and other IOs, where agreement is hashed out before ever setting foot in the formal boardroom. As Randall Stone explains, 'powerful countries can always find ways to stack the deck'

---

[34] For the stronger statements in this tradition, see Payer 1974; Peet 2009; Panitch and Gindin 2013.
[35] Momani 2004.
[36] Bhagwati 1998; Wade and Veneroso 1998; Kentikelenis and Babb 2019.
[37] Van Houtven 2002. Ikenberry suggests that an important factor in the composition of the Bretton Woods institutions is that the US has been cautious about appearing to dominate European states on policy and makes incremental adjustments to maintain legitimacy. Ikenberry 1992, 320.
[38] Dreher et al. 2009, 743.
[39] Dreher et al. 2009, 2015; Dreher and Vreeland 2014.
[40] Stone 2013, 125; also Stone 2008, 2011.

and hijack organizational governance unless this is explicitly prevented.[41] In this literature, the IMF looms large as an IO where informal governance is crucial in decision making, especially regarding the conditionality attached to its lending programs: The US informally intervenes in the design of conditionality for IMF borrowers 'when its security or broader strategic interests become involved, because these interests are not ordinarily represented in IMF objectives.'[42]

In its strongest version, this line of argument suggests that what goes on at the Board is mere kabuki theater: Executive Directors show up in meetings in their corporate attire, carrying their talking points, to play the role of a Board member, when in fact decisions have already been taken through backchannel negotiations and reflect the preferences of the US, other major shareholders, and associated horse trading with weaker IMF members. If this is indeed the case, the thousands of pages of Board transcripts that are produced from the discussions likely represent an elaborate performance to convince home authorities that deliberations are meaningful and that the Board rightly absorbs 8% of the IMF's administrative budget and employs 9% of total staff. Or, these transcripts reflect—at best—an attempt to put some discussions on the record to distribute within constituencies and to show to home authorities that Directors indeed behave as instructed. After all, why else would directors show up and talk for hours if everyone knows in advance what the outcome of a 'debate' will be? Furthermore, an overreliance on informal governance arguments to explain outcomes ignores the distribution of workloads among Executive Directors and the attention space for arguing positions within the limited time of meetings.[43] It is likely that Executive Directors representing lower-income countries with many IMF programs are overstretched and constrained in their capacity to develop positions on the range of topics that come to the IMF's Board for decision. In this sense, power asymmetries between the Global North and Global South are accentuated not only in the corridors but in the distribution of time and resources before and during Board meetings.[44]

We do not question the veracity of theories on the role of hegemonic powers, global bargaining, and informal governance—there is highly compelling quantitative and qualitative evidence to support these accounts. However, we raise concerns about their scope conditions. Building on the work of Stone,[45] we distinguish between high- and low-salience issues for IMF shareholders.

---

[41] Stone 2013, 125.
[42] Stone 2004, 596.
[43] Collins 2004.
[44] Our thanks to Martha Finnemore for this point.
[45] Stone 2008, 2011, 2013.

Stone points out that preference intensity of states—especially powerful ones—is central to the mode of governance that is pursued within an IO: The strong interests of powerful states are accommodated, both because they cannot be credibly bound by decisions that are counter to their interests and because they either have or can create more attractive outside options. But to avoid the reality of one or a few powerful states always dominating, which would alienate weaker members, the possibility of an 'inter-temporal exchange [emerges]: powerful states are granted temporary control of organizational policy when their interests are strongly affected, and in return weaker states are granted a share of formal control rights during ordinary times that is out of proportion to their capabilities.'[46]

Drawing on these arguments, we distinguish between three ways in which power is exercised on the IMF Board. First, there are cases where Board topics are perceived to be of low salience for everyone involved. Examples from the IMF Board's agenda here include the approval of an educational allowance for further training for staff, updating the travel policies of the organization, or discussing reallocation of office space—these are all issues that are unlikely to yield strong enough interest for the Fund's member states to expend effort or political capital to seek to materially influence outcomes. In these instances, Board power dynamics are only weakly expressed and deference to staff preferences likely occurs.

A second possibility is that the IMF Board considers an issue to be of high salience for some countries but low salience for others. Arguably, it is in this case that informal governance accounts maximize their explanatory power. Consider the case of IMF lending to countries in economic difficulties. These instances may feature a confluence of factors: A country has an important role in geopolitics (e.g., due to its UNSC temporary membership, economic importance, or global political positioning); the IMF has a significant role in this country through its lending activities; one or more major IMF shareholders have strong policy priorities that the IMF borrower can be instrumental in helping them achieve; and the majority of other IMF shareholders (major or minor) do not have strong preferences on this case. As the aforementioned scholarship has demonstrated, this is often enough the case.

A third possibility relates to IMF decision making on policies that would directly or indirectly affect all its members. As Stone explains, Board members' 'deference to management is much weaker on general policy issues than on lending, and the board takes a more active role in formulating policy.'[47] For

---

[46] Stone 2013, 125.
[47] Stone 2011, 71.

example, the development of a new lending instrument is a momentous decision for wealthy and poorer countries alike, as the former will be called upon to provide the funding while the latter are likely to turn to this instrument for financial support in times of need. The specification of new policies—on the use of capital controls, the definition of debt sustainability, or the development of a sovereign debt-restructuring mechanism—also is momentous for the global economy, and therefore of direct interest to the organization's entire membership. Isolated horse trading is unlikely to be effective here, as there likely are not enough favors to be exchanged to make a large enough majority of countries and their representatives go along with a decision that blatantly privileges the interests of only a small minority of IMF members. That is, in these cases, decisions are reached through extensive negotiations in the formal governance structures of the organization. This is not to say that backroom deals and informal coordination do not take place—there is ample evidence that it does.[48] But, still, formal decision making exhibits a degree of openness and uncertainty on what the ultimate decision will be, as this will inevitably reflect compromises between Board members and typically takes several rounds of discussions to be concluded.

In this book we suggest that this third possibility is where variation in scientific consensus and political contestation will be important for how the Board writes scripts. When both scientific consensus and political contestation are low, there is not much to talk about in analysis of actual decision making—without this excluding the possibility, however, that norm entrepreneurs within the organization might be working toward turning current nonissues into actionable items, a topic we return to in our conclusions. Where political contestation is low and scientific consensus is high, we expect the Board to rely on technocratic expertise to provide content for scriptwriting. In cases where political contestation is high—where there are clear political stakes at play—and the scientific consensus is weak, we expect many rounds of explicit debate, including what knowledge, models, theories, and benchmarks should be included in scripts. Last, in cases where both scientific consensus and political contestation are high, two outcomes are possible. The first is that political objectives clash with a scientific consensus, leading to extensive debate as Board members try to justify their arguments without recourse to coercion. In this sense, *how* Board members debate—by employing economic principles and theories—is important, since explicit strong-arming is frowned upon. The second outcome is that if political objectives align with a scientific consensus, then we expect to see the backgrounds of Board members

---

[48] Woods and Lombardi 2006.

as important to how they affirm the content of a new script. In such cases, Board *composition*—the number of central bankers relative to financiers, for example—may be important for scriptwriting.

Such high-salience issues form the core interest of this volume: how momentous policy scripts that codify norms and thus form the backbone of economic globalization are made. These processes do not exclusively take place in shadowy corridors where they can never be observed and are at best inferred, but they leave a voluminous paper trail, which—in combination with additional data—can help us piece together fine-grained explanations, and we do so in part III of the book. The first analytical step, however, is to turn our lens to the composition and actual functioning of the IMF Board. What are the educational and career backgrounds of Board members? How does the representation of these backgrounds on the Board vary over time? These are necessary (but only partial) components of our explanation of how scriptwriting occurs, and are the focus of the remainder of this chapter.

Mapping Executive Board Composition

While political representation is the raison d'être of the Executive Board and underpins the selection system for directors, reducing these individuals to mere mouthpieces of their home authorities, as implicitly or explicitly done in the relevant scholarship,[49] introduces important blind spots in analyses of organizational decision making. Board members are also experts in their own right, which gives them both additional power against whatever the bureaucracy proposes and additional epistemic authority in their interventions.[50] For this reason, a joint IMF–World Bank committee on the Executive Board outlined the importance of states' selecting individuals with appropriate knowledge and expertise: 'Given the dual function of Executive Directors as country representatives and as officers responsible for conducting the business of the institutions, they need to carry significant weight in their capitals to represent their countries adequately and, at the same time, to contribute effectively to the institutions' consensus building culture. This is particularly important in view of the increasing role of other—national and supranational—bodies in shaping decisions on the international financial architecture.'[51]

---

[49] For example, see Chwieroth 2010; Kentikelenis and Babb 2019.
[50] Forster 2024.
[51] World Bank 2004, 204.

As discussed in chapter 3, to identify the key attributes of Board members, we collected biographical data on the Executive Directors of the 1980–2009 period. Our dataset covers the entire career trajectories of the 727 individuals who held the rank of Executive Director or Alternate Executive Director.[52] Only 14 individuals whose tenures started in or before the 1970s could not be identified through their CVs and were thus excluded.[53] The Appendix to this chapter outlines how we coded this data to then use in the subsequent analyses.

Notwithstanding diverse national origins, IMF Board members have broadly similar educational profiles. Unsurprisingly, almost all were trained in economics or related disciplines, like finance or banking (86% of the identified 703 individuals who reported the subject of their degrees; 24 CVs did not include this information). Most of the remaining members held academic qualifications in public policy and administration, a discipline that includes training in economics. For example, two-thirds of the French representatives studied either at the École Nationale d'Administration (ENA) or the Institut d'Études Politiques de Paris (Sciences Po), both widely regarded as elite educational institutions for the emerging class of French public officials.[54]

Further, Board members lack diversity in terms of location of university studies, as shown in table 4.2. The 727 Board members hailed from 119 countries, yet nearly half of them received their most advanced degree from universities in the US or the UK. This is a clear sign that these individuals became embedded in channels of transnational norm circulation through higher education, as universities form key mechanisms for diffusing norms about the appropriateness and legitimacy of different policies.[55] In particular, the 18 top Anglo-American universities (15 from the US and 3 from the UK[56]), based on the rankings of their economics departments, accounted for the education of 26% of all Board members. Elite education is important because students are socialized not only into a worldview of

---

[52] Initially, we collected and coded the career trajectories of 738 individuals, but we removed 11 from our sample because they had pre-Board careers of less than five years (e.g., an individual joined their country's central bank for two years upon university graduation and then was sent to the IMF Board). Including these very short careers would have created theoretical quandaries (professional socialization is commonly assumed to occur over the medium run, not immediately upon entering a professional environment; see Djelic and Quack 2010) and empirical difficulties (the optimal matching analysis described later in this chapter performs more reliably when longer sequences are provided).

[53] We also do not have data for individuals holding the title of assistant to the Executive Director; these are junior officials who aid the Executive Directors and can occasionally participate in Board debates as 'Temporary Alternate Executive Directors' when none of the more senior staff are available. As per IMF procedures, the CVs of these junior officials are not circulated around the organization and consequently left no paper trail among archival documents.

[54] Bourdieu 1998.

[55] Frank and Meyer 2020; Schofer et al. 2000; Schofer and Meyer 2005.

[56] Coupé 2003.

Table 4.2 Educational Background of IMF Executive Board Members, 1980–2009

Country Income classification		Nationality	Number of Individuals	Site of University Studies		
				Elite US/UK[a]	Other US/UK	Total US/UK[b]
High income	*Major shareholders*	United States	23	48%	52%	100%
		Germany	32	3%	3%	6%
		Japan	30	67%	7%	73%
		France	36	6%	3%	9%
		United Kingdom	25	84%	12%	96%
	Other shareholders	21 nationalities	175	19%	15%	35%
	Total high income	26 nationalities	321	28%	14%	42%
Middle income		57 nationalities	264	27%	33%	59%
Low income		37 nationalities	142	21%	25%	46%
TOTAL		119 nationalities	727	26%	23%	49%

Note: Income classification of Board members' home authorities follows the World Bank's World Development Indicators in 1995, the midpoint in our data.
[a] We classified 18 universities as elite based on their economics departments' ranking: the top 15 from the US and the top 3 from the UK (Coupé 2003).
[b] Some rows do not total 100% due to rounding. *Source:* Authors, drawing on the curricula vitae of Board members available through the IMF archives.

how to tackle economic problems and what theories and models should be favored, but also in how to argue and network with others. For example, social cohesion among economists is especially intense around particular US and UK universities—notably the Chicago school of economics—that successfully propagated neoliberal economic ideas through its graduates, their publications, and their academic and policy networks.[57]

Clearer patterns emerge as we disaggregate Board members by income classification of appointing countries, relying on their income position in 1995—the midpoint in our data. High-income-country representatives comprise 44% of all Board members, who hailed from 26 nationalities, and more than one-quarter of them studied at a prestigious Anglo-American university. Elite education was particularly pronounced for the British, almost all of whom studied at Cambridge, Oxford, or the London School of Economics; and the Japanese, who often studied in universities like UC–Berkeley, Harvard, and Princeton, likely benefiting from the country's expansive study-abroad scholarship opportunities.[58] All US officials and almost all German and French officials studied in their respective countries, reflecting domestic educational hierarchies and preferences. Other high-income countries with representation on the Board (e.g., Austria, Belgium, Canada, Italy, and the Netherlands) also have comparatively few appointees (approximately one-third) who were educated in the US or UK, instead opting for training in their home country.

Turning to appointees from middle-income countries, we find that 59% of the 264 individuals, hailing from 57 countries, received their training in the US or the UK. For example, 9 of the 10 Mexican appointees, 8 of the 9 Indonesians, and 11 of the 12 Iranians studied in these two countries. Only appointees from post-communist countries were likely never to have studied abroad: Nearly all appointees from Estonia, Hungary, Lithuania, Latvia, Poland, Romania, Russia, Serbia/Yugoslavia, and Ukraine studied in their countries of origin, reflecting limited international educational opportunities.[59]

Last, 46% of low-income countries' appointees were also educated in the US or the UK. For this group, national educational cultures and linguistic similarities underpin study trajectories. Most Chinese appointees studied within their country, commonly in the Graduate School of the People's Bank of China. In contrast, half of the 22 Indian appointees were educated in country; the remainder opted for elite US and UK universities, with Cambridge and

---

[57] Henriksen et al. 2022.
[58] Ota 2018.
[59] On the importance of this training for post-communist central banking networks, see Johnson 2016.

Harvard educating five. Board appointees from francophone sub-Saharan African countries were primarily educated in France. However, unlike the clear patterns of French nationals in France being educated at prestigious domestic universities, all but one of the foreign-educated Board members from francophone Africa enrolled at the elite ENA or Sciences Po, instead primarily studying in a range of other French universities or in their home countries.

Comparing the educational credentials of Board members hailing from different countries reveals underlying global hierarchies but is not intended to signal our belief that developing-country nationals who have studied in national universities are necessarily trained differently. For example, given the degree of penetration of Chicago school economists in Chile,[60] it is highly plausible that students at Chilean universities over the 1970s and 1980s were exposed to the same type of training that their professors received at the University of Chicago.[61] Our main point is different: There are asymmetries in the mode of incorporation of individuals from developing countries in global decision making. High-income-country officials are accepted by the very fact of representing a major shareholder, regardless of their prior inclusion in transnational spaces of knowledge circulation. In contrast, individuals representing developing countries—with notable exceptions, like China or Eastern Europe—plausibly overcompensate for their more limited weight in formal decision making by having received advanced training at respected Anglo-American universities. This suggests that they are likely already well integrated into global circuits of knowledge distribution from their time at university.

Indeed, these individuals' command of mainstream macroeconomics as taught in broadly standardized curricula in US and UK universities—that is, their command of the epistemic language of the IMF—is likely what makes them attractive enough to their home authorities to send them to the IMF in the first place.[62] In short, the broad homogeneity in educational credentials and prestige suggests a degree of uniformity in the cultural frames on 'appropriate' policies that future Board members are exposed to during their training.

Similarity in educational backgrounds is only one part of what informs Board members' theorization and decision-making processes. The other part relates to pertinent characteristics beyond education that shape individuals.

---

[60] Dezalay and Garth 2002.
[61] As has been well documented, see Valdés 1995; Van Gunten 2015a.
[62] Fourcade 2006, 2009.

In this, the role of professional socialization in the pre-Board careers of Board members is key. Figure 4.1 presents the results from a sequence analysis, which yielded six career clusters: central bankers ($n = 379$), finance ministry officials ($n = 148$), political appointees ($n = 109$), IO officials ($n = 51$), academics ($n = 50$), and bankers and businesspeople ($n = 44$). Each line in the figure represents a career sequence, and the total number of such sequences is 781, as 54 individuals had two stints on the Board, thus re-entering the dataset each time they returned to the Board. That is, we assume that a Board member's career trajectory before their first and second stints might be different, and thereby could have a distinct imprint on their forms of rationalization while performing their duties.

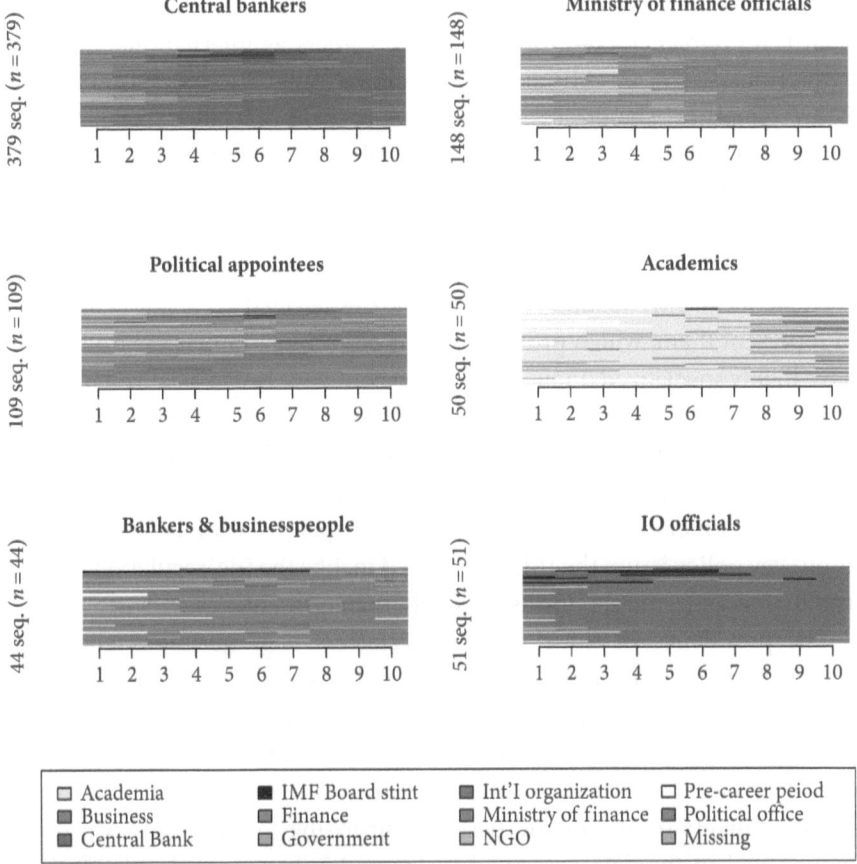

Figure 4.1 Career clusters of IMF Board members

Note: A color version of this figure is available in the online version of this book (open access).

Central bankers are the dominant group in the sample (49% of the total).[63] The central banking community is notable for its intense socialization within their professional field and technocratic independence from national governments.[64] The second-largest cluster (19%) is composed of finance ministry officials who move to the IMF. Unlike the prized autonomy of central bankers, these officials have spent their careers within the hierarchical structures of an important ministry, an experience that likely endowed them with cognitive models for how to conduct fiscal policy.[65] Third, political appointees (14%) represent a diverse group of individuals who mostly were selected from high public-office positions (e.g., deputy minister of economic affairs) to represent national interests. These are generally individuals who did not have straightforward bureaucratic careers but instead had posts at or near the top of their country's political leadership.

We also found three professional clusters that are less prevalent on the Board. IO bureaucrats—individuals with careers as international civil servants (most often, as IMF or World Bank officials)—account for 7% of all Board members. The professional skill set of these officials is likely indistinguishable from that of regular IO staff members. In-depth knowledge of how these organizations work may make these individuals desirable appointees for states that do not have available expertise domestically, as 80% of Board members in this cluster represent low- or middle-income countries, who are also core clients for IMF lending. Several countries selected academic economists to represent them, which provided 6% of our population. These individuals have highly specialized domain knowledge but have been socialized in different ways from those working in hierarchical environments like central banks or close to the center of political decision making like ministries of finance. Last, 6% of IMF Board members have backgrounds in private finance or business. These officials bring with them distinct expertise from the private sector about key policy issues the IMF is involved in, like the (de)regulation of trade and finance, structural reforms, and debt management.

The prevalence of these six career clusters begs questions about the appointment patterns of different IMF member states. To examine this issue, we isolated all 33 countries that had 10 or more representatives on the Board over the 1980–2009 period covered here and examined their distribution over different professional clusters. Given the overall prevalence of former central bankers on the Board, it is not surprising to see that they are well represented in the data presented in figure 4.2. For example, all Mexican,

---

[63] Woods 2006.
[64] Polillo and Guillén 2005; Johnson 2016; Harmon 2019.
[65] Broome and Seabrooke 2015.

Country	Central bankers	Finance ministers	Political appointees	Academics	Bankers & business	IO officials
Argentina	42%	33%	8%	8%	8%	
Australia		55%	45%			
Canada	35%	23%	35%		8%	
Chile	50%		30%	10%		10%
China	80%	7%		3%	7%	3%
France	29%	50%	11%	3%	5%	3%
Germany	52%	27%	6%	12%		3%
Iceland	64%	29%			7%	
India	45%	9%	41%			5%
Indonesia	78%	11%		11%		
Iran	62%		23%		8%	8%
Ireland	42%	8%	42%	8%		
Israel	100%					
Italy	57%	5%	5%	10%	10%	14%
Japan	37%	63%				
Korea		82%	18%			
Lebanon	18%		18%	18%	18%	27%
Malaysia	90%	10%				
Mexico	100%					
Netherlands	40%	47%			7%	7%
New Zealand	78%	22%				
Peru	80%				10%	10%
Philippines	90%		10%			
Russia	11%	22%		56%	11%	
Saudi Arabia	22%	22%		56%		
Spain	7%	47%	27%	13%	7%	
Sri Lanka	100%					
Sweden	78%	11%	11%			
Switzerland	44%	44%			11%	
Thailand	100%					
United Kingdom	54%	12%	27%			8%
United States	12%	44%	16%	12%	16%	
Venezuela	29%	7%	21%	7%	14%	21%

Share of country representatives within cluster: 1%–33%, 34%–66%, 67%–100%

Figure 4.2 Career clusters of IMF Board members by nationality.

Note: Some rows do not sum to 100% because of rounding.

Sri Lankan, and Thai representatives were central bankers. Of the major shareholders, China also stands out for being represented primarily by former officials of its central bank. In terms of finance ministry officials, Korea predominantly selects these types of professionals to join the IMF's Board.

In the cases of central bankers and finance ministry officials, their very high prevalence among some countries' representatives suggests that such appointments are often a matter of a bureaucratic selection procedure or—at minimum—selection from a very small pool of candidates (e.g., central bank officials of appropriate seniority and domain expertise), rather than a more open search-and-selection process.

In other instances, we observed that the professional backgrounds of many countries' representatives are highly diverse. Most notably, this is the case for US officials on the IMF's Board: 44% held previous posts at the Treasury, while the rest had backgrounds in private banking and business (e.g., Randal Quarles, who joined the Board in 2001, was previously the co-head of the financial institutions group at elite law firm Davis Polk & Wardwell), high-level politics (e.g., Quincy Krosby, who joined the Board in 1992, was previously assistant secretary of commerce in charge of export administration), academia, or the Federal Reserve. Similarly, other major shareholders, like France, Germany, and the UK, are also represented by individuals with diverse professional backgrounds. These patterns of representation point to selection processes that are not limited to fixed bureaucratic procedures and are thus more malleable to politics. For the US, this is explicit: Congress votes on all the country's senior appointments. For other countries, the degree of flexibility empowers ministers of finance to select appointees of their choice, whether due to their knowledge, expertise, and skills or—conceivably—to reward party loyalists or ideological affiliates with an IMF post as a sinecure.

At this point, an analytical clarification is necessary. The clustering of individuals in these distinct professional types is intended to document professional backgrounds present at the Board, and should not be mistaken as an argument that, by virtue of these backgrounds, these individuals hold similar knowledge and worldviews *across time*. Simply put, an individual with a central banking background trained in the 1950s and sitting on the Board in 1980 likely has different views on monetary policy from someone who was trained in the 2000s and joined the Board in 2009. There are many reasons for this, including changes in the discipline of economics and the curriculum offered in academic departments, new ideas on monetary policy, the experience of multiple global financial crises, changes in the importance of international capital mobility, and waves of financial deregulation. Thus, while the central bankers sitting on the Board in 1980 and 2009 might share key professional characteristics, they were not necessarily exposed to the same global norms that they may then seek to enact. In contrast, two contemporaneous Board members with very similar educational and professional trajectories likely interpret economic phenomena through similar epistemic lenses. Our analysis here, therefore, serves primarily to provide the building blocks for the in-depth analyses of how these malleable identities interact in Board deliberations that we pursue in subsequent chapters.

In sum, we have shown thus far that Board members are highly homogenous in terms of academic training, and almost half have studied in Anglo-American universities, thereby being exposed to similar norms on appropriate policy, which they carry forward with them in their professional lives. However, we have also documented a degree of heterogeneity of professional backgrounds—this is where the knowledge received at university becomes 'vernacularized' and adapted to particular circumstances.[66] That is, similarly trained individuals who thus initially inhabit similar epistemic spaces may update their priors in a way that helps them perform their professional duties. For example, consider two individuals who sat on the IMF Board at the same time. The Japanese representative who graduated with a master's in public administration from Harvard University in 1984 and the Malaysian representative who graduated from the same program in 1985. They studied the same curriculum, which provided them with a set of analytical tools for interpreting the economic world and with then-dominant norms on appropriate economic policies. Yet, in their subsequent professional lives, they probably had to tailor this knowledge to the specificities of the home countries where they returned: Japan, an open, high-income country; and Malaysia, a middle-income country with extensive restrictions on trade and finance.[67] In short, this knowledge—in correspondence to dominant global norms, but adapted and adjusted to their diverse professional experiences—provides these two individuals with distinct expertise, and this likely shapes how they perform their duties when interacting with other Board members. We elaborate on these issues next.

Script Negotiation in Action

The training and professional trajectories of Board members are key attributes that shape their worldviews and priorities. But the Board is not a static entity for these individuals to express platitudes on the topic du jour. Rather, it was intended as a system for vigorous debate on major economic

---

[66] Levitt and Merry 2009.
[67] Gygli et al. 2019.

policy issues that affect the lives of millions (in the case of IMF lending activities) or billions (in the case of normmaking activities on issues like sovereign debt or capital mobility), and all available evidence suggests that participants in these processes take this role seriously.[68] As such, interactions between participants in Board deliberations matter, because this iterative process shapes outcomes. It is our core contention that the types of backgrounds represented in the mix of Board members matter for the types of decisions the Board makes. In this section, we present initial evidence to substantiate our point. We return to these issues with in-depth analyses in the case studies presented in subsequent chapters.

As we have argued, the IMF's Board is composed of individuals that are dual loyalists: state representatives who also hold particular types of professional expertise by virtue of their pre-Board backgrounds. Within this dual loyalty, the first identity relates to underlying power imbalances on the Board: Simply put, countries in the Global North have more votes and more representatives in the IMF's governance structures, as already captured in table 4.1. But this formal governance structure is hardly interesting from an analytical standpoint, as votes rarely take place and decisions are taken by consensus. As this process is by definition deliberative, it becomes analytically necessary to move beyond the preceding static analyses of what credential or career a given Board member has and toward a dynamic account: How do the backgrounds of Board members aggregate to yield a particular Board composition?

To elaborate on this question, we illustrate the prevalence of different career types among sitting Board members between 1980 and 2009 in figure 4.3, using the results from the sequence analysis presented earlier. Consider points A (late 1980s) and B (early 2000s). In the former, more than 40% of Board members had a background in finance ministries or domestic political positions, nearly 15% were previously in the business of finance, and there was only one academic and nobody previously employed in IOs. By contrast, slightly more than a decade later, Board composition had shifted: Fewer than one in three were previously in finance ministries or domestic politics, while approximately 20% came from academia and 20% from IOs.

We contend that variation in the mix of professional backgrounds among those present on the Board will influence the types of interactions and debates that are had, and—by extension—the ultimate output of Board deliberations. That is, the IMF Board composed per point A would likely make different decisions than one having the composition at point B. Composition matters

---

[68] Boughton 2001; Woods and Lombardi 2006; Kentikelenis and Babb 2019; Forster et al. 2025.

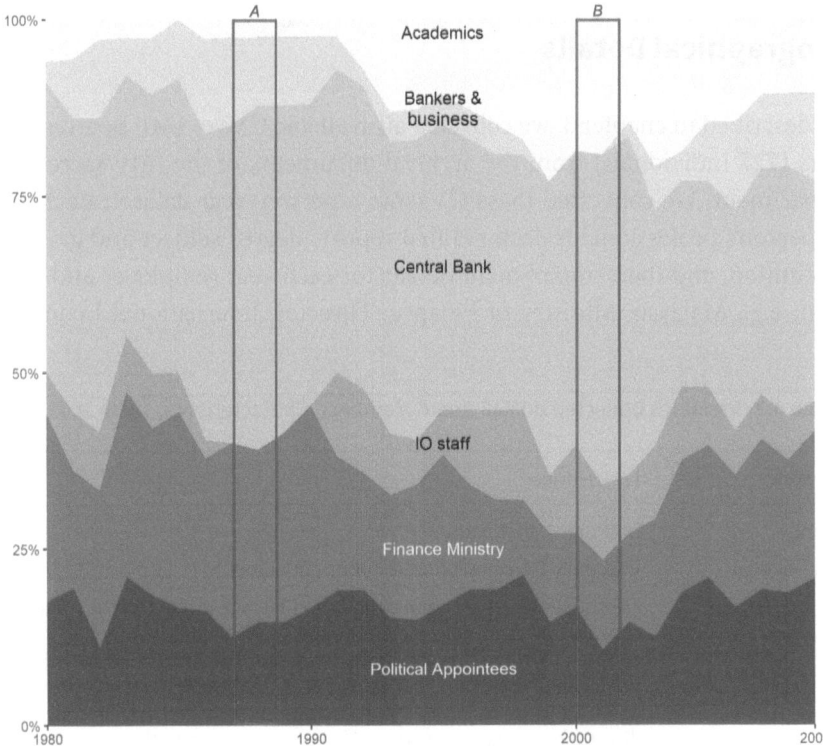

Figure 4.3 Evolution of professional backgrounds among IMF Board members

because different types of skills and knowledge are represented at both points. Substantiating this argument, however, encounters epistemological problems, as there is no possibility to observe perfect counterfactuals. The Board's composition changes, but so does the world: Financial crises, advances in economic thinking, and shifts in policy fads all can shape the types of decisions reached. A perfect counterfactual—that is, a comparison between outputs on the same issue area at the same time produced by differently composed Boards while holding everything else constant—will always be elusive.

Instead, to substantiate our point, we relied on the voluminous evidence collected across several periods—thus, different Board compositions—on the three issue areas covered in the three chapters of part III of this volume. In doing so, we employ abductive reasoning to propel the analysis. As discussed in chapter 3, this means that we have theoretically informed guesses on variation in scientific consensus and political contestation on different issues (sovereign debt management, capital controls, and value-added taxation).

Appendix: Data Collection and Coding of Board Member Biographical Details

As described in chapter 3, we collected all available CVs of IMF Board members (727 individuals) from the archival documents of the IMF secretary's department. We converted these CVs into a person–year dataset: Each row (a person's professional trajectory) first reports degree subject and granting institution, and then employment details for each year (employer and position; e.g., Malaysia Ministry of Finance: Director, International Economic

Table 4.3 Variables Collected on IMF Board Members' Characteristics, 1980–2009

Variable	Description
Name	Last name, first name
Nationality	Executive Director's country of origin name
Income Group	Executive Director's country of origin income group (low-income country, lower-middle-income country, upper-middle-income country, high-income country). To identify the income group, we use the mean of the 1990–2010 period (e.g., if a country is low income and transitions to lower-middle income over the period, we code the director's income group as whichever income group the country belonged to for most of the period). The source of income classifications is World Bank data.
Regional Group	Executive Director's country of origin regional group. Coding relies on the following World Bank conventions: EAS = East Asia & Pacific ECS = Europe & Central Asia LCN = Latin America & the Caribbean MEA = Middle East & North Africa NAC = North America SAS = South Asia SSF = Sub-Saharan Africa
Birth	Year of birth: If not stated in the Circular, we rely on the following conventions: BA graduation minus 23 years MA graduation minus 25 years PhD graduation minus 28 years
Representing	Names of countries represented by an Executive Director. Sources are the secretary's Circulars and/or IMF Annual Reports.
Education	We only code the last degree (incl. subject, year, and university).
1937–2009	Career coding, relying on the following convention: Non-Board posts: We consider the new post to cover the full first year of new employment (as we do not have monthly data). Board posts: Only coded as Board members if on the Board for 6+ months in a given year.

Table 4.4 Variables Collected on IMF Board Members' careers, 1980–2009

Code	Job Category	Description
CB	Central bank	Employed at a central bank (any level of seniority)
MF	Ministry of finance	Employed at a finance ministry (any level of seniority)
MFP	Ministry of finance: political office	Political post at a finance ministry (e.g., deputy minister of finance)
GO	Government	Government job outside the central bank or the ministry of finance (includes jobs in state-owned enterprises)
GOP	Government: political office	Political post in government outside the finance ministry
IO	International organization	International organization job, including in the IMF (any level of seniority)
EB	IMF Executive Board	Executive Director (ED); Alternate Executive Director (AED); or assistant, advisor, or senior advisor to Executive Director
FI	Private finance	Financial sector employment
BU	Business	Any private sector employment, excluding finance
NG	NGOs	Employed at nongovernmental organization (includes think tanks and the G-24)
AC	Academia	Employed at a university at any rank (excluding doctoral status)
OT	Other	Other
NA	Not available	Not available

Affairs Unit,' or 'Citibank: Sector Counsel and Associate General Counsel').[69] Table 4.3 summarizes the variables collected.

After collecting these raw data, we coded the professional positions held by an individual in a given year into distinct 'states,' as anticipated in the methodological discussion on optimal matching. To do this, we relied on the classification of job categories described in table 4.4. This coding exercise yielded the sequences that we analyzed through optimal matching methods to generate clusters of professionals with similar backgrounds. To improve the stability of the algorithm, our clustering only captures the 10 years of a person's career prior to joining the IMF's Executive Board.

---

[69] When a person changes employer or position in a year, we report the *new* post as covering the entire year, as the CVs do not provide information on the month of a job change.

5
Technocrats

Introduction

Scriptwriting relies on a workforce that can provide both content and direction.[1] While executive bodies such as the International Monetary Fund's (IMF) Executive Board provide oversight and have the authority to propose, negotiate, approve, adjust, or deny policy scripts, the intellectual and technical content is often originally derived from the technocracy. In principle, technocrats operate in a formal, rational system in which they have claims to expertise and control over information. Technocratic claims to expert,[2] epistemic,[3] or cognitive authority[4] are supported by recognized educational training and professional socialization. Technocracies in international organizations (IOs) are likely to have more influence over script content when the issues they are dealing with are *not* hot topics among their political masters.[5] Indeed, making script content more technical and scientific is one way of trying to minimize political interventions[6] while providing the technocrats autonomy from their line managers.[7] Technocrats are often active members of expert networks to access new knowledge and heighten their own autonomy through the propagation of their own concepts, ideas, and theories.[8] In short, technocrats can steer scripts when science has the upper hand over politics.

The technocracy of the IMF has expanded along with external demands on the organization. The Fund's bureaucracy increased from 500 staff in the early 1960s to 1,200 following the collapse of the Bretton Woods monetary order,[9] and to 1,700 by the late 1980s in the aftermath of the Third World

---

[1] Johnson and Urpelainen 2014; Ege et al. 2021; Liese et al. 2021.
[2] Best 2014.
[3] Pouliot 2021a.
[4] Broome 2010.
[5] Stone 2011; Bayerlein et al. 2020.
[6] Littoz-Monnet 2020.
[7] Babb 2003.
[8] Ban et al. 2016; Johnson 2016.
[9] de Vries 1985, 1010.

Making Global Norms. Alexandros Kentikelenis and Leonard Seabrooke, Oxford University Press.
© Oxford University Press (2025). DOI: 10.1093/9780197828656.003.0005

debt crisis.[10] It then steadily expanded in the 2000s to 2,500 staff until a lack of demand for IMF services, during a period of cheap loans, prompted plans for staff cuts in 2007.[11] Rejuvenated by the Global Financial Crisis, however, the Fund now has nearly 3,000 full-time employees.[12] The IMF technocracy occupies the organization's original brutalist building 'HQ1,' and its glass-encased sibling, 'HQ2,' on 19th Street in Washington, DC[13]—both a short walking distance from the US Treasury building. Most staff time is occupied with designing loan agreements for countries in crisis, conducting regular surveillance missions across the world, and developing economic analyses and positions for policy scripts.[14] The technocracy is divided into region- and function-based specializations, to customize the provision of funds, tools, and services for particular regions while positioning all content under the umbrella of uniform treatment for equal member-states.

The career of the IMF technocrat has transformed over time. In the Fund's early postwar history, staff were thought of as 'high-grade academic talent,' with Charles Kindleberger stating in 1951 that the IMF was 'training men [sic] fresh from graduate work who later go on into positions with more direct contact with problems and responsibilities.'[15] From the mid-1960s the Fund developed professional programs to attract staff for long-term technocratic careers, with a special emphasis from the late 1970s on reducing a reliance on US citizens (but not US-trained economists, as we will see hereafter). During this same period the Fund permitted its technocrats to have greater engagement with the economics profession, including formal academic publishing and conferences.[16] Joseph Stiglitz once derided IMF technocrats as 'third-rank students from first-rate universities.'[17]

In combining policy demands with economic sciences, the Fund's technocrats are self-described 'mini-Keyneses' who combine academic research and operational policy work.[18] On one hand, the Fund's technocrats must uphold principles of impartiality and fair treatment of all member states, calling on their expertise in the correct application of economic models to maintain states' confidence. Staff gain internal and external prestige and status by being recognized as academic innovators, including by writing working

[10] Seabrooke 2001, 95–98.
[11] Seabrooke and Nilsson 2015, 243.
[12] de Vries 1986, 85; Boughton 2001, 1019. Current figure from www.imf.org, accessed August 17, 2023.
[13] The 'welfare' brutalist versus 'neoliberal' glass contrast in architectural styling between HQ1 and HQ2 is also replicated at the European Investment Bank in Luxembourg. On such styles and what they mean for organizational signaling, see Burrell 2013.
[14] Moschella 2011; Breen and Doak 2021; Kentikelenis and Babb 2022.
[15] Kindleberger 1951, 41.
[16] de Vries 1985, 52.
[17] Stiglitz 2000b.
[18] Interview with IMF Junior Economists (group discussion), June 2009.

papers and formal academic publications.[19] On the other hand, they frame their analyses and proposals 'within the recognized limits imposed by major shareholder positions.'[20] As such, they must mediate politics and science, taking positions on what can be credibly communicated to the Board as scientifically rigorous while assessing Board representatives' preference intensity for particular issues. Fund staff are also actively involved in external training and technical assistance networks, where their view of economic policy common sense is propagated—even perhaps proselytized—so it may receive an easier reception when included in formal policy demands from the IMF.[21]

This chapter explores how technocrats deal with these political and scientific compromises, detailing where—and why—they make claims to settled knowledge, and their likely understanding of preference intensities in the Board. We discuss the characteristics of Fund technocrats, how they have contingent power over scriptwriting through providing material to the Board, and how they are active in diffusing scripts through surveillance, academic production, and the fostering of transnational training networks.

Who Are the Technocrats?

The typical IMF technocrat is a professionally trained economist who seeks a long-term career with the Fund. Diversity is now prominent among the IMF staff ranks. Among the 2,765 staff in 2018, 44% were women and 56% men, with 30% women and 70% men in senior positions. This is a considerable improvement from 1978, when no women occupied any senior roles, and from 2000, when 14% were women.[22] The IMF technocracy centers around those with scientific roles, ranging from 'A11' economist (PhD entry level) through to 'A15,' which includes deputy division chiefs, senior economists, and resident representatives.[23] For those entering the IMF via the Economist Program, the typical profile is a person with a doctorate in economics, younger than 34 years old, who 'want[s] to have influence on the global stage and who can bring the latest in economic thought and multidisciplinary approaches to help us address key global economic challenges.'[24] From the best data available on this group, approximately 39% are women and 61% men. From the total staff, those from 'underrepresented regions' include 8% of staff from sub-Saharan Africa, 14% from East Asia, and 5.5%

[19] Momani 2007.
[20] Clift 2018, 92.
[21] Broome and Seabrooke 2015; Johnson 2016.
[22] de Vries 1985, 1029; Weaver et al. 2022, 10.
[23] IMF 2017c.
[24] IMF 2023; for a review of the Economist Program in the 1980s and 1990s, see Momani 2005.

from the Middle East.[25] Europeans, followed by North Americans, then Latin and South Americans, are the most dominant regional groups for the Fund technocracy.[26] The Fund has increased the number of management staff from low- and middle-income countries from 25% in 2000 to 40% in 2019.[27]

To foster promise in their careers, IMF technocrats need to be viewed as credible to fellow staff while maintaining status and prestige with external audiences. One path is to be viewed as intellectually powerful in economic sciences by one's peers. Margaret Garritsen de Vries, an economist and then historian of the Fund, provides a clear view of this path in her portrait of William H. White, a senior Fund economist who joined in 1948 and had a 35-year career. As he was 'exceptionally well acquainted with the theoretical literature, Mr. White was an economist's economist, unusually sought after by his colleagues for discussions of economic ideas and for comments on their own work.'[28] Intellectual debates and discussions of what the Fund's views should be are based around both staffer's formal work but also informal networks. The importance of 'breakfast clubs' has been noted in the literature, with newly appointed technocrats waiting for invitations from veterans to join them, especially when the Fund had smaller staff numbers.[29]

Beyond the walls of the IMF, the Fund technocrat—certainly in the past few decades—is also expected to publish in academic journals and be active in the economics profession. Charles Kindleberger noted the importance of a modicum of academic vanity for the performance of the Fund's technocracy in 1955:

> It is important for this purpose to maintain a good professional reputation outside the confines of international bureaucracy. More significant perhaps is the contribution to harmonious personnel relations for professional staff members to feel that their contribution to the profession is not unrecognized. The narcissistic satisfaction of seeing one's name in print is perhaps a sign of immaturity. Yet it is real: agencies both intellectual and anonymous which want to employ high-class professional talent, as in intelligence, find it necessary to pay prices above those of positions which can offer the satisfaction of academic recognition or proximity to the seats of power.[30]

Scholarship has stressed the importance of educational training of IMF technocrats to connect their socialization in postgraduate economics

---

[25] IMF 2019, 4.
[26] IMF 2019, supplement, 4.
[27] Weaver et al. 2022, 8.
[28] de Vries 1985, 1030.
[29] Harper 1998, 79.
[30] Kindleberger 1955, 350.

programs, especially doctoral programs, with their likely behavior within the IMF. In terms of where the Fund technocrats get their education, 56.2% of technocrats in 2019 received their bachelor's degree, 58.2% their master's degree, and 59.1% their doctoral degree from the US. The UK was second for master's and doctoral degrees at 11.3% and 11.9%, respectively.[31] The dominance of Anglo-American training is especially prominent for those joining via the Economist Program.[32] The technocratic corpus is diverse in terms of nationality and gender while being centered on US economics training. The dominance of the US in the training of Fund technocrats has fed the idea that propinquity, being physically in close proximity, and indoctrination are important in generating homophily among Fund staff—being like 'birds of a feather.'[33] The notion that graduate training equips IMF technocrats with a predetermined mindset follows the logic that not only formal roles but also informal networks affirm their ideological positions.[34]

Jeffrey Chwieroth is clear on this view, arguing that the 'shared socializing experience of professional training in Anglo-American economics departments—which rests on a theoretical core stressing market efficiency and rationality—has helped instill in the Fund staff a shared way of forming policy judgments.'[35] Stephen Nelson makes a similar claim, with the view that the IMF's persistent recruitment of 'neoliberals'—those who '(1) earned an MA or higher at a top-ranked American economics department or (2) have significant experience with the IMF or World Bank'[36]—affirm neoliberal economic beliefs among staff. Those with neoliberal economics training carry those beliefs into how they negotiate with member-state officials when discussing loan conditionalities. Here, neoliberal IMF staff will be able to recognize their counterparts across the negotiation table, both finding a glint of Friedmanesque monetarism in each other's eyes.[37] Not recognizing this glint has big consequences for how many conditions may be attached to an IMF loan. As Chwieroth explains, 'When borrowing-country officials appear unsympathetic to the staff's normative orientations, thus demonstrating a weaker commitment to IMF policy goals, the staff may perceive a greater need to make any policy adjustments explicitly binding.'[38]

---

[31] IMF 2019, 7–9.
[32] Momani 2005, 174.
[33] McPherson et al. 2001; Heinzel et al. 2021.
[34] Van Gunten et al. 2016.
[35] Chwieroth 2015, 761.
[36] Nelson 2014, supplementary appendix.
[37] Personal interaction and the presence of 'mirror neurons' have been studied in diplomatic negotiations but are not part of the corpus of studies, to our knowledge, on the IMF. On diplomacy and mirror neurons, see Holmes 2013.
[38] Chwieroth 2015, 761.

To assert the presence of neoliberals in the IMF, Stephen Nelson collected data for 983 IMF staff hired between 1980 and 2000, finding that 47% were trained in top US economics departments and are thus classified as neoliberals.[39] The implication is that because the IMF's technocrats are neoliberals, they play favorites in how they allocate loan conditions, based on how they read their member-state counterparts in negotiations. But if the IMF technocracy is stuffed with neoliberals, then why do they refer to themselves as 'mini-Keyneses' rather than 'mini-Friedmans'? The logic here can be questioned, which is especially important if we wish to know who the IMF technocrats are.

Another way to approach the educational socialization of IMF technocrats is to follow the distinction in US economics between 'Freshwater' and 'Saltwater' schools of thought.[40] The distinction is important because to paint all technocrats trained in top American economics graduate programs as neoliberal fails to recognize that there are simultaneously different views on how the economy should work and the role of economic models within these normative dispositions.[41] In the Freshwater versus Saltwater distinction, the differences are theoretical and geographic. The Freshwater attack within US economics in the 1970s posited that conventional Keynesian macroeconomics was not up to task and that we needed to base economic modeling in microlevel individual choices, firm-level agency, rational expectations, and real business cycles.[42] This neoliberal attack came from places located near the Great Lakes, most notably the University of Chicago, Northwestern University, the University of Wisconsin–Madison, the University of Rochester, and others (including those not so close to the lakes, like the University of California, Los Angeles—sometimes jokingly referred to as the University of Chicago, Los Angeles).

The Saltwater retort was that Keynesian macroeconomics, rather than being replaced with universal laws of rationality, could be tinkered with. Irrationalities in economic life are important to understand and demand management for the macroeconomy is essential for addressing economic and social structural problems. Scholars from these universities were based in coastal cities and towns, like Harvard University, MIT, Columbia University, Princeton University, the University of California–Berkeley, and others. Prestigious overseas economics departments were also on the side of the 'salty,' including those at Cambridge University, Oxford University, the London

---

[39] Nelson 2014.
[40] Önder and Terviö 2015.
[41] Reay 2012; Helgadóttir 2022; Lang et al. 2024.
[42] Helgadóttir 2023.

School of Economics, and the Australian National University. Table 5.1 lists the top 'fresh' and 'salty' institutions for the 1990–2009 period, drawing on an analysis of citation networks.[43]

Henriksen and colleagues have demonstrated that Freshwater environments—especially the Chicago school—were much better at creating social cohesion among their graduate students than Saltwater universities like Harvard.[44] This social cohesion grew in the 1950s and 1960s and preceded the macroeconomic troubles that provided structural opportunities for the rise of neoliberalism from the mid-1970s.[45] Such

Table 5.1 Saltwater and Freshwater Universities in Economics

Saltwater	Freshwater	
Harvard	Chicago	University of Southern California
Massachusetts Institute of Technology	Northwestern	Washington
Stanford	Pennsylvania	Virginia
Princeton	Rochester	Penn State
Berkeley	New York University	Caltech
Yale	University of California Los Angeles	Indiana
Columbia	Wisconsin	Iowa
Michigan	Carnegie Mellon	University of North Carolina
London School of Economics	Minnesota	Brown
University of California San Diego	Cornell	Florida
Maryland	Illinois	Arizona
University of British Columbia	Duke	
Oxford	Hebrew	
Boston University	Tel Aviv	
Michigan State	Toronto	
Australian National University	University of California Davis	
University College London	Ohio State	
Cambridge	University of Texas at Austin	

Source: Önder and Terviö 2015, 1496; the authors include leading non-US universities in their classification.

---

[43] Önder and Terviö 2015.
[44] Henriksen et al. 2022.
[45] Stedman Jones 2012.

cohesion promotes ideological consistency over generations, especially the hardening of neoliberal right-wing views.[46] Successful intergenerational social cohesion increased the reproduction rate of prominent neoliberal economists, like Milton Friedman, who begat some 111 doctoral students over three generations, with him and his peers at Chicago outcompeting their rivals at Harvard and MIT.[47]

Given this, we should expect to find the IMF aflood with Freshwater folk. We recoded Nelson's data on 983 top-level IMF appointments between 1980 and 2000, locating them in the Freshwater and Saltwater universities list in Table 5.1. We found 384 Saltwater (39%) staff and 206 Freshwater (21%) staff in Nelson's data. Figure 5.1 shows the trends in appointments over time from Nelson's data, the proportion of Freshwater neoliberals compared to Saltwater Keynesians (and variations thereof), and other off-brand hires.

Studying the IMF's research output and citation networks identifies the organization as positively saline.[48] Henriksen and colleagues looked for elite

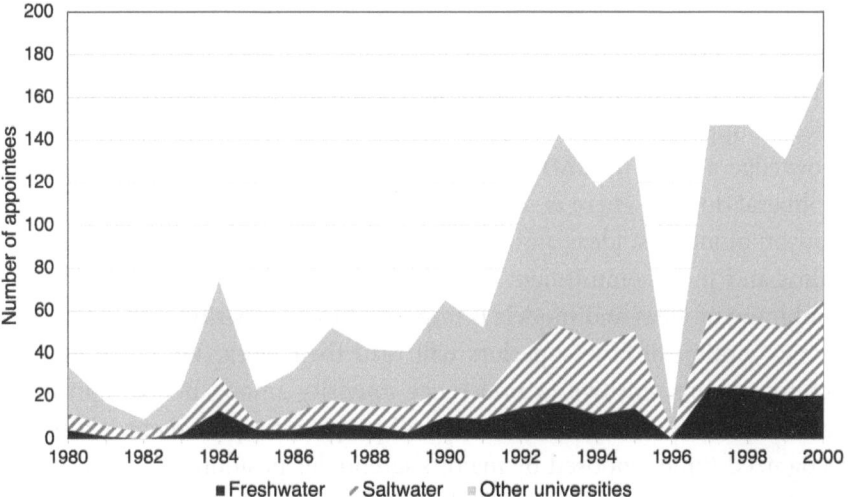

Figure 5.1 Freshwater and Saltwater top-level appointments at the IMF, 1980–2000

Note: While we could not find clear evidence explaining the drop in new appointments in 1996, the most likely explanation is that this was a period of internal reorganization at the IMF. In 1996 and 1997, the Asia and Pacific Department was created (by merging preexisting structures), a new regional office for Asia and the Pacific was established, and the Office of Internal Audit and Inspection was reformed; see Boughton 2012. It is likely that new senior appointments were on hold during this time.

Source: Adapted from Nelson 2014.

---

[46] Jelveh et al. 2014.
[47] Henriksen et al. 2022.
[48] Önder and Terviö 2015, 1497.

American universities not only in Nelson's data but also among IMF workingpaper authors from 1970 to 1995 and found that Harvard, Columbia, and Princeton were more prominent than Chicago, again suggesting more Saltwater than Freshwater.[49]

To verify the relative absence of Freshwater neoliberals, we wondered if this also applied to IMF staff sent on ordinary missions (e.g., tasks such as surveillance). We recoded Seabrooke and Nilsson's data for 141 IMF technocrats involved in the Financial Sector Assessment Program from its creation in 1999 until 2011.[50] Only 15% had doctorates, with 7 Freshwater and 12 Saltwater PhDs. Only one staff member trained at the University of Chicago.

What is the implication here? The first is that it is important to identify variation within the IMF technocracy, which leads to variation in the development of policy scripts.[51] The second is that it is not especially useful to treat being trained in a top US economics department as ipso facto evidence of neoliberal socialization. Third, a stress on socialization through education also misses the point that the IMF expends significant effort in shaping their new graduate hires into their own image, as commonly identified with global professional service firms.[52]

That the IMF technocracy is, on average, more salty than fresh also provides an opportunity to be surprised by variations in the degree of settled knowledge among the IMF staffers rather than assuming that they follow neoliberal dogma. There is simply greater complexity: IMF technocrats can draw on monetarist ideas and theories with 'no contradiction between these claims and their commitment to a Keynesian professional identity.'[53] Such combining of ideas and models is important in scriptwriting, as is the technocrats' notion of how superiors will read their work. We know that the technocrats are sensitive to preference intensity among Board representatives on particular issues—that they will propose script content 'within the recognized limits imposed by major shareholder positions.'[54] We know less about the degree of settled knowledge within the staff ranks, which provides a chance to identify variation in scriptwriting processes. This includes how IMF staff develop their own subcultures and how they engage in 'boundary work' to demarcate their policy territory relative to other IOs.[55] For example, Jacqueline Best has noted, from her interviews with IMF technocrats, tensions

---

[49] Henriksen et al. 2025.
[50] Seabrooke and Nilsson 2015.
[51] Kaya and Reay 2019.
[52] Suddaby et al. 2007; Spence and Carter 2014.
[53] Van Gunten 2015a, 331–33.
[54] Pauly 1997; Clift 2018, 92.
[55] Ban 2015; Kranke 2022.

between European and African department staff over whether the Fund should be interested in producing policy scripts for economic development rather than focusing on global financial and economic stability.[56] Such internal vignettes are of interest if we want to know how, and why, particular script content is being provided to the Board.

This is where the agency of technocrats is important to understand. As Ben Clift has described in detail, Fund technocrats can act as 'bricoleurs' to cobble together different economic ideas and propose solutions that appear nonthreatening to established paradigms. In his empirical case, Fund technocrats put forward the idea of 'fiscal space' to mix and match multiple economic ideas.[57] In recent years, many IMF technocrats have advocated supporting aggregate demand through countercyclical policy, infrastructure investment, and tackling inequality as key macroeconomic components of securing growth in advanced economies.[58] As Clift discusses, the 'Fund is wont to recommend tax rises and increasing the progressivity of income tax regimes in ways which seem beyond the pale, even for mainstream left parties, in many national political discourses.'[59] Viewed this way, Fund technocrats have strayed onto social-democratic economic policy terrain much more than one might have anticipated if we followed the neoliberal domination narrative.[60] The promotion of fiscal space as a conceptual container in which technocrats can combine ideas, and to which internal and external audiences can provide their own positive readings, is an example of what Ann Mische refers to as 'generality shifting,' a tactic more commonly associated with activists in social movements.[61]

Sources of Power in Scriptwriting

What sources of power do Fund technocrats possess in scriptwriting? We suggest they take two forms. The first form is through the content technocrats provide to the Board, which reflects a Fund technocratic worldview that the Board occasionally pushes back upon when political contestation is

---

[56] Best 2014, 211n22. The IMF's departments are split into Area and Functional roles as follows. The Area departments are the African Department (AFR), Asia and Pacific Department (APD), European Department (EUR), Middle East and Central Asia Department (MCD), and Western Hemisphere Department (WHD). The Functional departments are the Fiscal Affairs Department (FAD); Institute of Capacity Development (ICD); Money and Capital Markets Department (MCM); Research Department (RES); Statistics Department (STA); and Strategy, Policy and Review Department (SPR).
[57] Clift 2018.
[58] Ban and Patenaude 2019.
[59] Clift 2019, 212.
[60] Clift 2019, 208.
[61] Mische 2003.

high and differs from technocratic treatments.[62] The second form is in the crafting of governance objects through academic production that are shared with networks of technocrats and economists, and which establish the metrics and benchmarks that scriptwriting should take into account.[63] We deal with both of these in turn, using archival materials to show how this works in practice.

On material supplied to the Board to assist with scriptwriting, the key instruments are Staff Memoranda (known as 'SMs') and Executive Board Specials (known as 'EBSs'). SMs are staff-prepared studies and reports for the Board, including reports on country economic surveillance ('Article IVs'), Selected Issues reports with more in-depth analysis, statistical summaries, and policy papers. EBSs are more specialized because they feature staff reporting to the Board on the use of IMF resources, including overdue obligations.

Figure 5.2 provides an example of a SM on country experiences with the use and liberalization of capital controls. As we will see in chapter 7, scriptwriting for this issue was particularly contentious, with a high degree of scientific consensus among the technocrats hitting a wall of political contestation in the Board. Figure 5.2 provides some insight into the mechanics of this struggle. Note that this document is a revision and a supplement. It states that, given earlier debate,[64] revisions were required. Directors criticized the previous version for providing a position for the liberalization of capital controls, while the staff noted the use of capital controls as part of long-term development policy, in countries like China and India, rather than short-term contagion prevention.[65] The directors called for more information on short- and long-term effects of capital account liberalization, including the prudential macroeconomic and financial prerequisites for it to be effective. More was needed on the sequencing of capital account liberalization ('gradualism vs. big bang').[66] In figure 5.2 we can see that the technocrats have revised the document according to the directors' considerations and indicated where this is the case. Given that an edited version has been approved, unless a director raises an alarm the final product will appear in the Occasional Papers series, where it will provide the Fund's view on capital account liberalization and bona fide material for scriptwriting.

---

[62] Kentikelenis and Babb 2019.
[63] Best 2014.
[64] Documented in SM/99/60, BUFF/99/45, SM/99/214, and EBM/99/101. BUFF documents are informal papers composed of statements from staff representatives at Board meetings and remarks or summations from the Chair.
[65] Note that Executive Directors also submit positions on member states' views, known as 'Grays,' which have explicit preferences. See Carnegie et al. 2023.
[66] EBM/99/101, 6.

DOCUMENT OF INTERNATIONAL MONETARY FUND AND NOT FOR PUBLIC USE

IMMEDIATE ATTENTION

MASTER FILES
ROOM HQ C-525   0450

SM/99/214
Revision 1

November 18, 1999

To: Members of the Executive Board

From: The Acting Secretary

Subject: **Country Experience with the Use and Liberalization of Capital Controls**

Attached for the information of the Executive Directors is a revised version of the paper on country experience with the use and liberalization of capital controls (SM/99/214, 8/27/99), which was considered by the Executive Board on September 10, 1999. This paper incorporates the comments provided by the Executive Directors on details of respective country experiences. All changes have been indicated in the text of the paper, and relate to specific country experiences.

During its discussion on this topic, the Executive Board endorsed the publication of an edited version of this paper. It is not proposed to bring this matter to the agenda of the Executive Board for discussion unless an Executive Director so requests by noon on Monday, November 29, 1999. In the absence of such a request, this paper will be published in the *Occasional Papers* series.

Mr. Ariyoshi (ext. 39414) and Mr. Laurens (ext. 36534) are available to answer technical or factual questions relating to this paper.

Att: (1)

Other Distribution:
Department Heads

Figure 5.2 An IMF Staff Memorandum for the Executive Board
Source: IMF archives, SM/99/214, Revision 1

Figure 5.3 provides an example of an EBS on debt sustainability analysis (DSA) for the Heavily Indebted Poor Countries (see chapter 6). Here we can see some 'star power' in that the document has been approved by

INTERNATIONAL MONETARY FUND

**HIPC Initiative—Debt Sustainability Analysis and
Noncomplying Purchases and Disbursements**

Prepared by the Policy Development and Review and Legal Departments

Approved by Timothy Geithner and François Gianviti

February 1, 2002

1. This paper proposes an amendment of the HIPC Trust Instrument to provide for a change in the calculation of debt relief under the enhanced HIPC Initiative.[1]

2. Under existing procedures for the enhanced HIPC Initiative, the amount of assistance to be committed for a member is determined at the decision point on the basis of a debt sustainability analysis (DSA) using data available for the most recent calendar or fiscal year.[2] The DSA makes use of actual data for the stock of public and publicly guaranteed external debt as of the end of the relevant calendar or fiscal year, including debt owed to the Fund. It is possible that relevant amounts owed to the Fund may, between the reference date for the DSA and the completion point, be found to constitute noncomplying purchases/disbursements that are subject to early repurchase/repayment expectations under the Fund's Misreporting Guidelines.[3] The inclusion of such amounts in the stock of outstanding debt would result in an artificially high level of external debt and an unjustified amount of debt forgiveness as the member's outstanding debt would include amounts that the member, on the basis of accurate information, would not have been entitled to receive.

---

[1] See: *Instrument to Establish a Trust for Special PRGF Operations for the Heavily Indebted Poor Countries and Interim PRGF Subsidy Operations* (annexed to Decision No. 11436-(97/10), adopted February 4, 1997).

[2] The debt sustainability analysis is prepared jointly by the staffs of the Fund and the Bank and the relevant member.

[3] See: *Misreporting and Noncomplying Purchases in the General Resources Account – Guidelines on Corrective Action* (Decision No.12249-(00/77), adopted July 27, 2000); *Instrument to Establish the Poverty Reduction and Growth Facility Trust* (annexed to Decision No. 8759-(87/176) ESAF, adopted December 18, 1987), Appendix I.

Figure 5.3 An IMF staff-led Executive Board Special with a decision point
Source: IMF archives, EBS/02/18

Timothy Geithner, then the director of the Policy Development and Review Department. Geithner had moved to the IMF after being under secretary of the Treasury for international affairs under President Clinton and prior to becoming president of the Federal Reserve Bank of New York in 2003 (and US

Treasury secretary under President Obama in 2009). The document discusses how the DSA calculates debts owed according to fiscal year, and how differences between debt for this period and until the 'completion point'—whereby the member state has followed the conditions of a Poverty Reduction Strategy Paper for at least one year—may inflate the level of debt. Of particular interest here are the lines:

> It is not proposed to bring this matter to the agenda of the Executive Board for discussion unless an Executive Director so requests by noon on Friday, February 8, 2002. In the absence of such a request, the draft decision that appears on pages 3 and 4 will be deemed approved by the Executive Board.[67]

This is a clear example of a technocratic gambit. Those on the Board can question what is in the DSA, but doing so will then generate a Board discussion, with an implication that Geithner and the expertise of the Policy Development and Review Department would be questioned.

The technocratic development of a DSA as a key tool to be automatically factored into decisions authorized by the Board is, itself, a form of power wielded by the IMF staff. Sustainability assessments sort the member states with repayments into low-, medium-, and high-risk categories based on a baseline stress-test scenario. This includes conventional indicators like debt as a percentage of GDP, exports, and revenues, as well as debt service payments as a percentage of exports and revenues.[68] The categorization in weak, medium, and strong categories reflects what political economy literature discusses as state capacity.[69]

Jacqueline Best argues that not just the norms but the practices of Fund staff provide them with 'provisional expertise'—the development of positions that is 'open to revision or contradiction without losing its claim to expert authority.'[70] The development of standard forms of analysis and best practices become types of power through what is called 'inscription' in science and technology studies.[71] Put differently, standard treatments, like DSA, can be 'black boxed' and become normal and automatic, which then empowers the assumptions within the model, such as the primacy of the single rational individual in Real Business Cycles models.[72]

---

[67] EBS/02/18.
[68] Block-Lieb and Weidemaier 2016, 1621.
[69] Kentikelenis et al. 2016; Reinsberg et al. 2019.
[70] Best 2014, 5.
[71] Often defined as practices and technologies that are 'immutable, presentable, readable, and combinable' and ease calculability. See Latour 1986, 7.
[72] Helgadóttir 2023, 266.

Technocrats can use standard treatments to provide ready-made standards for how scripts should be thought about and discussed, using them as purportedly apolitical decision-making machines.[73] Ernst Haas recognized this long ago, arguing in 1962 that IO technical assistance to assess if member states met their obligations was one of the most powerful weapons in their arsenal, especially since it 'facilitates quantitative assessments of the degree of success achieved' that can be presented as politically neutral.[74]

From the IMF technocracy we have many examples of such automated decision-machines based on best practices, including the selection of statistical practices—defining how and what is measured[75]—and creation of compound indices like the Reports on the Observance of Standards and Codes (ROSCs) and the Special Data Dissemination Standard (SDDS). Both have been legitimated as efficient means for countries to report on economic performance to external audiences, especially private financial markets.[76]

Introduced in 1996 following Mexico's 1994 *tesobonos* debt crisis,[77] the SDDS requires standardized metadata to be provided to the IMF on the following sectors: fiscal (government operations and debt), financial (interest rates, stock market, central and commercial bank accounts), real (national accounts, production indices, consumer price index, employment and earnings data), and external (balances of payments, international reserves, exchange rates, merchandise trade, international investment position, and external debt). Heralded by the IMF technocracy as lowering the cost of issuance in government bond markets, SDDS can provide 'cost savings to the sovereign borrower and ultimately its taxpayers.'[78] Given that SDDS is legitimized as a mechanism for countries to effectively signal macroeconomic performance to financial markets, other analyses view SDDS as a private-sector failure, with traders unaware or unconcerned with it.[79]

ROSCs were launched in 1999 to integrate key economic indicators into a single document, including 12 areas of operational work for the IMF and the World Bank: accounting, auditing, banking supervision, corporate governance, creditor rights and insolvency, data dissemination, fiscal transparency, insurance supervision, monetary and financial policy transparency, payments systems, and securities regulation. In 2002, anti–money laundering and combating financial terrorism was also added. IMF staff justified this

---

[73] Steffek 2021.
[74] Haas 1962, 329.
[75] Mügge 2022.
[76] Lombardi and Woods 2008.
[77] Seabrooke 2001, 165; Best 2014, 131.
[78] Cady 2005, 516.
[79] Mosley 2003.

extensive exercise on the logic that it would provide more information on fiscal plans to financial markets, also encouraging governments not to backslide on commitments and enhancing their credibility in the marketplace.[80] IMF staff have heralded ROSCs as a success in reducing countries' borrowing costs.[81] However, while 130 countries had gone through ROSC reporting processes by 2006, creating 600 reports, there is little evidence of private-sector interest in them.[82]

Many of these standard treatments pass through the Board without comment, becoming part of the language of how the Board discusses issues. At other times, the Board has objected. For example, on the proposed formalization of DSA, a Board member exclaimed, 'We are not a ratings agency.'[83] What is clear is that such standard treatments can have power not only within the IMF but among peer institutions that recognize the importance of these best practices and affirm them.[84] As researchers have noted in recent years, IOs are important producers of benchmarks and ranking systems that have strong political and economic distributive outcomes[85] and thus are prone to gaming from powerful states and consultancies.[86]

The second form of power in scriptwriting comes from academic production that seeks to influence the content of policy scripts. As noted earlier, IMF technocrats hold onto a 'mini-Keynes' identity that encourages them to keep one foot in policymaking and the other in the economics profession.[87] Couching their work in technical and quantitative language provides Fund staff the opportunity to evade member states' political concerns and rely on economic models as rationalizations embedded in world culture.[88] This world culture, dominated by the US economics profession and its own clear hierarchy in knowledge production,[89] encourages internal intellectual competition that can also find an external audience in academic publishing.

About 10% of the IMF's administrative budget is dedicated to research activities, slightly more than the operational cost of the Board.[90] This work is supported by the Board as a key form of IMF 'propaganda,' with figures like Alexandre Kafka, an Executive Director for Brazil for more than three

---

[80] Best 2014, 33.
[81] Glennerster and Shin 2008.
[82] Mehrpouya and Salles-Djelic 2019, 22.
[83] Best 2014, 144.
[84] Broome and Seabrooke 2021.
[85] Honig and Weaver 2019.
[86] Broome 2022.
[87] Van Gunten 2015a, 331–33.
[88] Momani 2007, 47.
[89] Fourcade et al. 2015.
[90] Independent Evaluation Office of the International Monetary Fund 2013.

decades, commenting that staff studies should inform the academic community of economists that the IMF is more than a preacher of austerity.[91]

The key forms of IMF academic production are the Staff Papers, Occasional Papers, and Working Papers. Figure 5.4 provides an example of a Staff Paper, which is intended to provide academic debate around best practices for policy. The paper's author is Vito Tanzi, who was director of the Fiscal Affairs Department of the IMF from 1981 to 2000, and it outlines the relationship between tax levels and macroeconomic stability, arguing for tax reforms that can help developing countries cope with external shocks. Tanzi provides a justification for how stabilizing government revenues through reliable broader taxes—such as a value-added tax (see chapter 7)—can neutralize a dependence on trade taxes and help adjust to changing monetary and financial shocks, such as sudden exchange-rate adjustments and interest rate hikes. In short, the paper provides the intellectual reasoning for the IMF's fundamental position on fiscal matters.

A second site of academic production is the Working Paper series, with an example illustrated in Figure 5.5. One of the most prominent IMF technocrats, Jacques Polak, initially dismissed the Working Paper series as an unnecessary distraction, given that 'Staff Papers was the main organ of Fund propaganda.'[92] Nevertheless, the series emerged in 1986 with a first paper on indirect taxation in developing countries. Since then, it has boomed, developing a different profile from the Staff Papers. Dennis Essers and coauthors found that the IMF produced 6,152 papers between 1990 and 2017, with 3,918 distinct authors.[93] This rate of production is nearly fourfold that at the World Bank, when accounting for staff size.[94] Sixty percent of these papers are from the functional departments, especially the Research Department and the Fiscal Affairs Department,[95] with area departments making up the remainder. The authors are, understandably, mainly IMF staff (54.2%), followed by visiting scholars (24.6%) and central bankers (6.6%).[96]

A crucial element of the Working Papers series is demonstrating the IMF technocracy's ties to prominent academic economists, like Barry Eichengreen and Carmen Reinhart. Essers et al.'s study of IMF Working Paper citation networks found 'a network architecture where interlinked "star" authors act as

---

[91] EBM/86/158, 36. See also Kaya and Reay 2019, 395.
[92] EBM/86/158, 37. Polak was director of research and statistics (1958–1979) and an Executive Director (1981–1986).
[93] Essers et al. 2022, 7171.
[94] Aizenman et al. 2011, 20.
[95] The Fiscal Affairs Department is one of the key intellectual innovators within the Fund; see Clift 2018.
[96] Essers et al. 2022, 7177.

IMF *Staff Papers*
Vol. 36, No. 3 (September 1989)
© 1989 International Monetary Fund

The Impact of Macroeconomic Policies on the Level of Taxation and the Fiscal Balance in Developing Countries

VITO TANZI*

In recent years the taxation level in many developing countries has changed dramatically over relatively short periods. These changes are too large and too sudden to be attributed fully to a deterioration in tax administration or to changes in the traditional determinants of tax levels. They can be attributed, to a considerable extent, to the connection between tax levels and macroeconomic policies—in particular, exchange rate, import substitution, trade liberalization, inflation, public debt, and financial policies. Thus, more attention should be paid to these relationships, and tax reform should aim to neutralize some of their effects. [JEL 121, 320, 431]

THE LEVEL of taxation, expressed as a percentage of gross domestic product (T/GDP), varies considerably among the world's developing countries. In a few of them, it is below 10 percent. In a few others, it is above 30 percent. For the majority of developing countries, however, the level ranges between these two limits, with an overall average of about 18 percent and a substantial proportion in the 15–25 percent range (see Tanzi (1987)).[1]

---

* Mr. Tanzi is Director of the Fiscal Affairs Department of the Fund. He holds a Ph.D. in Economics from Harvard University.

An earlier and much shorter version of this paper was presented at the "XX Jornadas de Finanzas Públicas," Córdoba (Argentina), September 23–25, 1987. The author would like to thank Sebastian Edwards, Brian Pinto, and colleagues from the Fund for valuable comments on an earlier draft.

[1] For the Organization for Economic Cooperation and Development (OECD) countries the average in 1980–85 was between 35 percent and 37 percent of gross domestic product (GDP). For a few countries, in 1985 it exceeded 45 percent of GDP (Belgium, Denmark, France, the Netherlands, Norway, and Sweden). See OECD (1987).

633

Figure 5.4 An IMF Staff Paper

MASTER FILES
ROOM C-525

0440

IMF WORKING PAPER

© 1990 International Monetary Fund

This is a working paper and the author would welcome any comments on the present text. Citations should refer to an unpublished manuscript, mentioning the author and the date of issuance by the International Monetary Fund. The views expressed are those of the author and do not necessarily represent those of the Fund.

WP/90/51

INTERNATIONAL MONETARY FUND

Central Banking Department

Capital Controls and International Portfolio Theory:
A Microeconomic Approach

Prepared by Marjorie B. Rose*

Authorized for Distribution by Sérgio Pereira Leite

June 1990

Abstract

This paper examines the effects of capital controls on asset prices. A closed-form valuation model by Eun and Janakirimanan (1986) is extended to analyze the impact of three restrictions on international portfolio investment: a percentage quantity constraint on the amount of foreign securities a domestic resident may hold in her portfolio; a constraint on the absolute amount of foreign securities a domestic resident may hold; and a percentage tax on the domestic purchase price of a foreign security. Comparative statics and numerical analysis are used to reveal the effects of these distortions on domestic and world equilibrium prices.

JEL Classification No.
441

---

*/ Ms. Rose was an economist in the Central Banking Department when this paper was prepared. She is now in the African Department. Comments by Sérgio Pereira Leite, Douglas Irwin, David Hirshliefer, and Cheol Eun are gratefully acknowledged. The author is solely responsible for any remaining errors.

Figure 5.5 An IMF Working Paper
Source: IMF archives, WP/90/51

connectors of different clusters in the overall network.'[97] Within this network, the competing technocratic organizations are respective Federal Reserve offices, the Organisation for Economic Co-operation and Development, and the World Bank.

Ayse Kaya and Mike Reay's analysis of 12,000 IMF documents published between 1982 and 2011, including Board minutes, Article IV staff reports (discussed hereafter), and Working Papers, provides great insights in identifying whether the technocracy leads or follows the Board in providing content for policy scripts.[98] They found that IMF Working Papers used pro-market language more prominently than the Executive Board on themes like tax reform, privatization, interest rate liberalization, and foreign direct investment. There are clear patterns where staff increased the use of particular terms after they were used prominently in the Executive Board, on themes like central bank independence, structural adjustment, fiscal discipline, and capital-account openness. They further show that the staff have led on themes like poverty, inequality, education, and healthcare.[99] IMF staff have also led on the introduction of climate-change-related policies, using their mission experience as a spur to innovate.[100] Whether the head wags the tail, or vice versa, depends on the script being written.

Diffusing Scripts to Support Norms

IMF technocrats diffuse policy scripts through lending mission work, technical assistance, and surveillance, as well as through transnational training networks. Given that our interest in this book is in scriptwriting, we highlight three processes by which the IMF technocracy provides direct and indirect support for script implementation that also feeds back into scriptwriting. First, IMF lending is the most direct and conspicuous way in which staff can ensure that dominant policy scripts are diffused and institutionalized. This process is often termed 'coercive diffusion,'[101] as it relies on the organization's power to condition loan disbursement to the introduction of certain reforms, to be introduced over multiple reviews of the original program.[102] Fund technocrats are in the driver's seat at all stages of IMF loans, including preparations for negotiations with member-state governments, direct

[97] Essers et al. 2022, 7189.
[98] Kaya and Reay 2019.
[99] Kaya and Reay 2019, 397.
[100] Clark and Zucker 2023.
[101] Simmons et al. 2008.
[102] Kentikelenis and Stubbs 2023.

discussions between IMF mission staff and member-state officials, and internal discussions within the Fund, and they ultimately prepare the relevant documentation for Board discussion and approval.

The role of Fund staff in determining the number and type of loan conditions during negotiations with member states has attracted consistent academic attention,[103] with the implication being that the educational socialization of technocrats as neoliberal economists is important for playing favorites with like-minded counterparts.[104] The Fund technocrats are known for their general-application economic knowledge rather than their long-standing country expertise (staff rotate in and out of different country teams or regional departments every few years), which provides a contrast with how member states value advice from the World Bank.[105] Importantly, given the time-sensitive aspect of IMF lending—as recipient countries are commonly in crisis—the Board rarely rejects a loan agreement negotiated by staff, but it does voice its opinions, preferences, or reservations in order to guide staff negotiating positions during subsequent reviews.

The second process, also direct, is the surveillance work of member states' economic policies. This is the regular, noncrisis work of the organization, which relies on staff producing a report—called an Article IV consultation—following a mission visiting a member state for a general economic health check-up.[106] Article IVs provide the bulk of IMF surveillance around 120 are conducted annually.[107] They are used to not only document what is happening within countries but to compare them regionally and culturally.[108] The Article IV process permits IMF staff from the relevant regional department to provide a country-specific mission brief, which is circulated among relevant functional departments. Four or five IMF staff visit the country for one or two weeks; the mission team meets with various government agencies, and the concerned member state informs them about macroeconomic conditions and forecasts. Such surveillance is a 'one-way process' with little room for peer-to-peer learning between IMF mission team and member-state officials.[109] Much of this activity is, to quote Armin Schäfer, about 'getting the numbers

---

[103] Caraway et al. 2012; Rickard and Caraway 2014, 2018.
[104] Nelson 2014; Chwieroth 2015. Similar claims have been made about the World Bank, with the dominant nationality within teams important in determining outcomes; see Clark and Dolan 2021.
[105] Heinzel 2022.
[106] Moschella 2012.
[107] Lopez 2017, 107.
[108] For example, Australia and New Zealand were part of the IMF's European Department, based on cultural and economic affinities, but were reassigned in 1992 to what was then called the Southeast Asia and Pacific Department. See Broome and Seabrooke 2007, 585.
[109] Lombardi and Woods 2008, 733.

right.'¹¹⁰ The Fund staff then provide a mission-concluding statement, which includes staff recommendations, and the head of mission is responsible for drafting a back-to-office report and, back in Washington, a staff report. The Board then discusses this staff report, but—as the subject matter is economic surveillance—makes no explicit decision. The IMF also releases its findings in a Public Information Notice.¹¹¹ This makes Article IV work part of the IMF's public-facing activities, even though there is little evidence that domestic policymakers are actually interested.¹¹²

There is interest in Article IV surveillance, however, from those working in sovereign debt markets, with analysts assigned to large developing countries—such as Brazil and Romania—considering them a 'de-facto gold standard' in information provision and adjusting their investments accordingly.¹¹³ From the IMF's viewpoint, Fund staff can use Article IVs as a form of 'defensive surveillance' to help member states with significant debt to promote their macroeconomic health and lower the costs of sovereign debt servicing.¹¹⁴

In general, the IMF staff work via Article IVs to provide some variation—but mainly continuity—in their economic ideas and what they consider appropriate content for script implementation.¹¹⁵ Staff use of Article IVs differs according to the income-level of the member state involved, with low-income countries receiving reform goals and implementation advice, and high-income countries receiving advice on policy tools.¹¹⁶ Differences among Article IVs are important to recognize because they also provide a way to identify political contestations. Contrasts between Article IV staff recommendations and Board opinions provide one way to see when great powers intervene, as Bessma Momani has demonstrated with US intervention to support a pro-Western regime in Egypt in 1987 and 1991.¹¹⁷

This regular use of Article IVs for macro-level surveillance has been expanded into particular sectors, which provides an example of how IMF staff use mission work to support the diffusion of scripts and feedback to the Fund's Board and technocracy. Multilateral surveillance is currently 13% of IMF spending. Of these programs, an especially important one is the Financial Sector Assessment Program (FSAP), established in 1999 following the

---

[110] Schäfer 2006, 75.
[111] Schäfer 2006, 75–76.
[112] Edwards and Senger 2015.
[113] Breen and Doak 2021, 323.
[114] Fratzscher and Reynaud 2011.
[115] Broome 2015; Hernandez 2020.
[116] Schlaufer 2019.
[117] Momani 2005.

Asian Financial Crisis, in which the severity of IMF loan conditions was attributed to the Fund technocracy and its 'silent revolution' in steering script content.[118] The IMF responded by strengthening its surveillance of financial systems, partly to address its significant legitimacy gap with Asian member states,[119] especially given a rise in member states' scapegoating the Fund for unpopular reforms.[120]

FSAPs fostered better utilization of limited expert resources on financial systems between the IMF and the World Bank, with the latter supplying staff to be involved in FSAPs in low-income member states. FSAPs are conducted as missions, staffed mainly by IMF technocrats and external consultants. Missions begin with a scoping process to develop a Terms of Reference document that details what is to be studied and discussed. In this process IMF staff must address a macroeconomic relevance test,[121] in that they should connect the member state's financial system to core macroeconomic concerns.[122] The mission team visits the country for two to three weeks to discuss and analyze data made available by local authorities. Especially important for measuring financial-sector resilience are Financial Soundness Indicators, which were 'envisioned as a macro version of a bank value at risk model.'[123] Such indicators establish a standard treatment for financial data provided by governments. FSAP mission analyses are then funneled into a ROSC, as discussed earlier, and the mission team produces a Financial Structure Stability Assessment. The point here is that the IMF technocracy expands standard treatments across new sectors.

The third process by which IMF technocrats support the diffusion of their preferred policy scripts is through technical assistance and their participation in transnational training networks. This process is indirect insofar as it relies on Global South bureaucrats internalizing the IMF-endorsed scripts and applying them in their day-to-day work, unlike lending and surveillance, in which the IMF staffers directly tell a country what policies it should implement. In other words, technical assistance—recently rebranded by the IMF as 'capacity development'—encourages national policymakers to 'see like' the IMF in how they devise policy solutions to economic problems.[124] That is, they should foster and support sympathetic interlocutors at the national

---

[118] Chwieroth 2013.
[119] Seabrooke 2007.
[120] Vreeland 2003.
[121] Gola and Spadafora 2009, 45.
[122] Vetterlein and Moschella 2014.
[123] Kupiec 2005, 77.
[124] Broome and Seabrooke 2007.

level—policymakers who are 'both willing and able to embrace the priorities preferred by the [international financial] institutions.'[125] In short, the Fund technocracy has an interest in supporting and bolstering national officials who are 'especially attuned' to working in similar ways,[126] which has been articulated through a Capacity Development strategy that absorbs about 10% of the IMF's spending and has support with funding from Japan and European countries.

IMF training occurs in Washington, DC, but also in regional training centers in Austria, Brazil, China, Côte d'Ivoire, Georgia, India, Kuwait, Mauritius, and Singapore. Of these, the most prominent is the Joint Vienna Institute (JVI), which was established in 1992 as a collaboration between five IOs and Austrian authorities to retrain Soviet-trained economic policy officials and bring them into the fold and way of thinking of the Bretton Woods institutions.[127] Since 1992 the JVI has trained more than 50,000 officials, using intensive courses over seven weeks to provide a shared language and treatment of data and models used in IMF surveillance and lending. Interviews with IMF staff engaged in JVI training have revealed that the aim of training is to 'improve capacity for Article IV consultations' and to 'learn to speak the language the IMF speaks.'[128]

Training from Fund staff focuses not only on economic ideas—both Saltwater and Freshwater—but also stresses situated learning through simulations. Figure 5.6 reproduces a figure from a textbook used in the core JVI training course, Applied Economic Policy. Participants must work in groups to deal with core budget issues for a case study based on Ukraine. This long-established example within the JVI system demonstrates how situated learning—a lab environment with common computers and software, where small teams work to solve a common problem—is mixed with simulated learning. The problem to be solved in the exercise is balancing Ukraine's budget for the early 2000s. Students work through their exercise jointly on computers, and the lecturer extensively uses a projected image of the students' Excel worksheet to discuss various components and issues. Participants are free to develop solutions to the Ukrainian budget problem within the boundaries of the taught material, using IMF indicators for economic activity. Students are also presented with comparative national and regional data to assess Ukraine's options.[129]

---

[125] Woods 2006, 10; Heinzel and Liese 2021.
[126] Haas 1990, 130.
[127] Broome 2010.
[128] Broome and Seabrooke 2015, 966.
[129] Broome and Seabrooke 2015, 967–68.

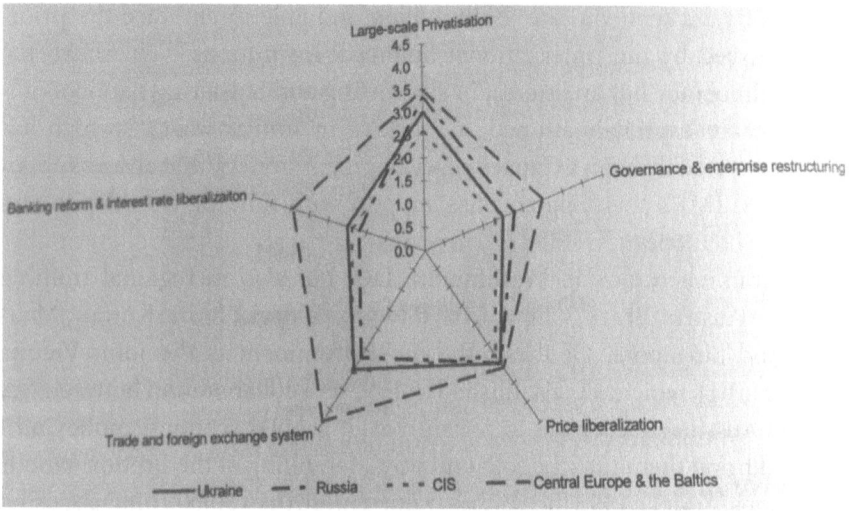

Figure 5.6 Ukrainian constraints example from JVI case book
Source: Author's photograph of JVI training materials

Note that the 0–4.5 scale in Figure 5.6 indicates the degree of need to reform listed aspects of the economy, with 0 meaning no reform and 4.5 a complete overhaul for a transition to a market economy. Importantly, the presentation of the documents and the language used is very similar to that of IMF annual reports and staff reports on loan conditions. The simulation teaches the participants the language of the Fund and the general parameters of what is considered acceptable and legitimate by its international technocrats. The IMF's own staff makes clear the link between training networks to develop sympathetic interlocutors and scriptwriting. Dealing with member states whose officials have been through training, like the JVI, 'increases the likelihood that a subsequent IMF program provides a window of opportunity for reforms in which IMF conditionality and governments' reform ownership reinforce each other.'[130]

In sum, for Fund scriptwriting, its technocracy is a source of direct inputs through its policy and intellectual work (which feeds into official Board decision making) and its development of standard treatments (which binds how those involved in scriptwriting consider what is relevant and appropriate to consider); and of indirect inputs through mission work and training networks (which feed back into the legitimacy of its expertise).

---

[130] Arezki et al. 2012.

PART III
NEGOTIATIONS

6
Sovereign Debt

Introduction

Few issues animate policy debates in international political economy and development circles as much as questions over sovereign debt.[1] The conventional starting point for contemporary global attempts to deal with (over)indebtedness problems is the so-called Third World debt crisis, which started with Mexico's August 1982 announcement that it could no longer service its debts, and then quickly spread across the developing world. This crisis followed on from consecutive external shocks over the 1970s that contributed to rising debt burdens in the Global South—most notably, the two oil crises of the decade drastically increased energy prices as the prices of many other commodities fell, leading to major fiscal problems.[2] At the same time, the economic slowdown and protectionist measures in the Global North, the major export market for developing countries, slowed economic growth and trade expansion in the latter.[3] While these developments were economically squeezing the Global South, access to finance became easier and cheaper through the rise of American interbank lending, not least because the oil revenues accruing to oil-exporting countries were channeled to major private banks in search of high returns.[4] The average size of large US international banks doubled in the late 1970s, with some interbank syndicates offering 'jumbo' ($500 million) and 'mammoth' ($1 billion) loans.[5] Of this lending, 80% went to developing countries, which started borrowing to offset increased import costs, but did so under interest rates that were pegged to the base lending rate set by the US Federal Reserve. When its chairman, Paul Volcker, hiked interest rates in the late 1970s to deal with domestic economic problems, this quickly translated into an increase in debtors' interest rates from 10% to 20% in just two years and exploded debt service requirements.[6]

[1] Roos 2018.
[2] Boughton 2001.
[3] Watson and Regling 1992.
[4] Braun et al. 2021.
[5] Seabrooke 2001, 95.
[6] Singh 1990; Frieden 2020, 374.

Making Global Norms. Alexandros Kentikelenis and Leonard Seabrooke, Oxford University Press.
© Oxford University Press (2025). DOI: 10.1093/9780197828656.003.0006

This mix of factors meant that by the early 1980s, the debt situation had become unsustainable for many countries in the Global South. In the immediate aftermath of the crisis, developing countries resorted to international financial institutions for fresh financing and requested the rescheduling of debt service obligations. Yet this approach proved too limited to turn their economic fortunes around. In 1984, Latin American countries sought to develop a unified voice against the creditors, who already had formalized cooperation and coordination in the form of the long-standing Paris Club (where the International Monetary Fund [IMF] is also a formal participant in discussions, having observer status). This attempt yielded the Group of Cartagena, named after a meeting of 11 Latin American finance ministers in the Colombian city, and promoted 'a "positive" type of adjustment' that would limit debt service, lower interest rates, and restructure debt obligations.[7] Infighting and lack of cohesion of this group, however, limited its ability to mount effective opposition as a debtors' cartel and a collective counterpart to the Paris Club. By 1988, after failing to secure any concessions by creditors, Brazilian President José Sarney lamented that 'the fact is that we cannot destroy the international system…we can scratch it, but it can destroy us.'[8]

This meant that the only solutions left on the table for dealing with debt issues passed through multilateral institutions, especially the IMF, which served as the focal point for the development of policy scripts on handling debt problems.[9] These problems related to three types of sovereign debt: debt to multilateral creditors, like the IMF and the development banks; debt to official creditors (i.e., other countries), most of which were members of the Paris Club; and debt to the private sector. While these debt problems were intertwined, each type of debt required different treatment and elicited a different role for the IMF, as we briefly cover below.

As debt issues are of core concern to all countries (debtors and creditors alike), they were unsurprisingly highly politicized. For countries in the Global South, debt problems absorbed their policy attention for over a decade or more, limited their growth potential, and made them dependent on decisions taken elsewhere—in bank headquarters or Global North capitals—regarding their economic fortunes.[10] In rich countries, these issues were equally political: Early developing-country defaults could have thrust their banking systems in deep crisis with inevitable spillover effects, and any debt relief on

---

[7] IMF 1985.
[8] Quoted in James 1996, 400.
[9] Herman et al. 2010; Tan 2014.
[10] Stiglitz 2002.

bilateral debt could prove politically treacherous at home. For example, the lead US government entity in charge of developing a policy response to the debt crisis was not the Treasury or the Federal Reserve, but the National Security Council—a clear sign of the fundamental importance the US ascribed to developing-country debt problems. Thus, this case offers appropriate empirical ground to examine the remit of political-versus-scientific decision-making on the development and application of global norms. How were the debt-related policy scripts developed through multilateral processes?

Sovereign Debt Problems and the IMF

Given its mandate as 'a permanent institution [offering] the machinery of consultation and collaboration on international monetary problems'[11] as well as a reputational intermediary[12] between debtors and creditors, the IMF has been at the epicenter of discussions over sovereign debt problems. In the early phases of the Third World debt crisis, it provided emergency financial assistance to affected countries while encouraging other creditor groups (official and private) to maintain credit lines and restructure medium- and long-term debt payments. Given that the willingness of many creditors to do so was highly limited due to these countries' payment difficulties, the IMF also sought to assume a coordinating role to enable concerted lending: Private banks and official creditors were encouraged to increase their exposure to countries undergoing debt restructuring and simultaneously implementing an IMF program.[13] Banks showed little appetite to do so, and simultaneously demanded—with the support of the IMF—harsh terms from the debtors and receipt of their interest payments in full.[14] Official creditors offered nonconcessional 'flow reschedulings' negotiated at the Paris Club, in effect pausing debtors' repayment for the period that an IMF program was in place.

While this strategy avoided potential sovereign defaults and their highly destabilizing effects on the global financial system,[15] it did not generate the desired result of kick-starting economic recovery that would allow countries to grow out of their debt problems. Meanwhile, it increased the value of outstanding debt stocks, as debt service payments were only paused for

---

[11] IMF 2011a.
[12] Broome 2008.
[13] Watson and Regling 1992.
[14] Sachs 1989b; Lissakers 1991.
[15] The exposure of large US banks to Latin American countries stood at 177% of bank capital in 1982, meaning that a default of Latin American debtors would immediately pose systemic stability issues for the US financial sector; see James 1996, 399.

the IMF-supported adjustment period.[16] A new approach was widely deemed necessary, and this was offered by the new US Treasury secretary, James Baker, who in 1985 announced his eponymous plan. Per the Baker Plan, countries would gain access to new financing if they implemented far-ranging IMF programs that would now target their 'structural problems'—a moniker for a range of policies seen as overly statist and impeding the functioning of markets, including state exploitation of natural resources, state involvement in production through state-owned enterprises, tight regulation of trade, and purportedly burdensome labor market policies.[17] The IMF was envisaged to have the central role in this process, as it would oversee the implementation of 'market-oriented policies for growth.'[18] This initiative also marked the birth of the IMF's new Structural Adjustment Facility (later renamed the Enhanced Structural Adjustment Facility), which would form a key lending vehicle to underpin the introduction of structural reforms. At its core, the Baker Plan substantially expanded what countries needed to implement in order to gain access to some debt rescheduling on market terms, while resisting any discussions over debt reduction. Importantly, all negotiations between debtors and creditors had to take place on a case-by-case basis—thus preempting the emergence of a coordinated debtor position.[19]

This approach also failed to generate the intended results: Countries' growth performance was lackluster and the private sector never meaningfully got behind offering fresh money to those implementing IMF-designed structural reforms.[20] To make sense of the persistent debt problems, policy debates started centering around the problem of debt overhang, in which debtors' debt burdens were so high that they discouraged potential creditors from providing fresh capital and required excessively high levels of taxation to meet debt service obligations, which in turn reduced the likelihood of economic growth. To address these problems, in 1989 Nicholas Brady, Baker's successor at the US Treasury, put forward a plan that would spur debt reduction by giving private banks a menu of options to voluntarily reduce the value of their claims.[21] This plan primarily related to debts of middle-income countries, the main debtors to international banks. At the same time, the Paris Club was already beginning to either reschedule on a concessional basis or partially cancel the debts of some low-income

---

[16] Daseking and Powell 1999.
[17] Babb and Kentikelenis 2021.
[18] Baker 1985.
[19] Tan 2014.
[20] Kentikelenis and Babb 2019.
[21] Sachs 1989a.

countries.[22] The constants throughout these plans and efforts, however, were the role of the IMF in guaranteeing that indebted countries would adopt the gamut of policies that their creditors deemed credible, and the underlying case-by-case principle that foreclosed any comprehensive response to debt problems.

While this approach did help some middle-income countries (primarily in Latin America) overcome debt overhang problems and raise new private capital,[23] the Brady Plan approach likewise proved inadequate on the whole. Many private banks had little incentive to join the voluntary Brady Plan debt relief; if the debt reduction was adequate for debtors to become creditworthy again, then the holdout debt that was not covered by the debt reduction plan would return to face value.[24] Further, official sector debt was not covered by the Plan and remained at high levels. Thus, even though the various debt initiatives of the 1980s were able to somewhat reduce the debt service paid (as a share of goods and services exports), the present value of debt remained persistently high. This meant that policy attention gradually started to shift from debt flows to addressing debt stock problems. These problems were particularly pressing for low-income countries with large debt burdens, which faced a dismal growth performance and to which disbursement of funds—whether by private banks or the official sector—had dried up, leaving debt service very high.[25] This group of countries came to be known as the Heavily Indebted Poor Countries (HIPCs).

Over the first half of the 1990s, successive rounds of Paris Club initiatives targeted debt service reduction for developing countries with excessive debt burdens by introducing long grace periods and extending debt maturities. But the watershed moment was the introduction of the HIPC Initiative in 1996, which reduced the debt stock in order to bring the debt-to-export ratio under 200% for 41 countries. To qualify for relief, HIPCs needed to be under IMF- and World Bank–supported conditional lending programs and adhering to the reform measures set out in Poverty Reduction Strategy Papers that they had to develop and submit to the IMF and other creditors. This was envisaged to be a long process: Relief eligibility would be assessed after the successful implementation of IMF programs for at least six years (the 'decision point'), and relief would actually be granted after another three years of stable macroeconomic conditions (the 'completion point').[26]

---

[22] Daseking and Powell 1999.
[23] Krugman 1990; Bulmer-Thomas 2003.
[24] Sachs 1989a.
[25] Birdsall and Williamson 2002.
[26] Birdsall and Williamson 2002.

Only about seven countries made meaningful progress within a few years of the HIPC Initiative, leading to sharp criticisms by developing countries and civil society.

In 1999, high-income countries, revamping the original HIPC terms and responding to some of the criticisms, changed both the ambitions and terms for relief. Under the Enhanced HIPC Initiative, the debt-to-export ratio benchmark was lowered to 150% and the IMF-mandated structural-reform implementation period was drastically shortened to three years before qualifying for the completion point. The qualification criteria of an ongoing IMF lending program and the implementation of measures set out in a Poverty Reduction Strategy Paper remained the same. That same year, to keep up with the jargon of the times that linked debt relief to poverty reduction—and to jettison the tarnished reputation of its Enhanced Structural Adjustment Facility—the IMF simply renamed it the Poverty Reduction and Growth Facility, without meaningfully altering the policy content of mandated reforms.[27]

For all the good intentions behind the HIPC approach, only few countries were eligible at first, and the scale of their debt problems remained obdurate. Partly this was because the IMF and the development banks had also scaled up lending over the 1990s, and the time had come for their borrowers to service this debt—in other words, while official sector debt was being reduced, multilateral debt had been increasing, thus keeping debt service at high levels.[28] Recognizing these problems, in 2005 high-income countries agreed to expand the HIPC Initiative with the introduction of the Multilateral Debt Relief Initiative, which would provide full cancellation of the debt stock owed to the IMF, the World Bank, the African Development Bank, and—from 2006—the Inter-American Development Bank.[29] To gain access to the initiative, countries needed to meet the same criteria as for meeting the completion point of the Enhanced HIPC. In turn, donor countries would provide the financial resources these multilateral institutions needed to cancel debts without threatening their balance sheet and impeding their ability to lend to other countries.

In sum, throughout the long period of debt problems and the multiple attempts to address them covered here, the IMF was at the epicenter of all relevant policy debates. The most conspicuous role for the organization was that of providing financial assistance through its conditional lending programs,

---

[27] Kentikelenis and Stubbs 2023.
[28] Dijkstra 2013.
[29] Tan 2007.

which were fundamentally transformed over the mid-1980s to target 'structural' reforms. But the IMF was also an active participant in the development of debt management norms and their operationalization in scripts, for two reasons: the staff's hands-on experience in dealing with debt crises (and the prowess of its Research Department in developing analyses of the debt situation), and because its Executive Board was a core venue where relevant debates could play out. Indeed, this was the only apex global economic governance forum where both creditors and debtors were represented en masse,[30] and could engage in closed-door technical as well as political debate on what was to be done about debt problems.

As one World Bank official summarized, 'The major evolution of the treatment of sovereign debt was the move from debt collection, to debt rescheduling, to aid and structural adjustment, to debt "sustainability," to forgiveness and poverty reduction.'[31] It should come as no surprise that this policy roller coaster entailed both highly complex technical problems on the treatment of debt and intractable (geo)political problems. Figure 6.1 schematically simplifies the evolution of norms and corresponding scripts over how to deal with sovereign indebtedness problems.

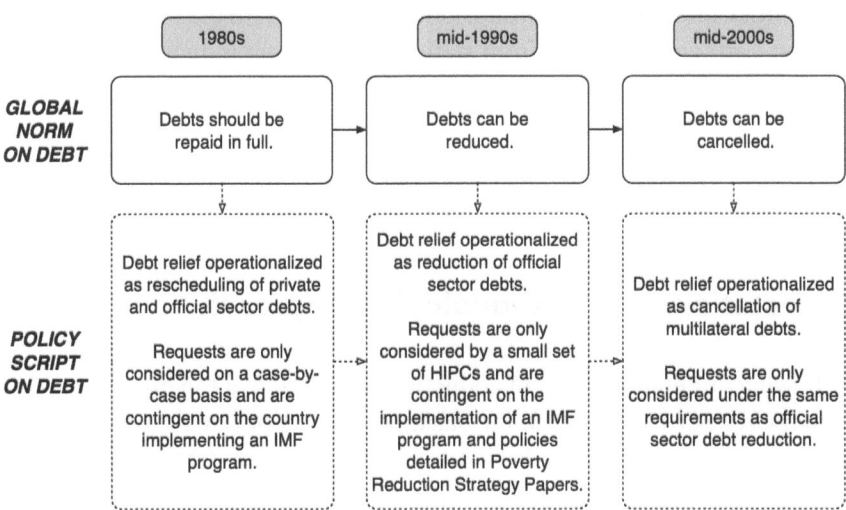

Figure 6.1 Evolution of global norms over sovereign indebtedness

---

[30] High-income countries developed joint positions primarily through the Group of 7, and then saw these through in the context of Paris Club negotiations. Developing countries also had venues of coordination—most notably, the Group of 77 and the Group of 24—but their ability to meaningfully influence creditors' decision making was limited by the scale of their debt problems and their creditors' unwillingness to deviate from the case-by-case approach for dealing with debt problems until the mid-1990s.

[31] Gautam 2003, 10.

The remainder of this chapter traces the intra-organizational technocratic and political struggles at the IMF over the development of these scripts through our extended computational case study. First, we lay out our expectations, based on our use of abductive logic, and the methodological approach. Second, we present a systematic comparison of policy positions by IMF staff and Board members, to identify any similarities or differences between these participants in script writing. Third, we turn our attention to a more structured comparison of the policy positions articulated by Board members (i.e., those with a formal authority over decision making), disaggregated by their prior professional experience and whether they represented a high-income or developing country. In these last two analytical steps, our aim is not to provide a qualitative analysis of the nuances of everyone's policy positioning—an exercise that would delve into the minutiae of multiple debates over three decades and yield an overly complex mapping of scriptwriting participants' views. Instead, we leverage computational methods to present stylized comparisons of use of concepts across many speaker clusters in a way that qualitative analysis cannot easily accomplish. Documenting linguistic similarities and differences then allows us to link these findings back to our motivational questions over the role of political decision making versus that of scientific knowledge and professional socialization in the making of policy scripts. Last, we shift gears from statically examining individuals' interventions in debates to dynamically examining interactions: Who engages with whom, with what valence, and to what intended policy goal? Qualitative analysis here can yield the necessary evidence to document the dynamic nature of scriptwriting processes and how politics and expertise clash.

Expectations and Methodological Approach

Following our endorsement of abductive reasoning and the broad empirical strategy set out in chapter 3, the starting point of our analysis is articulating the expectations for the behavior of participants in debt-related debates at the IMF. Given the centrality of debt and debt service issues for domestic economic management, as well as the implications of this issue for global financial stability, we expect the home authorities of all participants in normmaking and scriptwriting processes over debt issues to have a keen interest—and a policy position—in these debates. Indeed, a consistent body of scholarship has documented that views on how to deal with debt problems diverge along creditor–debtor country classifications.[32] The creditors are

---

[32] DeWitt and Petras 1980; Strange 1998; Wade and Veneroso 1998; Lissakers 1991; Lipson 1992.

likely to band together in an attempt to be repaid, while debtors will seek relief or rescheduling. Consequently, high-salience topics for IMF member states are likely also the ones where they transmit clear guidelines to their representatives, who correspondingly have limited leeway to veer too far off these guidelines. This means that the representation function is likely dominant, with the effects of professional expertise being only secondary. Given the political nature of these discussions and the lack of settled academic opinion on how to deal with debt problems, the role of the IMF bureaucracy is also likely to be muted, primarily elaborating on the options requested by the Board and seeking streamlining of the policy response. We return to these expectations and fine-tune them in line of our empirical analyses throughout this chapter, in line with the abductive logic.

The analysis here makes use of a battery of archival data. As shown in table 6.1, we initially searched our database of all IMF Board discussions for debt-related terms, of which we ultimately selected 131 discussions as directly pertinent to relevant normmaking processes. This represents the universe of Board discussions on debt issues, where the comments of Board members with available CVs amount to 2.4 million words.[33] In addition, we collected all IMF background documents submitted to the Board for consideration (a total of 379 documents).

The first systematic analytical step is to examine word embeddings. Using this method, we are first able to compare two types of text. The content of IMF staff documents that are used as background for Board meetings provides insights into prevalent themes in the technocrats' work, while the statements

Table 6.1 Search Strategy and Results for IMF Board Discussions, 1980–2009

Search Terms	Initial Hits	…of Which Were Excluded:	Transcripts Used
'debt,' 'sovereign,' 'bond,' 'creditor,' 'collective action clause,' and 'HIPC' (Highly Indebted Poor Countries)	494	283 country-specific discussions (e.g., on Zambia's debt relief), 51 items for which there was no discussion (i.e., items for information only), 25 on topics not of substantive relevance (primarily related to raising funds for the Enhanced Structural Adjustment Facility, an IMF lending instrument relevant to low-income countries) and 5 unavailable transcripts	131 (~2.4 million words)

---

[33] Additionally, Board members with unavailable CVs said about 371,000 words; as discussed in chapter 2, these are almost always junior advisors in an Executive Director's office, who participate as 'Temporary Alternate Executive Directors.' These statements are not part of our analysis.

on the IMF Board capture the preferences expressed by the organization's political leadership. We treat this text as a whole to compare the embedding of text by IMF staff with that of Board members, split on whether they are representing Global North or Global South countries. Subsequently, we further parse Board members' text by the six professional background clusters drawn from the optimal matching (OM) analysis presented in chapter 3. This means that Board members' overall text is allocated to 12 mutually exclusive clusters: high-income-country central bankers, low- and middle-income-country central bankers, high-income-country finance ministry officials, low- and middle-income finance ministry officials, and so on. We can now compare the content of their speeches among one another.

To choose the terms for embeddings analysis, we used a simple topic-modeling algorithm—known as the term frequency (TF)/inverse document frequency (IDF) algorithm, or simply TF/IDF—to find the salient terms in the corpus. TF/IDF ranks the most frequent terms in a document, compared to a larger collection of documents, resulting in terms that are significant to the document examined. We used our domain knowledge vis-à-vis the empirical focus to choose from these salient terms the ones we highlight in our analysis. This method promotes the discovery of salient terms alongside the terms we already knew to be important for the analysis. Since semantically meaningful terms in our highly technical domain are often longer than a single word, we allowed for terms of up to four words long. For example, we selected 'burden sharing' from the terms that were identified by the TF/IDF analysis as significant, as we already knew that it is a meaningful term in global debates over debt.

We then extracted the embeddings for those terms, and collected their 10 nearest neighbors, meaning the 10 terms with the closest vectors. To calculate vectors, we used the Gensim library Word2Vec implementation in Python and set up the hyperparameters to optimize for semantic significance. We lemmatized the text to further generalize it[34] and generated one- to four-word sequences while observing sentence boundaries. We empirically evaluated thresholds for minimal word counts, removing terms on the long tail of the corpus; here, we present terms that appear at least four times in the discussions. We configured vector size and negative sampling to accommodate the relatively concise size of our corpus.[35]

For the second systematic analytical step, we turned to a supervised approach to strengthen the robustness of our findings on word embeddings.

---

[34] That means that we transformed words to obtain their root form. For example, the lemma of 'repaying' is 'repay' and of 'servicing' is 'service.'

[35] For comparison, word-embeddings models are often used on datasets of billions of words, like Wikipedia or X; see Stoltz and Taylor 2021.

Table 6.2 Ad Hoc Dictionary for Frequency Analysis

Topic	Theme	Dictionary Terms
Sovereign debt management	Creditor rights	creditor equity, creditor equality, moral hazard, creditor right*, bank advisory, investor*, prudential, credibility, insurance, contract, litigat*, enforce*
	Debtor concerns	grace, good faith, good-faith, vulnerability, fiscal space, burden-sharing, burden sharing, poverty, social spending, social expenditure*, social issue*, labor standard*, social target*

Note: An asterisk indicates search for term including the stem; e.g., 'litigat*' includes litigation, litigate, litigated, and so on.

Rather than asking an algorithm to extract information on prevalent terms and their textual surroundings, we relied on our own knowledge from reading dozens of Board meetings to extract terms that we considered analytically relevant, then examined the frequency with which they appeared in the comments of different clusters of Board members. Table 6.2 shows the ad hoc dictionary we created for themes associated with sovereign debt management.

Last, we switched to qualitative methods to illustrate the negotiations between the differently situated and socialized Board members. As the transcripts of all these debates are too voluminous for systematic qualitative treatment, we selected as a subset for closer analysis those pertaining to the HIPC Initiative: the treatment of sovereign debt to multilateral creditors (mainly the IMF and the World Bank) over the 1995–96 period. We studied the five lengthy meetings—their transcripts number 226 pages—that shaped the initiative. In doing so, we focused on the dynamic elements of deliberation: how speakers articulated their positions in relation to one another. It is through this process of negotiation that the Board makes decisions.

Policy Positioning of IMF Staff and Board Members

To provide a window into how technocratic and political positions differ, we isolated three terms that signal different elements of scriptwriting. The first relates to 'debt distress.' In this context, the substantive content of debates pertains to establishing principled thresholds for classifying debt profiles and risks of distress. The second is distributional in working out who, in principle, should be on the hook for the costs of debt relief. We located this in 'burden sharing,' a commonly used term within the Fund when discussing this issue. The third is for what terms and words are associated with a normative commitment to a common good. We assessed this through 'international community.' In all three cases we differentiated the IMF technocracy, Global North Board members, and Global South Board members.

What can we expect to find? If power-politics accounts are correct, we should expect a lot of similarity between IMF staff and Global North Board members, given that principal–agent dynamics would suggest that the technocracy does what it is told by major shareholders. In contrast, we should expect a high degree of divergence in topics covered by Global North and Global South Board members, given their diverging interests and priorities. A World Polity approach may suggest that we can expect to see the IMF staff diverge from both the Global North and Global South, as they have a distinct esprit de corps, irreducible to the preferences of its political masters. If the technocracy is engaging in scientization and rationalization, reflecting norms in world culture, they want to produce scientific alignment and are thus careful not to appear too politically aligned with any one constituency on the Board. In other words, we should not expect to see much textual similarity among any of these three intra-IMF actors.

Figure 6.2 presents the findings on 'debt distress,' divided into panels according to the IMF staff, Global North Board members, and Global South Board members. The text contained in IMF staff reports (panel A) appears squarely technical. Technocrats present to Board members their preferred 'debt indicators,' 'stress tests,' and 'risk ratings' in a well-established strategy used by IOs to scientize policy areas,[36] as it puts themselves in the drivers' seat in devising methodologies and deciding on the appropriate risk ratings. Similarly, discussions of 'debt thresholds' are in line with debates in economics; indeed, Kenneth Rogoff—a leading academic studying the economic impact of different debt thresholds[37]—was IMF chief economist between 2001 and 2003, thus providing a hint on how scientific agendas can make their way into the IMF technocracy. Turning to Board members' comments, we observe that Global North representatives (panel B) pick up on some key issues discussed by staff. Most notably, debt distress appears collocated with comments on 'debt thresholds,' in line with the staff proposals. In addition, they—unsurprisingly—refer to terms related to money ('new borrowing') and the conditions for its disbursement ('concessional' or 'non-concessional'). In

---

[36] Broome et al. 2017.
[37] For example, from Rogoff's time as IMF chief economist, see Reinhart et al. 2003. Coauthors Carmen Reinhart and Miguel Savastano were based in the IMF Research Department when Rogoff was with the Fund.

Sovereign Debt 139

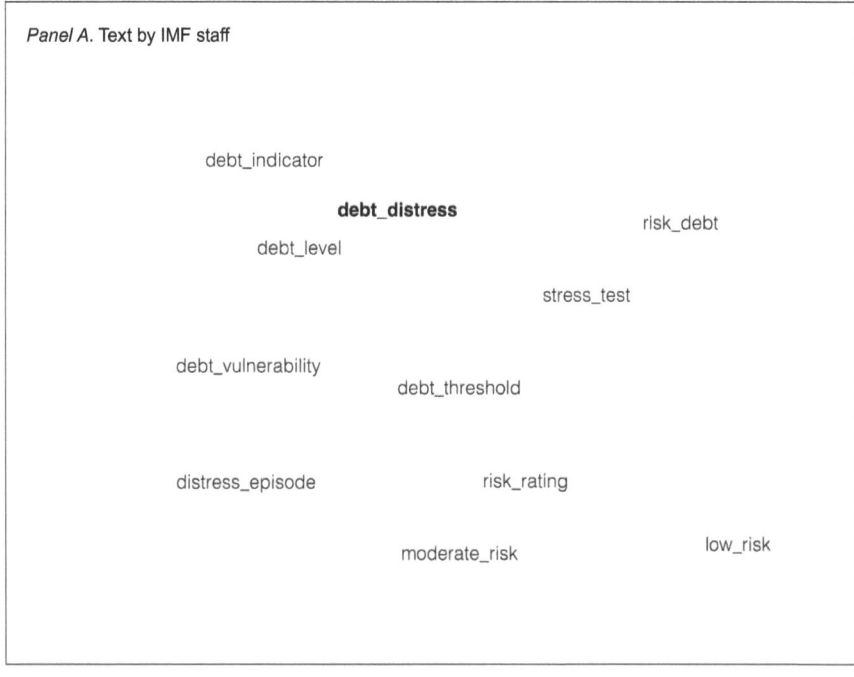

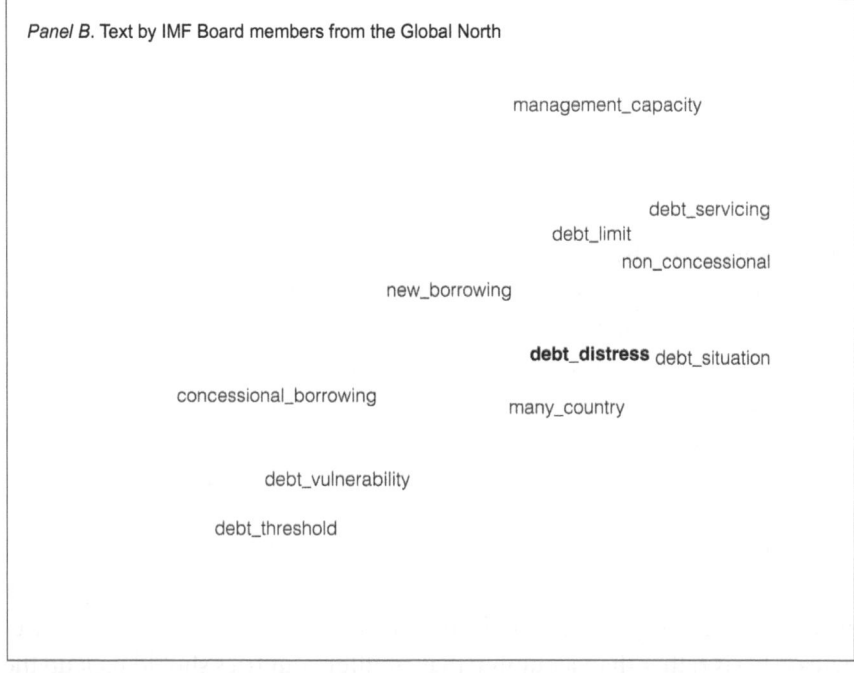

Figure 6.2 Word-embedding comparisons of IMF staff and Board members on 'debt distress.'

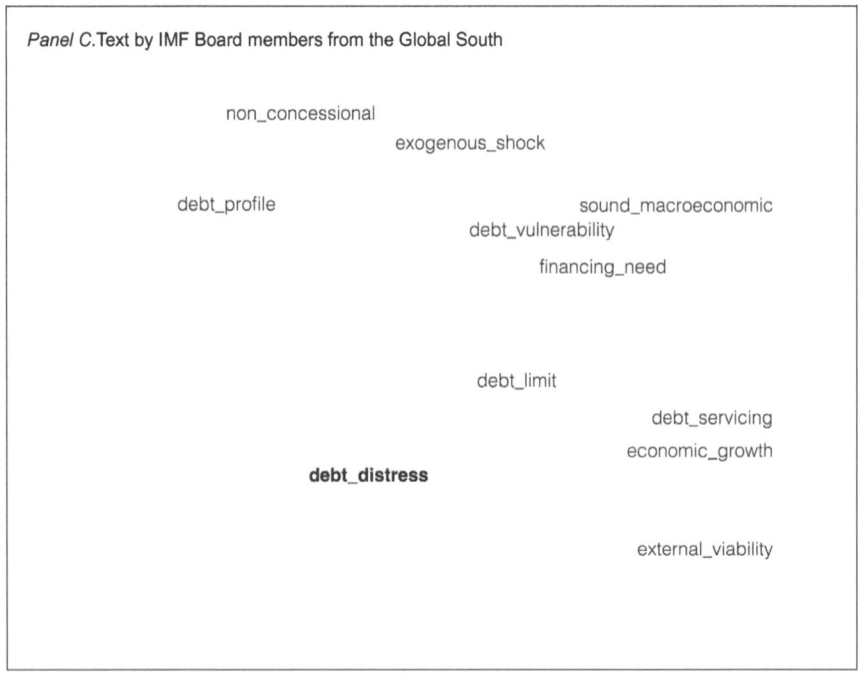

Figure 6.2 *Continued*

contrast, Global South Board members' mentions of debt distress in panel C are near terms that seek to bring into the frame the economic performance of countries ('economic growth' and 'sound macroeconomic policies'), the sources of debt distress ('exogenous shocks'), and their needs ('debt servicing,' 'financing needs,' 'external viability').

In figure 6.3 we focus on 'burden sharing,' and the results are striking, showing divergence among the three groups of actors. In panel A, we can see that the technocracy links burden sharing to the potential behavior of creditors. In 'indicated willingness' and 'sharing approach,' we can see that the basic positioning is to establish what is a credible claim on creditors within the overall framework. This differs strongly from the Global North Board members in panel B, where we can see that the terms closely linked to 'burden sharing' are 'moral hazard,' 'commercial creditor,' and 'bilateral contribution.' This language is concerned with caution, to *not* establish general principles that encourage debt forgiveness, and the need take on debt rescheduling on a case-by-case basis rather than assuming that creditor countries should pick up the check. In panel C, we can see that the Global South Board members disagree: Terms close to 'burden sharing' are 'progress made,' 'multilateral institution,' 'debt rescheduling,' and 'debt operation.' This language supports the idea that

Sovereign Debt 141

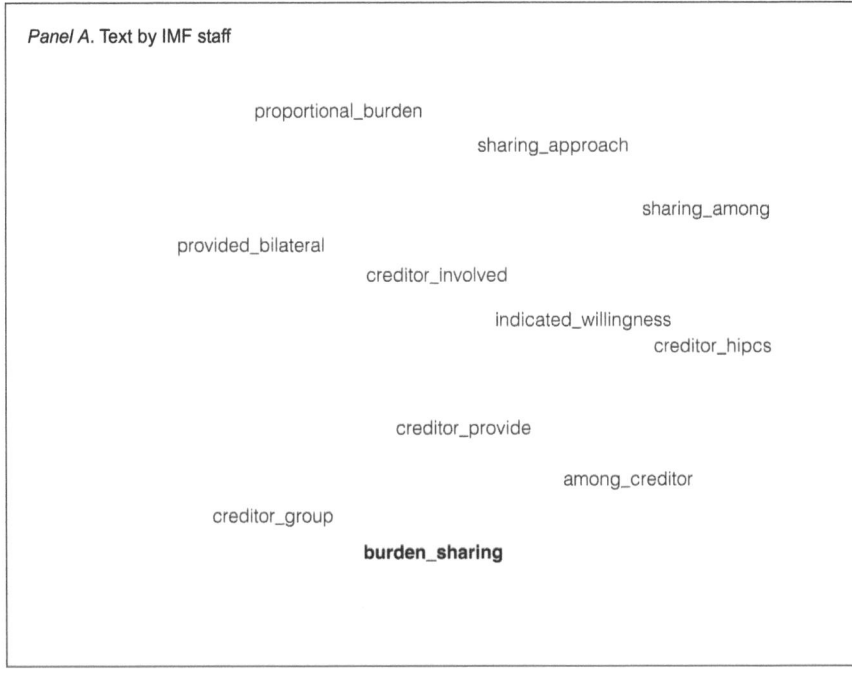

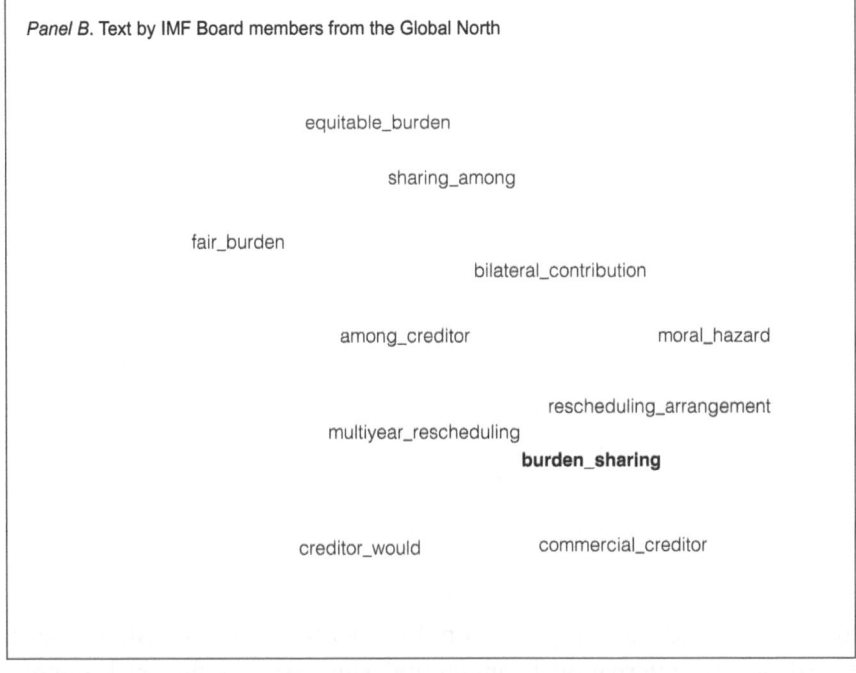

Figure 6.3 Word-embedding comparisons of IMF staff and Board members on 'burden sharing.'

142 Making Global Norms

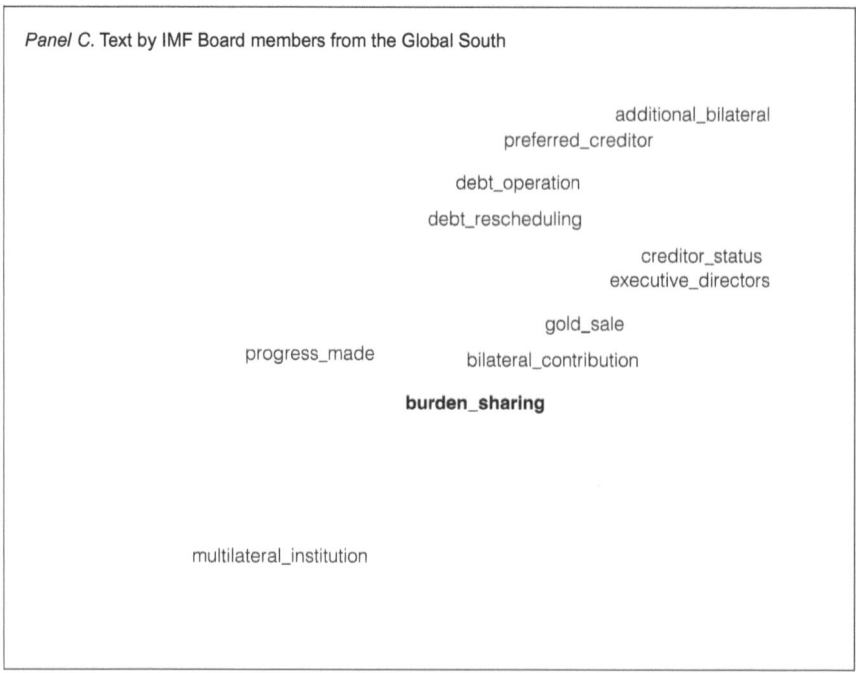

Figure 6.3 *Continued*

scripts for sovereign debt should give multilateral debt forgiveness a prominent role, embedding debt rescheduling into a shared-principle framework in which developing countries can advance. In sum, the technocracy seeks principles creditors can sign on to, the creditors want to pick and choose, and the debtors want a principled multilateral framework.

Figure 6.4 examines how the different participants in these debates treat the term 'international community'. From IMF staff in panel A we can see in-principle commitments through terms like 'important role,' 'play important,' and 'help country,' as well as references to technocratic competence in 'best practice' and norms like 'transparency and accountability'.[38] But this is no free lunch, given that the need to avoid providing 'moral hazard' is especially prominent, in line with arguments from economics on the role of the IMF.[39] Thus we have a good approximation in panel A of how the IMF technocracy sees its own role: as providers of scientific best practice to help member states in a prudent and frugal organization. In panel B we have the Global North Board view on 'international community,' which stresses 'financial support,'

[38] Kim and Sharman 2014.
[39] Vaubel 1983.

Sovereign Debt 143

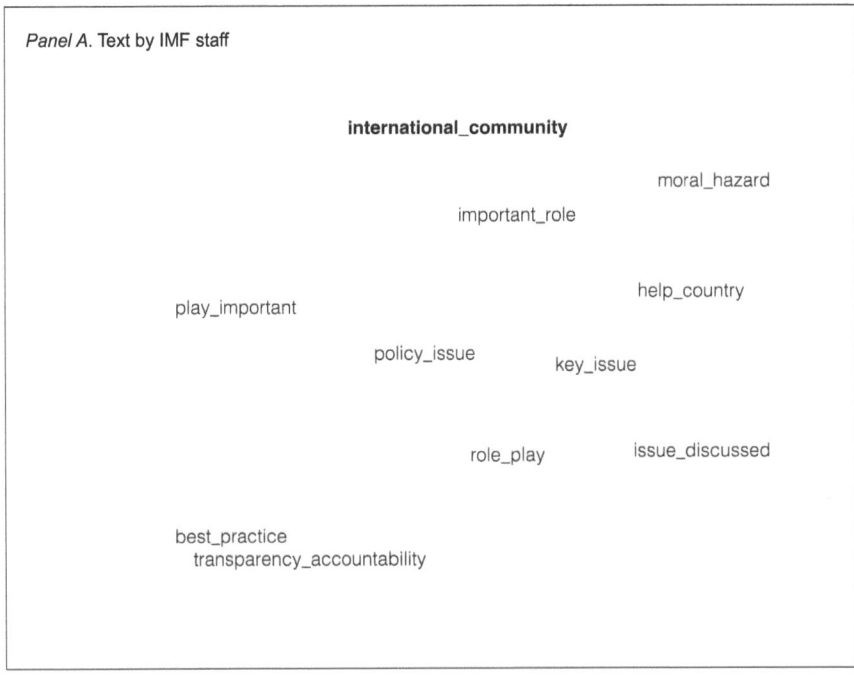

Figure 6.4 Word-embedding comparisons of IMF staff and Board members on 'international community.'

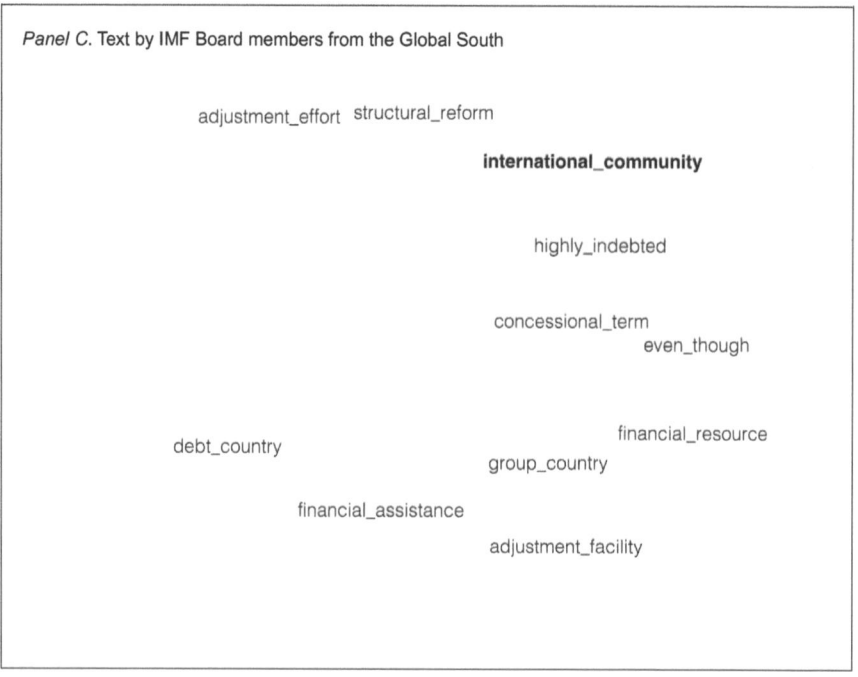

Figure 6.4 *Continued*

'external financing,' and the 'debt crisis'—this reflects a view of the IMF as a crisis manager. From the terms 'development assistance,' 'problem country,' and 'sub-Saharan,' we can infer that, for the Global North members, international community has a key role in dealing with ongoing 'problem' countries. Global South Board members in panel C associate international community with 'structural reform' and 'adjustment effort'—not a surprise given the experience of these countries with receiving international financial assistance that is conditioned on economic reform.[40] But these Board members also call for greater 'financial assistance' and 'financial resources' on 'concessional term[s].'

In sum, the word embeddings linked to the technocracy, Global North, and Global South paint a mixed picture. On debt-distress issues—a key term in discussions of sovereign debt management, as it evokes a need for action—we see that IMF staff and Global North Board members have overlaps in what they emphasize (namely, questions of debt thresholds and vulnerabilities) and associated risks. In contrast, when it comes to burden sharing and the role of the international community, we find wide differentiation. Text by

[40] Kentikelenis and Stubbs 2023.

IMF staff shows little overlap with that of Board members, suggesting that any staff attempts to influence debates over these normative issues were unsuccessful. Further, remarks by Global North and South representatives appear orthogonal: The former are interested in the *terms* of their financial assistance, while the latter emphasize the importance of increasing the *quantity* of financial assistance by bilateral and multilateral actors, as well as the progress they have already made with structural reforms.

Politics Versus Science in Boardroom Debates

Having documented how the technocracy, Global North, and Global South Board members distinguish themselves on thresholds, distributions, and larger normative commitments, we now dig deeper into the observed positioning of IMF Board members. We examine the content of statements by each representative, and trace variation along two axes: their state representation function (their political role) and their professional expertise (their science-infused background). In other words, and in line with the preliminary evidence in the preceding section as well as extant scholarship, we first expect Board members to vary in their policy positions depending on whether they represent a high-income country or one in the Global South.

As we have anticipated, we hypothesize that this is not the sole influence on their positions. Thus, second, we want to explore whether and how professional socialization matters, and whether individuals with different career trajectories diverge in what they choose to comment on during boardroom debates. How exactly do we expect them to vary? From the findings presented in chapter 4, we know that central bankers account for nearly half (49%) of all Board members. Scholarship on central bankers has consistently documented that they belong to a transnational epistemic community where professional socialization is strongly enforced across country income levels.[41] Given that a quarter of central bankers on the Board were trained in elite Anglo-American universities, we also expect exposure to similar training to encourage use of similar terms. As such, we anticipate a high degree of convergence for this professional group for Board members from the Global North and the Global South.

In contrast, we expect that Board members with such professional backgrounds as politicians and finance ministry officials (together, about a third of total Board members) are more likely to use terms that overtly reflect

---

[41] Verdun 1999; Polillo and Guillén 2005; Johnson 2016.

the political preferences of their home authorities.[42] These professionals have spent their work lives devising or implementing economic policies—commonly contentious and contested. Unlike staff in independent central banks, these individuals have likely been thoroughly socialized in professional careers imbued by politics and attuned to the domestic political-economic implications of different globally devised policies and exogenous shocks. In short, having been in or around high-level politics over the course of their careers, those with backgrounds in finance ministries and politics are as close to being seamless extensions of state preferences as we can expect. We also expect the same of those with backgrounds in business and private finance,[43] where 'bang for the buck' logics may be prominent for those from the Global North (while avoiding moral hazards), while those from the Global South will favor business-led solutions to problems, like increased foreign investment and business protections to assure those with capital that their funds are secure.

For former staff of IOs, we expect they will generally align themselves with the proposals of IMF staff, given that not long ago they were in the position of preparing policy papers and discussion notes for the boards of the IMF, the World Bank or another international financial institution. Last, in line with findings on normative change on fiscal policy at the IMF,[44] we expect that academics will adhere to theoretical principles with no particular stake in script outcomes.

Mirroring the presentation of word embeddings just reviewed, we first resorted to quantitative text analysis using word embeddings to document variation. As our analysis relates to the text of Board interventions, sorted by the professional background of speakers and the income classification of their home authorities, this means that we sorted text into 12 categories, per the 6 professional clusters identified in chapter 4 and the Global North–South divide. Because complexity can kick in quickly when presenting findings, for word embeddings, we present findings from terms that illustrate this breakdown for a subset of groups. As done earlier, we have chosen terms that reflect three aspects of sovereign debt management: thresholds, distributions, and normative commitments. For consistency, we keep the terms 'debt distress,' 'burden sharing,' and 'international community.'

In figure 6.5 we compare central bankers along with private bankers and businesspeople, distinguishing by career socialization and by Global North and South. We expected that the central bankers would align regardless of

---

[42] Woods and Lombardi 2006.
[43] Abdelal 2007, 141.
[44] See Ban and Patenaude 2019.

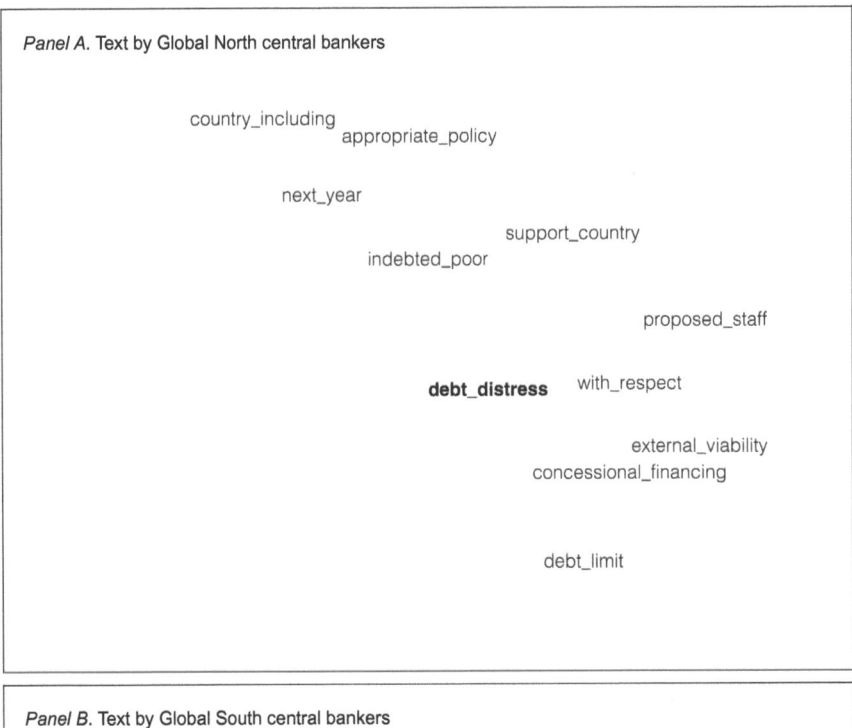
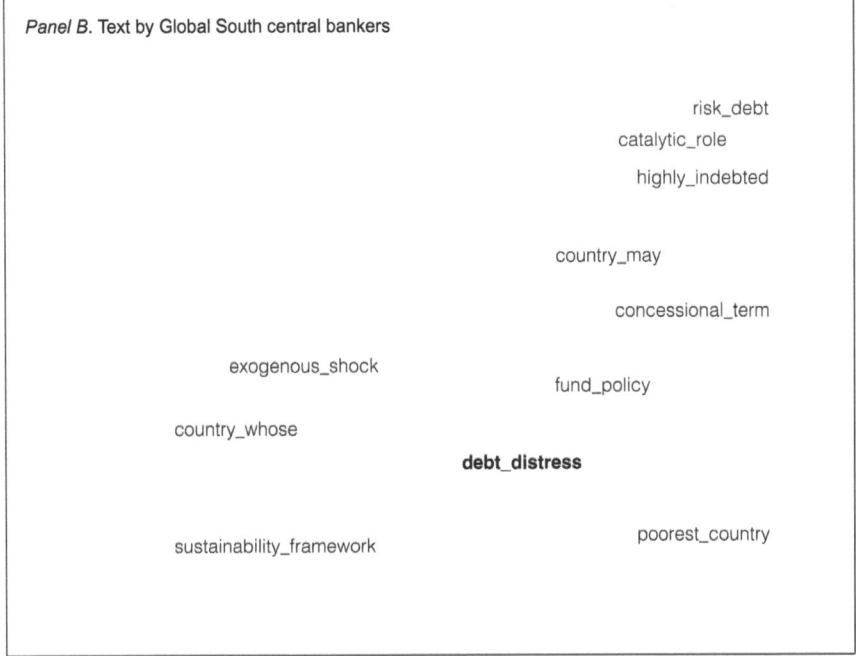

Figure 6.5 Word-embedding comparisons of Board member clusters on 'debt distress.'

148 Making Global Norms

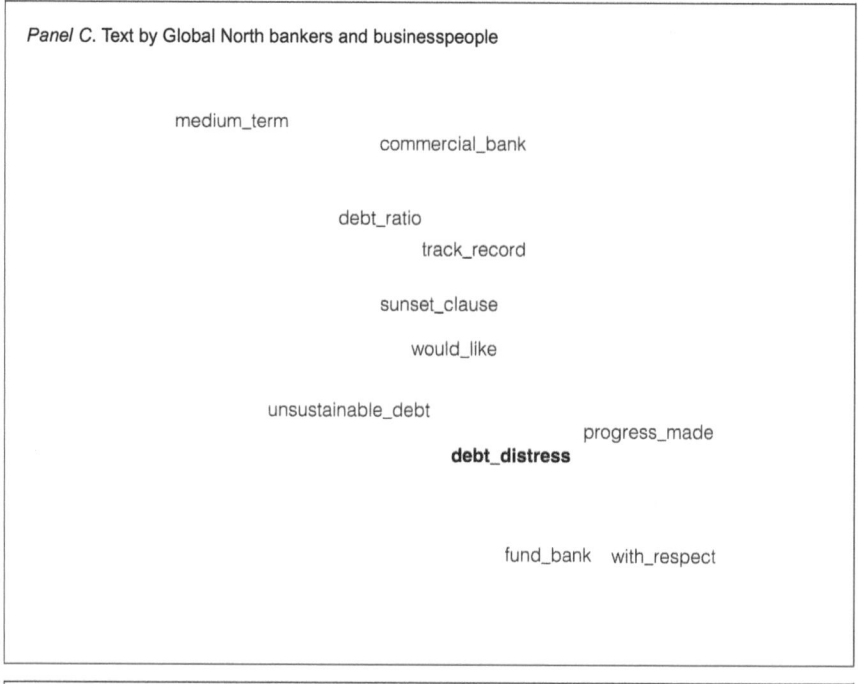

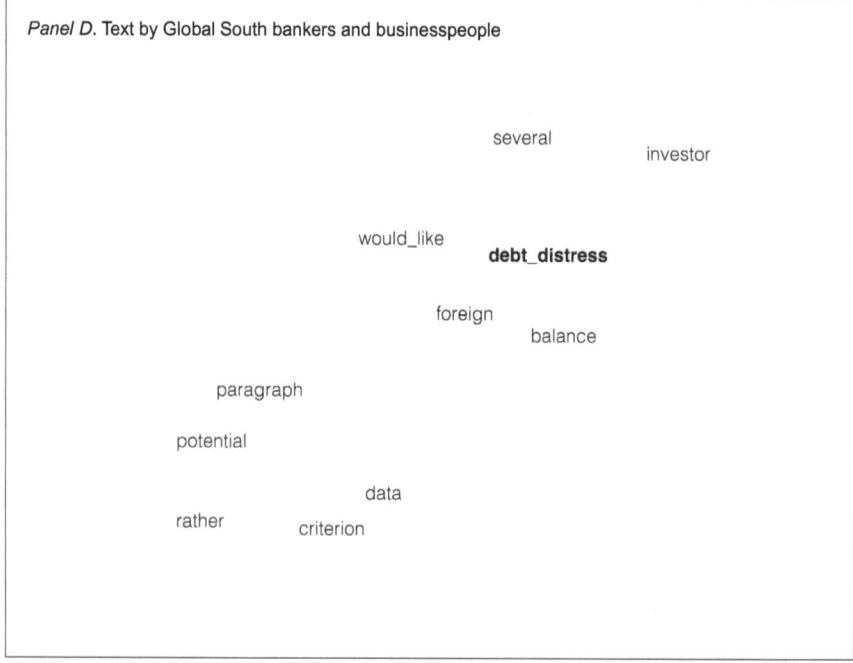

Figure 6.5 *Continued*

income level, given the extensive literature on their scientization that fits well with world polity explanations. Panels A and B show this to be more than less true. Across the North–South divide, the terms used by central bankers signal the same kind of content, with (i) 'support country' and 'poorest country,' (ii) 'appropriate policy' and 'fund policy,' and (iii) 'concessional financing' and 'concessional term' all appearing close to debt distress. There is some variation, with Global North central bankers concerned with 'external viability' and Global South bankers with 'exogenous shock,' suggesting the reasons behind countries' debt problems in the first place, but otherwise there is strong alignment.

For the bankers and businesspeople, our expectation was that they would split not over distributions (should the Global North compensate?), but over solutions to debt distress involving the private sector. This is indeed what we see in panels C and D, with the Global North associating debt distress with terms like 'commercial bank,' 'track record,' 'progress made,' and 'sunset clause'—terms related to a country's capacity to access and maintain private capital. For the Global South, the terms associated with debt distress are more linked to solutions, such as 'investor,' 'foreign [investor],' and 'potential.' We note that the amount of text for Global South bankers and businesspeople is thin, given their relatively small numbers on the Board, which helps explain the prevalence of more generic terms in word embeddings (i.e., our text analysis models did not have a very large amount of data to be trained on).

Turning to 'burden sharing' in figure 6.6, we contrast former finance ministry officials and political appointees—as noted earlier, we expected each group to behave in line with the North–South divide in policy positions. Our findings broadly confirm this hypothesis. Northern finance ministry officials (panel A) link burden sharing most closely to 'moral hazard,' 'adjustment efforts,' and the role of the 'Fund and Bank,' explicitly noting that they 'agree with staff' proposals. For Southern officials (panel B), 'market access,' 'capital markets,' and 'cash flow' issues are collocated with burden sharing, thus indicating their core concern with raising fresh funds to cover fiscal holes. The term 'Mrs. Filardo' also appears, meaning that these officials tend to refer to the remarks by Leonor Filardo—the Venezuelan Board member between 1986 and 1990—who was highly active in the Board debates over burden sharing.

Political appointees (panels C and D) also position themselves in ways anticipated by power politics arguments. Those hailing from the Global North emphasize the involvement of 'commercial creditors' and the role of 'export credits' (a way for high-income countries to provide loans to

150   Making Global Norms

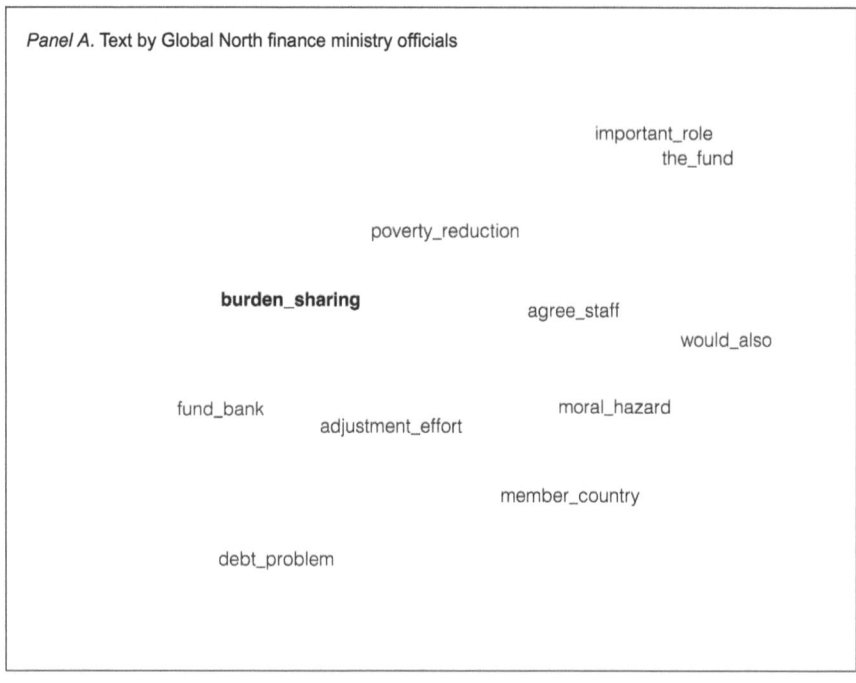

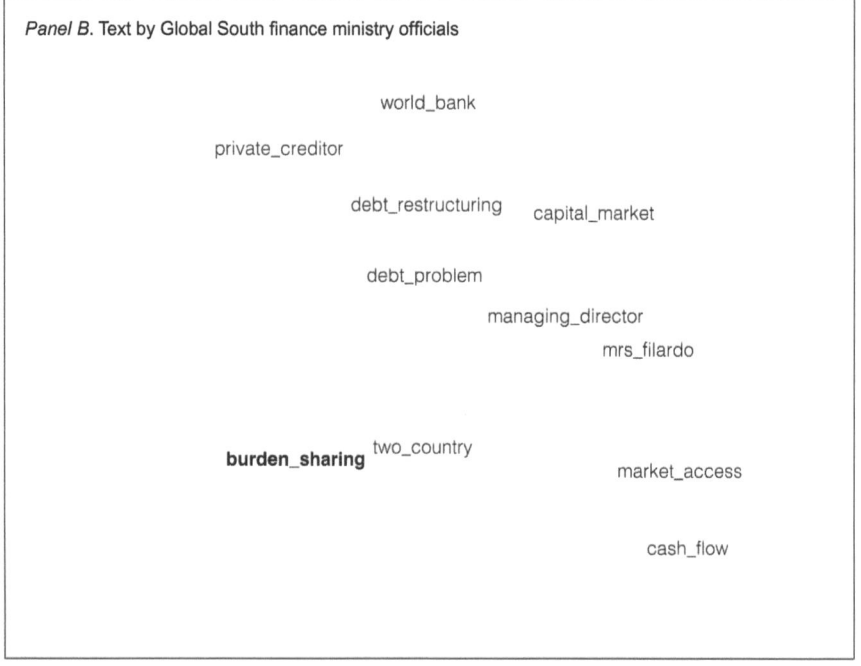

Figure 6.6   Word-embedding comparisons of Board member clusters on 'burden sharing.'

Panel C. Text by Global North political appointees

    take_account

            balance_payment
set_aside

      self_sustained look_forward
                export_credit
                          esaf_hipc

            commercial_creditor
            burden_sharing   fund_staff

                          exogenous_shock

Panel D. Text by Global South political appointees

                          executive_board
                  gold_sale

        burden_sharing
                        debt_export

      reserve_account   staff_view

  debt_stock potentially_eligible
      protracted_arrears
                sovereign_bond
     progress_made

Figure 6.6 *Continued*

developing ones for them to purchase goods from the creditor's own private sector),[45] and defer to 'Fund staff.' In contrast, Global South representatives use terms associated with assessing funds that can be used for relief, such as 'gold sale' and 'reserve account,' while also referring to technocratic analysis to support their claims with terms such as 'staff view.' We can also see a contrast between Global North and South in a distributive temporal view of burden sharing, with political appointees from the Global North emphasizing 'set aside [accounts]' (an IMF funding scheme for debt service reduction) and 'self-sustained,' while Global South political appointees use the terms 'potentially eligible' and 'progress made.'

Figure 6.7 compares those with careers in finance ministries and academia from the Global North and South on 'international community,' a term associated with normative commitments. Our theoretical expectation here was that the finance ministry officials will split sharply following political interests associated with their income level: The Global North will be miserly, the Global South will want mechanisms of relief. Panels A and B do not reflect such extremes but do show concerns that align with our expectations. The Global North finance ministry officials associate international community with 'external viability,' 'financing package,' and 'financial assistance,' as well as 'unsustainable debt,' emphasizing the costs of maintaining the international community. For the Global South, international community is about a framework being established to provide debt relief, with terms like 'long term,' 'multilateral institution,' 'World Bank,' 'debt problem,' and 'creditor country' prominent.

Panel C and D show what terms academics from the Global North and South associate with international community. Our theoretical expectation here was randomness, as academics—having a reputation for being professional contrarians—are likely hard for their home authorities to control. In the case of academics from the Global North, we see that international community is associated with 'multilateral creditor,' 'moral hazard,' 'the Fund,' and 'World Bank.' From the Global South, we see 'bilateral debt,' 'progress made,' and 'macroeconomic performance' as key terms that these Board members use. In both cases the academics use terms that reflect the institutional order and dominant logics within it—often terms associated with the opposite of their income-based preferences. Contrarians indeed.

To verify the evidence from the word-embedding analyses, we built an ad hoc dictionary on two key themes, creditor rights and debtor concerns, and calculated the prevalence of associated terms. The terms for creditor rights

---

[45] Daseking and Powell 1999.

Sovereign Debt 153

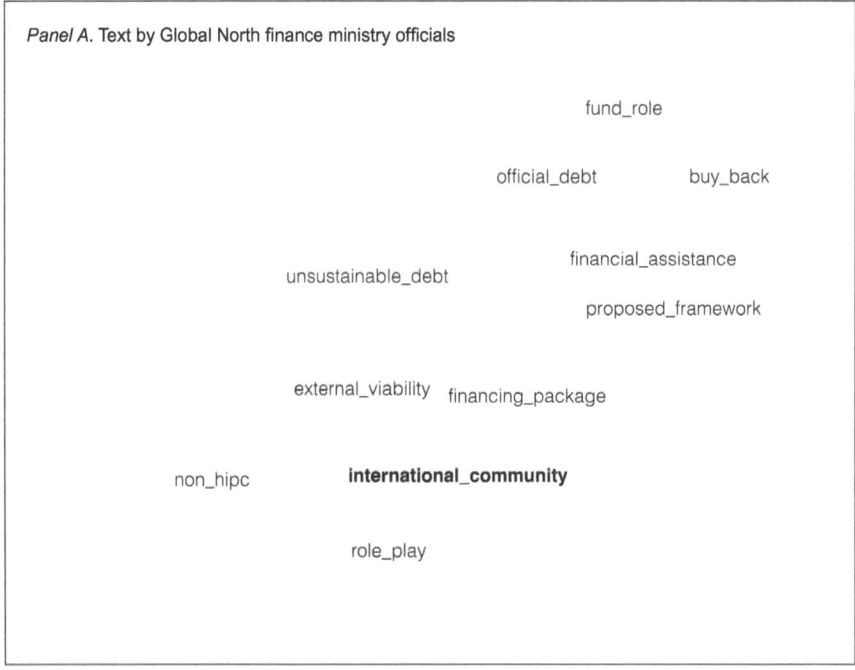

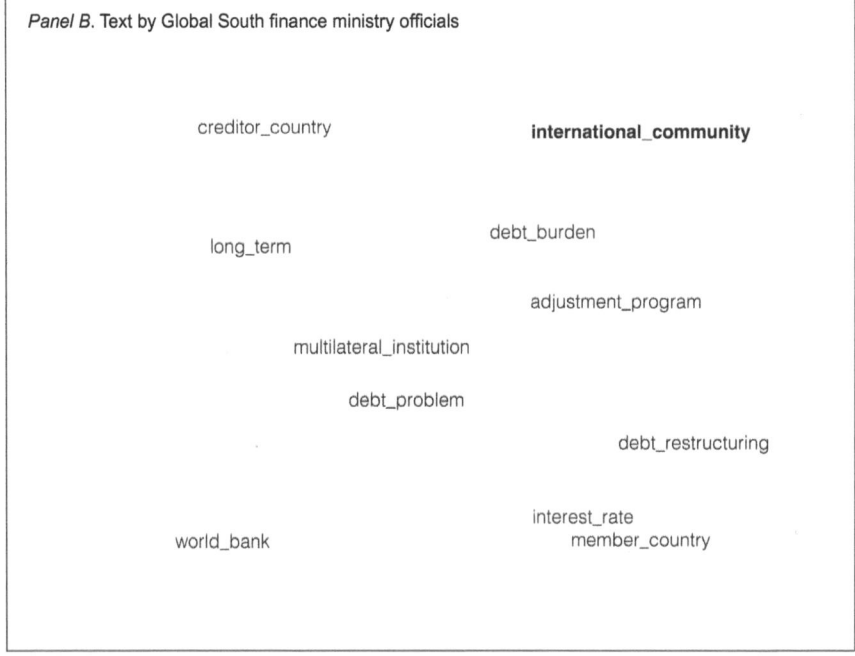

Figure 6.7 Word-embedding comparisons of Board member clusters on 'international community.'

154 Making Global Norms

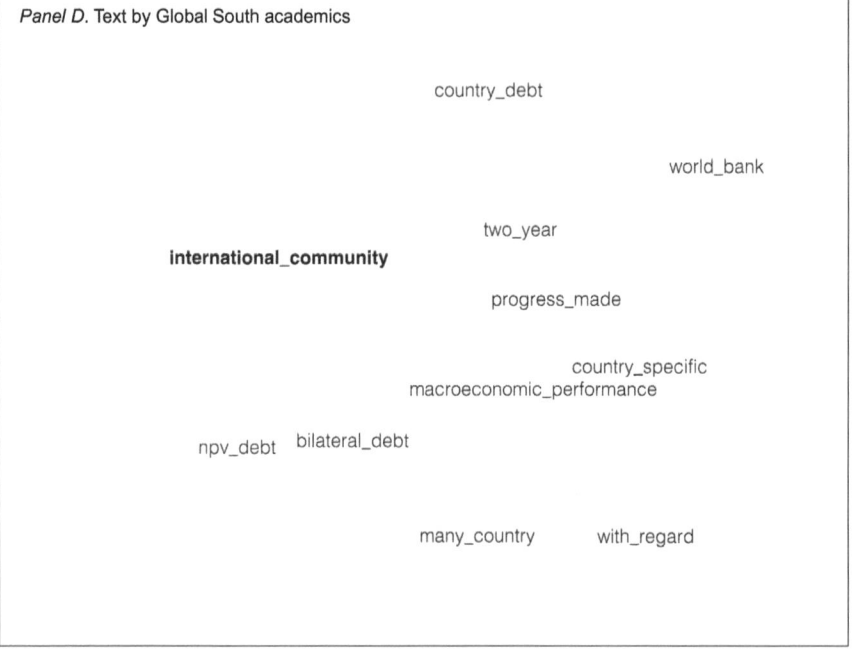

Panel C. Text by Global North academics

balance_payment
commercial_debt
      moral_hazard
the_fund

fund_bank
international_community
                    would_also
esaf_hipc

financing_hipc
multilateral_creditor
developing_country

Panel D. Text by Global South academics

country_debt

world_bank

two_year
international_community
progress_made

country_specific
macroeconomic_performance

npv_debt   bilateral_debt

many_country   with_regard

Figure 6.7 *Continued*

capture key words associated with the empowerment of creditors, such as 'moral hazard,' 'prudential,' 'litigation,' and the like. Similarly, the terms for debtor concerns are linked to likely positioning on debtor relief, such as 'burden-sharing,' 'good-faith,' 'fiscal space,' and others. Our reading of the dozens of these debates suggests that the use of such terms is generally associated with taking a position on what should be included in or excluded from the sovereign-debt management policy script. This reliance on our domain knowledge of these issues makes this approach 'supervised.'

Our analysis on text prevalence offers a picture broadly consistent with the one yielded by the word-embedding approach: There is meaningful variation in Board members' intervention during debt-management-related scriptwriting that is explained not only by the income level of their home authorities but also by these individuals' expert backgrounds. Figure 6.8 schematizes the findings. Overall, our main hypotheses are broadly confirmed. Most strikingly, central bankers converge in the frequency of their use of terms across the Global North–South divide. Given that this group is known as the most professionally socialized, this finding aligns with arguments that highlight how central bankers view economic policy as being above national concerns and best treated with technocratic solutions.[46] Our hypothesis that political appointees and finance ministry professionals, as well as former bankers and businesspeople, would use terms that reflect national political positions with respect to high-income and developing countries is also supported by these findings. That is, we expected that individuals from the Global North who held such previous professional experience would comment more using terms that reflect the economic interests of their countries (creditor rights), while those hailing from the Global South would discuss debtor concerns more. This is indeed what figure 6.8 shows.

Turning to Board members with previous careers as IO staff, we find that they spend more time on debtor concerns than on creditor rights. There can be two explanations for this. First, such professionals have extensive experience working on debt issues in Global South countries, thus potentially becoming sympathetic to their concerns—similar to how IMF staff who have hands-on engagement with climate issues in country-level work are likely to promote climate engagement in their subsequent postings.[47] Second, this pattern may itself be a function of past professional socialization within global economic governance, where staff members may appear to take on the concerns of developing countries to expand the mandate of their organizations under the guise of being responsive to demands. Once these former

---

[46] Polillo and Guillén 2005.
[47] Clark and Zucker 2023.

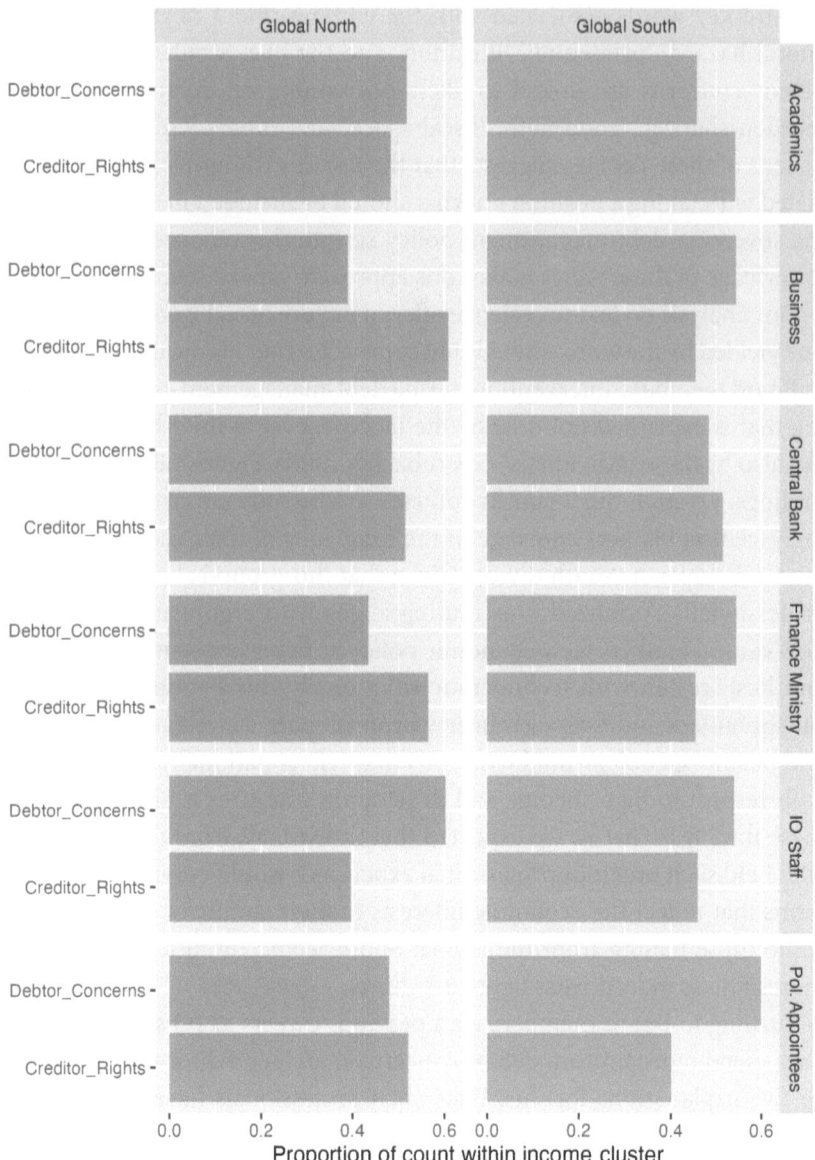

Figure 6.8 Frequency of key themes from IMF Board members, by professional cluster and income

staffers become Board members, they likely still support policies that can bolster organizational activities, including 'mission creep'–based organizational expansion.[48]

---

[48] Weaver 2008.

Our findings on former academics—accounting for approximately 5.5% of Board members—are harder to interpret, and we have limited theoretical priors to explain their behavior. Interestingly, academics from developing countries talk more about creditor rights than about debtor concerns. A third of this group has been trained in elite Anglo-American universities, where theories that favor property rights, avoidance of moral hazard, and reduction of transaction holdups dominate curricula and have been transnationalized across the profession.[49] So, even though they represent countries that might be credibly skeptical toward the application of these theories, the professional background of these Board members may dominate the issues to which they choose to devote attention.

Scriptwriting Through Boardroom Interactions

We now move beyond the static analysis of what Board members say in the boardroom to a dynamic analysis of the system of which they are part, as their interactions in this venue are what yields new or modified policy scripts. As we saw in chapter 4, the raison d'être of these Board debates is to generate the broadest possible consensus among Executive Directors, which is at core a discursive process of collectively 'puzzling' and 'persuading,' rather than simply 'powering' through one's preferred policy position.[50] We expect that variation in the mix of professional backgrounds among those present will influence the types of interactions and debates that are had, and—by extension—the ultimate output of Board deliberations.

To examine how trends at the individual level across the period play out in interactions at the boardroom level (where formal decisions on script modification are made), we focus on the debates over the HIPC Initiative over 1995–96, pertaining to the treatment of sovereign debt to multilateral creditors. The established script was that such debts should be paid in full, as they were owed to global public institutions with preferred creditor status, meaning that distressed countries had to prioritize repaying these over debts to other creditors. Following major IMF and World Bank lending in the aftermath of the debt crises of the 1980s, debts to multilateral creditors increased rapidly, adding up to 44% of all debts of HIPCs.[51] From the perspective of developing countries, this debt—together with additional debts to bilateral and private lenders—became unsustainable. In 1996, the script was altered

---

[49] Fourcade 2009.
[50] Blyth 2007.
[51] Birdsall and Williamson 2002, 24.

to offer a reduction of debt to multilateral lenders by about 20%, if a debtor country agreed to surveillance and control of its economic policy by the IMF and the World Bank for a period of at least six years.

Figure 6.9 depicts interactions from the initial Board meeting to change this policy script. The figure illustrates script positions taken by Board members, their country and its income level, and their professional cluster. The figure is arranged to show how the professional and income categories cluster into different positions for script modification. The speakers are arranged in the order in which they spoke within their script position groups. We also include a 'Via' column, which illustrates how their statements refer to other representatives. Such statements reflect interaction in the board as the representatives perform their role as dual loyalists. Straight lines leading to Via entries show a reference to another speaker's comments that is either positive or signals openness to other ideas in case of limited support for one's own. Crossed lines indicates a negative reference, where the speaker is making their own position in opposition to other Board members. Both types of references are common, sometimes combined, and occasionally selective (i.e., one speaker agrees with one aspect of another's comments but not another). In other words, these references signal interactions in the process of refining the policy script.

Four positions are prominent within the meeting as our dual loyalists articulate viewpoints that mediate between their professional-socialization background and their political-representation function. The first is the view that *technocratic extension* is the best solution to the debt overhang issue. This involves making the existing Enhanced Structural Adjustment Facility (ESAF) permanent to provide ongoing concessional lending, ensure continued policy surveillance, and devise appropriate conditionality (i.e., mandated policy reforms) for borrowing countries. The second position is *creditor enforcement*, which rejects the need for a permanent ESAF and prefers treatment of debtors on a case-by-case basis to minimize moral hazards and maximize the chance of repayment of nonconcessional loans. The third position is *debt forgiveness*, which promotes a view that IMF operating surpluses could be used to increase concessional lending and also provide debt forgiveness for extreme cases. Last, the fourth position is the *status quo*, which holds that the current system is adequate and the policy script should not be modified.

Figure 6.9 also includes examples of iterations during this meeting, indicated by the vertical lines that join the same speaker in the Representative column. Autheman in the technocracy group, Lissakers in the creditor group, and Geethakrishnan in the debtor group are all particularly important in

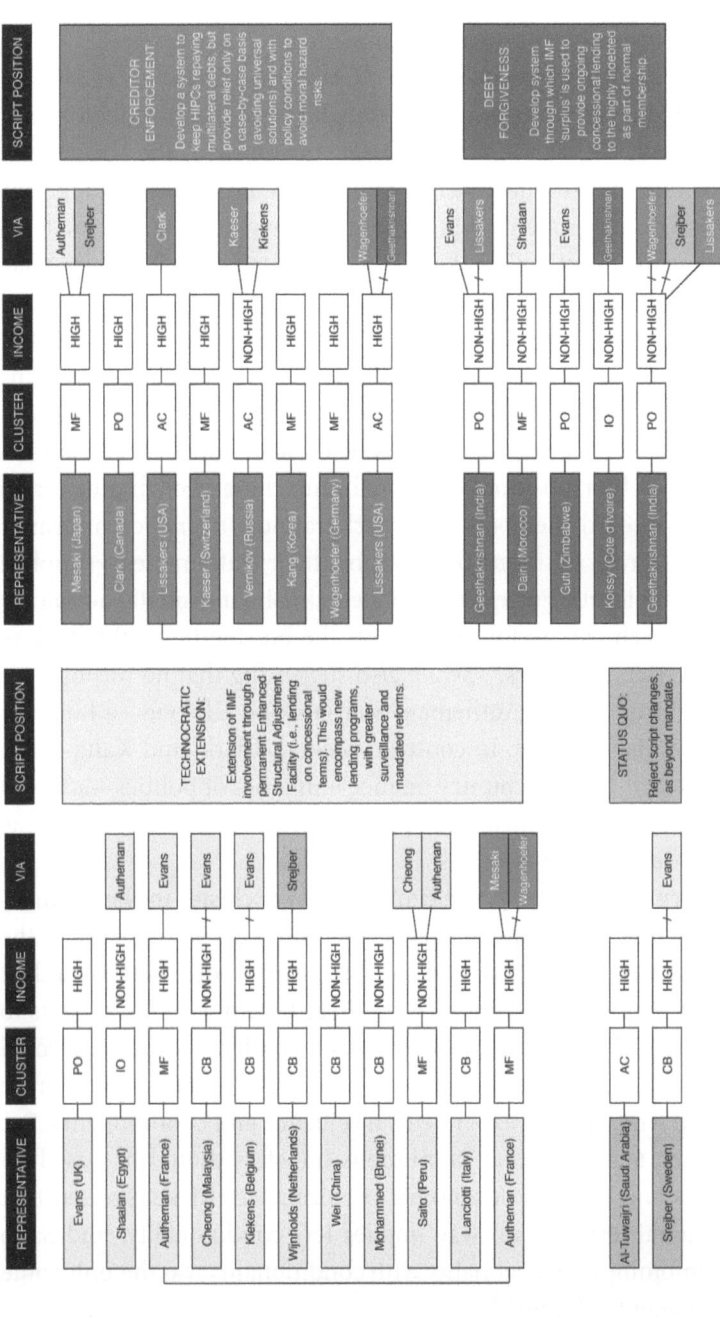

Figure 6.9 Board interactions in the modification of a policy script

Note: Two letter codes in the cluster column refer to the professional backgrounds of speakers: AC = academic, CB = central banker, IO = former international organization staff, MF = ministry of finance, and PO = political appointee. HIPC refers to Heavily Indebted Poor Countries.

articulating script positions in this meeting. Autheman supports Evans initially and then counters an extreme creditor position articulated by Wagenhoefer, while showing favor toward Mesaki, who is also in the creditor group (Mesaki also shows support to Autheman while rejecting Srejber's position in the status quo group). Lissakers supports Clark, who is also in the creditor group, and then later supports Wagenhoefer while rejecting the debtor position articulated by Geethakrishnan. As Lissakers represents the US, we may expect her position to carry more weight than others'. From the debtor group, Geethakrishnan's initial statement gives some support to Evans in the technocracy group while rejecting Lissakers. In a later statement, Geethakrishnan rejects the Wagenhoefer creditor position, and also Srejber's status quo position, while showing support to Lissakers's openness in considering alternative financing arrangements. Such is the micropolitics of the meeting in coming to a script position that wins broad consensus.

On the relationship between professional clusters and script positions, the creditor and debtor positions map well onto the earlier findings from the text analysis. Board members with backgrounds in finance ministries and high politics favor positions that support their state interests (implied from their income level). For example, Geethakrishnan initially adopted a maximalist approach calling for 'writing off the outstanding debt stock of Sub-Saharan African countries,'[52] while also suggesting that he was open to considering the proposals of Autheman, Shaalan, and Cheong—a hint of a possible compromise position. In contrast, Mesaki, Clark, and Kang—with backgrounds in high-income country finance ministries or politics—adopted a pro-creditor stance, pointing to the moral hazard problems from agreeing on multilateral-debt write-offs.

Across country income levels, the central bankers cluster in the technocracy group, which seeks to expand surveillance and give permanence to the IMF's lending vehicle—the ESAF—as an instrument to deal with high debt burdens. In comment after comment, these Board members closed ranks to promote ESAF as adequate to handle the debt problems of over-indebted countries. The consistent argument here was to have a permanent vehicle for concessional lending with expanded surveillance and conditionality. For example, Cheong suggested that 'continuous transfers should be based on individual cases and linked to economic performance,' Kiekens stated that 'more concessional terms in no way implies less conditionality,' and Saito argued that combining concessionality with conditionality was the 'only route towards a permanent solution.'[53]

---

[52] EBM/95/19, 32.
[53] EBM/95/19, 32, 34, 54.

Over the course of the two subsequent Board meetings, positions started converging as a compromise was being worked out. In the third meeting, taking place 11 months after the one just referenced, there was already wide agreement about the path to be taken. The IMF's technocratic infrastructure would be extended, but would follow a case-by-case approach in that HIPCs' eligibility for debt relief would be contingent on implementing extensive and stringent policy reforms over six years. This approach was an amalgam of the technocratic-extension and creditor-enforcement positions pursued in earlier interactions. For example, Lissakers found it 'pleasing to note that the [updated proposal under debate] incorporates the central principles that this chair and others have suggested in previous discussions,'[54] and Kaeser was satisfied as the updated general framework 'responds to many of my previous concerns.'[55] Former advocates of more debtor-friendly positions registered some objections; for example, Dairi noted that 'the lack of a guarantee for eventual debt relief could serve as a disincentive for some countries to put forth their maximum reform efforts.'[56] But even these objections were muted and only came at the very end of the Board discussion. The main contours of the script had taken shape, and the next two meetings[57] only finessed the general approach, to be rubber-stamped by countries' finance ministers and central bankers.

The script position on expanding technocratic surveillance is the one that eventually won out. In other words, the modification of this policy script for multilateral debt management was strongly conditioned by the professional socialization among central bankers, who favored the scientization of the problem with some political accommodations.

Overall, the finding from these debates was that the policy script over treating sovereign over-indebtedness of low-income countries changed from their needing to repay all their debts to multilateral institutions to being eligible to receive a discount on their obligations if they agreed to heightened technocratic surveillance of their economy by the IMF. This outcome was reached through the interactions of Board members whose professional and educational socialization has important explanatory power for their observed behavior. An analysis that relied solely on the Executive Directors' country affiliations would have been consistent with the dominant arguments in academic scholarship around these issues, but ultimately would have been unable to fully explain the outcome of these deliberations. In turn, our findings support two arguments: First, Board members are not merely

---

[54] EBM/96/24, 16.
[55] EBM/96/24, 11.
[56] EBM/96/24, 56.
[57] EBM/96/34; EBM/96/58.

political tools of their appointing governments; and second, the interplay between political representation and professional socialization explains the positions taken in the boardroom.

Conclusions

Our aim in this chapter was to delve into the scriptwriting process on sovereign debt, an issue on which global norms changed significantly from 'debts should be repaid in full,' to 'debts can be reduced,' to 'debts can be canceled.' These changes required constant modifications to the IMF's scripts on sovereign debt management that relied on multiple rounds of exchange between the Fund technocracy and the Board members. We have employed our abductive reasoning and extended computational case toolkit to assess how the IMF arrived at scripts that support the cancellation of debts. Starting from the expectation that the issue of sovereign debt would posit a basic creditor-versus-debtor conflict, our findings suggest a more interesting story and add up to three key points.

First, when it comes to the relationship between the staff technocrats and Board members (whether hailing from the Global North or South), we revealed different patterns of argumentation. Some overlap existed between the content of staff recommendations and Global North representatives' policy positions on how to respond to broad debt-distress problems, in line with expectations from the literature on staff needing support from major shareholders before committing to decisions that entail financial commitments (whether in terms of new money or rescheduled obligations) for IMF members. Overall, however, there was no clear alignment between staff and any Board members.

Second, we found evidence of similarities in how Board members with similar prior professional experiences position themselves. Those with a central banking background—regardless of where they hail from—tend to devote attention to similar issues and have overlaps in their views about the appropriate policy path forward. Those who had experiences at the heart of domestic policy—whether through senior ministerial appointments or careers spent in finance ministries—acted more consistently, as a North–South divide would suggest. That is, their political representation function trumped their independent expertise credentials.

Third, once we shifted our attention to how these individuals interact with each other, we found that they group together not only in a North versus South way, but also in line with their professional backgrounds, which shape how they approach the policy issues at hand. This reveals the limits of trying to interpret the outcomes of these processes with a binary understanding of actorhood. Instead, our approach highlights these individuals as dual loyalists—both to their countries and their expertise derived through education and professionalization. In other words, Board-level interactions, we argue, are not simply a reflection of basic political interests from the Global North and the Global South. Rather, they are mediated by professional socialization, and we have shown how the career backgrounds of Board members are important for what terms and arguments they are willing to make.

Of course, these findings have nothing to say on whether the decisions reached were ultimately the 'right' ones—this depends on where one stands, politically as well as epistemically. In the case of the debt relief offered, the historical record shows that its economic and social impact was at best limited,[58] and that the IMF's policy packages actually undermined developing countries' administrative capacity.[59] Instead, our analysis is intended to beg a different sort of question on the dynamics of relevant policymaking: Would a different Board composition have yielded a different outcome? We posit that this is likely. For example, it was the strong voice of central bankers that successfully pushed for increasing the IMF's role in developing scripts on appropriate policy reforms and conditionality. A possible Board composition with higher prevalence of professionals with backgrounds in high political offices, finance ministries, and academia—all skeptical, albeit for different reasons, of augmenting the IMF's role—would have plausibly handed less leeway to the organization.

---

[58] Chauvin and Kraay 2005; Djimeu 2018.
[59] Reinsberg et al. 2019.

7
Capital Controls

Introduction

The promise of unrestricted international capital flows is alluring—at least according to orthodox neoclassical economics—for many reasons. When firms or households can move their money abroad, they can diversify their financial portfolios and smooth out any fluctuations stemming from economic shocks affecting their home country. This enables them to reduce their risk and—hopefully—secure high rates of return, which may in turn feed into subsequent growth-enhancing investment. Thus, capital mobility can offer firms and households income-maximization opportunities that would have been foreclosed if they had been limited to keeping their money in their home country. Meanwhile, from the vantage points of states, fostering international capital flows also makes good economic sense: It allows them to raise capital at competitive interest rates for a variety of public investments. The benefits of unshackling capital are also systemic. International competition for capital means that countries should maintain a favorable business environment, lest financial inflows cease. Even if a crisis occurs, open capital markets can come to the rescue, because international investors will pour money into countries with undervalued assets or lower wages, thereby stimulating growth.[1]

Given these advertised benefits, it should initially come as a surprise that the merits of unrestricted cross-border capital flows are heavily contested. Nearly a century ago, John Maynard Keynes was already worried about the consequences of finance becoming internationalized because of the destabilizing effects, *contra* the rosy neoclassical account, that this would have on national economies.[2] This line of argument focused on what came to be known as capital flight—hot money outflows in response to a wide range of economic changes, like crises, increased taxation, a forecast devaluation, hyperinflation, or even sizable international interest-rate differentials. In

---

[1] For a more extensive exposition of these issues, see Eichengreen and Mussa 1998; Fischer 1998; Stiglitz 2000a; Moschella 2009, 2010.
[2] Crotty 1983.

Making Global Norms. Alexandros Kentikelenis and Leonard Seabrooke, Oxford University Press.
© Oxford University Press (2025). DOI: 10.1093/9780197828656.003.0007

these cases, firms and households may anticipate hardship or merely a lower rate of return to capital and opt to send their money abroad.

Such an exit of capital—especially in the form of short-term speculative movements—can create a range of pressing problems for the economy experiencing the outflow. First, large-scale capital outflows have follow-on implications for exchange rates, and central banks may attempt to intervene to stabilize them at the cost of depleting foreign currency reserves. Second, capital that leaves a country in search of low-risk, high-yield investments instead could have been invested domestically, thus bolstering economic activity. And, of course, once capital leaves, there is no guarantee that it will ever return to feed into domestic investment. Third and relatedly, fiscal policy is directly affected by runaway capital, as the domestic tax base becomes eroded: Taxation of domestic money holdings becomes less efficient, and the ability of tax authorities to trace income or wealth kept abroad is notoriously poor.[3]

Further, Global South countries are particularly severely affected by capital flight; one reason is economic, and the other is political. On the economic front, there is a discrepancy between the social rates of return on capital—for example, due to improved infrastructure or investment in health and education—and the private incentives of firms and households. This is because capital availability is often limited, so retaining money inside the domestic financial system opens up a cycle for reinvestment that is virtuous for domestic development trajectories but can be subpar compared to the rates of return that capital could attract abroad.[4] On the political front, capital flight creates legitimacy problems for development models that rely on extensive state intervention in the economy. This is because the state, in its effort to stabilize the economy, ends up assuming debt that was initially contracted by the private sector, even though that sector's foreign assets remain private. In short, the end result is large-scale reverse redistribution, at the cost of ballooning public-sector debt.[5]

These major risks of unrestricted capital flows beg a core political economy question: Who stands to benefit the most? As we have seen, neoclassical economic theory would suggest that capital account liberalization enhances welfare, as it aids the global-level efficient allocation of capital. An alternative reading—advanced by international political economy scholars[6]—sees this policy as extending and entrenching the financial dominance of the Global North, and especially the US. Following Robert Wade's pioneering

---

[3] This discussion closely follows Cuddington 1986.
[4] Cuddington 1986.
[5] Diaz-Alejandro 1984.
[6] Block 1996; Helleiner 1996; Strange 1996; Wade 1998; Wade and Veneroso 1998; Kirshner 1999.

analysis,[7] there are three main reasons for this. First, the US favors a high degree of world financial market integration, as its own domestic savings are generally low and the country thus needs to tap into savings from the rest of the world.[8] Capital outflows from developing countries are often inflows to the US or other advanced economies. Second, such financial integration also foregrounds the role of Wall Street banks, which see opportunities for business expansion in developing countries where they can search for high-return opportunities. Last, the US 'sees free capital movement as a wedge that will force other economies to move in its direction' in terms of the rules it has on international finance and transnational corporations: shareholder dominance, low taxes, and low regulation.[9] The entanglement of US policy positions and Wall Street preferences vis-à-vis capital account liberalization even prompted Jagdish Bhagwati—a prominent trade economist and free-market advocate—to point to a 'Wall Street–Treasury complex [that] is unable to look much beyond the interest of Wall Street, which it equates with the good of the world.'[10]

This entire debate culminates into questions over countries' use of so-called capital controls—that is, restrictions on the movement of capital in and out of their borders. These discussions have taken place within the International Monetary Fund (IMF). As we will see, the organizational bureaucracy and major shareholders were enthusiastic proponents of financial liberalization and the removal of capital controls, and even sought amending the IMF's founding treaty to that end. Developing countries were skeptical or outright hostile to these ideas. This chapter traces the contentious scriptwriting over how countries should manage capital flows and what the role of the IMF in this process should be.

Capital Controls and the IMF

While attempts to globalize finance have a long history,[11] the latest round of policy debates over the merits of capital account liberalization took place between the late 1980s and late 1990s. As we have seen, for proponents of the policy, capital was understood to be like any other good, and its free movement was expected to spur benefits for lenders and borrowers alike: higher output, increased efficiency, and greater economic stability. Consequently,

---

[7] Wade 1998.
[8] Strange 1990.
[9] Wade 1998, 47.
[10] Bhagwati 1998, 11.
[11] Helleiner 1996; Abdelal 2007; Moschella 2009, 2010; Chwieroth 2010.

removing restrictions on capital flows was simply good economic policy and a prime candidate for becoming institutionalized in the normative apparatus of globalization.

Given its globalizing mission,[12] the IMF was the most prominent participant in the global normmaking process over capital account liberalization, in particular the use of capital controls. The IMF's founding treaty, the Articles of Agreement, explicitly permitted reliance on capital controls: 'Members may exercise such controls as are necessary to regulate international capital movements.'[13] This is unsurprising given Keynes's ardent opposition to globalized finance, which also informed his negotiating priorities at the Bretton Woods conference.[14] Yet, as scholarly debates—influenced by the ascendancy of free-market ideas in the 1970s and 1980s—started centering on the relative merits of capital account liberalization, the organization's mandate on promoting related policies came up for discussion.

In this chapter, we trace scriptwriting in the IMF vis-à-vis capital controls, one central element of the broader debates over capital account management norms. What was the role of scientific evidence, and what was the remit of politics? Prominent accounts in political science focus on how IMF staff came to believe that capital controls were unworkable, with politics and contention operating primarily in the background.[15] For example, Manuela Moschella has shown the ideational shifts within the IMF's bureaucracy who came to see capital controls as 'ineffective in stemming capital flight, retaining domestic savings, and assisting stabilization efforts.'[16] Instead, we seek to foreground the role of the bureaucracy's political masters, who set the tone for what the bureaucracy considers appropriate and legitimate activity,[17] and their interactions with the bureaucracy and with each other.

The evolution of global norms on capital flows followed a pendulum movement from regulation to deregulation and back.[18] As shown in figure 7.1, underlying scripts on capital controls similarly passed from a period of stability to concerted—and ultimately unsuccessful—attempts to change the underlying script and ban the use of capital controls unless the IMF granted explicit permission. In other words, there was an attempt to institutionalize a 'no capital controls' script on the part of powerful shareholders and the bureaucracy that failed, thus marking the restabilization of the former status quo that permitted the use of capital controls at any government's discretion.

[12] Woods 2006.
[13] IMF 2011a, 20.
[14] Keynes 1943.
[15] Abdelal 2007; Chwieroth 2010.
[16] Moschella 2009, 865.
[17] Pauly 1997.
[18] Gallagher 2014, 2015a, 2015b.

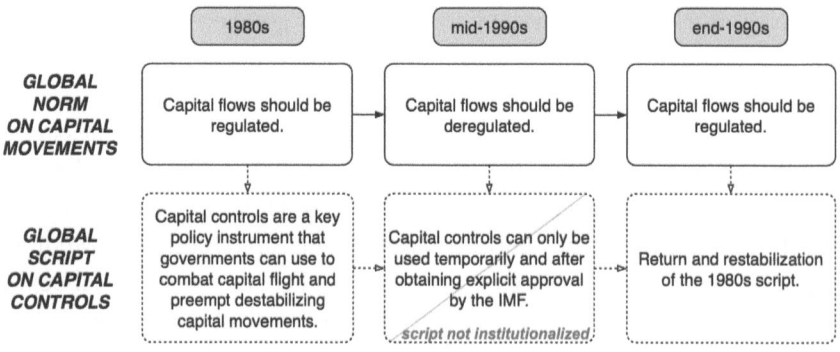

Figure 7.1 Evolution of global norms over capital flows

This chapter traces the contentious scriptwriting processes over the use of capital controls, with reference to both their political and technocratic inputs. Mirroring the empirical setup of chapter 6, we first juxtapose the policy positioning of IMF staff and Board members, as reflected in background reports and verbatim boardroom statements, respectively. Next, we focus our attention on Board members only, disaggregated by income classification of their home authorities and their previous professional experience. We pursue these analyses using computational methods, as these allow us to process extensive statements from the various participants in these processes. Last, we change our methodological approach and rely on a qualitative analysis of Board debates. This approach enables a more dynamic investigation into what happens inside the IMF boardroom: What discursive tools do Board members use, how do they position themselves vis-à-vis IMF staff, how do they relate to each other, and how do these interactions yield the eventual outcome of the scriptwriting process?

Expectations and Methodological Approach

The empirical strategy pursued here closely follows that of chapter 6. To briefly recapitulate our approach, we leaned on abductive reasoning to make 'good guesses' on what we expected to find on the issue of capital controls. The shorthand here is that we expected the IMF technocracy to support capital liberalization, given what we know about their training and socialization, and that Global North Board members would want to open markets for their businesses while Global South Board members would want protections. We also

Table 7.1 Search Strategy and Results for IMF Board Discussions, 1980–2009

Search Terms	Initial Hits	…of which were Excluded:	Transcripts Used
'capital,' 'liberalization,' and 'controls'	122	41 items on the capital budget and related topics, 31 annual discussions of developments in international capital markets, 15 items on topics not of substantive relevance, and 12 items for which there was no discussion (i.e., items for information only)	20 (~586,000 words)

expected professional clusters to matter, especially alignment among central bankers—given their socialization as 'priests of prosperity.'[19]

In terms of data, we searched our database of all IMF Board discussions for terms related to capital flows and identified 20 pertinent discussions (summarized in table 7.1) that added up to 335,000 words of verbatim statements.[20] While this textual corpus is sizable from a human-coding perspective, it is small from a computational perspective—many such analyses use tens of millions of words, and even the sovereign debt study in chapter 6 pertained to underlying Board debates of 2.4 million words. The reason behind the smaller textual corpus of debates on capital account liberalization is that they were highly concentrated (15 of the 20 relevant debates took place in the 1995–99 period), unlike the frequently recurring debt discussions. As we will describe, this has implications for the scope of our empirical analyses. We also collected the 55 background reports that were put to the Board for consideration.

Employing these data, we first identified the terms to be employed in the word-embedding analysis through the use of a topic-modeling algorithm, and relying on our own domain knowledge. For the word embeddings, we again generated one- to four-word sequences (as the terms of interest are commonly longer than a single word; e.g., 'capital account liberalization' or 'structural reform'), then applied a threshold of appearing at least twice in each speaker's interventions.[21] Subsequently, we proceeded with comparisons of word embeddings: between IMF staff and Board members from the Global North and the Global South; and between Board members, as parsed by their professional affiliation and income classification of their country of origin.

---

[19] Johnson 2016.

[20] This figure excludes another 22,000 words spoken by Board members without available CVs (and therefore excluded from the analysis).

[21] We set a lower threshold here compared to the sovereign debt analysis in chapter 6 (minimum of four appearances) because the textual corpus of capital controls is considerably smaller.

Unlike the sovereign debt analyses, we did not use supervised approaches on the capital controls text, because our reading of the relevant Board debates did not reveal clear patterns of different term usage between policy alternatives. All discussions revolved around whether to ban the use of capital controls, so all participants in these processes used broadly the same language (e.g., they talked about inflows, outflows, IMF jurisdiction, volatility, and capital flight). Such textual similarities made frequency analysis too crude a tool to pick up nuance.

Last, we turned to a qualitative analysis of negotiations over capital controls. As the textual corpus is smaller and the debates more tightly focused than in the case of sovereign debt, we analyzed the entirety of the deliberations. In doing so, we matched each speaker to their country of origin and prior professional experience, then qualitatively traced how they interacted with other Board members: who was supporting whom, who was dissenting, and how they related to proposals stemming from the IMF's technocratic staff.

Policy Positioning of IMF Staff and Board Members

Our first analytical task was a comparison of the policy positioning of IMF staff and Board members from the Global North and the Global South. We pursued this by drawing on two key terms employed in these discussions. First, we examined references to 'international capital,' as this was the key target of the policy change under discussion. Subsequently, we turned our attention to 'structural reform,' as this concept underpinned the IMF's explanation for the merits of removing capital controls. If the IMF proposal for banning controls had been approved, governments no longer would have been able to use restrictions on international capital mobility as an economic policy tool, and instead would have needed to engage in structural reforms to deal with the purported underlying weaknesses that prompted the use of capital controls in the first place.

Reflecting our theoretical setup, our interest here was in similarities and differences among the three types of participants in scriptwriting. Our framework asserts that we can distinguish how policy scripts are crafted by differentiating the intensity of political contention over the issue, as well as the intensity of scientific alignment. When both are low, there is incoherence. When politics is dormant but scientific alignment is high, then experts will dominate (see chapter 8 on taxation). When scientific alignment is weak but political contention high, then power politics will assert itself (see chapter 6 on sovereign debt). When both scientific alignment and political contention are high, there will be contestation if dominant political interests and the science clash, and congruity if they align.

This latter combination of high scientific alignment and high political contestation is the more likely one on the issue of capital controls. As we know from the scholarship reviewed earlier, the IMF technocrats were advocates of capital account liberalization and more than happy to provide scientific justifications for it. But how did Board members position themselves in this scriptwriting process? Potential similarities between the policy positioning of IMF staff and Global North representatives on the Board would provide evidence of either major shareholder interference in shaping the priorities of the technocracy or simply a confluence of opinion between these two policy actors. In either case, the observable implication would be the same: agreement on the merits of capital account liberalization. Alternatively, if we were to see differentiation across all three types of participants, then this would open questions over the distinct political and scientific frames that these actors bring to scriptwriting.

Figure 7.2 presents the findings on how 'international capital' is embedded in its textual corpus, divided into panels for each of the actors under study. The text by IMF staff (panel A) links international capital to the economic trajectories of countries, as it shapes 'development prospects' and the 'role of growth.' At the same time, IMF staff point to policy challenges associated with capital movements to 'deliver efficient' financial support for growth, such as ensuring that flows are 'adequate,' that 'prudential' measures are in place, and that countries can secure 'renewed access.' This word-use pattern does not suggest high degrees of epistemic doubt or political contention but instead implies that the issue at hand is primarily technical. Panel B shows the textual context of references to international capital by Global North Board members. These individuals primarily use positive valence terms like 'capital inflows,' 'strengthening domestic' economic conditions, and improving the 'balance of payments' position. Importantly, they also link their views on international capital to those of 'the staff' and their background papers, thus hinting at the support and legitimation of staff policy positions and proposals. In contrast, Board members from the Global South have a less rosy picture of international capital (panel C). These individuals are especially focused on its impact on 'developing countries' and their 'exchange rates,' and on the role of 'short term' capital movements, especially those viewed as 'excessive[ly] short'—what Keynes would associate with unfettered capital flows.[22] Indeed, the 'risks' involved appear clearly in their policy statements.

---

[22] Kirshner 1999, 321.

172 Making Global Norms

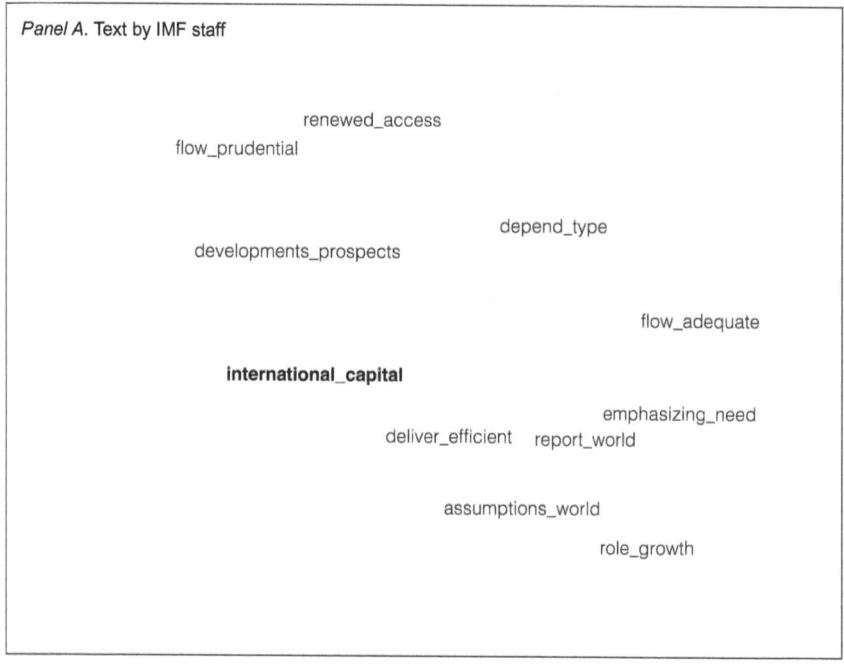

Figure 7.2 Word-embedding comparisons of IMF staff and Board members on 'international capital.'

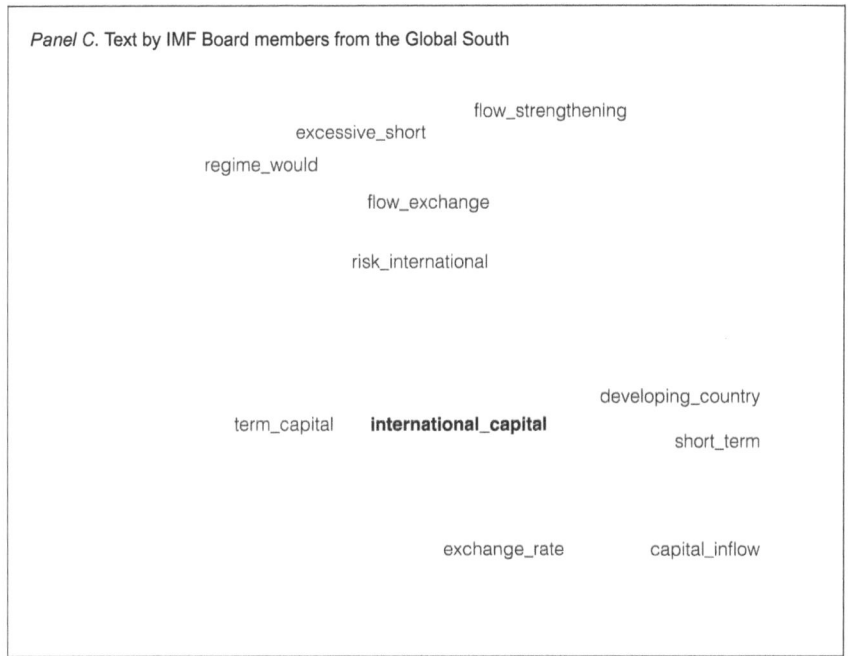

Figure 7.2 *Continued*

In figure 7.3 we turn our attention to the role of 'structural reforms' in discussions over capital controls. Unsurprisingly, IMF staff (panel A) link structural reform to the 'banking sector,' 'prudential regulations,' 'macroeconomic policy,' and 'trade liberalization'—all seen as crucial policies to prevent or preempt 'banking crises' and (speculative) 'attacks.' These are all standard policies advanced by the IMF in its lending programs, and an expanded mandate for the organization on capital flow issues would also grant staff a stronger hand in promoting their preferred structural reforms. Global North officials (panel B) also emphasize the various reforms that these Board members see as necessary ('economic policy,' 'monetary and financial,' 'prudential'), and are promoting reliance on 'technical assistance' for their implementation. In other words, their comments dovetail with the policy positions of IMF staff, who would ultimately be the ones diffusing such policies through their technical assistance missions, which are in turn primarily funded by high-income countries, as we saw in chapter 5. By contrast, Global South (panel C) Board members associate structural reform with access to Fund resources, technical assistance, reform of the financial system, and an 'extension' of macroeconomic management in accordance with Fund policy. IMF technical assistance and the introduction of prudential controls go hand

174 Making Global Norms

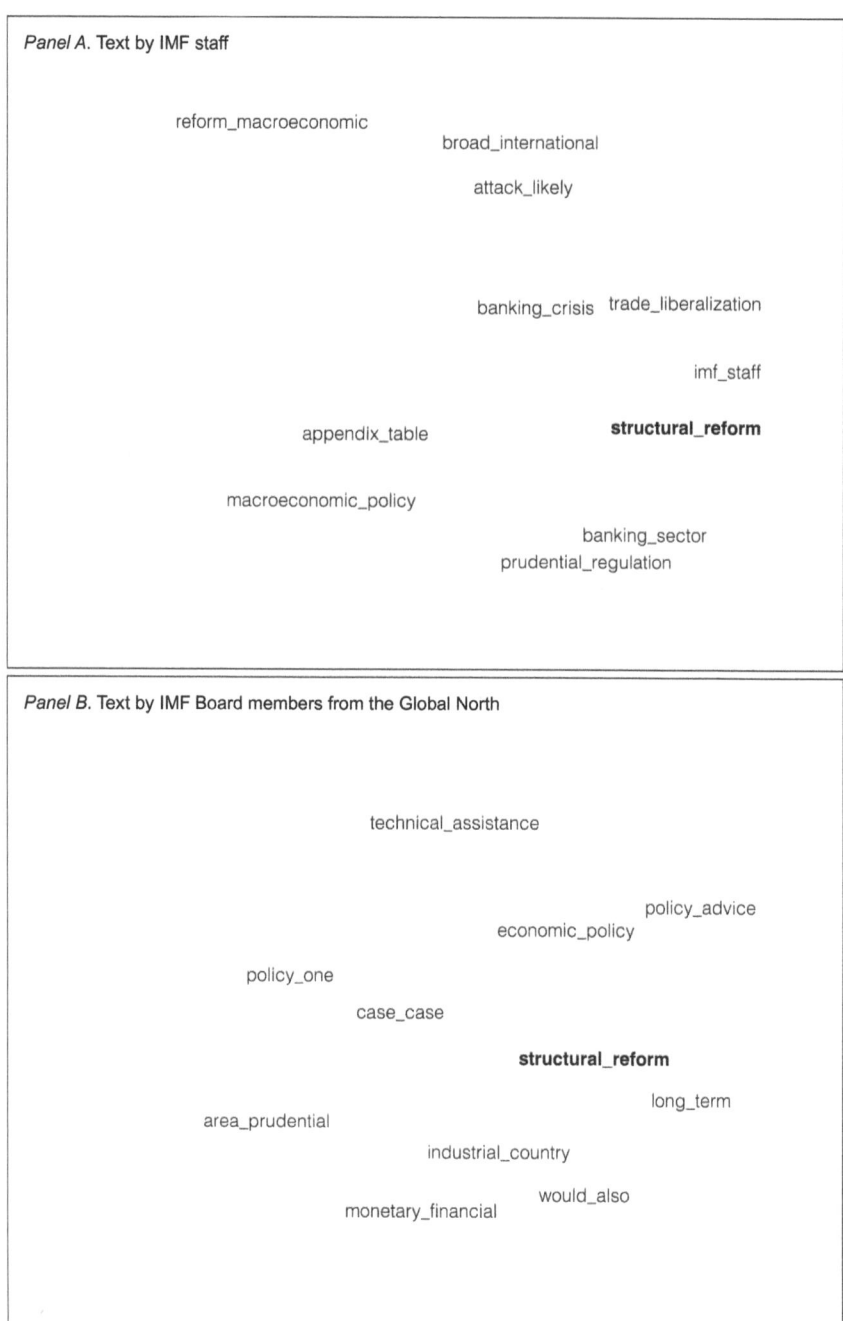

Figure 7.3 Word-embedding comparisons of IMF staff and Board members on 'structural reform.'

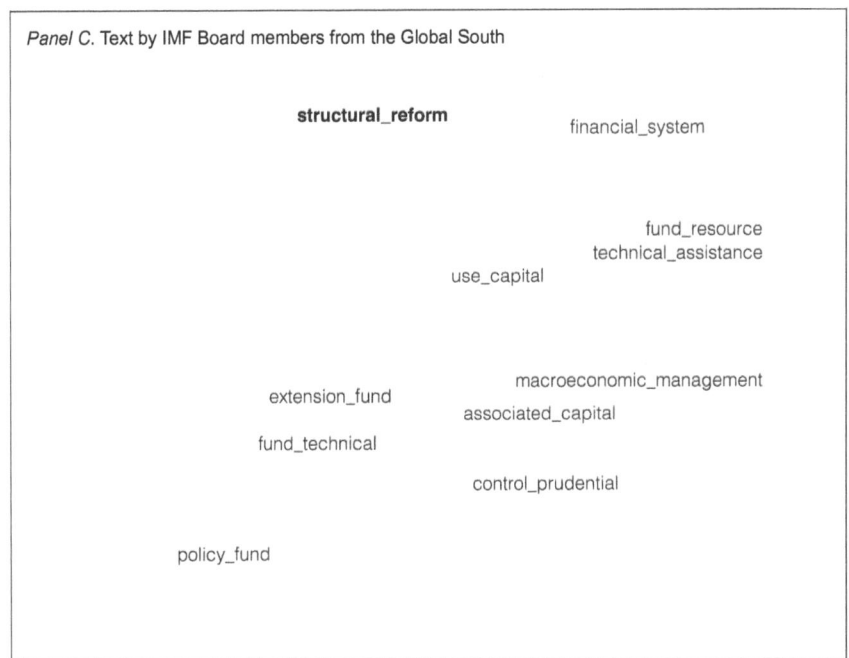

Figure 7.3 *Continued*

in hand with structural reforms in discussions around capital account liberalization. Put differently, structural reform means opening the capital account to allow inflows and outflows, but with more external scrutiny into domestic macroeconomic management.

To sum up, in the case of debates over capital controls, we see affinities between the policy positions of Global North representatives and IMF staff, while Board members from the Global South are skeptical. These patterns of word usage present prima facie evidence of dissent by developing countries against a unified staff–Global North front. Such dissent is important as it sets out the odds that developing countries faced in their attempts to influence scriptwriting over capital controls.

Politics Versus Science in Boardroom Debates

As in chapter 6, we now delve deeper into Board discussions, investigating whether there is a difference in policy positioning according not only to income group (Global North or South) but also to the professional background of individual Board members. Our interest here is to assess if the scientization of capital controls from the IMF technocracy[23] resonated with a particular professional audience in the Board, or if more blunt political preferences over whether to loosen or tighten capital controls were supreme.

Knowing that nearly half the IMF Executive Board members have a background in central banking—a community with a strong preference for capital account liberalization in line with trade interdependence and multilateral lending[24]—we expected to see them align across the Global North–South income divide. As many of these central bankers have gone through the same Anglo-American educational institutions, they likely would share a vocabulary positively disposed toward capital openness and its supposed cornucopia of benefits. Other Board members are less likely to be enamored with capital controls. We expected that those with finance ministry backgrounds and political appointees would reflect a Global North–South divide. The former would want to open up markets, arguing that capital liberalization stimulates inward investment and economic growth, and is simply part of the institutional evolution into being a full member of the capitalist world economy. The latter would suggest that opening up brings dangers, including excessive short-term risks, threats of capital flight for reasons exogenous to the member state, and a looming sense that a path toward capital liberalization would bring more technocratic oversight and interference.[25]

In figure 7.4 we can see the word embeddings for 'capital account.' Panels A and B show the key terms associated with Global North and Global South central bankers. In both panels we can see an emphasis on 'account liberalization.' The Global North central bankers are also concerned with 'promoting' and 'liberalizing' capital 'flows.' Global South central bankers share some language with their Northern counterparts, even though they infuse their comments with concerns over 'definitions' and 'obligations' of capital—these remarks are in line with considerations of central banks in monitoring and classifying international capital flows. In short, Board members with central banking backgrounds, regardless of their income level, use language that suggests a positive predisposition toward loosening controls on the capital account, or—at a minimum—the lack of clear and vocal opposition.

In contrast, we observe dissent among finance ministry officials, shown in panels C and D. Those from the Global North emphasize the benefits of releasing capital controls, particularly noting that capital account

---

[23] Chwieroth 2007.
[24] Polillo and Guillén 2005.
[25] As noted earlier, our textual corpus of Board debates on capital controls is only modestly sized, which means that for professional clusters with lower prevalence (i.e., businesspeople and private bankers, academics, and IO staff), we only have limited data. As ensuing inferences would be weak, we do not devote much attention to their policy positioning during Board debates.

Panel A. Text by Global North central bankers

                                                          account_liberalization
                                    international_capital
                                                              capital_movement

            capital_flow
                  liberalization_capital

                                      capital_account

                                                            debate_fund
                                                           direction_capital

                           respect_international
    promoting_capital jurisdiction_international

Panel B. Text by Global South central bankers

                                                  respect_capital
                                           industrialized_country

                                                successful_capital

                         definition_capital
                                        liberalization_would

                             liberalization_developing
                                      obligation_capital

                 account_convertibility

                                    full_capital
     capital_account
                  account_liberalization

Figure 7.4 Word-embedding comparisons of Board member clusters on 'capital account.'

178 Making Global Norms

Figure 7.4 *Continued*

liberalization must be properly 'sequenced' and 'paced' to ensure that institutional evolution can meet international financial-market expectations. Consequently, they favor policies that 'promote' and 'encourage' liberalization, which they expect will spur 'benefits.' This perspective differs from that of Global South finance ministry professionals, who highlight the particular concerns for 'developing countries' and the use of 'capital controls' while linking these discussions to the IMF's 'jurisdiction.' Terms like 'capital inflows' and 'direct investment' suggest that these officials are cognizant of the potential benefits of opening; however, they also point to the need for customized 'transitional arrangements' (vs. general sequencing) and for reducing 'exchange rate' volatility. In sum, Global North and South finance ministers split over the likely benefits of capital account liberalization, the former proposing a positive view, the latter emphasizing the need for caution.

We turn next to Board members' discussions around the Articles of Agreement (figure 7.5). What was at stake here was a fundamental revision to the Articles—the Fund's official mandate that applies to all member states—to include capital account liberalization. This push to revise the Articles, concentrated in the 1990s (discussed in detail hereafter), was to formally make the Fund's treatment of the capital account akin to the current account. On the current account, the Fund has a clear mandate to establish a 'multilateral system of payments in respect of current transactions between members and in the elimination of foreign exchange restrictions which hamper the growth of world trade.'[26] The stress is on the facilitation of payments, rather than the transactions themselves. When there is a significant balance-of-payments issue, Article IV of the Articles of Agreement specifies that to avoid a member state needing to draw on IMF resources, the 'Fund may request a member to exercise controls' on capital transfers.[27] As such, the need for a change in the Articles to promote capital account liberalization explicitly recognizes that capital controls should be phased out, implying both greater economic integration but also greater reliance on the IMF. A fundamental issue here is whether the capital account should be liberalized to facilitate transactions, significantly expanding the Fund's jurisdiction beyond 'payments' and potentially increased surveillance over financial systems.

In panels A and B, we can see that those with a central banking background support capital account liberalization, agreeing with both the Fund approach and the staff. Yet they also reflect how their constituencies benefit

---

[26] IMF 2011a, 2.
[27] IMF 2011a, 20.

180 Making Global Norms

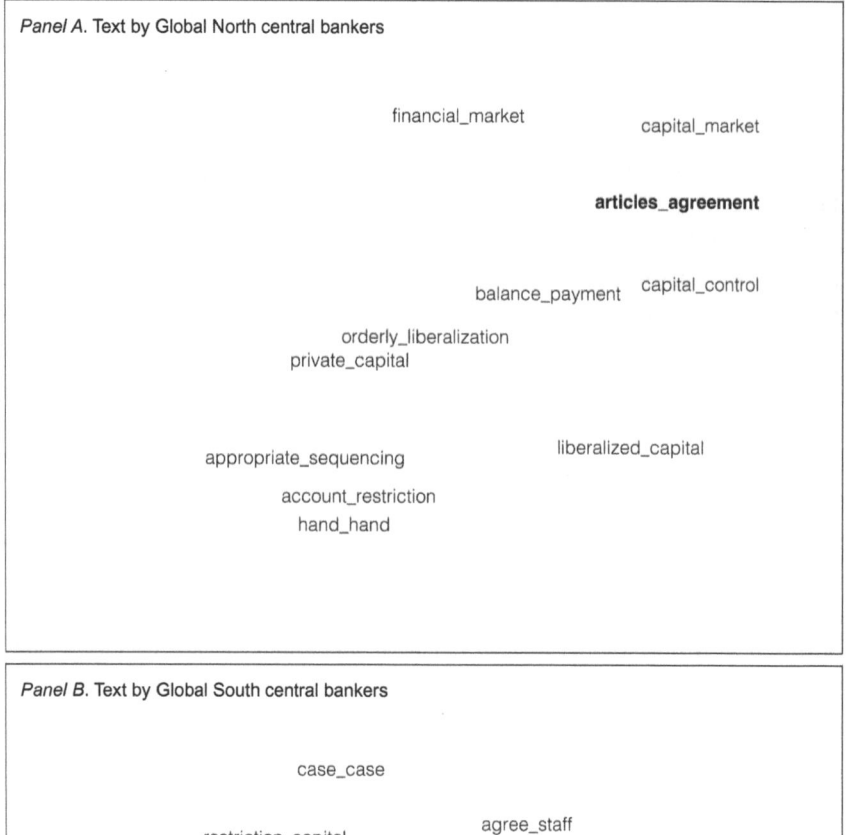

Figure 7.5 Word-embedding comparisons of Board member clusters on 'Articles of Agreement.'

Figure 7.5 *Continued*

from or think about a potential change to the Articles of Agreement. For the Global North, the terms 'orderly liberalization' and 'liberalized capital' tell us that an amendment to the Articles should take place to maximize capital freedoms, while for the Global South, the terms 'transitional arrangement' and 'technical assistance' show how a change to the Articles must be accompanied by Fund expertise over a longer period. Furthermore, the stress on capital restrictions and case-by-case basis reflects a need to accommodate potential exceptions rather than a new universal ruling. In short, the central bankers generally support an amendment to the Articles while noting the likely institutional pathways.

In panels C and D, we see the terms that Global North and South political appointees use in association with Articles of Agreement. Those from the Global North appear to support an amendment, believing that it would spur 'inward direct investment' and should be fostered with necessary 'technical assistance' and an expansion of the Fund's 'jurisdiction.' For Global South members, the emphasis is linked to concerns of 'developing countries' and 'emerging markets,' and they refer to terms associated with caution, such as 'exchange rate' risks and dangers from rapid 'capital inflows.' Both Global North and South political appointees stress the need for policies to be approved, reflecting underlying dynamics of a change to the Articles of Agreement that would require approval by the IMF's member states.

This section has shown the tensions between different professional clusters and between Global North and South representatives. Those with central banking backgrounds appear somewhat aligned, notwithstanding some critical terms used by Global South representatives. Instead, those with backgrounds in finance ministries or high politics are more sharply split: Those from the Global North are endorsing treaty change and relying heavily on the staff's analyses to support their arguments, while those from the Global South appear more skeptical of the merits of this policy change. Here we have clear hints of disputes over the scientific merits of banning capital controls, as well as the political decisions over what is to be done vis-à-vis amending the IMF's Articles of Agreement—a process that requires a high majority (three-fifths of member states, having 85% of total votes). Ultimately, these inferences reveal the types of reasoning of different actors but do not uncover the dynamic nature of scriptwriting, to which we now turn.[28]

---

[28] As we note in chapter 3, our reading of these Board discussions did not reveal usage of terms with very clear valence vis-à-vis the merits of capital controls, unlike the sovereign debt case presented in chapter 6. Instead, interventions use mostly uniform language to refer to the IMF's impending decision on whether to prohibit or allow capital controls (e.g., terms commonly employed by all are 'inflows,' 'outflows,' 'IMF jurisdiction,' 'volatility,' and 'capital flight'). In this context, frequency analysis is insufficiently refined to detect subtle differences, and therefore we chose not to use this method.

Scriptwriting Through Boardroom Interactions

Having seen the broad priorities of staff and Board members, as reflected in word embeddings, we shift our attention to the interactive element of these debates: Who says what in reaction to whom? It is through discussions that consensus is built among Executive Directors; qualitative analysis is thus required to uncover the relevant power dynamics and types of (scientific or political) reasoning. Given that scientific expertise (in the form of academic knowledge taken on and promoted by staff) had a key role in these processes, we focus on the positioning and interactions between IMF technocrats and the Board members, with reference to their representation function and prior professional expertise.

Initial discussions over capital controls in the work of the IMF started in the mid-1980s, when—at the behest of the Executive Board—IMF staff considered relevant issues. At the time, the IMF was assessing the costs and benefits of multiple currency practices, one way in which governments sought to control capital movements. A Staff Paper confirmed that the IMF had refrained from pronouncing judgments on its members' multiple currency practices relating to capital movements, as the Board had 'not yet settled the issue *expressis verbis*.'[29] However, at the same time, staff made the case for granting the IMF jurisdiction over these practices. In this view, there was economic and legal support for interpreting the intention of the Articles of Agreement as expanding the remit of the IMF in this area, as this 'would contribute to policy consistency.'[30]

This interpretation gained no traction on the Board, even among Global North representatives of various professional backgrounds, who duly blocked any further consideration of the issue. For example, German Director Grosche noted that he 'could not easily accept the staff's argument,'[31] and Dutch Director de Groote found the staff arguments 'somewhat contrived…[due to the attempt] to extend the Fund's jurisdiction to [issues that] did not fall within the Fund's legal province,' and complained that staff tried 'to force an interpretation on the Executive Board.'[32] Indeed, French Director de Maulde emphasized that 'the selective treatment by the staff of the Articles of Agreement…did not reinforce the credibility of the Legal Department.'[33] These views and concerns were echoed by a range of other representatives from industrialized and developing countries alike.

[29] SM/85/19, 2.
[30] SM/84/64, 18; SM/85/19.
[31] EBM/85/23, 3.
[32] EBM/85/23, 5–6.
[33] EBM/85/23, 10.

Importantly, two key directors expressed support to staff positions: Charles Dallara from the United States and Nigel Wicks from the United Kingdom, both with backgrounds in the finance ministries of their respective countries. Dallara acknowledged that the economics of the issue were contentious, but favored the staff's interpretation of the mandate, despite other Board members' serious reservations: 'If the Board accepted the staff's legal opinion…[the IMF] would have the duty of exercising the jurisdiction emanating from the legal analysis.'[34]

Unable to garner requisite support, this attempt—initiated by staff and supported by some powerful directors—at granting the IMF jurisdiction over a form of capital controls failed. Given this unfavorable outcome, staff retreated to a less contentious activity: producing research on the topic.[35] To give new thrust to this kind of work, in 1987 the IMF recruited two economists from the University of Chicago, a locus of pioneering research in the monetarist tradition in economics, which favored limiting government intervention in the economy.[36] Most importantly, Chicago-trained Jacob Frenkel was hired as director of the IMF's Research Department. Frenkel was aided by Michael Dooley, author of several IMF studies on capital account liberalization and formerly a faculty member at Chicago's economics department.

In 1990, staff returned to the issue with their first systematic treatment intended for Executive Board discussion.[37] This 90-page report noted with concern that developing countries—compared to industrialized ones—generally maintained regulated capital flows, even though 'experiences with capital flight…suggest that these restrictions are far from effective.'[38] Indeed, staff reported 'a growing consensus that capital flight needs to be addressed by dealing with the underlying distortions or policy inadequacies at the source, rather than by attempting to restrict the symptom or manifestation of these inadequacies (i.e., the capital flow itself).'[39]

This time, the staff proposals were greeted with considerable enthusiasm by representatives from high-income countries on the Board. Yet, some directors took issue with the assertion that removal of capital controls forces governments to adopt 'good' economic policies. For instance, Saudi Director Al-Jasser, a former finance ministry official, posited that staff insights '[do]

---

[34] EBM/85/23, 12–13.
[35] Penati and Dooley 1984; Gros 1987; Dooley 1988; Dooley et al. 1988.
[36] Dezalay and Garth 2002; Henriksen et al. 2022.
[37] SM/90/128.
[38] SM/90/128, 66.
[39] SM/90/128, 66.

not often apply to developing countries,[40] as their economic systems were fundamentally different from those of industrialized countries. However, many Global North Executive Directors set a broad tone in favor of dismantling capital controls. As Spanish Director Fernandez Ordonez, another former finance ministry official, noted:

> If we all [i.e., the Executive Board] agree that the possibility of imposing restrictions on capital flows is an instrument that should never be used by governments, the time has come for this consensus to become law. We should initiate a process to arrive at an international agreement on the freedom of capital flows....In my view, the Fund is well placed to play a role here.[41]

In sum, by the early 1990s, a consensus had emerged among staff and powerful shareholders about the desirability of extending IMF jurisdiction to issues related to capital controls. The emerging policy script was a simple one: Reliance on capital controls posed a policy problem, as they were ineffectual, counterproductive, and props for misguided domestic economic policies—their removal would only spur benefits. Nonetheless, given the IMF's restrictive mandate, no concrete policy changes occurred at this stage, other than production of research output that would serve as fodder for the battle to come over expanding the IMF's jurisdiction. In 1991, Frenkel left the IMF's Research Department and was replaced by Michael Mussa, who also studied at the University of Chicago at the same time and under the same supervisor as Frenkel. Prior to this appointment, Mussa—known for his contributions to international economics—was a professor of economics at Chicago and a member of Ronald Reagan's Council of Economic Advisers (1986–88).

Building on the support for capital account liberalization by major shareholders on the Executive Board, staff started incorporating such proposals into their policy advice and technical assistance to member states. For instance, IMF missions to Korea, Chile, and Botswana 'encouraged' the removal of capital controls.[42] Yet, even though staff acknowledged 'a general distaste for such controls,'[43] the Articles of Agreement prohibited any direct action on the topic. To this end, staff raised the issue of whether the IMF

---

[40] EBM/90/121.
[41] EBM/90/121, 20–21.
[42] SM/95/164, 10.
[43] SM/95/164, 10–11.

should adhere to the mandate's provisions, which 'were framed in a different era, and are no longer in harmony with the new international system,' or extend the IMF's jurisdiction to cover capital account issues, thereby aiding policy harmonization worldwide and yielding 'clear systemic benefits' for the global economy.[44] In other words, staff were attempting to institutionalize their preferred policy script on capital controls by enshrining it in the mandate, thereby giving them automatic responsibility to diffuse ('harmonize') the norm across the world.

Given the boldness of the recommendations, this attempt at institutionalizing the policy script attracted controversy on the Board. Directors from high-income countries praised the staff analysis, which 'add[ed] impressive ammunition' to the liberalization efforts.[45] US Director Lissakers—a former international finance professor at Columbia University—commended Michael Dooley, author of the literature review that informed staff recommendations,[46] for 'remind[ing] us that there is a compelling theoretical argument that free capital movements are likely to be welfare enhancing, identical to the argument for the gains from trade in goods and services....Careful research suggests capital controls are more frequently a device for preserving suboptimal macro policies.'[47] As noted, Dooley—now recruited as a consultant to draft this report—was previously a senior staff member of the IMF's Research Department, and author of several IMF reports opposing capital controls.[48]

For high-income-country directors, the evidence presented by staff was adequate for them to conclude that removing capital controls was desirable, as they only 'impair the efficient allocation of resources, preserve vested interests...and can be expected to be of only limited impact because markets almost certainly will find ways to circumvent them' (German representative Bernd Esdar, formerly at the country's finance ministry).[49] As Swiss Director and former finance ministry official Daniel Kaeser suggested, 'Capital account liberalization should be an irreversible process...[because] economic agents prefer to act in an environment in which the rules of the game are predictable.'[50] Further, US Director Lissakers noted that the US 'would also be

[44] SM/95/164, 15.
[45] EBM/95/73, 5.
[46] SM/95/164, Supplement 3.
[47] EBM/95/73, 22.
[48] Revealing the ideological provenance of his recommendations, Dooley drew on the public choice school (SM/95/164, Supplement 3), known for its critical stance toward state interventions and its free-market bias (e.g., Niskanen 1971).
[49] EBM/95/73, 27.
[50] EBM/95/73, 14.

willing to look seriously at the idea of amending the Articles of Agreement' or support other activist approaches for the removal of controls.⁵¹

Notwithstanding such enthusiastic endorsements, developing country representatives were skeptical. Malaysian Director Latifah Cheong, a former central banker, took the lead in attacking the staff report for misrepresenting country experiences, and disagreed with the conclusion 'that capital control measures delay policy adaptations,'⁵² as IMF staff contended. Instead, such measures 'provided a breathing space to enable more fundamental macro-policies to be implemented subsequently,'⁵³ a comment repeated by the Chinese, Colombian, Indian, Iranian, and Venezuelan directors, among others. Hinting at double standards for developed versus developing countries, Russian Director and former finance ministry official Dmitri Tulin complained:

> The fact that a vast majority of the industrial countries had exercised controls on capital flows for decades, until they felt themselves prepared to liberalize their regulations, attests to the nonincidental nature of this phenomenon. General and unqualified appeals to remove capital controls from industrial nations known for recent sophisticated protectionism in this area would not sound very convincing to the rest of the world.⁵⁴

To support their positions, developing country directors drew on the experiences of their own countries and even reports by the IMF's sibling institution, the World Bank, that suggested that short-term capital controls made 'eminent sense.'⁵⁵ These directors attacked the economic logic of staff arguments, offering instead a joint line that the use of 'capital controls may be decided by [national] authorities at their own discretion and without review by the Fund' (Iranian Director).⁵⁶ In this view, the existing mandate was sufficient to allow the Fund to provide informal suggestions on the use of capital controls, 'without making [liberalization] an end in itself' (Indian Director).⁵⁷

Even though high-income-country directors with their large voting shares were in favor of banning capital controls, the Board was not able to reach a consensus over the desirability of the policy or the need to amend the Articles

---

[51] EBM/95/73, 26.
[52] EBM/95/73, 6.
[53] EBM/95/73, 6.
[54] EBM/95/73, 50.
[55] EBM/95/73, 48.
[56] EBM/95/73, 9.
[57] EBM/95/73, 58.

of Agreement. Consequently, no decision was reached, and a general commitment was made to revisit the issue in the future. Reacting to this outcome with disappointment, American Director Lissakers noted that the US 'would not rule out further consideration of an amendment of the Articles at a relatively early date, [and suggested] that the Board would revisit the issue sooner rather than later.'[58]

The 1995 attempt of IMF staff and powerful shareholders to institutionalize their preferred 'no capital controls' policy script drew on frontier academic work and the IMF's own research and policy proposals. These bases of legitimation for the new approach—giving the IMF jurisdiction to demand removal of capital controls—were cast into doubt due to contention on the Board. In a concerted effort, developing-country directors managed to forestall any changes to the Articles by drawing not only on their countries' experiences but also their social skills: They couched opposition to a treaty change in terms of the adequacy of existing arrangements and by framing the merits of capital controls as a topic under debate (rather than being one on which consensus exists, as staff and developed-country directors contended).

Following this failed 1995 attempt, IMF staff initiated a pilot data-collection project on capital controls in 29 countries and suggested the collection of data for all members as 'a central element of the Fund's intensified efforts in this area.'[59] The research revealed a 'generally guarded approach to the use of capital controls as a sustained response to dealing with swings in capital flows.'[60] Building on these findings, staff reiterated their call for expanding the IMF's jurisdiction over capital account management, including the power to stipulate the removal of capital controls.[61] As a concession to concerns raised by developing countries on the Board, the IMF acknowledged that temporary imposition of capital controls may in some instances be beneficial. These cases would require the explicit approval of the IMF,[62] even though—as a staff report mentioned—the IMF had 'never found it necessary to formally request a member to impose capital controls.'[63]

These staff proposals still elicited objections from developing countries. For instance, M. R. Sivaraman—a former secretary of the Indian finance ministry—noted his dissent with putting the IMF 'in a final position to approve such temporary controls which could mean that the Fund impinges

[58] EBM/95/73, 71.
[59] SM/97/32, Supplement 1, 4.
[60] SM/97/32, 36.
[61] SM/97/32.
[62] SM/97/86, SM/97/209.
[63] SM/97/32, 28.

on the prerogatives of governments to do what is best to prevent a crisis in their country,'[64] a remark echoed by other Global South directors.[65] Bypassing such opposition, Managing Director Camdessus reported that the general view of the Board was that the IMF was 'well placed to determine when the temporary imposition of controls could provide an appropriate means of addressing surges in capital inflows and outflows.'[66]

As in the earlier attempt by staff to institutionalize their preferred policy script, a concerted effort by several directors—primarily from developing countries—sought to avoid a substantial expansion of the IMF's jurisdiction to capital-account management issues. Importantly, in the draft report for the Interim Committee—a decision-making body overseeing the Executive Board composed of 24 finance ministers—IMF staff sought a wholesale overhaul of their mandate. The report suggested that liberalization of capital movements not only should be under the jurisdiction of the IMF but also that it should become one of the purposes of the organization.[67] Responding to the statement, the Egyptian and Canadian directors chastised the staff for promoting an issue that 'had not been discussed in the Board.'[68] Indeed, reflecting the absence of overall consensus about the exact content of the mandate changes, Executive Directors preferred a very general statement of intent rather than specific measures.[69]

At the time of these discussions, the Asian financial crises had captured global attention. Starting in Thailand and spreading to other countries in the region, the crisis became pivotal for determining the fate of the attempt to institutionalize the 'no capital controls' policy script. The Asian crisis was intricately linked to capital account issues: Indonesia, Korea, Malaysia, the Philippines, and Thailand had received net private capital inflows of $93 billion in 1996, which reversed to $12.1 billion in private capital outflows in 1997.[70] Among such capital movements, the key contributors to the outflow were commercial banks and portfolio investments, both having been identified by developing countries in Board meetings as key capital flows that required regulation.

These crises invigorated debates over the utility of free capital flows at a time when it appeared that IMF staff and powerful shareholders were closer

[64] EBM/97/38, 7.
[65] EBM/97/38, 31.
[66] EBM/97/38, 41.
[67] SM/97/230, 2–3.
[68] EBM/97/93, 5.
[69] EBM/97/93, 5.
[70] Radelet and Sachs 1998, 3–4.

to achieving their preferred outcome: expanding the organization's jurisdiction to cover these issues. A number of prominent economists suggested that open capital markets were partly to blame for these crises, which might have been avoided had these countries maintained the use of capital controls.[71] In reaction to these debates, IMF staff attempted to propagate an argument that suggested few—if any—links between the Asian crises and capital account liberalization. For instance, the IMF's flagship *World Economic Outlook* attributed the crises to underlying domestic policies,[72] and the IMF's first deputy managing director, Stanley Fischer, commented that 'the Asian crisis forcefully raises the questions of whether capital-account liberalization has moved too quickly...I reject this view.'[73] Indeed, as Fischer explained in a seminar on 'Asia and the IMF' just two months after the onset of the crisis, capital account liberalization 'is an inevitable step on the path of development, which cannot be avoided and therefore should be adapted to. In support of this view, we may note that all the most advanced economies have open capital accounts.'[74] Speaking to an audience of Asian policymakers, Fischer noted that 'what I would like to do is to persuade those of you who remain skeptical about capital account liberalization...that an amendment of the Fund's Articles of Agreement is the best way of ensuring that [it] is carried out in an orderly, non-disruptive way.'[75]

Making similar arguments, IMF Managing Director Camdessus told the Executive Board that 'the Asian crisis had been a powerful argument for added jurisdiction. If it were to rely on technical assistance and surveillance, the Fund would not be able to prevent such crises from happening again.'[76] In this position, he was supported by US Director Lissakers, who agreed that the Asian 'developments argue for speed and some ambition in our amendment [of the Articles].'[77] Other high-income-country representatives further supported the view that the IMF should move forward with the plans to expand its jurisdiction, and took issue with influential accounts of the Asian crises that accorded a role to free capital flows. For instance, Icelandic Director and former central banker Axel Palmason took issue with the views of then-World Bank chief economist Joseph Stiglitz, instead supporting the views of Charles Dallara, formerly US Executive Director at the IMF and at the time head of the main lobby of international banks, the Institute of International Finance:

---

[71] Bhagwati 1998; Rodrik 1998; Wade 1998; Wade and Veneroso 1998.
[72] IMF 1997, 2.
[73] Fischer 1998, 2.
[74] Fischer 1997.
[75] Fischer 1997.
[76] EBM/98/38, 9.
[77] EBM/98/38, 10.

I found less convincing the Stiglitz metaphor that, although an ill-repaired boat is more likely to sink, the force of powerful waves can cause even a perfectly sound vessel to founder, particularly smaller ones. Hence, short-term capital controls are called for. The problem with this analogy is that capital controls won't help anyone sail to where they need to go. Controls won't make the big waves smaller nor will they make the small boats bigger. In fact, it is not the boat's size that determines its ability to sail on the ocean. Rowboats have made it across the Atlantic but the Titanic sank. It is all up to the captain, but he needs clear rules for navigation. …Dallara of the Institute of International Finance made the point that inward direct investment was a better way of balancing capital flows than the practice of short-term controls.[78]

Nonetheless, the tide against expanding the IMF's jurisdiction was turning. Even US Director Lissakers acknowledged that—in light of the Asian crises— 'a number of [IMF] members want to reopen the issue of jurisdiction [over the capital account], which I think is a terrible idea, but so be it.'[79] Indeed, many directors, mostly from developing countries (India, Egypt, Russia, and Zimbabwe), raised important challenges to the view that capital controls were ineffective, and that the benefits of capital account liberalization outweighed any potential costs.[80] Further, the purported economic merits of removing capital controls—as promoted by staff—now came under increased scrutiny, and were characterized as 'misleading' by Greek Director Spraos, formerly a professor of economics at University College London.[81]

Starting in early 1999, directors from Angola, Canada, Egypt, India, Japan, Saudi Arabia, and Thailand were explicitly skeptical about expanding the IMF's jurisdiction.[82] Some support by high-income countries remained for an amendment but had lost momentum compared to the period before the Asian crisis. Proposals for changing the Articles of Agreement soon ceased altogether.

Conclusions

What does the attempt to institutionalize the 'no capital controls' policy script suggest about scriptwriting within IOs? Unlike the case of sovereign debt,

---

[78] EBM/98/38, 22–23.
[79] EBM/98/38, 10.
[80] EBM/98/38, 10.
[81] EBM/98/85.
[82] EBM/99/31.

where there was no scientific consensus on how to deal with debt problems, the case of capital account management is marked by strong predictions from academic economists on the benefits that liberalization would bring. But this case was also marked from the outset by intense political jostling to influence the eventual outcome of the scriptwriting process, which would no less than fundamentally reshape international financial integration and countries' available policy space. In other words, this was a contentious process manifesting as political and epistemic struggles on the IMF's Board. Staff and powerful IMF shareholders tried to institutionalize their preferred policy script in several ways—for example, by producing research, advancing a new legal reading of the mandate, or misrepresenting the nature of developing countries' concerns. At the same time, developing-country representatives sought to stave off the institutionalization of the script—for example, by building coalitions and repeating the same message; casting their disagreements with staff and other directors in terms of economic theory; and using rhetorical tools, such as acknowledging that while open capital accounts are generally desirable, there are many instances where controls are useful.

Our initial abductive logic for this case was that the technocracy would support the liberalization of capital controls, the Global North and South Board members would differ strongly, and members' professional backgrounds might be important in moderating this fight. While these expectations were mainly on target, the relative importance of Board members' professional background appears limited. There is some evidence for central bankers' taking similar positions, in line with theoretical expectations. However, as we documented in the qualitative part of the analysis, Board members with backgrounds in finance ministries and high politics were the most vocal and dominated discussions. They engaged with the scientific frames put forth by the staff yet rebutted rosy perspectives on the promises of capital account liberalization. Importantly, these Board members also presented a unified front: Allied speakers often referenced each other and leveraged the IMF's procedures for consensus building to stave off attempts at institutionalizing the 'no capital controls' policy script. To be sure, the Asian financial crisis was crucial in demonstrating the importance of capital controls and derailing efforts to ban them. But even without this crisis, it is far from certain that this policy script could have been institutionalized, given the expansive majority needed to amend the Articles of Agreement.

In short, the capital account liberalization case is marked by the primacy of North versus South political dynamics. The scientific basis for advancing this policy script was clear and advanced by the bureaucracy, with the support of powerful Global North representatives. Yet it was not enough to trump the high-level politics behind a momentous change that had the potential to substantially transform the nature of global capitalism. For this reason, the role of Board members' professional backgrounds appears more muted compared to the sovereign debt case presented in chapter 6. When policy scripts were developed that could have political, economic, and social implications for the entire IMF membership, the state-representation function of participants in these processes overrode their individual worldviews. The stakes were simply too high, and politics dominated.

8
Taxation

Introduction

There is a long-standing consensus that what undergirds sustainable economic and political development is a reliable tax system. Tax revenues enable governments to invest in infrastructure, education, welfare, and defense. These revenues can come from direct and indirect taxes. The former are taxes on income and profits and typically are directed at individuals, households, and businesses. The latter are taxes on goods and services that are collected through an intermediary. The most contemporary popular example of the latter is the value-added tax (VAT), in which the tax is added to the price paid by the consumer, with the seller collecting the tax to pass on to the government, minus their own rebates. Historically, trade has been a strong source of tax revenue, with tariffs a direct tax on the importation of goods and duties an indirect tax passed on to consumers. Such import taxes are typically easier to collect and do not challenge powerful social groups that do not want redistribution via income taxation.

In the postwar period, a concerted and broadly successful effort has shifted tax burdens away from tariffs and duties and onto household incomes and consumption. The logic here has been that to accelerate economic interdependence—what we call globalization—states must lower the costs of trade and expand consumer choice. At the same time, states cannot engage the global economy without a strong tax base, since that is how they nurture and maintain 'human capital' while securing the means to cope with external shocks. Thus, global economic integration demands that states have two things at once: economic growth through trade and investment, and robust fiscal systems. In short, taxes have to come from somewhere, and that means political trade-offs must be engaged.

Extensive research on 'state capacity' has investigated political trade-offs in the development of countries' revenue systems.[1] Rely too heavily on taxing imports like grain, and you may end up with mass protests as bread prices

---

[1] Skocpol 1979; Mann 1986.

Making Global Norms. Alexandros Kentikelenis and Leonard Seabrooke, Oxford University Press.
© Oxford University Press (2025). DOI: 10.1093/9780197828656.003.0008

increase.² Tax the rich too heavily on their income or wealth, and they too will find means to revolt.³ Lean too much on taxing businesses, and those with monies will threaten to relocate it.⁴ The hackneyed quote from Jean-Baptiste Colbert, Louis XIV's finance minister and key architect of centralized economic policy decision-making, goes as follows: 'The art of taxation consists of plucking the goose so as to obtain the most feathers with the least squawking.'⁵

The International Monetary Fund (IMF) is on the front line in advising its member states on how they can best extract the most feathers.⁶ To do so, the Fund has placed significant resources into making its powerful Fiscal Affairs Department (FAD) a global intellectual leader on tax policy and providing extensive technical assistance to member states to redesign their tax systems. The Fund's pro–economic globalization mindset seeks to balance global economic integration with fiscal robustness, aiming for 'growth-friendly fiscal policies [that] remove the distortions that are holding more productive firms back.'⁷ This pro-growth agenda is mixed with recognition that the tax systems of many of its member states were established by colonizers importing 'home' systems into contexts where they are difficult to administer or have not been legitimated.⁸ As such, the Fund is actively involved in encouraging—sometimes forcing—the redesign of taxation systems, which, by its own account, it seeks to do in the most depoliticized and scientized manner possible. An additional rationale for reforming tax systems is to reduce reliance on sovereign borrowing, since debt is 'really just a promise of deferred taxation.'⁹

How has the Fund encouraged the redesign of fiscal systems? One logic here has been to follow the 'Laffer curve,' which embodies the belief of its creator, Arthur Laffer, that there are good reasons to not have high marginal taxes, especially on personal income. Laffer attributed the logic to Ibn Khaldun's writings in his *Muqaddimah* from 1381:

> The Laffer curve, by the way, was not invented by me. For example, Ibn Khaldun, a 14th-century Muslim philosopher, wrote in his work The Muqaddimah: 'It should be known that at the beginning of the dynasty, taxation yields a large revenue from small assessments. At the end of the dynasty, taxation yields a small revenue from large assessments.'¹⁰

---

² Hobson 1997.
³ Martin 2015.
⁴ Tilly 1992.
⁵ Martin and Gabay 2018, 663.
⁶ Stewart and Jogarajan 2004; James 2015; Stewart 2024.
⁷ IMF 2017b.
⁸ Goode 1993, 37.
⁹ Keen and Slemrod 2022, 47.
¹⁰ Laffer 2004.

The Fund has critically engaged with the Laffer curve, recognizing it as both an American conservative 'propaganda device'[11] and also the basis for reasoning through the appropriate level of tax rates.[12] This talks directly to the Fund's aim to help member states pluck the most feathers with the least squawking. The clever plucker applies taxes on the consumption of the broad population through a VAT, where these taxes can be built into pricing and purchasing, becoming automatic and natural rather than additional burdens.

The evolution of global norms on taxation is one of immersion into the VAT tax revolution, the decline of tariffs as a key source of revenue, and the simplification of other taxes. The idea behind the VAT is commonly attributed to the German industrialist Wilhelm von Siemens, who proposed it in 1918. Versions of it were created in France in the 1920s, and it was introduced as an experiment within General Douglas MacArthur's economic reforms in occupied postwar Japan.[13] It was later revived by French economist Maurice Lauré, vice-director of Direction Générale des Impôts, and introduced in France in 1954. Subsequently, the VAT became a key component of economic policy harmonization in the European Union during the late 1960s, and was instituted in the 1970s as the fiscal cornerstone of the European Community.[14] The notion that the VAT is hidden from the general public has been explained as part of its popularity for policymakers. Critics of VAT contend that is regressive, given the rich and the poor pay the same amount of tax when buying a carton of milk.[15]

As shown in figure 8.1, the tax was also adopted in South America in the 1960s and in East Asia in the 1970s and 1980s, followed by significant rollouts of VAT reforms in African and former Soviet economies in the 1990s. In this process, upper- and middle-income countries replaced 45%–60% of tariff revenues with other taxes, and the VAT bolstered central government revenues while being treated as hidden from the public.[16] In developing countries, approximately 30% of tariff revenues were replaced by other forms of taxation; VAT was the most prominent fiscal tool introduced—often at the behest of the IMF—to boost administrative capacity and public revenues.[17]

From the 1980s onward, the rollout of the VAT became a core element of the IMF's policy script for taxation. As shown in figure 8.2, this script evolved from a view that taxes, such as income and excise taxes, were too complicated,

---

[11] Tanzi 2014, 29.
[12] Tanzi 1989, 636n8.
[13] Kato 1994; Brownlee 2009.
[14] Kentikelenis and Seabrooke 2017.
[15] Emran and Stiglitz 2004; Stiglitz and Emran 2007; Stiglitz 2010; Stewart 2016.
[16] Steinmo 1993, 199–200; Prasad 2006, 176.
[17] Baunsgaard and Keen 2010.

Figure 8.1 The global spread of the VAT
Source: Ebrill et al. 2001, xiv–xv.

and that relying on tariffs was negative for global economic integration. Tax exemptions were commonplace and part of state–business relationships, and were accepted largely as political realities. This script evolved in the 1990s to a clear view that consumption taxes should replace tariffs, and that income taxes on households and corporations should be simplified and lowered. In the 2000s, following significant efforts from the IMF to spread the VAT— backed by technical assistance—consumption taxes become a key staple of revenue, and exemptions for all tax classes were frowned upon as creating distortions for economies competing under globalization.

The framework in this book helps us to distinguish how scripts are crafted through a combination of politics and science. The intensity of political contention over issues melds with the intensity of scientific consensus on how the issue should be treated by the technocratic parts of the organization. Variations in these intensities tip the balance between more scientized scripts that reflect technocratic preferences on how an issue should be treated, and politicized scripts that reflect great-power political interests that often split along Global North and Global South income lines (see chapter 1). This book explores variation in politics-versus-science contests to write scripts that inform global norms. We can see that when scientific alignment is lacking and political contestation is intense, power politics emerges, often seeking an

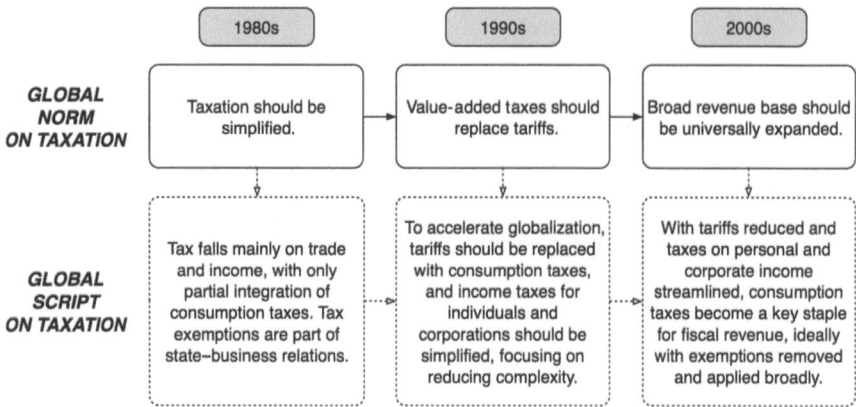

Figure 8.2 Evolution of global norms over taxation

alliance with technocratic interests (see chapter 6 on sovereign debt). When scientific alignment and political contestation are both high, we suggest that script content will either follow congruities between the dominant political interests and the science, or there will be a clash (see chapter 7 on capital controls). This chapter on taxation explores a scenario where scientific alignment is high and political contestation is low, allowing the technocracy to dominate the provision of content for policy scripts and, indeed, have a deep influence on global norms. The IMF's Board only devoted one discussion solely on tax policy over the three decades under study here, meaning that the bulk of Board member statements on tax issues are haphazardly scattered around country-specific discussions and do not add up to a coherently articulated view by the Executive Board.

As this chapter details, the IMF technocracy has significant claims to success in creating a global tax revolution, especially in spearheading the VAT, which has become a bedrock of revenue in more than 130 IMF member states, providing between 20% and 33% of overall fiscal revenue.[18] One explanation for a reliance on the VAT has been that—by virtue of being an indirect tax—it is invisible to many taxpayers, especially in richer economies.[19] The VAT is, however, a contentious tax that frequently invokes political backlash.[20] It must be actively depoliticized, ideally through policy scripts that stress best scientific practice rather than distributional issues. The IMF technocracy has gone to great lengths to 'scientize' the rollout of the VAT across its member states. This chapter traces how the IMF technocracy led the way on reforming fiscal

---

[18] Ebrill et al. 2001; Stotsky and WoldeMariam 2002; Keen and Lockwood 2010.
[19] Wilensky 2002, 363.
[20] Kato 1994; Martin and Gabay 2018.

systems and developing a policy script that has revolutionized taxation across much of the globe, with only encouraging whispers from its Executive Board. In the sole ad hoc Board discussion on tax policy coordination, Muhammad Al-Jasser, a Board member from Saudi Arabia, exemplifies the body's attitude on why the technocrats should provide content for policy scripts on taxation: 'The Fund is the natural institution to undertake such coordination. It has the largest database and an established and accepted mechanism for surveillance.'[21] To put this differently, Vito Tanzi, the longtime director of FAD (1981–2000), publicly noted that the Board 'does not have an official view of tax reform,' and that tax opinions attributed to the IMF must be viewed as staff opinions.[22]

Expectations and Methodological Approach

Few aspects of domestic economic policy are as overtly political as taxation, given that its distributional implications are immediately felt by populations. We should expect the states present on the IMF Board to engage in repeated debates on the organization's tax policy advice, and to seek to closely monitor the activities of its technocrats on these issues. But this expectation was wholly disconfirmed by our examination of the archival record; there was no direct engagement of the Board in the development of the IMF's tax policy prescriptions. The political contestation we expected to encounter was absent. In fact, Board members found little conflict when discussing tax policy scripts, generally encouraging the rolling out and application of the Fund technocracy's standard treatments. Those who were vocal in Board meetings on tax issues were typically junior figures, with 'heavy hitters' rarely intervening. All this speaks to the power of the Fund technocracy in producing policy scripts on tax issues, especially on consumption taxes, that are well elaborated and grounded with economic concepts and models. As we cover in this chapter, such scripts read as literal 'to do' lists with a great amount of detail.[23]

Our empirical strategy for this chapter focused on a close reading of tax-related documents from the IMF technocracy in the Staff Papers, Working Papers, and explicit IMF tax policy handbooks.[24] Because the Fiscal Affairs Department is second highest in its rate of academic and policy production

---

[21] EBM/90/116, 5.
[22] Tanzi 1994, 465.
[23] Tait 1988.
[24] Shome 1995.

within the Fund (only outcompeted by the Research Department; see chapter 5), we knew we had a wealth of material to review. Previous work on IMF tax policy engagement with Australasian and Southeast Asian member states provided examples of how the IMF staff consistently advocated for lowering tariffs, simplifying corporate and personal income taxes, and introducing a broad consumption tax.[25] We consulted Article IV surveillance reports to the Board and various documents on reform progress for the 1980–2009 period to trace the evolution of IMF tax policy scripts. We also knew, from work linking tax issues to loan conditionality, which countries received more tax-related conditions.[26] We delved into Board minutes linked to member states, like Romania and Tanzania, to find most-likely cases where the Board had something to say—but it didn't say much.

Accordingly, unlike the sovereign debt and capital controls cases that precede this one, we have not used word embeddings to locate positions between the technocracy and various professional affiliations held by Global North and Global South Board members. That would be bringing a bazooka to a knife fight, overcomplicating matters for little analytical benefit. Our approach in this chapter relies more on our close reading of relevant policy documents, IMF academic papers, and selected Board minutes.

Taxation and the IMF

A common trope within the IMF is that the organization's acronym stands for 'It's Mostly Fiscal,' meaning that many solutions to member states' economic problems can be addressed through fiscal means, such as public-budget spending cuts and deficit reduction.[27] When considering what is appropriate for a tax system, Tanzi provided the following policy determinants:

> (1) use of particular tax sources (for example, whether a country does or does not use a value-added tax); (2) number of taxes in the country's tax system; (3) level of tax rates; and (4) use of tax incentives and tax expenditures in general.[28]

The IMF's long-term emphasis has been to move taxes away from trade tariffs and toward consumption (ideally a VAT), to reduce the number of taxes in an economy, consider Laffer curve effects when establishing tax rates, and

---

[25] Broome and Seabrooke 2007; Seabrooke 2010.
[26] Reinsberg et al. 2020.
[27] Clift 2018, 1.
[28] Tanzi 1989, 635–36.

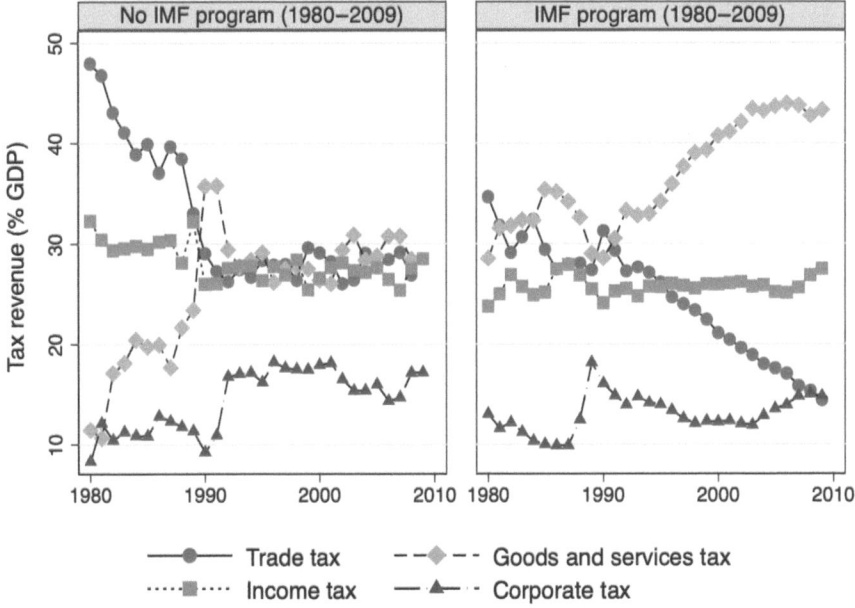

Figure 8.3 Evolution of tax revenues by IMF exposure

Source: Reinsberg et al. 2020, based on 110 IMF program countries and 31 non-IMF program countries.

remove tax incentives that artificially prop up parts of the economy that are unprofitable. The stress within the FAD, and for the IMF more broadly, has been to *simplify* tax systems, making the articulation of tax brackets and exemptions more explainable not only to domestic but also international audiences. The IMF language for tax items it doesn't like typically refers to 'distortions' and 'disincentives.' For example, two of the FAD's key architects said that 'developing countries will need to reduce sharply their reliance on foreign trade taxes, without at the same time creating economic disincentives, especially in raising more revenue from personal income tax.'[29] Once more, a key means of doing this is through the introduction of a VAT.

Research on how IMF programs have transformed tax systems shows that the FAD has been particularly successful in getting its way. A recent study by Bernhard Reinsberg and colleagues demonstrated that while trade taxes have come down in most countries, those with IMF programs have, overwhelmingly, introduced goods and services taxes (i.e., a VAT) to compensate.[30] Figure 8.3 uses their data for 1980–2009. We can clearly see the

[29] Tanzi and Zee 2001.
[30] Reinsberg et al. 2020.

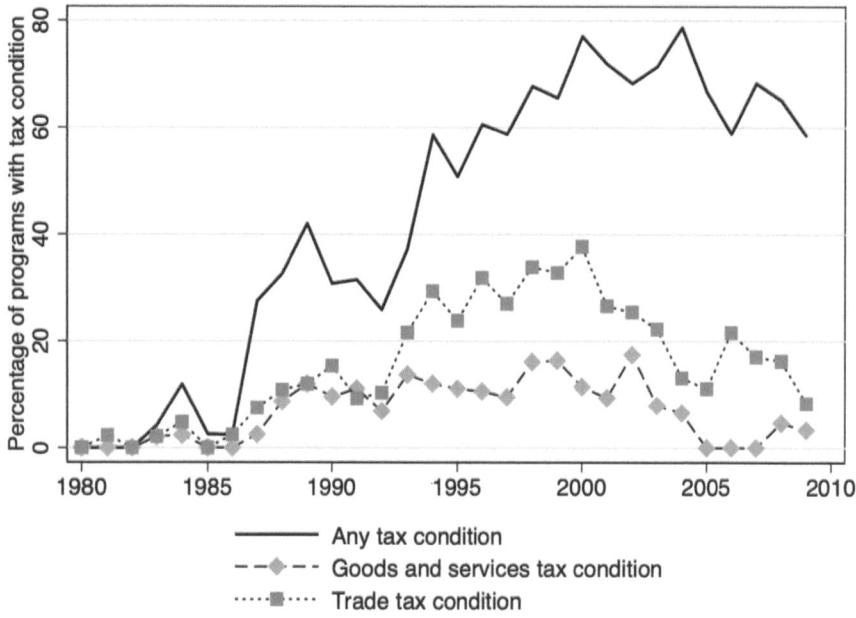

Figure 8.4 The use of tax conditionality in IMF programs over time
Source: Reinsberg et al. 2020.

ascendency of VAT after 1990, following the development of a clear policy script on how it should be rolled out (discussed later in this chapter).[31] This affirms the IMF's view that trade taxes create distortions and should be removed,[32] and that personal income taxes generally should not be increased.[33] Figure 8.3 shows that there is no overall significant increase in revenue but a clear shift in what is being taxed that follows the IMF's formula. Personal income taxes and corporate taxes are kept at steady rates in accordance with Laffer curve logic.

A key issue for the Fund on taxation is that many member states fail to meet their fiscal targets, with 60% of those with IMF loans falling into this category. The problem has been attributed to 'political will' and 'political economy distortions'.[34] Accordingly, the Fund has stressed tax reform as a key element of loan conditionality.[35] Figure 8.4 demonstrates the trends for our period of study: Overall, tax conditions increased, with more than half of programs including them since the mid-1990s. A key element here is the

[31] Tait 1988.
[32] Tait 1989, 7.
[33] IMF 2017b.
[34] Tanzi and Zee 2001; Bird 2003, 94–95.
[35] Reinsberg et al. 2020.

use of conditions to remove trade tariffs, which some developing countries have retained as a source of revenue. The use of loan conditionality for VAT is also common and follows its self-reinforcing logic: Once VAT is introduced and the administrative apparatus for collecting it is in place, it is difficult for countries to backtrack. To solidify the VAT's role in the domestic tax system, the Fund leans heavily on technical assistance to member states.

One notable case of tax conditionality is Tanzania, which stands out as one of the countries with the most tax policy reforms mandated in its IMF loans from 1985 to 2014.[36] Between 1980 and 2009, Tanzania was under no IMF program, and associated policy reforms, for only six years. While prominent staff—notably, Michael Keen, then head of the FAD's Tax Policy and Tax Coordination divisions—was involved in the country's tax reforms, the Executive Board also exerted considerable pressure, as it saw the introduction of VAT as necessary, given the overall insufficient implementation of IMF-mandated reforms in Africa.[37] In 1992, IMF staff intended for Tanzania to implement VAT by 1994, and a FAD technical assistance mission was quickly agreed upon.[38] A few years later, Tanzania entered a series of consecutive IMF lending programs from 1996 until 2006 that mandated and micromanaged the introduction of VAT. During Board discussions over these programs, directors commented on the importance of VAT in relation to other taxes. For example, German Director Donecker, a central banker, noted while the 'so-called Laffer curve approach did not work…a more rapid introduction of the value-added tax would not only improve the revenue situation but also allow a faster reduction of custom tariffs.'[39] Reflecting such views, IMF-mandated policy reforms for Tanzania included a condition for 'VAT legislation to be passed by Parliament' in 1997.[40] This VAT was then introduced in 1998 and subsequently broadened with further IMF technical assistance.

Through loan conditions and technical assistance, the IMF has been successful in transforming tax systems in most regions, with the exception of sub-Saharan Africa, where IMF programs decreased rather than increased revenue.[41] The IMF's technocracy attributes such problems to poor institutional quality, the proliferation of exemptions for political reasons, a lack of training among tax officials, and straightforward corruption.[42] For IMF

---

[36] Kentikelenis and Stubbs 2023.
[37] On the Ghanaian case, see Terkper 1996.
[38] EBS/92/170, 29, 44.
[39] EBM/96/101, 24.
[40] EBS/96/165, 59.
[41] Brun et al. 2011.
[42] Bird and Gendron 2007; Keen and Lockwood 2010.

staff, the solution to these problems was to extend surveillance, heighten the level of administrative and technical training, and advise the IMF Board on what they should include in loan conditions. In short, the answer to tax problem is the technocratic determination of a clear policy script supported by a boots-on-the-ground approach to technical support.

Policy Positioning Among the IMF Staff and Board

The notion that the IMF has a singular mind on what economic models and theories should be pursued, including on fiscal matters, has been dismissed.[43] One way to distinguish how the IMF technocracy treats tax issues is to look at variation in how they advise different types of member states and develop standard treatments to differentiate which economies need a bit more help. A comparison between IMF staff requests and states from the Global North and South is instructive on how scientized scripts are aligned to what is considered possible within types of member states. When the Board does speak, it is to affirm how IMF staff advice should be put into practice in particular member states.

On the Global North, André Broome and one of this book's co-authors provided an early version of content analysis to trace tax advice from the IMF, through standard Article IV consultations, to states in the Global North—in their case, Australia and New Zealand, and Denmark and Sweden.[44] They coded the development of 'IMF-friendly' tax advice, noting advice from the IMF staff and the Board to introduce or simplify a VAT, reduce tariffs, and broaden and simplify income taxes. The New Zealand case provides particular insight into how the IMF thinks. Like Australia, New Zealand was located in the European department in the 1970s until moved to the Southeast Asia and Pacific Department in 1992 (renamed the Asia and Pacific Department in 1997), when the IMF accommodated new Eastern European member states and aligned the Australasian economies more with their geography than their settler cultures.

For New Zealand, IMF staff advocated the introduction of a VAT in the early 1980s and sought to locate tax reform in the context of negotiating a new social compact among the government, employers, and trade unions. The IMF's guidance to domestic policymakers was that they should 'raise the community's awareness of the conflict between the goal of reducing the

---
[43] Clift 2018.
[44] Broome and Seabrooke 2007.

tax burden and that of safeguarding long-standing social preferences for income equity and high levels of welfare.'[45] The New Zealand government's negotiations with trade unions over a 'wage-tax trade-off' had failed, leading them to impose a freeze on wages and prices in 1982, and to reduce top marginal income tax from 66% to 33%. The New Zealand government then requested technical assistance on the design and implementation of its VAT (or GST, goods and services tax),[46] with its representative stating to the Board that their new economic strategy relied on successful tripartite negotiations between the government, employers' associations, and trade unions, that the new VAT would help welfare provision for low-income earners, and that inflation (and wage pressures) would be curtailed. In short, with IMF support, New Zealand's new economic strategy was 'courageous, enlightened and well founded.'[47] A VAT was introduced to New Zealand in 1986. This period of New Zealand's economic history is often referred to as Rogernomics, after Minister of Finance Roger Douglas, who 'made Thatcher look timid' in applying neoliberal economic ideas with negative social outcomes.[48]

In the Australian case, the Fund also advocated a VAT in the 1980s and suggested the same view that it could be part of a new social pact. However, an Australian GST was consistently blocked. Instead, the Australian government enfolded trade unions and the public sector into 'productivity-enhancing reorganization plans from the fiscal bureaus.'[49] While the IMF technocracy continued to complain about the 'excessive complexity of the tax code' and high marginal tax rates,[50] a VAT did not break through until a right-wing government introduced it in 2001.

On the Global South, we can compare how the IMF engaged on tax issues with Southeast Asian member states. In this context, the Philippines and Thailand provide good examples of IMF staff and Board positions. Both countries are especially suitable: The Philippines had eight lending agreements during the period of study (1980–2009), most of them in the 1980s, and Thailand had four, with three in the early to mid-1980s and then one to cope with the Asian financial crisis in 1997. Within these arrangements, the reduction of tariffs, a simplification of personal and corporate taxes, and the introduction of a VAT were all put forward.[51] This is the standard IMF policy script for taxation. What is noteworthy, however, are discussions of how to get

---

[45] SM/83/19, 14.
[46] EBD/85/35.
[47] BUFF/85/103. Statement by Mr. Rye on New Zealand to the IMF Executive Board, June 6, 1985, 4.
[48] Menz 2005. Notably, child poverty increased from 12% in 1988 to 35% in 1994.
[49] Schwartz 1994, 548.
[50] SM/98/211, 12, 14
[51] Seabrooke 2010.

the reforms into place, especially on introducing consumption taxes, which was delayed many times in both countries during the 1980s.

In the Philippines' case, the ongoing inability to implement a VAT and reliance on trade tariffs was a frustration for the IMF staff, until it came into place in 1988. In a staff report on the Philippines in 1988, the IMF note that 'although there has been widespread opposition to the VAT, the Government intends to resist pressure for a weakening of the new tax.'[52] This rare view on politics is of note because the Board also commented that progress in fiscal reform faced the threat of a presidential veto in the Philippines.[53] In other words, both staff and Board note the unpopularity of a VAT and how its success relies on political salience.[54] Part of the notion here is that once VAT is in place, it is subject to less political bargaining, as direct taxes for income and on corporations would be.[55] But the trick is to get it in the statutes in the first place.

In the Thai case, tax reform was included as a key requirement—but not a formal condition—of a 1985 loan that included a VAT. IMF technical assistance was launched, but implementation of the VAT was postponed until 1992 and then introduced, following popular protest, at a rate of 7% rather than the 10% advised by the Fund. The staff commented that the VAT was not introduced in a revenue-neutral manner, but that 'it had been important to set the rate at a level that would gain public acceptance.'[56] Both the Fund staff and the Board noted the importance of elections for the timing of the tax reform, with no major changes taking place before a potential new government, and that tax reforms should be accelerated if earlier elections could be completed.

As to the Board, our scouring of country-specific documents found that the Board supports the IMF staff view on policy scripts for taxation. One note of interest in much of these discussions is the absence of Executive Directors and the prominence of Alternate Directors and Temporary Alternate Directors—the lowest-ranked staff in each constituency's office. There is perhaps no better indicator of a lack of political contention than the absence of heavy hitters. For example, in relation to the cases just presented, only two Executive Directors were present in a 1987 discussion on Thailand, leaving the discussion to alternates. On Thai tax reform, Ian Sliper, a Temporary

---

[52] SM/88/113, 21
[53] EBM/88/34, 38.
[54] Vreeland 2003, 51.
[55] Joshi and Ayee 2008, 208.
[56] SM/92/90, 5.

Alternate Director from New Zealand with a background career in its finance ministry, stated the following:

> The [Thai] authorities are thinking of excluding a range of expenditures from the value-added tax, namely, on food, health care, education, and transportation, which account for about 40% of domestic expenditure. I seriously question the exclusion of so large a group of expenditures, and hope that if the decisions have not been made final, the authorities would reconsider these exclusions.[57]

A Canadian Temporary Alternate Director, Glen Hogdson, then added, 'The planned introduction of a value-added tax, along with a restructuring of personal and corporate income taxes is welcome, although I share Mr. Sliper's questions about the coverage of a value-added tax.'[58] In short, the Board has little to say that does not simply default to the IMF staff's well-known position.

When the Board has intervened, it has been to question the political consequences of VAT universalism. For example, in the Romanian case—which has had 53 revenue and tax policy conditions, including requirements for its parliament to pass tax legislation by certain deadlines[59]—the difficult implementation of VAT in the mid-1990s included many exemptions. The staff sought to wipe these out, leading to concern from Wieslaw Szczuka, an Alternate Director for Poland with a finance ministry background. In a 2000 Executive Board meeting reviewing Romania's progress and the staff's plans, he stated that

> the unification of VAT rates implies an increase from 11% to 19% of the rate for some essential items like basic food products, medical and pharmaceutical products, and urban transportation. Moreover, VAT for energy was increased from zero to 19% at the beginning of the second quarter of 2000. The staff report does not say anything about the likely impact of these rate increases on prices.[60]

But there was little follow-up, which is unsurprising when less politically powerful actors are the only ones complaining. We can see some political action in the Board on the thorny issue of removing tax arrears for enterprises in post-Soviet countries. Tanzi reflected that, in the post-Soviet context, tax arrears were not simply an institutional problem but a political problem.[61] In the Romanian case, tax arrears to enterprises were a hot political topic

---

[57] EBM/87/165, 8.
[58] EBM/87/165, 17.
[59] Kentikelenis and Stubbs 2023.
[60] EBM/00/57, 142
[61] Tanzi 1992; Walder et al. 2015, 452–53.

in Board discussions. In a 2002 discussion on the reasons behind Romania's stalled tax reform, Andy Baukol, US Temporary Alternate Executive Director with a finance ministry background, stated that

> while we understand the staff's desire to streamline conditionality, we are disappointed that it has removed the element of the program pertaining to tax arrears, downgrading it from an indicative target to ongoing monitoring…these arrears produce an uneven playing field for private enterprises and reduce the incentives for tax compliance.[62]

Frank Vermaeten, a Canadian Temporary Alternate Executive Director with (again) a finance ministry background, then piled in, protesting that 'the process is dragged out by an uninspiring privatization team and by public servants that, in the words of the Oxford Analytica report, "exhibit a chronic lack of professionalism."'[63] The practical issue here was that forcing firms to pay their dues would have led to the collapse of many social institutions. The solution was to introduce a tax that was less visible, and to retrain finance ministries and tax departments to collect it. Complaints only from minor shareholders in the Board have simply affirmed the dominance of the Fund technocracy as primary author of IMF tax scripts.

How does the IMF staff get its way with so little comment from the Board? One means of doing so is through the production of standard treatments that are then readily accepted as scientific best practice. An example here is the IMF technocracy's development of 'C-efficiency'. This term—the C stands for Consumption—is 'an indicator of the departure of the VAT from a perfectly enforced tax levied at a uniform rate on all consumption.'[64] A ratio of 1:1 means there are no exemptions and optimal efficiency. A ratio of 0.6:1 is where 40% of goods that could come under a consumption tax are missing, and so on. Key figures in the IMF's FAD based this benchmarking best-practice measure on an ideal type to compare countries and regions.[65] This is explicitly referred to as an 'ideal' or 'normative' VAT system.[66]

How do countries of different income levels do in a C-efficiency test? High-income countries do best, with a consistent ratio of around 60% over a 20-year period. These are the same countries where VAT is imposed at a high rate (around 18% for 1993–2012) and where VAT is the largest share of overall tax revenue (around 7%). Low-income countries do poorly on C-efficiency,

---

[62] EBM/02/89, 123.
[63] EBM/02/89, 126–27.
[64] Keen 2013, 1.
[65] IMF 2013, 29.
[66] Ueda 2017, 7.

due to exemptions that undermine the breadth of the tax base. Notably, some regions, like the Asia-Pacific, Middle East and Central Asia, lowered their C-efficiency in the 1990s.[67] The clear implication here is that to improve VAT as a source of revenue, as is the case in Europe, exemptions must be cut.[68] Standard treatments, like C-efficiency, provide justifications for technocratic best practices and the rollout of VAT.

Scriptwriting Through Technocratic Prowess

The rollout of the VAT is considered, including by its authors, to be an 'unparalleled tax phenomenon' in the postwar capitalist order.[69] How did the IMF technocracy roll out the VAT across its member states to create a global tax revolution? The leading actors in the FAD on VAT-related issues were a group of policy economists—Alan Tait, Vito Tanzi, and Michael Keen—who developed the IMF policy script on VAT. An obituary in *The Times* points to Tait's charismatic leadership within the technocracy as fundamental to the diffusion of the VAT:

> Its spread is due, at least in part, to the leadership provided by Tait. His locus classicus, *Value Added Tax: International Practice and Problems,* is still a respected reference point for any discussions of policy and administrative issues. As much as Tait was a recognized figure in public finance, his contribution to the work of the IMF was also a product of his broad wisdom as an economist, his diplomatic skill, his charm and wit and the breadth of his knowledge and his ability to draw on his wide reading and his experiences gained in travelling and working throughout the world.[70]

Tait's charms worked to great effect, showing how social skill is an important aspect of mobilizing normative change within organizations.[71] Tait was especially important in developing and then proselytizing for a policy script on how to roll out a VAT in about 18 months in any member state.[72] Figure 8.5 displays part of the script. Tait argued that 'the more examples [of the VAT] there are to follow, the less likelihood of mistakes. Legislation and regulations

---

[67] Keen 2013, 5, 9.
[68] The creation of such governance objects, including visualizations for benchmarks, 'risk dashboards,' and the like, has been prominent not only among technocrats but also for activist organizations pursuing tax reform. See Seabrooke and Wigan 2015; Baker and Murphy 2019.
[69] Tait 1988, 3.
[70] *The Times of London* 2009.
[71] Fligstein 2001; Kentikelenis and Babb 2019, 1727.
[72] Tait 1988, 409–16.

APPENDIX II

Chronological Schedule of Work to Be Done to Introduce a VAT in About Eighteen Months

The following timetable sets out broad guidelines for the work that needs to be done month by month starting July 1988 to introduce a VAT by, say, January 1, 1990, and enforce it effectively thereafter. It might be intended as an aide-mémoire for the head of the VAT committee and for the heads of the various subcommittees preparing the VAT. Progress should be monitored regularly to identify any failure that could jeopardize the planning or the proper implementation of the VAT on the target date. It has to be pointed out that while the list may appear reasonably comprehensive, there will inevitably still be many unrecorded auxiliary activities to which attention has to be given if the VAT is to be implemented successfully and on time.

Month	Tasks

By end 1988	1. Settle policy proposals on the scope and the structure of the VAT, including a cost-benefit analysis, and on transitional measures, and obtain the relevant ministerial approval with regard to policy, the funding plan, and so on.
	2. Training subcommittee prepares training plan, identifies training courses and orientation seminars for executives and managers, selects training staff, and identifies the need for other training resources, such as office space, photocopiers, and secretarial support.
	3. Design and present an orientation seminar on the basic principles of VAT for executives and managers at the revenue, customs, and excise departments.
	4. Prepare a course for training all supervisors and operating personnel concerned with the VAT in the revenue and customs departments on the basic principles of VAT operation.
	5. Design VAT return form, VAT payment form, and application form for VAT registration.
	6. Within the revenue department, determine the administrative framework of the VAT, such as detailed procedures for the registration of taxpayers, processing of VAT returns, audit for VAT, and collection procedures.
	7. Start discussion on the extent of computer support in VAT administration and the system's design.
	8. Identify the resource needs for implementation of the VAT, with particular attention to funding and the filling of outstanding vacancies.
	9. Legal subcommittee starts discussion on VAT and drafts laws and basic regulations.
	10. Make final decisions, both within the revenue department and with the customs department, on registration procedures and the incorporation of VAT registration information in the tax master file.
	11. Discuss with the customs department the role of customs in the enforcement of the VAT.
	12. Decide on computer involvement and consequently determine the needs for changes in existing programs and/or the development of new programs.
	13. Determine the broad setup of the administrative system for VAT and examine possible consequences for the organization of the revenue department.
	14. Draft a simple VAT information booklet for press and public use, for distribution in February 1989.
	15. Produce a trial list of potential VAT taxpayers based on the information available in:
	  • The revenue department's computer system (data on business tax and income tax).
	  • The customs department (exporters and importers).
	  • Local manual listings, knowledge and surveys, including press advertisements and telephone directories.
	16. Make a preliminary estimate of staff required in each office to administer the VAT at the beginning of each month as registration, educational visits, collection, enforcement, and verification progress. The estimate should be based on the numbers of likely taxpayers on the list at 15 above.
	17. Begin preparation of a staff manual on the VAT legislation and procedures.
	18. Draft staff manual on VAT registration procedures.
	19. Start preparations for extensive publicity campaign to be held from May 1989, including the production of publicity literature.

January 1989	1. Review all actions to date and monitor progress to identify delays. 2. Complete preliminary draft of the VAT law for full committee review. 3. Give course on VAT principles to relevant supervisors and operating personnel. 4. Design forms for VAT administration. 5. Design general audit policy for VAT. 6. Work out curriculum for VAT auditors' training, determine content of manuals for that training, and select instructors. 7. Establish VAT units in each regional, provincial, district, and area offices.
February 1989	1. Complete drafting of VAT law and submit draft for government approval. 2. Conduct first media campaign to inform the

Figure 8.5 Policy scripts in practice: Introducing the VAT
Note: Only first two pages presented for illustration purposes.
Source: Tait 1988, 409–16.

can be adopted to suit the particular contingencies of a country, but it is better to have half a dozen alternative laws and experiences to start from than none at all.'[73] Tait's script details the need to train subcommittees to educate executives and managers in revenue departments on the design of VAT return forms, computerize data for those in a VAT registration database, systematically collect data on income and corporate taxpayers as well as exporters and importers, prepare legislation for government approval, create a public media campaign, and even address requirements such as access to photocopying equipment. In short, the VAT script became an 'off-the-shelf' policy model.[74] Other Fund technocrats affirmed the importance of the script as a best practice, fostering both cohesion among the ranks and a clear signal to the Board when it was discussed in policy reports. In short, once the VAT could be established as the key tax reform of the postwar period, the 'power of its inner logic is likely to be felt more strongly.'[75]

Part of the logic here is an insistence on scientific best practice that is technical and apolitical while recognizing that welfare concerns have political economy effects. One must recognize that the IMF staff can keep welfare concerns in mind while seeking to develop a universal approach to scientific best practice.[76] IMF staff recognized that a country's tax/GNP ratio is a political choice, and they sought to offer tax advice that provides a stable revenue stream without aggravating intergenerational equity concerns. The staff supported the VAT because it is 'grounded on solid microeconomic foundations [...and is] capable of addressing also normative issues.'[77]

The Fund's technocrats also prefer the VAT because it is relatively easy to collect, with half of this tax collected in developing countries at the border,[78] and because it supports a reduction in trade tariffs and the embrace of economic globalization—ideally with a system of no capital controls.[79] In short, the VAT affirms trade and capital openness. Making the VAT *the* policy script for IMF member states is a way of automating some revenue stability into globalization in a manner that allows feathers to be extracted without too much squawking.

Greater scientization and less politicization has helped standard tax policies to be rolled out via IMF staff and external experts who shared the same rationalization. Indeed, the power of the VAT policy script also lies in its capacity to be implemented by professionals other than those in the IMF.[80]

---

[73] Tait 1988, 25.
[74] James 2015, 41
[75] Ebrill et al. 2001, 1999.
[76] Clift 2018.
[77] Frenkel and Razin 1988, 19.
[78] Baunsgaard and Keen 2010, 564.
[79] Zee 2000.
[80] A parallel here can be found in the diffusion of bankruptcy scripts; see Halliday and Carruthers 2009.

The Fund's preferred policy script has been implemented not only by IMF staff but also by hired professionals.[81] This further affirmed a consensus, with the OECD supporting the IMF's script, encouraging an overall 'impression that a consensus had been formed and that fiscal reform should be technical rather than political.'[82] The indoctrination of officials from former Soviet economies has also been important here, especially at the Joint Vienna Institute, which was established in 1992 and has since trained more than 50,000 officials to follow IMF scripts (see chapter 5).[83] Where variations have emerged, notably 'flat tax' experiments in some former Soviet economies, the IMF has objected, with Tanzi dismissing flat taxes as inappropriate for countries going through significant economic transitions.[84] Importantly, the 'baking in' of the VAT within the European Union—a high C-efficiency performer—means that countries that wish closer economic integration with the European Community have an additional incentive to implement a broad and universal consumption tax.[85] In general, while the Fund technocracy holds the pen in developing global tax scripts like the VAT, the implementation also relies on external professional networks and affirming political pressures that further embed the script as an appropriate rationalization.

Conclusion

What does the IMF's rollout of the VAT as a global tax revolution tell us about scriptwriting within IOs? In stark contrast to the chapters on sovereign debt (chapter 6) and capital controls (chapter 7), the taxation case exhibits the maximalist version of scientization and the minimalist version of political contestation. It would appear that the Fund's technocracy knows the key game at play in the political economy on taxation: how to extract the most feathers from the population with the least squawking. Taxation is a clear case where the technocratic arm of an IO provides intellectual leadership on a policy solution and then aggressively scientizes it to make it appear technical and nonpolitical. We would not have this finding if we treated taxation as only a politically distributive issue that state representatives care about. Getting to our finding requires digging into the technocracy machinery.

The FAD has promoted the value-added tax as a technical and nonpolitical solution to meet the twin challenge of taxation in a globalized economy:

[81] Shome 1995; Tait 1988.
[82] Appel 2011, 34.
[83] Broome and Seabrooke 2015.
[84] Appel 2011, 111.
[85] Gehlbach 2008, 26.

to encourage member states to drop their tariffs and economically integrate trade and capital flows, while having a robust fiscal base to be able to invest in human and physical capital and withstand exogenous shocks. For the FAD, this meant promoting the elimination of tariffs, the simplification and reduction of personal and corporate income taxes, and the introduction of a consumption tax—the VAT—that should be as broad and universal as possible.

As this chapter has shown, the Fund technocracy has succeeded in its mission. The global norm on taxation has changed from being reliant on tariffs and exemptions that reflected state–business compromises, to the introduction of a consumption tax as a pillar of revenue-generation, and then the removal of tax exemptions to broaden and universalize principles for revenue collection. The IMF technocracy's use of concepts like C-efficiency have helped propel an 'ideal' or 'normative' consumption tax system,[86] spotlighting how the Global North is more efficient and stable compared to the Global South and its exemptions.

case of taxation also shows how a scientized best practice can lead to Board inattention. While we know that tax-related conditions have increased,[87] the Board doesn't have much to say on tax issues, and certainly nothing that counters the script presented by the IMF staff. When the Board does speak up on taxation, it is normally about the need to eliminate exemptions and tax arrears to propel privatization, or to hasten implementation of the VAT. And those who speak, as detailed earlier, are most commonly minor players on the Board. The heavy hitters rarely speak out on taxation.

In sum, the case of taxation is one where the IMF technocracy successfully developed a policy script on a highly distributive politico-economic issue—what taxes should be paid and who should pay them—that the Board endorses with little question. Certainly, we can attribute some of this consensus to the fact that it propels economic integration, separates the state and business clearly, and provides no challenge to dominant class interests within or across societies. The proselytization of IMF tax policy, epitomized by the VAT, shows how norms can be transformed by forms of scientization that do not threaten global capitalism.

[86] Ueda 2017, 7.
[87] Reinsberg et al. 2020.

PART IV
EXTENSIONS

9
Politics Versus Science Across Global Organizations

Introduction

Our goal in this book is a simple one: to examine how struggles between politics and science over policy scripts in international organizations (IOs) help us understand how global norms are codified and eventually changed. In the contemporary period of economic and political globalization, several apex organizations have an outsized influence on how norms are determined and guided. These organizations dedicate their time to developing policy scripts that operationalize norms and help diffuse them worldwide. Our empirical focus has been on the International Monetary Fund (IMF), a central actor in global economic governance. On the issues discussed in the empirical chapters—sovereign debt, capital controls, and taxation—the IMF is *the* international organization that, in the postwar period, has had a mandate to develop policy scripts in the interests of all member states. This has legitimated the expansion of a technocracy of scientific professionals to feed into the development of these scripts, and an Executive Board of political representatives, also highly trained in economics, to negotiate precise script content.

The intensity of preferences among Board members matters. Here, our innovation is that—in contrast to much scholarship—we ought not understand these individuals simply as state representatives. This is only one part of their identity. The other part derives from their own professional and educational backgrounds, which offer individuals distinct ways of viewing policy problems and the world. In turn, these political and expert identities can and do show up when these individuals perform their duties. This means that merely examining global normmaking with reference to the positions of participants from the Global North or South is inadequate. The types of knowledge and expertise participants in normmaking have are also important determinants for the decisions they make. The implication is that Boards with different mixes of expertise will likely reach different decisions, even

Making Global Norms. Alexandros Kentikelenis and Leonard Seabrooke, Oxford University Press.
© Oxford University Press (2025). DOI: 10.1093/9780197828656.003.0009

if the underlying voting shares remain the same. Thus, echoing recent calls for more attention to individuals in global governance,[1] we direct academic attention to these microfoundations of global normmaking.

In our approach, the focus on the micro-level is not an analytical endpoint, but a central building block toward explaining macro-level institutional change. Making this micro-to-macro connection has long been a challenge for social scientists,[2] one that requires a recursive logic. Initially, we are interested in how global norms are reflected from the macro-level of institutions all the way down to the individuals that enact their vernacularized variants. Once we know these individuals' attributes, we can then piece together how they work toward generating new versions of these norms—though accompanying scripts—and thus change important planks of globalization along the way. We show how these individuals come together at the meso-level: the organizational structures where different types of actors negotiate. The outcome of these negotiations—new or modified scripts codifying appropriate policy—then forms part of the evolving macro-level normative apparatus of globalization that is diffused anew to students and professionals who will carry these ideas with them when they are called on to participate in global normmaking. These processes obviously take years or decades, and our theoretical and methodological approach helps bridge this long arc of global normmaking.

Our case studies show variation in how scripts are made according to differences in political contestation and scientific consensus. We demonstrate how common assumptions about state preferences, typically expressed as battles between member states of different income levels (the Global North and Global South), are conditioned by whether there is scientific consensus within the technocracy, as well as the amount of political and scientific contestation among board members. Our broader point here is that it would be simple to posit that policy scripts for sovereign debt follow creditor-versus-debtor dynamics, or that a script on capital controls follows capital-open versus capital-closed dynamics, or that one on taxation follows rich-versus-poor-country dynamics. Our approach posits that these proxies can be correct, but we also cannot rely on them without leaning too heavily on priors. Our commitment to abductive reasoning also tells us that while good guesses and mastery of the literature are essential, we should engage in empirical analyses with a theoretical and empirical framework versatile enough to surprise us.[3] In the empirical chapters, we have shown that, as a general argument for

---

[1] Copelovitch and Rickard 2021; Clark and Zucker 2023; Heinzel et al. 2024; Lang et al. 2024.
[2] Collins 1981b.
[3] Timmermans and Tavory 2022.

how IOs work, the prevalent 'Global North versus Global South' explanatory lens simply misses too much of the variation, underestimating the role of professional socialization among Board members while underplaying the role of technocracy in providing standard treatments that guide script content as it passes the Board's eyes.

In the case of sovereign debt (chapter 6), we showed that some overlap existed between technocratic recommendations and those from Board members with central-banking career backgrounds, regardless of whether they were from the Global North or the Global South. By contrast, Board members with careers that embedded them in national economic policy, like finance ministry posts and political appointments, split along creditor-versus-debtor positions reflecting the Global North or South. Overall, the clustering of arguments and opinions on the Board reflects their professional backgrounds as much as it does their political-representation function. In this sense, Board members are dual loyalists. The evolution of this policy script into a position that debt can be canceled when accompanied by significant additional technocratic surveillance reflects politics-versus-science interactions in the Board, particularly central bankers seeing eye to eye on the logic of scientized technocratic extension over sovereign debt management.

Chapter 7 provided the case on capital controls, where an intended policy script from the IMF technocracy faced significant Board opposition. While Fund staff drew from economic theories on the benefits of liberalization, the issue was highly contentious within the Board, with a sharp division between Global North and Global South officials, especially from those with finance ministry and political appointee backgrounds. A technocratic attempt to amend the Fund's Articles of Agreement to include capital account liberalization was blocked, leading to a reversion to more ad hoc regulation of the capital account in line with the Fund's original Articles and the wishes of many states from the Global South. In this case, Global North versus Global South dynamics provide the broader contours of the story, but the rejection of technocratic scientific sequencing of capital liberalization, as part of normal market-institution evolution, provides a finer explanation.

The case of taxation in chapter 8 provides a clear example of how strong scientific alignment within a technocracy can determine the content of a policy script with little manipulation from the Board. The IMF is the key agent behind the global tax revolution of rolling out consumption taxes—namely the value-added tax (VAT)—across its member states. The VAT has been pushed to meet two objectives. The first is to encourage member states to drop trade tariffs and integrate flows of goods and capital to propel economic globalization. The second is to support states in building fiscal resilience so they can invest in human and physical infrastructure, as well as cope with exogenous shocks from the global economy. Led by key figures in the Fiscal Affairs Department (FAD), the IMF technocracy developed a policy script to drop tariffs, simplify personal and corporate taxes, and introduce a broad and universal VAT. On all of this the Board had little to say, other than occasional interventions from minor Global North officials, with those having finance ministry backgrounds (*again*) pushing for faster reforms. In sum, the taxation case shows that coherent scientization can preempt or neutralize political contestation at the global level.

In the remainder of this concluding chapter, we seek to spell out the scope conditions of our arguments and outline how this work advances theoretical frontiers within the social sciences on how global norms are made. We conclude by reflecting on current and future challenges pressing IOs' capacity to create policy scripts that can influence global norms.

Internal Validity

Given our empirical focus on the IMF, how does our framework apply beyond our selected timeframe (1980–2009)? Recent work on the IMF has pointed to how the technocracy and the Board have consistently expanded the organizational remit to a growing array of policies that are now legitimated as 'macro-critical' and therefore covered by the Fund's mandate.[4] Thus, the IMF's traditional focus on fiscal and monetary policy, debt, and the financial sector is now joined by a more hands-on engagement with issues of inequality, gender, and the environment. To achieve this, the Fund has explicitly discussed since 2009 how creating policy space is important for its member, especially those the Global South.[5] This policy space is fostered through a focus on macroeconomic stability, the stabilization of fiscal revenue sources, and (purportedly) more customized program conditions for member states with IMF loans. However, available evidence suggests that a fundamental transformation in post-2009 programs did not occur, and that classic structural adjustment measures—such as economic deregulation and privatization—actually increased since 2008.[6] The IMF's 2017 introduction of a new Policy Coordination Instrument to allow closer dialogue between itself and member states follows the logic of developing policy space through

---

[4] Van Waeyenberge et al. 2013; Clift 2018; Clift and Robles 2021; Ramos et al. 2022; Kentikelenis and Stubbs 2025.
[5] IMF 2009.
[6] Kentikelenis et al. 2016.

flexibility, with no qualification criteria, 'but countries would have to commit to policies strong enough to constitute the basis for a Fund-supported [conditional lending] program.'[7] This is an example of the Fund's tendency to add 'ever-more layers of ceremonial reforms and rhetoric.'[8]

What has changed is that the Fund places more stress on 'resilience' and the identification of 'political economy' issues. The creation of a Resilience and Sustainability Trust in 2021 explicitly notes the need to augment policy space, to allow member states to adjust to 'spillovers from geopolitical shocks, and long-standing structural problems.'[9] The Fund's own flagging of political economy in recent years includes an interest in issues like climate change, money laundering and terrorism, gender diversity, and more long-standing concerns like central bank transparency and poverty reduction. We return to how the Fund has integrated climate change later on in this chapter. But first, we must consider how the cases presented in chapters 6 to 8 have been treated in recent years. We begin with sovereign debt, follow with capital controls, and end with taxation.

On sovereign debt, the development of the debt sustainability analysis (DSA) toolkit discussed in chapter 5 is an example of a standard treatment developed by the IMF technocracy and then embedded in Highly Indebted Poor Countries (HIPC) and the Enhanced HIPC Initiative, discussed in chapter 6. The DSA grew out of the IMF's structural-adjustment lending facilities and required extensive negotiations and compromises on the part of Board members, who leaned on their professional backgrounds to align with the IMF-proposed technocratic extensions. The DSA has been undergoing transformations and ever-greater expansions in what it will cover and how. For example, in 2021 the IMF Board approved the awkwardly titled Market Access Countries Sovereign Risk and Debt Sustainability Framework (MAC SRDSF) for member states with ready access to international capital markets.[10] This framework includes a new template for Sovereign Risk and Debt Sustainability Analysis. The recognition and codification of peculiarities of market-access countries versus those without market access has also led to an extension of the technocratic infrastructures: The IMF bureaucracy developed a public-facing, open-access tool for experimentation with different debt scenarios and modification of debt sustainability assumptions. This is an IMF attempt at making its scientized logic more transparent[11] while

---

[7] IMF 2017a, 5.
[8] Kentikelenis et al. 2016, 546.
[9] IMF 2022b, 1.
[10] IMF 2022c.
[11] Tallberg et al. 2013.

providing resources to interested publics on how to use the MAC SRDSF 'to detect and discourage overly optimistic debt, fiscal, and macroeconomic projections.'[12]

On capital controls, the failed deregulation attempts of the late 1990s (discussed in chapter 7) did not lead to the abandonment of interest in capital liberalization among the Fund technocracy. In the years following the Asian financial crisis, the IMF took up the issue of capital controls again, only to ultimately reach an altogether different conclusion. In 2012, the IMF published a new 'institutional view' on 'capital flow management measures.'[13] Unlike the organization's previous self-assured condemnations of capital controls, the new view begrudgingly acknowledged that they have a role to play as a macroeconomic management tool, even though they are generally still best avoided and should only be temporary measures en route to ever-greater capital account liberalization.[14] In his analyses of how this institutional volte-face came about, Kevin Gallagher highlights the political contention emanating from rising powers within the IMF (most notably the BRICS countries: Brazil, Russia, India, China, and South Africa), as well as the role of scientific advances. On the latter issue, the IMF technocrats imported insights from the 'new welfare economics' and econometric methods in order to develop a new policy script that was more tolerant of the use of capital controls; these script changes could be achieved 'because they were founded in a fundamental new breakthrough in economic science.'[15] Similar to our account, here we have a complex interplay between politics and science, with geopolitical rebalancing and scientific developments being reflected in new global norms that were gradually codified in the new policy script.

On taxation (chapter 8), while staff from the FAD demonstrated enough intellectual flexibility to rethink fiscal policies more commonly associated with demand management, through the ideational vector of fiscal space,[16] core post-2009 Fund views reflect a staunch technocratic continuity on the VAT. This was the case despite serious modifications to global norms on other taxes, especially information exchange on corporate taxation.[17] But the IMF's position is not surprising, given how the Board barely mentioned taxation while the staff developed an ironclad policy script to diffuse through technical assistance, loan programs, and training. Recent Fund work points,

[12] IMF 2022c, 7.
[13] IMF 2012.
[14] Gallagher and Ocampo 2013.
[15] Gallagher 2015b, 27; 2014, 2015a; Ban and Gallagher 2015.
[16] Ban 2015; Clift 2018; Ban and Patenaude 2019.
[17] Christensen and Hearson 2019.

predictably, to the elimination of VAT exemptions and reducing VAT fraud, including the release of a new 'How To' series of policy notes from the FAD.[18] The encouragement of a standard VAT rate with broad and universal application is still the mantra, with current technocratic production referring to the heyday of VAT scriptwriting highlighted in chapter 8. The C-efficiency measure is still included as a basic metric.[19] It is with little irony that IMF staff note, in a discussion of the relative benefits of a VAT compared to retail sales tax, that the 'economic and practical advantages of the VAT are also illustrated by revealed preferences, as most governments use a VAT.'[20] The reliance on VAT by governments in the Global South would likely look very different if the IMF had not persistently and forcefully worked toward diffusing this policy script around the world, as we discussed in chapter 8.

In short, these recent developments provide hints for how the analyses presented in chapters 6 to 8 could, with sufficient access to the underlying staff documents and boardroom transcripts, be rerun for the post-2009 period. The abductive logic of discovery would still hold for this extended period, and incorporating new data would allow us to interrogate the previous findings. In line with our insistence on abductive reasoning, we cannot state that the exact same result would be replicated with perfect certainty. That's the point. But our 'good guesses' on what we expect to find from the technocracy, Global North and Global South Board members, and professional clusters within the Board provide excellent starting points for studying the processes and interactions that compose scriptwriting. They can provide the springboard for structured, focused comparisons that illuminate the ever-changing nature of global normmaking.

The three cases presented in this book cover different combinations of political contention and scientific consensus, as illustrated in figure 1.2. What did not receive any treatment, however, is the quadrant of low scientific consensus and low political contention—issues where the science is not settled and the politics largely absent. Yet even in these instances our framework can offer empirical entry points for theoretically informed explanation. Consider climate change: Until relatively recently, this issue was mostly absent from discussions of global economic governance and the IMF mandate. The treatment of this policy problem from a macroeconomic perspective was broadly limited, and state representatives at the IMF did not thematize it, as it was broadly considered foreign to the IMF remit. Indicatively, the IMF's 2003

---

[18] Andrew and Baer 2023.
[19] Benitez et al. 2023, 10.
[20] Swistak and Vernon 2023, 5n4.

Annual Report mentioned the terms 'environment' and 'climate' 4 times,[21] the 2013 Report again 4 times, and the 2023 Report 37 times. What was previously a marginal issue is now prominent. How has this happened?

To be sure, the consequences of climate change have become increasingly visible in recent years, which has prompted the IMF—and many other IOs—to increase their engagement. But this is not an adequate explanation; the fact that climate change poses existential threats to humanity has been the subject of many rounds of prominent climate negotiations since at least the 1990s.[22] What explains the IMF's rising interest in the last decade or so? We cannot do justice to this story here,[23] but we posit that the core claims advanced in this book are also applicable to this case. First, the issue was taken up by IMF member states, which used institutional avenues to push the Board to engage with it. The first IMF Board discussion dedicated to the environment was in the context of a seminar on 'The Fiscal Implications of Climate Change' in 2008, which senior members of the Board chose to skip; only four participants were Executive Directors. In 2015, the Board returned to these questions by holding a debate on 'Addressing Global Climate Change—The Role of the Fund.' This coincides with the efforts of then–Managing Director Christine Lagarde to raise the profile of climate issues within the IMF by branding them as 'macro-critical.'[24] Over the subsequent years, this topic gained further traction on the Board, culminating in the decision to integrate climate change into IMF surveillance missions in May 2021,[25] the development of a new 'Strategy to Help Members Address Climate Change Related Policy Challenges' that July,[26] and the seminal introduction that November of the Resilience and Sustainability Facility to provide financing to deal with long-term challenges like climate change.[27] All these were developments that the Board had to debate and approve, and thus also represented spaces for high-level politics to take place.

Second, staff also showed a growing scientific interest in the macroeconomic impacts of climate change. Perhaps unsurprisingly, the main initial entry point for such engagement was fiscal.[28] Countries' reliance on energy subsidies was identified as inappropriate, as they had negative fiscal and

---

[21] Excluding mentions of the term in an economic context, like 'global economic environment,' 'policy environment,' or 'business climate.'
[22] Gupta 2014.
[23] See Gallagher et al. 2021; Skovgaard 2021; TCDIMF 2021; Kentikelenis et al. 2022; Ramos et al. 2022; Kentikelenis and Stubbs 2025.
[24] Lagarde 2015.
[25] IMF 2021b.
[26] IMF 2021a.
[27] IMF 2021c.
[28] Skovgaard 2021.

environmental consequences: Staff saw subsidies as draining the public budget, while simultaneously shielding consumers from the true price of carbon, and thus supporting overconsumption that leads to higher emissions.[29] Consequently, the IMF set out to develop policy scripts on how to phase out energy subsidies, a policy seen as operationalizing global norms on fiscal management and climate-friendly economic policies. The IMF bureaucracy eventually started a publication series called 'Staff Climate Notes,' delivered online courses on environmental issues, and sought to upgrade the technical skill set of existing staff with climate-relevant economic tools. In short, it worked to infuse global climate change norms with its own scientized economic logic—one that emphasizes market mechanisms while muting alternative or complementary approaches like green industrial policies or green research-and-development subsidies.[30]

Whether the staff or the Board was taking the lead in 'greening' the IMF is not something we can adjudicate here. Similarly, we cannot pronounce judgment on the internal conflicts over the development of the relevant scripts. The available data on these questions are still classified. But future analyses of these issues can use the analytical lenses provided here to begin to explain what happened. In doing so, such accounts can also illuminate how low-scientific-consensus, low-political-contestation issues can become more scientifically and politically contested over time, and what implications this has for normmaking and scriptwriting in these areas.

External Validity

This volume has built up a theoretical apparatus that we systematically applied to three instances of scriptwriting within the IMF. This immediately begs the question: How representative is this organization of the broader universe of global governance institutions? To be sure, the IMF stands out for the financial resources, epistemic authority, and convening power it has. Indeed, these characteristics are what make it such an appropriate empirical setting for theory building and methodological innovation. Its centrality within global governance surfaces political and scientific dynamics that might remain obscure in other organizational environments, hidden behind lack of academic scrutiny, opaque archival access policies, and layers of jargon. But this is not to say that they are absent from other global organizational settings.

---

[29] Clements et al. 2013.
[30] Kentikelenis and Stubbs 2025.

We propose that our theoretical argument and methodological approach can be exported to the study of a range of other empirical cases. Moreover, following our arguments in chapter 3, we suggest that applying our model with abductive reasoning can reveal new information—even surprises—rather than only working deductively to theory-test, or inductively to build cases from the ground up.

We contend that any organization involved in scriptwriting and steered by a governing body can be analyzed through our model, given access to sufficient data on board composition, careers, and content of board deliberations. As previously noted, our framework works best with regularity: when there is scheduled political representation by board members, and when there is a well-staffed technocracy capable of establishing a scientific consensus. This is the case for prominent IOs, and certainly those regarded by member states as performing well and capable of producing their own policy scripts.[31] The challenge in locating politics-versus-science struggles is data availability, given that many organizations have extensive minutes from their own governing body meetings but do not publicly disclose them. Pushes from activist organizations to access these meetings are admirable,[32] and making transcripts accessible to researchers would enable exploring how scriptwriting occurs as a politics-versus-science process across a range of issue areas and global norms.

Our framework has four extensions. The first is a straightforward application to cases where board meetings set policy within singular organizations. The most obvious cases are those of the large group of apex intergovernmental organizations that—similarly to the IMF—are governed by a board of directors.[33] This is the case, for example, for the World Health Organization, which has 34 'technically qualified members,' and for many UN specialized agencies. It is also the case for the important (and relatively unexplored) regional development banks.[34] For example, the Asian Development Bank, European Investment Bank, and Inter-American Development Bank all name the executives attending their board meetings. Matching the executives to political and scientific preferences is possible in all these cases, and likely to reveal previously undiscovered forms of politicking, as well as reliance on different aspect of world culture.

A second obvious application is to large international nongovernmental organizations (NGOs), like Greenpeace or Oxfam, which typically comprise

---

[31] Lall 2023.
[32] Tallberg et al. 2013.
[33] Martinez-Diaz 2009.
[34] Park and Strand 2015; Kentikelenis and Babb 2022; Park 2022.

national chapters and a secretariat. These are venues for struggles between politics and science, with clashes where science points in a particular direction but power dynamics make national chapter representatives object. Although less able to compel compliance, these organizations can still heavily influence the content of policy scripts.[35] In the case of Amnesty International, the professionalization of the bureaucracy is considered by the first generation of activists as hollowing out the organization's purpose and conceding on issues to retain funding.[36] Or, to take different examples, Human Rights Watch chose to be inactive on the issue of conscription, and the International Committee of the Red Cross on 'future combat systems,' because it would politically associate them with peace movements and harm relations with the US.[37] Pressures on these organizations, mainly political, force many to develop their 'advocacy niche' for survival.[38] In cases where NGO gatekeepers can be circumvented, such action relies on transnational professional networks, often science-based ones, in which professionals assert issue control over what script content is appropriate.[39]

A third application is to standard-setting organizations that rely on deliberation and technical expertise. Jean-Christophe Graz's work on 'hybrid authority' in the International Standards Organization shows how the ISO 9000 standard—often seen as a sticker on the back of trucks—is a quality management system developed in the UK that was then diffused through the ISO and its 160 national-standard-body members.[40] The interplay of politics and science here is straightforward: Those who can get a scientific standard in place that becomes a requirement for engaging globalization gain political leverage. Indeed, this is what others have found with ISO 9000, arguing that it permits powerful states and multinational enterprises to enforce a coercive isomorphism around foreign direct investment, in which 'scientific and technical knowledge provides a normative template.'[41] In such cases, who has the right to attend and deliberate at a body's meetings—and who can afford to be in the ISO meeting rooms in Geneva—is of relevance.

In this vein of research, Susan Block-Lieb and Terence Halliday's ethnographic accounts of standard setting in the United Nations Commission on International Trade Law, on items such as determining insurance liabilities for goods carried over oceans, show that it is not only which member-state

---

[35] Stroup and Wong 2017.
[36] Hopgood 2006.
[37] Carpenter 2011.
[38] Eilstrup-Sangiovanni 2023.
[39] Breen and Eilstrup-Sangiovanni 2023.
[40] Graz 2019.
[41] Guler et al. 2002.

representatives show up to the meetings that counts, but also the capacity to exhibit technical prowess and establish a credible reputation among peers.[42] Other examples of politics-versus-science battles can be seen in supranational standard-setting bodies across a range of areas, including accounting and finance.[43] Similar dynamics can also be found in organizations engaged in global benchmarking,[44] which involves both politics versus science within their respective meeting rooms and also outside shenanigans from global consultancies.[45]

Fourth, a similar logic applies to multistakeholder forums, which blend private, public, and civil society organizations to create best practices in transnational governance.[46] A common view in this literature is that transnational boards provide 'clear infrastructures for coordinated political action,'[47] often to legitimize private interests. We also know from this literature that negotiations among those involved often lead to the thinning of hard-law governance, with a preference for soft-law governance that follows privatized best practices. Luc Fransen and Genevieve LeBaron's example of the role of the Big Four global accounting firms (Deloitte, Ernst & Young, KPMG, and PriceWaterhouseCoopers) in determining modern slavery regulations and standards is an especially striking example where 'scientific' auditing best practices erode formal political accountability, to the benefit of private interests.[48]

Theoretical Frontiers

Our model of scriptwriting enriches scholarship on IOs by unpacking change at different levels of aggregation.[49] Specifying the politics and science beneath what becomes rationalized and diffused allows us to understand how norms can be contested, even if the overall framework of global capitalism is not. An even deeper dive into the Board members could establish if they belong to left or right political ideologies,[50] but such information should be moderated by their professional socialization, as we've shown earlier.

---

[42] Block-Lieb and Halliday 2017.
[43] Mattli and Büthe 2005; Seabrooke and Stenström 2023.
[44] Broome and Quirk 2015; Kelley and Simmons 2019.
[45] Broome 2022; Tsingou 2022.
[46] Fransen 2012.
[47] Bartley 2018, 149.
[48] Fransen and LeBaron 2019.
[49] Beckfield 2010.
[50] Copelovitch and Rickard 2021.

One gripe against our work may be that we've taken a rather one-dimensional approach toward the science part of our explanation—science is simply 'there' in academic economics and other university departments as well as in different professional fields, and from there it finds its way into the development of policy through the individuals who enact it. While this reduces complexity in our account, a reasonable objection would point to science itself being infused by political struggles and power asymmetries.

One point of departure here is that available science is limited to what is thought to be politically acceptable. We know, anecdotally, a case in which a left-wing government sending a representative to the IMF Executive Board chose a neoclassical economist, rather than a more heterodox bedfellow, because they thought it was the only way the representative's peers would view them as credible. We can speculate that there is a shadow of hegemony in what science can be brought to the table. That is, what is seen as legitimate knowledge in different global governance settings carries the imprint of politics, and reflects the functioning of hegemony: Major powers seek to institutionalize their way of interpreting the world, identifying policy problems and spelling out acceptable solutions.[51] For example, Annabelle Littoz-Monnet has demonstrated how expertise on global mental health issues is exclusive and circular, and how the WHO's strategy to address the burden of mental health issues in the Global South is funneled through Western psychiatric categories, including those that are heavily contested in the Global North.[52] Such situations come at the expense of alternative ways of viewing the same issues from other actors. To draw on a case study of this volume, how one views capital account liberalization depends on where one sits: Global South representatives, painfully aware of the highly destabilizing periodic capital flight from their countries, were highly skeptical of the arguments, legitimated through academic prestige, that the IMF's technocrats and their Global North counterparts brought to the table.

Our empirical account hinted at some of these dynamics by documenting the lack of educational diversity among key IMF policymakers. Despite the highly diverse national origins of IMF Board members, about half of them studied in the US or the UK; a quarter in elite universities therein. What does this monoculture mean for decisions taken, and what are the chances that it can engage with ideas and arguments that have diverse origins? This is question relevant not only to the IMF but to the whole of global governance. For example, a constant ideational struggle within global public

---

[51] Haas 1990; Kentikelenis et al. 2023.
[52] Littoz-Monnet 2022, 16.

health pertains to forms of knowledge that emphasize a security approach toward health—primarily articulated in and by institutions in the Global North and reflecting anxieties over potential spread of disease from South to North—versus approaches to health that are homegrown in the Global South and emphasize the strengthening of domestic primary healthcare systems as the main tools to protect global health and limit the spread of infections.[53] It is hard not to see these struggles over what is the appropriate scientific approach toward safeguarding health without reference to colonial dynamics and global power asymmetries.[54]

A second concern with our account could be that it is simply not complex enough to capture the current state of affairs in global governance. As Mette Eilstrup-Sangiovanni and Oliver Westerwinter have recently documented, a growing range of policy spheres—from the environment to public health, and from intellectual property rights to civil aviation—are governed by 'clusters of overlapping institutions and actors.'[55] Our explicit attempt in this volume was to add multiple layers to how we understand global normmaking within one organization, but what happens when normmaking boundaries are porous, and multiple organizations—whether solely multilateral, or a mix of governmental, nongovernmental, and intergovernmental—are involved in the relevant processes?

Global governance complexes are also centrally concerned with devising norms and scripts on their mandated policy areas, but analytical dissection of their underlying processes is more difficult. Consider the case of global health.[56] The complex underpinning it includes—at minimum—the WHO, the World Bank (in particular, its Health, Nutrition and Population Global Practice), the Global Vaccine Alliance (Gavi), and the Global Fund Against AIDS, Tuberculosis and Malaria, as well as purely private initiatives, most notably the Gates Foundation. A range of additional organizations, like the UN Children's Fund (UNICEF), UNWomen, and UNAIDS, also have core functions that impinge on global health. The WHO is not even necessarily at the epicenter of relative normmaking and scriptwriting; indeed, institutions like UNAIDS or Gavi emerged partly in response to perceived failures of the WHO. Moreover, the Gates Foundation and other private foundations bankroll many global health initiatives. This is clearly a world of more distributed governance far removed from the case

---

[53] Wenham 2019; Wenham et al. 2023.
[54] Harris and White 2019; White 2020, 2023; Devakumar et al. 2022.
[55] Eilstrup-Sangiovanni and Westerwinter 2022, 233.
[56] Hanrieder 2015; Clinton and Sridhar 2017.

of the IMF and its undisputed centrality within the sphere of global financial governance.

How are we to make sense of these dynamics? The theoretical and empirical challenge becomes one of aggregation. Each organization involved has to deal with its own internal political and scientific struggles while engaging with other organizations that—unsurprisingly—have different priorities and perspectives. But this is not merely a problem of interorganizational negotiation and coordination. Rather, within global governance complexes, 'mandates, functions and memberships overlap, and [...] jointly address a specific policy problem.'[57] This means that the same actors may be pushing for their preferred policy agendas from different positions. To stick with the global health example: The US is a major shareholder in the World Bank, provides extensive financing to the WHO, and has board representation in both Gavi and the Global Fund; these positions give the country the opportunity to pull strings from different directions to steer this complex in a favorable direction.

Thus, the researcher's empirical task is to be able to trace these processes and determine whether they cohere and how. In other words, who is doing what, when, and why? Integrating these elements into a unified account is certainly a tall order, but it is certainly feasible. For example, Mette Eilstrup-Sangiovanni has shown how the evolution of the global civil aviation regime entailed both political bargaining and expert involvement with technical aspects of this policy issue.[58] Similarly, Stephanie Hofmann and Patryk Pawlak show how emergent policy issues like artificial intelligence and cyberspace lead to organizational jostling for being at the frontier of developing new norms and scripts to regulate these spheres, and how issue-area expertise feeds into the political discussions on appropriate policy responses.[59] In other words, these cases too entail the same types of inputs into normmaking and scriptwriting as the ones covered in this volume, but take place across additional layers of inter- and intra-organizational action.

A third concern with our account might pertain to the emergence of more shadowy forms of global governance. Traditional multilateralism and even global governance complexes ultimately leave ample paper trails. It is generally easy to identify who was involved, what roles they had, what decision-making structures existed, how formal processes unfolded, and what the outcome of these discussions and negotiations was. Where available, transcripts from meetings further illuminate these processes, as was the case of the

---

[57] Eilstrup-Sangiovanni and Westerwinter 2022, 234.
[58] Eilstrup-Sangiovanni 2022.
[59] Hofmann and Pawlak 2023.

IMF in this volume. But a growing trend in informal global governance has been to shift to more opaque forms of decision making.[60]

One instance of this phenomenon is the rise of so-called ad hoc coalitions in global governance. These are arrangements characterized by 'their short-notice creation, task-specific purpose and their temporarily circumscribed existence.'[61] For example, the Joint Force of the Group of Five Sahel and the Access to COVID-19 Tools (ACT) Accelerator coalition were both established as special-purpose vehicles with, respectively, international security and global health objectives. While these coalitions generally slip into the ether once their mandate expires, they have tangible decision-making power over the course of their short lives. For example, the ACT Accelerator was behind the creation of the COVAX initiative that promoted vaccine donation from the Global North to the Global South, thus shaping global norms around vaccine distribution.[62]

A second instance of this phenomenon can be found in the rise of global professional service firms. Included here are the Big Three global consulting firms (McKinsey, Boston Consulting Group, and Bain & Company), as well as the Big Four global accounting firms noted earlier. Compelling evidence suggests that these actors are taking on a larger roles within and around IOs.[63] They also actively monitor potential challengers to their own scripts, be it from IOs, civil society actors, or others.[64]

Global professional service firms also have a strong influence on how governments interpret and implement scripts.[65] We have little detail on how politics-versus-science debates play out in the executive meetings of these firms. While we know how they are legally formed—as national chapters with a global 'brand' as the executive—these structures help the firms avoid accountability, including by concealing insights into decision making.[66] These same organizations have been viewed as critical to the maintenance of neo-imperial and neocolonial networks of domination by controlling knowledge management to implement scripts.[67] Our framework on how struggles between science and politics are waged within organizations to influence global norms provides one starting point to help us get our heads around these lesser-known sides of political and economic globalization.

---

[60] Squatrito and Sommerer 2024.
[61] Reykers et al. 2023, 740.
[62] Storeng et al. 2021; de Bengy Puyvallée and Storeng 2022.
[63] Seabrooke and Sending 2020; Stone et al. 2021; Eckl and Hanrieder 2023.
[64] Christensen and Seabrooke 2022.
[65] Jones 2019; Broome 2022; Tsingou 2022.
[66] Stausholm et al. 2025.
[67] Boussebaa et al. 2012; Boussebaa and Faulconbridge 2019.

Norm Contestation and the Future of Globalization

Our claim in this book is that examining battles of politics versus science provides us with new knowledge on how scripts are crafted within organizations, which tells us how they codify or modify global norms. Our syncretic model draws on theoretical approaches that stress the primacy of both power politics and world culture. Which 'side' explains the most depends on the case. Our abductive approach to extended computational cases suggests that we should first work from best guesses and then delve into the empirical material, allowing ourselves to be surprised.[68] Our findings in the empirical cases provide new revelations, even if the organization, the IMF, is well known to many. This is in fact the promise of the abductive method: that our multimethod approach can explore details such as career compositions and word embeddings and incorporate them into long-arch accounts; in our case, by linking micro-level attributes to meso-level organizational behavior and interactions, and ultimately to macro-level outcomes. By doing so we gain a richer understanding of the apex organizations that shape global norms, as well as the behavior of the executives and technocrats that drive them.

Our fundamental view is that norms are the product of contestation. We can see that, in our empirical case of the IMF from 1980 to 2009—a period in which globalization took off—the process of producing scripts to support the modification of global norms was conflictual. While theories of how norms are created and diffuse emphasize the onward march of world culture, any changes have distributional effects. Political economy, with all its winners and losers, kicks in. But, then again, not all is hard-nosed bargaining between those who have and those who lack. Professional and educational socialization matter in shaping how those who have the power to craft, interpret, and decide—the scriptwriters—put forward their arguments. At the micro-level of interaction, these actors—our Board members and technocrats—lean on their priors and how they have been socialized in advancing their views. In short, variations in scientific consensus and political contestation matter for scriptwriting and the modification of global norms. We have shown how variations in science versus politics matter across issues within a singular (albeit very important) organization. As just discussed, a number of parallels can be drawn to other global organizations, including how multiple organizations can have overlapping influence on the same issue.

What can we expect for how IOs will continue to make and modify global norms? Three matters come to mind. The first relates to ongoing debates

---

[68] Timmermans and Tavory 2022.

about the rise of populism and deglobalization. We can see this in the growing populism in a range of countries that explicitly reject IOs (or at least those forged at Bretton Woods). Indeed, many countries are willing to pay the costs of lesser economic interdependence so they can engage in status and identity politics, what Rebecca Adler-Nissen and Ayşe Zarakol call recognition struggles.[69] The second is the proliferation of alternative private organizations providing global governance solutions,[70] as well as the establishment of IOs that encroach on already well-established turf. The most prominent example here is China's creation of the Asian Infrastructure Investment Bank in 2015, which mirrors the World Bank in many ways but has been described as 'indifferent to core liberal ideas'.[71] With these developments and other geopolitical transformations among rising powers,[72] we can expect the character of scientific consensus and political contestation to change in scriptwriting.

The third and most important matter is the capacity of IOs to deal with the existential politics of climate change.[73] As Matthew Paterson has warned, our current IOs were built in the postwar period to provide gradual progress on particular agendas, not radical transformation.[74] It is difficult to imagine the creation of IOs that could provide timely and needed changes while permitting the deliberation we currently enjoy. As distributional battles swell amid climate breakdown, we can expect to see the heightened relevance of analytically investigating what is scientific consensus and what is political contestation.

---

[69] Adler-Nissen and Zarakol 2021.
[70] Abbott et al. 2016; Lake 2021.
[71] Stephen and Skidmore 2019, 91.
[72] Mukherjee 2022.
[73] Colgan et al. 2021.
[74] Paterson 2021.

List of Archival Documents Cited

BUFF Documents (Draft statements by IMF staff at Board meetings)

BUFF/85/103	Statement by Mr. Rye on New Zealand—EBM (6/10/85)
BUFF/99/45	Summing Up by the Acting Chairman—Countries' Experiences with the Use of Controls on Capital Movements and Issues in Their Orderly Liberalization

Executive Board Documents (EBD)

EBD/85/35	New Zealand—Request for Technical Assistance

Executive Board Minutes (EBM)

EBM/00/57	Romania—Stand-By Arrangement—Review, Extension, Augmentation, Modification, and Waiver of Performance Criteria
EBM/02/89	Romania—Stand-By Arrangement—Reviews, Modification, and Waiver of Performance Criteria
EBM/85/23	Multiple Currency Practices Applicable Solely to Capital Transactions
EBM/86/158	IMF Working Papers—Establishment of Document Series
EBM/87/165	Thailand—1987 Article IV Consultation
EBM/88/34	Philippines—Stand-By Arrangement—Request for Extension
EBM/88/53	Debt Situation—Developments, Issues and Role of Fund
EBM/90/121	Capital Flows—Determinants and Systemic Consequences
EBM/95/19	Issues and Developments in Multilateral Debt and Financing for the Heavily Indebted Poor Countries—Preliminary Considerations
EBM/95/73	Capital Account Convertibility—Review of Experience and Implications for Fund Policies
EBM/96/101	Tanzania—1996 Article IV Consultation; and Enhanced Structural Adjustment Arrangement
EBM/96/24	Proposed Initiative for Assisting Heavily Indebted Poor Countries
EBM/96/34	Debt Problems of Heavily Indebted Poor Countries—Framework for Action—Draft Report to Interim and Development Committees
EBM/96/58	Enhanced Structural Adjustment Facility and Fund Participation in HIPC Initiative—Proposed Framework
EBM/97/38	Capital Account Convertibility—Consideration of Possible Amendment of Articles of Agreement—Further Considerations
EBM/97/93	Capital Movements Under an Amendment of the Articles of Agreement—Draft Report of Executive Board to Interim Committee
EBM/98/38	Liberalization of Capital Movements Under an Amendment of Articles—Statement by Managing Director
EBM/98/85	Capital Account Liberalization—Theoretical and Practical Aspects

Continued

Continued

BUFF Documents (Draft statements by IMF staff at Board meetings)

EBM/99/101	Use and Liberalization of Capital Controls—Country Experiences
EBM/99/31	Use of Controls on Capital Movements and Issues in Their Orderly Liberalization—Countries' Experiences List of Archival Documents Citedy

Executive Board Specials (EBS) (Background reports by IMF staff for the Board)

EBS/02/18	HIPC Initiative—Debt Sustainability Analysis and Noncomplying Purchases and Disbursements
EBS/92/170	Tanzania—Staff Report for the 1992 Article IV Consultation and Request for the Second Annual Arrangement Under the Enhanced Structural Adjustment Facility
EBS/96/165	Tanzania—Staff Report for the 1996 Article IV Consultation and Request for Arrangements Under the Enhanced Structural Adjustment Facilit

Staff Memoranda (SM) (Studies and reports by IMF staff for the Board)

SM/83/19	New Zealand—Staff Report for the 1982 Article IV Consultation
SM/84/64	Review of Experience with Multiple Exchange Rate Regimes
SM/85/19	Multiple Currency Practices Applicable Solely to Capital Transactions
SM/88/113	Philippines—Staff Report for the 1988 Article IV Consultation
SM/90/128	The Determinants and Systemic Consequences of International Capital Flows
SM/92/90	Thailand—Staff Report for the 1992 Interim Article IV Consultation
SM/95/164	Capital Account Convertibility—Review of Experience and Implications for Fund Policies
SM/95/164, Supplement 3	A Survey of Academic Literature on Controls over International Capital Transactions
SM/97/209	Legal Aspects of Capital Movements Under an Amendment of the Articles—Further Considerations
SM/97/230	Draft Report to the Interim Committee on the Liberalization of Capital Movements Under an Amendment of the Articles
SM/97/32	Capital Account Convertibility and the Role of the Fund—Review of Experience and Consideration of a Possible Amendment of the Articles
SM/97/32, Supplement 1	Review of Experience with Capital Account Liberalization and Strengthened Procedures Adopted by the Fund
SM/97/86	Capital Account Convertibility and a Possible Amendment of the Articles—Further Considerations
SM/98/211	Australia—Staff Report for the 1998 Article IV Consultation
SM/99/214	Country Experiences with the Use and Liberalization of Capital Controls
SM/99/60	Countries' Experiences with the Use of Controls on Capital Movements and Issues in Their Orderly Liberalization

Working papers (WP)

WP/90/51	Capital Controls and International Portfolio Theory: A Microeconomic Approach

References

Abbasi, Kamran. 1999. "The World Bank and World Health: Under Fire." *BMJ* 318 (7189): 1003–6.
Abbott, Andrew Delano. 2001a. *Time Matters: On Theory and Method*. University of Chicago Press.
Abbott, Andrew Delano. 2001b. *Chaos of Disciplines*. University of Chicago Press.
Abbott, Andrew, and Stanley DeViney. 1992. "The Welfare State as Transnational Event: Evidence from Sequences of Policy Adoption." *Social Science History* 16 (2): 245–74.
Abbott, Andrew, and Alexandra Hrycak. 1990. "Measuring Resemblance in Sequence Data: An Optimal Matching Analysis of Musicians' Careers." *American Journal of Sociology* 96 (1): 144–85.
Abbott, Andrew, and Angela Tsay. 2000. "Sequence Analysis and Optimal Matching Methods in Sociology: Review and Prospect." *Sociological Methods & Research* 29 (1): 3–33.
Abbott, Kenneth W., Jessica F. Green, and Robert O. Keohane. 2016. "Organizational Ecology and Institutional Change in Global Governance." *International Organization* 70 (2): 247–77.
Abdelal, Rawi. 2007. *Capital Rules: The Construction of Global Finance*. Harvard University Press.
Adler-Nissen, Rebecca, and Ayşe Zarakol. 2021. "Struggles for Recognition: The Liberal International Order and the Merger of Its Discontents." *International Organization* 75 (2): 611–34.
Adolph, Christopher. 2013. *Bankers, Bureaucrats, and Central Bank Politics: The Myth of Neutrality*. Cambridge University Press.
Aizenman, Joshua, Hali Edison, Larissa Leony, and Yi Sun. 2011. *Evaluating the Quality of IMF Research: A Citation Study*. IMF Independent Evaluation Office.
Akin, John S., Nancy Birdsall, and David M. De Ferranti. 1987. *Financing Health Services in Developing Countries: An Agenda for Reform*. World Bank.
Allen, William L., and Evan Easton-Calabria. 2022. "Combining Computational and Archival Methods to Study International Organizations: Refugees and the International Labour Organization, 1919–2015." *International Studies Quarterly* 66 (3): sqac044.
Andonova, Liliana. 2017. *Governance Entrepreneurs: International Organizations and the Rise of Global Public-Private Partnerships*. Cambridge University Press.
Andrew, Cedric, and Katherine Baer. 2023. *How to Combat Value-Added Tax Refund Fraud*. Fiscal Affairs Department, International Monetary Fund.
Apeldoorn, Bastiaan van, and Nana Andrea de Graaff. 2016. *American Grand Strategy and Corporate Elite Networks: The Open Door Since the End of the Cold War*. Routledge.
Appel, Hillary. 2011. *Tax Politics in Eastern Europe: Globalization, Regional Integration, and the Democratic Compromise*. University of Michigan Press.
Aragão, Roberto, and Lukas Linsi. 2022. "Many Shades of Wrong: What Governments Do When They Manipulate Statistics." *Review of International Political Economy* 29 (1): 88–113.
Arezki, Rabah, Marc G. Quintyn, and Frederik G. Toscani. 2012. *Structural Reforms, IMF Programs and Capacity Building: An Empirical Investigation* (IMF Working Paper 232). International Monetary Fund.

Arseniev-Koehler, Alina. 2022. "Theoretical Foundations and Limits of Word Embeddings: What Types of Meaning Can They Capture?" *Sociological Methods & Research* 53 (4): 1753–93.

Avant, Deborah D., Martha Finnemore, and Susan K. Sell, eds. 2010. *Who Governs the Globe?* Cambridge University Press.

Aykut, Stefan C., Edouard Morena, and Jean Foyer. 2021. "'Incantatory' Governance: Global Climate Politics' Performative Turn and Its Wider Significance for Global Politics." *International Politics* 58 (4): 519–40.

Ayoub, Phillip M. 2014. "With Arms Wide Shut: Threat Perception, Norm Reception, and Mobilized Resistance to LGBT Rights." *Journal of Human Rights* 13 (3): 337–62.

Ayoub, Phillip M. 2015. "Contested Norms in New-Adopter States: International Determinants of LGBT Rights Legislation." *European Journal of International Relations* 21 (2): 293–322.

Ayoub, Phillip M., and Kristina Stoeckl. 2023. "The Double-Helix Entanglements of Transnational Advocacy: Moral Conservative Resistance to LGBTI Rights." *Review of International Studies* 50 (2): 289–311.

Babb, Sarah L. 2003. "The IMF in Sociological Perspective: A Tale of Organizational Slippage." *Studies in Comparative International Development* 38 (2): 3–27.

Babb, Sarah L. 2009. *Behind the Development Banks: Washington Politics, World Poverty, and the Wealth of Nations*. University of Chicago Press.

Babb, Sarah L., and Nitsan Chorev. 2016. "International Organizations: Loose and Tight Coupling in the Development Regime." *Studies in Comparative International Development* 51 (1): 81–102.

Babb, Sarah L., and Alexander E. Kentikelenis. 2021. "Markets Everywhere: The Washington Consensus and the Sociology of Global Institutional Change." *Annual Review of Sociology* 47 (1): 521–41.

Baker, Andrew. 2017. "Esteem as Professional Currency and Consolidation: The Rise of the Macroprudential Cognoscenti." In *Professional Networks in Transnational Governance*, edited by L. Seabrooke and L. F. Henriksen. Cambridge University Press.

Baker, Andrew, and Richard Murphy. 2019. "The Political Economy of 'Tax Spillover': A New Multilateral Framework." *Global Policy* 10 (2): 178–92.

Baker, James A. 1985. "Remarks." In *Summary Proceedings: 1985 Annual Meetings of the Boards of Governors*. International Bank for Reconstruction and Development, International Finance Corporation, and International Development Association.

Ballakrishnen, Swethaa S., and Sara Dezalay, eds. 2020. *Invisible Institutionalisms: Collective Reflections on the Shadows of Legal Globalisation*. Hart.

Ban, Cornel. 2013. "Brazil's Liberal Neo-developmentalism: New Paradigm or Edited Orthodoxy?" *Review of International Political Economy* 20 (2): 298–331.

Ban, Cornel. 2015. "Austerity Versus Stimulus? Understanding Fiscal Policy Change at the International Monetary Fund Since the Great Recession." *Governance* 28 (2): 167–183.

Ban, Cornel. 2025. "Content Analysis in International Political Economy." In *The Oxford Handbook of International Political Economy*, edited by Jon C. W. Pevehouse and Leonard Seabrooke. Oxford University Press.

Ban, Cornel, and Kevin P. Gallagher. 2015. "Recalibrating Policy Orthodoxy: The IMF Since the Great Recession." *Governance* 28 (2): 131–46.

Ban, Cornel, and Bryan Patenaude. 2019. "The Professional Politics of the Austerity Debate: A Comparative Field Analysis of the European Central Bank and the International Monetary Fund." *Public Administration* 97 (3): 530–45.

Ban, Cornel, Leonard Seabrooke, and Sarah Freitas. 2016. "Grey Matter in Shadow Banking: International Organizations and Expert Strategies in Global Financial Governance." *Review of International Political Economy* 23 (6): 1000–1033.

Barnett, Michael N., and Martha Finnemore. 1999. "The Politics, Power, and Pathologies of International Organizations." *International Organization* 53 (4): 699–732.

Barnett, Michael N., and Martha Finnemore. 2004. *Rules for the World: International Organizations in Global Politics.* Cornell University Press.

Bartley, Tim. 2022. "Power and the Practice of Transnational Private Regulation." *New Political Economy* 27 (2): 188–202.

Bartley, Tim. 2018. "Transnational Corporations and Global Governance." *Annual Review of Sociology* 44 (1): 145–65.

Baturo, Alexander, Niheer Dasandi, and Slava J. Mikhaylov. 2017. "Understanding State Preferences with Text as Data: Introducing the UN General Debate Corpus." *Research & Politics* 4 (2): 1–9.

Baunsgaard, Thomas, and Michael Keen. 2010. "Tax Revenue and (or?) Trade Liberalization." *Journal of Public Economics* 94 (9–10): 563–77.

Bayerlein, Louisa, Christoph Knill, and Yves Steinebach. 2020. *A Matter of Style? Organizational Agency in Global Public Policy.* Cambridge University Press.

Beckfield, Jason. 2010. "The Social Structure of the World Polity." *American Journal of Sociology* 115 (4): 1018–68.

de Bengy Puyvallée, Antoine, and Katerini Tagmatarchi Storeng. 2022. "COVAX, Vaccine Donations and the Politics of Global Vaccine Inequity." *Globalization and Health* 18 (1): 26.

Benitez, Juan Carlos, Mario Mansour, Miguel Pecho, and Charles Vellutini. 2023. "Building Tax Capacity in Developing Countries." *IMF Staff Discussion Notes* 2023/006.

Ben-Josef Hirsch, Michal, and Jennifer M. Dixon. 2021. "Conceptualizing and Assessing Norm Strength in International Relations." *European Journal of International Relations* 27 (2): 521–47.

Berge, Tarald Laudal, and Taylor St John. 2021. "Asymmetric Diffusion: World Bank 'Best Practice' and the Spread of Arbitration in National Investment Laws. *Review of International Political Economy* 28 (3): 584–610.

Best, Jacqueline. 2012. "Bureaucratic Ambiguity." *Economy and Society* 41 (1): 84–106.

Best, Jacqueline. 2014. *Governing Failure: Provisional Expertise and the Transformation of Global Development Finance.* Cambridge University Press.

Bhagwati, Jagdish N. 1998. "The Capital Myth: The Difference Between Trade in Widgets and Dollars." *Foreign Affairs* 77 (3): 7–12.

Binder, Martin, and Monika Heupel. 2015. "The Legitimacy of the UN Security Council: Evidence from Recent General Assembly Debates." *International Studies Quarterly* 59 (2): 238–50.

Bird, Graham. 2003. *The IMF and the Future.* London: Routledge.

Bird, Richard M., and Pierre-Pascal Gendron. 2007. *The VAT in Developing and Transitional Countries.* Cambridge University Press.

Birdsall, Nancy, and John Williamson. 2002. *Delivering on Debt Relief: From IMF Gold to a New Aid Architecture.* Institute for International Economics.

Birn, Anne-Emanuelle, and Klaudia Dmitrienko. 2005. "The World Bank: Global Health or Global Harm?" *American Journal of Public Health* 95 (7): 1091–92.

Blair-Loy, Mary. 1999. "Career Patterns of Executive Women in Finance: An Optimal Matching Analysis." *American Journal of Sociology* 104 (5): 1346–97.

Block, Fred. 1996. "Controlling Global Finance." *World Policy Journal* 13 (3): 24–34.

Block-Lieb, Susan, and Terence C. Halliday. 2017. *Global Lawmakers: International Organizations in the Crafting of World Markets.* Cambridge University Press.

Block-Lieb, Susan, and Mark C. Weidemaier. 2016. "Lenders' Roles and Responsibilities in Sovereign Debt Markets." *University of Illinois Law Review* 5: 1589–1636.

Blondeel, Mathieu, Jeff Colgan, and Thijs Van de Graaf. 2019. "What Drives Norm Success? Evidence from Anti-Fossil Fuel Campaigns." *Global Environmental Politics* 19 (4): 63-84.

Blyth, Mark. 2007. "Powering, Puzzling, or Persuading? The Mechanisms of Building Institutional Orders." *International Studies Quarterly* 51 (4): 761-77.

Bockman, Johanna, and Gil Eyal. 2002. "Eastern Europe as a Laboratory for Economic Knowledge: The Transnational Roots of Neoliberalism." *American Journal of Sociology* 108 (2): 310-52.

Boli, John, and George M. Thomas. 1997. World Culture in the World Polity: a Century of International Non-Governmental Organization. *American Sociological Review* 62 (2): 171-190.

Boughton, James M. 2001. *Silent Revolution: International Monetary Fund, 1979-1989*. International Monetary Fund.

Boughton, James M. 2012. *Tearing Down Walls: The International Monetary Fund, 1990-1999*. International Monetary Fund.

Bourdieu, Pierre. 1998. *The State Nobility: Elite Schools in the Field of Power*. Stanford University Press.

Boussebaa, Mehdi, Glenn Morgan, and Andrew Sturdy. 2012. "Constructing Global Firms? National, Transnational and Neocolonial Effects in International Management Consultancies." *Organization Studies* 33 (4): 465-86.

Boussebaa, Mehdi, and James R. Faulconbridge. 2019. "Professional Service Firms as Agents of Economic Globalization: A Political Perspective." *Journal of Professions and Organization* 6 (1): 72-90.

Boy, John. 2020. "Textnets: A Python Package for Text Analysis with Networks." *Journal of Open Source Software* 5 (54): 2594.

Boyle, Elizabeth H., Minzee Kim, and Wesley Longhofer. 2015. "Abortion Liberalization in World Society, 1960-2009." *American Journal of Sociology* 121 (3): 882-913.

Boyle, Elizabeth Heger. 2002. *Female Genital Cutting: Cultural Conflict in the Global Community*. Johns Hopkins University Press.

Boyle, Elizabeth Heger, and John W Meyer. 1998. "Modern Law as a Secularized and Global Model: Implications for the Sociology of Law." *Soziale Welt* 49 (3): 213-32.

Brandt, Philipp, and Stefan Timmermans. 2021. "Abductive Logic of Inquiry for Quantitative Research in the Digital Age." *Sociological Science* 8: 191-210.

Braun, Benjamin, Arie Krampf, and Steffen Murau. 2021. "Financial Globalization as Positive Integration: Monetary Technocrats and the Eurodollar Market in the 1970s." *Review of International Political Economy* 28 (4): 794-819.

Breen, Laura, and Mette Eilstrup-Sangiovanni. 2023. "Issue-Adoption and Campaign Structure in Transnational Advocacy Campaigns: A Longitudinal Network Analysis." *European Journal of International Relations* 30 (2): 486-516.

Breen, Michael, and Elliott Doak. 2021. The IMF as a global monitor: surveillance, information, and financial markets. *Review of International Political Economy* 30 (1): 307-31.

Bromley, Patricia, and John W. Meyer. 2015. *Hyper-organization: Global Organizational Expansion*. Oxford University Press.

Broome, André. 2015. "Back to Basics: The Great Recession and the Narrowing of IMF Policy Advice." *Governance* 28 (2): 147-65.

Broome, André. 2008. "The Importance of Being Earnest: The IMF as a Reputational Intermediary." *New Political Economy* 13 (2): 125-51.

Broome, André. 2010. *The Currency of Power*. Palgrave Macmillan.

Broome, André. 2022. "Gaming Country Rankings: Consultancies as Knowledge Brokers for Global Benchmarks." *Public Administration* 100 (3): 554-70.

Broome, André, Alexandra Homolar, and Matthias Kranke. 2017. "Bad Science: International Organizations and the Indirect Power of Global Benchmarking." *European Journal of International Relations* 20 (4): 469–84.

Broome, André, and Joel Quirk. 2015. "Governing the World at a Distance: The Practice of Global Benchmarking." *Review of International Studies* 41 (5): 819–41.

Broome, André, and Leonard Seabrooke. 2007. "Seeing Like the IMF: Institutional Change in Small Open Economies." *Review of International Political Economy* 14 (4): 576–601.

Broome, André, and Leonard Seabrooke. 2015. "Shaping Policy Curves: Cognitive Authority in Transnational Capacity Building." *Public Administration* 93 (4): 956–72.

Broome, André, and Leonard Seabrooke. 2021. "Recursive Recognition in the International Political Economy." *Review of International Political Economy* 28 (2): 369–81.

Brosig, Malte, and John Karlsrud. 2024. "How Ad Hoc Coalitions Deinstitutionalize International Institutions." *International Affairs* 100 (2): 771–89.

Brownlee, W. Elliot. 2009. "The Shoup Mission to Japan: Two Political Economies Intersect." In *The New Fiscal Sociology: Taxation in Comparative and Historical Perspective*, edited by I. W. Martin, A. K. Mehrotra, and M. Prasad. Cambridge University Press.

Broz, J. Lawrence, Jeffry Frieden, and Stephen Weymouth. 2021. "Populism in Place: The Economic Geography of the Globalization Backlash." *International Organization* 75 (2): 464–94.

Brun, Jean-François, Gérard Chambas, and Bertrand Laporte. 2011. "IMF Programs and Tax Effort: What Role for Institutions in Africa" (CERDI Working Paper 33). *HAL Open Science*: halshs-00552206.

Bruzelius, Cecilia. 2023. "Problems Chasing Missing Solutions: The Politics of Placing Emigration on the EU Agenda." *Journal of European Public Policy* 32 (1): 296–321.

Bühlmann, Felix, Christoph Houman Ellersgaard, Anton Grau Larsen, and Jacob Aagaard Lunding. 2023. "How Career Hubs Shape the Global Corporate Elite." *Global Networks*: e12430.

Buira, Ariel. 2003. "The Governance of the International Monetary Fund." In *Providing Global Public Goods*, edited by Inge Kaul, Pedro Conceição, Katell Le Goulven, and Ronald U Mendoza. Oxford University Press.

Bulmer-Thomas, Victor. 2003. *The Economic History of Latin America Since Independence*. Cambridge University Press.

Bunea, Adriana, and Raimondas Ibenskas. 2015. "Quantitative Text Analysis and the Study of EU Lobbying and Interest Groups." *European Union Politics* 16 (3): 429–55.

Burawoy, Michael. 1989. "Two Methods in Search of Science: Skocpol Versus Trotsky." *Theory and Society* 18 (6): 759–805.

Burrell, Gibson. 2013. *Styles of Organizing: The Will to Form*. Oxford University Press.

Buse, Kent, and Gill Walt. 2000. "Role Conflict? The World Bank and the World's Health." *Social Science & Medicine* 50 (2): 177–79.

Cady, John. 2005. "Does SDDS Subscription Reduce Borrowing Costs for Emerging Market Economies?" *IMF Staff Papers* 52 (3): 503–17.

Caraway, Teri L., Stephanie J. Rickard, and Mark S. Anner. 2012. "International Negotiations and Domestic Politics: The Case of IMF Labor Market Conditionality. *International Organization* 66 (1): 27–61.

Carnegie, Allison, Richard Clark, and Ayse Kaya. 2023. "Private Participation: How Populists Engage with International Organizations." *The Journal of Politics* 86 (3): 877–91.

Carpenter, Charli, and Alexander H. Montgomery. 2020. "The Stopping Power of Norms: Saturation Bombing, Civilian Immunity, and U.S. Attitudes Toward the Laws of War." *International Security* 45 (2): 140–69.

Carpenter, R. Charli. 2007. "Setting the Advocacy Agenda: Theorizing Issue Emergence and Nonemergence in Transnational Advocacy Networks." *International Studies Quarterly* 51 (1): 99–120.

Carpenter, R. Charli. 2011. "Vetting the Advocacy Agenda: Network Centrality and the Paradox of Weapons Norms." *International Organization* 65 (1): 69–102.

Carruthers, Bruce G., and Terence C. Halliday. 2006. "Negotiating Globalization: Global Scripts and Intermediation in the Construction of Asian Insolvency Regimes." *Law & Social Inquiry* 31 (3): 521–84.

Centeno, Miguel Angel. 1994. *Democracy Within Reason: Technocratic Revolution in Mexico*. Pennsylvania State University Press.

Chase-Dunn, Christopher K. 1998. *Global Formation: Structures of the World-Economy*. Rowman & Littlefield.

Chauvin, Nicolas Depetris, and Aart Kraay. 2005, September. "What Has 100 Billion Dollars Worth of Debt Relief Done for Low-Income Countries?" https://econwpa.ub.uni-muenchen.de/econ-wp/if/papers/0510/0510001.pdf.

Chelsky, Jeff. 2009. "Summarizing the Views of the IMF Executive Board." In *Studies of IMF Governance: A Compendium*, edited by Ruben Lamdany and Leonardo Martinez-Diaz. Washington, DC: IMF Independent Evaluation Office.

Chorev, Nitsan. 2012a. "Changing Global Norms Through Reactive Diffusion: The Case of Intellectual Property Protection of AIDS Drugs." *American Sociological Review* 77 (5): 831–53.

Chorev, Nitsan. 2012b. *The World Health Organization Between North and South*. Cornell University Press.

Christensen, R. C., and M. Hearson. 2019. "The New Politics of Global Tax Governance: Taking Stock a Decade After the Financial Crisis." *Review of International Political Economy* 26 (5): 1068–88.

Christensen, R. C., and L. Seabrooke. 2022. "The Big 4 Under Pressure: Scanning Work in Transnational Fields." *Contemporary Accounting Research* 39 (4): 2941–69.

Chwieroth, Jeffrey M. 2007. "Neoliberal Economists and Capital Account Liberalization in Emerging Markets." *International Organization* 61 (2): 443–63.

Chwieroth, Jeffrey M. 2010. *Capital Ideas: The IMF and the Rise of Financial Liberalization*. Princeton University Press.

Chwieroth, Jeffrey M. 2013. "The Silent Revolution:" How the Staff Exercise Informal Governance over IMF Lending." *The Review of International Organizations* 8 (2): 265–90.

Chwieroth, Jeffrey M. 2015. "Professional Ties That Bind: How Normative Orientations Shape IMF Conditionality." *Review of International Political Economy* 22 (4): 757–87.

Clark, Richard, and Lindsay R. Dolan. 2021. "Pleasing the Principal: U.S. Influence in World Bank Policymaking." *American Journal of Political Science* 65 (1): 36–51.

Clark, Richard, and Noah Zucker. 2023. "Climate Cascades: IOs and the Prioritization of Climate Action." *American Journal of Political Science* 68 (4): 1299–314.

Clements, Benedict J., David Coady, Stefania Fabrizio, Sanjeev Gupta, Trevor Serge Coleridge Alleyne, and Carlo A Sdralevich, eds. 2013. *Energy Subsidy Reform: Lessons and Implications*. International Monetary Fund.

Clift, Ben. 2018. *The IMF and the Politics of Austerity in the Wake of the Global Financial Crisis*. Oxford University Press.

Clift, Ben. 2019. "Unusual Bedfellows? The IMF, Tackling Inequality and Social Democratic Policy Renewal." In *Diverging Capitalisms*, edited by Colin Hay and Daniel Bailey. Palgrave Macmillan.

Clift, Ben, and Te-Anne Robles. 2021. "The IMF, Tackling Inequality, and Post-neoliberal 'Reglobalization': The Paradoxes of Political Legitimation Within Economistic Parameters." *Globalizations* 18 (1): 39–54.

Clift, Ben, and Jim Tomlinson. 2008. "Negotiating Credibility: Britain and the International Monetary Fund, 1956–1976." *Contemporary European History* 17 (4): 545–66.

Clinton, Chelsea, and Devi Sridhar. 2017. *Governing Global Health: Who Runs the World and Why?* Oxford University Press.

Colantone, Italo, Gianmarco Ottaviano, and Piero Stanig. 2022. The Backlash of Globalization. In *Handbook of International Economics*, vol. 5, edited by Gita Gopinath, Elhanan Helpman, and Kenneth Rogoff. Elsevier.

Colgan, Jeff D., Jessica F. Green, and Thomas N. Hale. 2021. "Asset Revaluation and the Existential Politics of Climate Change." *International Organization* 75 (2): 586–610.

Collins, H. M. 1981a. "The Place of the 'Core-Set' in Modern Science: Social Contingency with Methodological Propriety in Science." *History of Science* 19 (1): 6–19.

Collins, Randall. 1981b. "On the Microfoundations of Macrosociology." *American Journal of Sociology* 86 (5): 984–1014.

Collins, Randall. 2004. *Interaction Ritual Chains*. Princeton University Press.

Coman, Ramona. 2020. "Transnational Economists in the Eurozone Crisis: Professional Structures, Networks and Ideas." *New Political Economy* 25 (6): 978–91.

Copelovitch, Mark, and Stephanie Rickard. 2021. "Partisan Technocrats: How Leaders Matter in International Organizations." *Global Studies Quarterly* 1 (3): ksab021.

Copelovitch, Mark S. 2010a. "Master or Servant? Common Agency and the Political Economy of IMF Lending." *International Studies Quarterly* 54 (1): 49–77.

Copelovitch, Mark S. 2010b. *The International Monetary Fund in the Global Economy: Banks, Bonds, and Bailouts*. Cambridge University Press.

Cormier, Ben, and Mark S. Manger. 2022. "Power, Ideas, and World Bank Conditionality." *The Review of International Organizations* 17 (3): 397–425.

Coupé, Tom. 2003. "Revealed Performances: Worldwide Rankings of Economists and Economics Departments, 1990–2000." *Journal of the European Economic Association* 1 (6): 1309–45.

Crotty, James R. 1983. "On Keynes and Capital Flight." *Journal of Economic Literature* 21 (1): 59–65.

Cuddington, John T. 1986, September. *Capital Flight: Estimates, Issues, and Explanations*. Princeton Studies in International Finance 58.

Daseking, Christina, and Robert Powell. 1999. "From Toronto Terms to the HIPC Initiative: A Brief History of Debt Relief for Low-Income Countries." *IMF Working Papers* 99 (142): 1–29.

Devakumar, Delan, Sujitha Selvarajah, Ibrahim Abubakar, Seung-Sup Kim, Martin McKee, Nidhi S. Sabharwal, Angela Saini, Geordan Shannon, Alexandre I. R. White, and E. Tendayi Achiume. 2022. "Racism, Xenophobia, Discrimination, and the Determination of Health." *Lancet* 400 (10368): 2097–2108.

DeWitt, R. Peter, and James F. Petras. 1980. "Political Economy of International Debt: The Dynamics of Financial Capital." In *Debt and the Less Developed Countries*, edited by Jonathan David Aronson. Routledge.

Dezalay, Yves, and Bryant G. Garth. 2002. *The Internationalization of Palace Wars: Lawyers, Economists, and the Contest to Transform Latin American States*. University of Chicago Press.

Diaz-Alejandro, Carlos F. 1984. "Latin American Debt: I Don't Think We Are in Kansas Anymore." *Brookings Papers on Economic Activity* 1984 (2): 335–403.

DiCaprio, Alisa, and Kevin P. Gallagher. 2006. "The WTO and the Shrinking of Development Space." *Journal of World Investment and Trade* 7 (5): 781–803.

Dijkstra, Anneke Geske. 2013. *The Impact of International Debt Relief*. Routledge.

Ding, Iza. 2020. "Performative Governance." *World Politics* 72 (4): 525–56.

Djelic, Marie-Laure, and Sigrid Quack, eds. 2010. *Transnational Communities: Shaping Global Economic Governance*. Cambridge University Press.

Djimeu, Eric W. 2018. "The Impact of the Heavily Indebted Poor Countries Initiative on Growth and Investment in Africa." *World Development* 104: 108–127.

Dobbin, Frank, Beth Simmons, and Geoffrey Garrett. 2007. "The Global Diffusion of Public Policies: Social Construction, Coercion, Competition, or Learning?" *Annual Review of Sociology* 33 (1): 449–72.

Dooley, Michael P. 1988. "Capital Flight: A Response to Differences in Financial Risks." *IMF Staff Papers* 35 (3): 422–36.

Dooley, Michael P., Jeffrey Frankel, and Donald J. Mathieson. 1988. "International Capital Mobility: What Do Saving-Investment Correlations Tell Us? Reply to Miller." *IMF Staff Papers* 35 (2): 397–98.

Dreher, Axel, Jan-Egbert Sturm, and James Raymond Vreeland. 2009. "Global Horse Trading: IMF Loans for Votes in the United Nations Security Council." *European Economic Review* 53 (7): 742–57.

Dreher, Axel, Jan-Egbert Sturm, and James Raymond Vreeland. 2015. "Politics and IMF Conditionality." *Journal of Conflict Resolution* 59 (1): 120–48.

Dreher, Axel, and James Raymond Vreeland. 2014. *The Political Economy of the United Nations Security Council*. Cambridge University Press.

Drori, Gili S. 2006. "Scientization: Making a World Safe for Organizing." In *Transnational Governance: Institutional Dynamics of Regulation*, edited by Marie-Laure Djelic and Kerstin Sahlin-Andersson. Cambridge University Press.

Drori, Gili S. 2009. "Institutionalism and Globalization Studies." In *The SAGE Handbook of Organizational Institutionalism*, edited by Royston Greenwood, Christine Oliver, Roy Suddaby, and Kerstin Sahlin-Andersson. SAGE.

Drori, Gili S., and John W. Meyer. 2006. "Global Scientization: An Environment for Expanded Organization." In *Globalization and Organization: World Society and Organizational Change*, edited by Gili S. Drori, John W. Meyer, and Hokyu Hwang. Oxford University Press.

Durkheim, Emile. 2001. *The Elementary Forms of Religious Life*. Oxford University Press.

Ebrill, Liam, Jean-Paul Bodin, Michael Keen, and Victoria Summers, eds. 2001. *The Modern VAT*. International Monetary Fund.

Eckhard, Steffen, Ronny Patz, Mirco Schönfeld, and Hilde van Meegdenburg. 2023. "International Bureaucrats in the UN Security Council Debates: A Speaker-Topic Network Analysis." *Journal of European Public Policy* 30 (2): 214–33.

Eckl, Julian, and Tine Hanrieder. 2023. "The Political Economy of Consulting Firms in Reform Processes: The Case of the World Health Organization." *Review of International Political Economy* 30 (6): 2309–32.

Edelmann, Achim, Tom Wolff, Danielle Montagne, and Christopher A. Bail. 2020. "Computational Social Science and Sociology." *Annual Review of Sociology* 46 (1): 61–81.

Edwards, Martin S., and Stephanie Senger. 2015. "Listening to Advice: Assessing the External Impact of IMF Article IV Consultations of the United States, 2010–2011." *International Studies Perspectives* 16 (3): 312–26.

Ege, Jörn, Michael W. Bauer, and Nora Wagner. 2021. "How Do International Bureaucrats Affect Policy Outputs? Studying Administrative Influence Strategies in International Organizations." *International Review of Administrative Sciences* 87 (4): 737–54.

Eichengreen, Barry, and Michael Mussa. 1998. "Capital Account Liberalization and the IMF." *Finance and Development* 35 (4): 16–19.

Eilstrup-Sangiovanni, Mette. 2022. "Ordering Global Governance Complexes: The Evolution of the Governance Complex for International Civil Aviation." *The Review of International Organizations* 17 (2): 293–322.

Eilstrup-Sangiovanni, Mette. 2023. "Competition and Strategic Differentiation Among Transnational Advocacy Groups." In *Advocacy Group Effects in Global Governance: Populations, Strategies, and Political Opportunity Structures*, edited by Lisa M. Dellmuth and Elizabeth A. Bloodgood. Palgrave Macmillan.

Eilstrup-Sangiovanni, Mette, and Oliver Westerwinter. 2022. "The Global Governance Complexity Cube: Varieties of Institutional Complexity in Global Governance. *The Review of International Organizations* 17 (2): 233–62.

Ellersgaard, Christoph Houman, Jacob Aagaard Lunding, Lasse Folke Henriksen, and Anton Grau Larsen. 2019. "Pathways to the Power Elite: The Organizational Landscape of Elite Careers." *The Sociological Review* 67 (5): 1170–92.

Emirbayer, Mustafa. 1997. "Manifesto for a Relational Sociology." *American Journal of Sociology* 103 (2): 281–317.

Emran, M. Shahe, and Joseph E. Stiglitz. 2004. "Price-Neutral Tax Reform with an Informal Economy." *Public Economics* 0407010.

Essers, Dennis, Francesco Grigoli, and Evgenia Pugacheva. 2022. "Network Effects and Research Collaborations: Evidence from IMF Working Paper Co-authorship." *Scientometrics* 127 (12): 7169–92.

Eyal, Gil. 2019. *The Crisis of Expertise*. Polity.

Ferguson, Jason L. 2022. "'There is an Eye on us': International Imitation, Popular Representation, and the Regulation of Homosexuality in Senegal." *American Sociological Review* 86 (4): 700–27.

Finnemore, Martha. 1996. "Norms, Culture, and World Politics: Insights from Sociology's Institutionalism." *International Organization* 50 (2): 325–47.

Finnemore, Martha. 2013. *The Purpose of Intervention: Changing Beliefs About the Use of Force*. Cornell University Press.

Finnemore, Martha, and Kathryn Sikkink. 1998. "International Norm Dynamics and Political Change." *International Organization* 52 (4): 887–917.

Firth, John Rupert. 1957. "A Synopsis of Linguistic Theory 1930–1955." In *Studies in Linguistic Analysis: Special Volume of the Philological Society*. Blackwell. https://cs.brown.edu/courses/csci2952d/readings/lecture1-firth.pdf.

Fischer, Stanley. 1997, September 19. "Seminar—Asia and the IMF." International Monetary Fund. https://www.imf.org/external/np/speeches/1997/091997.htm.

Fischer, Stanley. 1998. "Capital-Account Liberalization and the Role of the IMF." In *Should the IMF Pursue Capital-Account Convertibility?*, edited by Stanley Fischer, Richard N. Cooper, Rudiger Dornbusch, Peter M. Garber, Carlos Massad, Jacques J. Polak, Dani Rodrik, and Savak S. Tarapore. Princeton Essays in International Finance.

Fligstein, Neil. 2001. "Social Skill and the Theory of Fields." *Sociological Theory* 19 (2): 105–25.

Fligstein, Neil, and Iona Mara-Drita. 1996. "How to Make a Market: Reflections on the Attempt to Create a Single Market in the European Union." *American Journal of Sociology* 102 (1): 1–33.

Forster, Timon. 2024. "Respected Individuals: When State Representatives Wield Outsize Influence in International Organizations." *International Affairs* 100 (1): 261–81.

Forster, Timon, Dan Honig, and Alexandros Kentikelenis. 2025. "Formal Governance Matters: When, How, and Why States Act on the IMF Executive Board." *Review of International Political Economy*: 1–29. https://doi.org/10.1080/09692290.2024.2441136.

Fourcade, Marion. 2006. "The Construction of a Global Profession: The Transnationalization of Economics." *American Journal of Sociology* 112 (1): 145–94.

Fourcade, Marion. 2009. *Economists and Societies: Discipline and Profession in the United States, Britain, and France, 1890s to 1990s*. Princeton University Press.

Fourcade, Marion, Etienne Ollion, and Yann Algan. 2015. "The Superiority of Economists." *Journal of Economic Perspectives* 29 (1): 89–114.

Frank, David J., and John W. Meyer. 2020. *The University and the Global Knowledge Society*. Princeton University Press.

Fransen, Luc, and Genevieve LeBaron. 2019. "Big Audit Firms as Regulatory Intermediaries in Transnational Labor Governance." *Regulation & Governance* 13 (2): 260–79.

Fransen, Luc. 2012. "Multi-stakeholder Governance and Voluntary Programme Interactions: Legitimation Politics in the Institutional Design of Corporate Social Responsibility." *Socio-Economic Review* 10 (1): 163–92.

Fratzscher, Marcel, and Julien Reynaud. 2011. "IMF Surveillance and Financial Markets—A Political Economy Analysis." *European Journal of Political Economy* 27 (3): 405–22.

Frenkel, Jacob A., and Assaf Razin. 1988. *International Effects of Tax Reforms* (IMF Working Paper 62). International Monetary Fund.

Frieden, Jeffry. 2019. "The Backlash Against Globalization and the Future of the International Economic Order." In *The Crisis of Globalization: Democracy, Capitalism and Inequality in the Twenty-First Century*, edited by Patrick Diamond. I. B. Tauris.

Frieden, Jeffry A. 2020. *Global Capitalism*. W. W. Norton & Company.

Friedrichs, Jörg, and Friedrich Kratochwil. 2009. "On Acting and Knowing: How Pragmatism Can Advance International Relations Research and Methodology." *International Organization* 63 (4): 701–31.

Gallagher, Kevin P, ed. 2005. *Putting Development First: The Importance of Policy Space in the WTO and IFIs*. Zed Books.

Gallagher, Kevin P. 2014. "Countervailing Monetary Power: Re-regulating Capital Flows in Brazil and South Korea." *Review of International Political Economy* 22 (1): 77–102.

Gallagher, Kevin P. 2015a. "Contesting the Governance of Capital Flows at the IMF." *Governance* 28 (2): 185–98.

Gallagher, Kevin P. 2015b. *Ruling Capital: Emerging Markets and the Reregulation of Cross-Border Finance*. Cornell University Press.

Gallagher, Kevin P., and José Antonio Ocampo. 2013. "IMF's New View on Capital Controls." *Economic and Political Weekly* XLVIII (12): 10–13.

Gallagher, Kevin P., Luma Ramos, Corinne Stephenson, and Irene Monasterolo. 2021. "Climate Change and IMF Surveillance: The Need for Ambition." *GEGI Policy Brief* 013.

Gardner, Richard. 1956. *Sterling-Dollar Diplomacy: Anglo-American Collaboration in the Reconstruction of Multilateral Trade*. Clarendon Press.

Gautam, Madhur. 2003. *Debt Relief for the Poorest: An OED Review of the HIPC Initiative*. World Bank.

Gautier Morin, Johanna, and Thierry Rossier. 2021. "The Interaction of Elite Networks in the Pinochet Regime's Macroeconomic Policies." *Global Networks* 21 (2): 339–64.

Gehlbach, Scott. 2008. *Representation Through Taxation: Revenue, Politics, and Development in Postcommunist States*. Cambridge University Press.

Genovese, Federica, Richard J. McAlexander, and Johannes Urpelainen. 2023. "Institutional Roots of International Alliances: Party Groupings and Position Similarity at Global Climate Negotiations." *The Review of International Organizations* 18 (2): 329–359.

Glennerster, Rachel, and Yongseok Shin. 2008. "Does Transparency Pay?" *IMF Staff Papers* 55 (1): 183–209.

Goertz, Gary, and James Mahoney. 2012. *A Tale of Two Cultures: Qualitative and Quantitative Research in the Social Sciences*. Princeton University Press.

Goetze, Catherine. 2017. *The Distinction of Peace: A Social Analysis of Peacebuilding*. University of Michigan Press.
Gola, Carlo, and Francesco Spadafora. 2009. *Financial Sector Surveillance and the IMF* (IMF Working Paper 247). International Monetary Fund.
Goode, Richard. 1993. "Tax Advice to Developing Countries: An Historical Survey." *World Development* 21 (1): 37–53.
Goyal, Rishi, and Ratna Sahay. 2023. "Integrating Gender into the IMF's Work." *IMF Gender Notes* 2023/01.
Gray, Ian, and Jean-Philippe Cointet. 2023. Multilateralism of the Marginal: Least Developed Countries and International Climate Negotiations, 1995–2016. *American Journal of Sociology* 129 (3): 796–855.
Graz, Jean-Christophe. 2019. *The Power of Standards: Hybrid Authority and the Globalisation of Services*. Cambridge University Press.
Grigorescu, Alexandru. 2020. *The Ebb and Flow of Global Governance: Intergovernmentalism vs. Nongovernmentalism in World Politics*. Cambridge University Press.
Grimmer, Justin, Margaret E. Roberts, and Brandon M. Stewart. 2022. *Text As Data: A New Framework for Machine Learning and the Social Sciences*. Princeton University Press.
Gros, Daniel. 1987. "The Effectiveness of Capital Controls: Implications for Monetary Autonomy in the Presence of Incomplete Market Separation. *IMF Staff Papers* 34 (4): 621–642.
Guillén, Mauro F. 2001. *The Limits of Convergence: Globalization and Organizational Change in Argentina, South Korea, and Spain*. Princeton University Press.
Guler, Isin, Mauro F. Guillén, and John Muir Macpherson. 2002. "Global Competition, Institutions, and the Diffusion of Organizational Practices: The International Spread of ISO 9000 Quality Certificates." *Administrative Science Quarterly* 47 (2): 207–32.
Gupta, Abhinav, and Adam J. Wowak. 2017. "The Elephant (or Donkey) in the Boardroom: How Board Political Ideology Affects CEO Pay." *Administrative Science Quarterly* 62 (1): 1–30.
Gupta, Joyeeta. 2014. *The History of Global Climate Governance*. Cambridge University Press.
Gurciullo, Stefano, and Slava J. Mikhaylov. 2017. "Detecting Policy Preferences and Dynamics in the UN General Debate with Neural Word Embeddings. In *2017 International Conference on the Frontiers and Advances in Data Science (FADS)*, 74–79. http://ieeexplore.ieee.org/document/8253197/.
Gygli, Savina, Florian Haelg, Niklas Potrafke, and Jan-Egbert Sturm. 2019. "The KOF Globalisation Index–Revisited." *The Review of International Organizations* 14 (3): 543–74.
Haas, Ernst B. 1962. "System and Process in the International Labor Organization: A Statistical Afterthought." *World Politics* 14 (2): 322–52.
Haas, Ernst B. 1990. *When Knowledge Is Power: Three Models of Change in International Organizations*. University of California Press.
Haas, Peter M. 1992. "Introduction: Epistemic Communities and International Policy Coordination." *International Organization* 46 (1): 1–35.
Hafsi, Taïeb, and Gokhan Turgut. 2013. "Boardroom Diversity and Its Effect on Social Performance: Conceptualization and Empirical Evidence." *Journal of Business Ethics* 112 (3): 463–79.
Halliday, Terence C., Susan Block-Lieb, and Bruce G. Carruthers. 2010. Rhetorical Legitimation: Global Scripts as Strategic Devices of International Organizations. *Socio-Economic Review* 8 (1): 77–112.
Halliday, Terence C., and Bruce G. Carruthers. 2007. "The Recursivity of Law: Global Norm Making and National Lawmaking in the Globalization of Corporate Insolvency Regimes." *American Journal of Sociology* 112 (4): 1135–1202.
Halliday, Terence C., and Bruce G. Carruthers. 2009. *Bankrupt: Global Lawmaking and Systemic Financial Crisis*. Stanford University Press.

Halliday, Terence C., Josh Pacewicz, and Susan Block-Lieb. 2013. "Who Governs? Delegations and Delegates in Global Trade Lawmaking." *Regulation & Governance* 7 (3): 279–98.

Hanrieder, Tine. 2015. *International Organization in Time: Fragmentation and Reform.* Oxford University Press.

Harmon, Derek J. 2019. "When the Fed Speaks: Arguments, Emotions, and the Microfoundations of Institutions." *Administrative Science Quarterly* 64 (3): 542–75.

Harper, Richard H. R. 1998. *Inside the IMF: An Ethnography of Documents, Technology and Organizational Action.* Academic Press.

Harris, Joseph, and Alexandre White. 2019. "The Sociology of Global Health." *Sociology of Development* 5 (1): 9–30.

Hasselbalch, Jacob A., and Leonard Seabrooke. 2021. "Prosopography." In *Research Methods in the Social Sciences*, edited by Jean-Frédéric Morin, Christian Olsson, and Ece Özlem Atikcan. Oxford University Press.

Hearson, Martin. 2018. "Transnational Expertise and the Expansion of the International Tax Regime: Imposing 'Acceptable' Standards." *Review of International Political Economy* 25 (5): 647–71.

Heinzel, Mirko. 2022. "International Bureaucrats and Organizational Performance. Country-Specific Knowledge and Sectoral Knowledge in World Bank Projects." *International Studies Quarterly* 66 (2): sqac013.

Heinzel, Mirko, Ben Cormier, and Bernhard Reinsberg. 2023. "Earmarked Funding and the Control-Performance Trade-Off in International Development Organizations." *International Organization* 77 (2): 475–95.

Heinzel, Mirko, and Andrea Liese. 2021. "Managing Performance and Winning Trust: How World Bank Staff Shape Recipient Performance." *The Review of International Organizations* 16 (3): 625–53.

Heinzel, Mirko, Jonas Richter, Per-Olof Busch, Hauke Feil, Jana Herold, and Andrea Liese. 2021. "Birds of a Feather? The Determinants of Impartiality Perceptions of the IMF and the World Bank." *Review of International Political Economy* 28 (5): 1249–73.

Heinzel, Mirko, Catherine Weaver, and Samantha Jorgensen. 2024. "Bureaucratic Representation and Gender Mainstreaming in International Organizations: Evidence from the World Bank." *American Political Science Review* 119 (1): 1–17.

Helgadóttir, Oddný. 2022. "Seeing Like a Macroeconomist: Varieties of Formalisation, Professional Incentives and Academic Ideational Change." *New Political Economy* 27 (3): 426–40.

Helgadóttir, Oddný. 2023. "How to Make a Super-Model: Professional Incentives and the Birth of Contemporary Macroeconomics.: *Review of International Political Economy* 30 (1): 252–80.

Helleiner, Eric. 1996. *States and the Reemergence of Global Finance: From Bretton Woods to the 1990s.* Cornell University Press.

Helleiner, Eric. 2014. *Forgotten Foundations of Bretton Woods: International Development and the Making of the Postwar Order.* Cornell University Press.

Helleiner, Eric. 2019. "The Life and Times of Embedded Liberalism: Legacies and Innovations Since Bretton Woods." *Review of International Political Economy* 26 (6): 1112–35.

Hendriksen, C. 2022. "Navigating Norms and Invisible Rules: Explaining the Case of Business Influence in International Shipping Regulation." *Business and Politics* 24 (1): 79–95.

Henning, C. Randall. 2017. *Tangled Governance: International Regime Complexity, the Troika, and the Euro Crisis.* Oxford University Press.

Henriksen, Lasse Folke, and Leonard Seabrooke. 2016. "Transnational Organizing: Issue Professionals in Environmental Sustainability Networks." *Organization* 23 (5): 722–41.

Henriksen, Lasse Folke, Leonard Seabrooke, and Kevin L Young. 2022. "Intellectual Rivalry in American Economics: Intergenerational Social Cohesion and the Rise of the Chicago School." *Socio-Economic Review* 20 (3): 989?–1013.

Herman, Barry, José Antonio Ocampo, and Shari Spiegel. 2010. "Towards a Comprehensive Sovereign Bankruptcy Regime." In *Overcoming Developing Country Debt Crises*, edited by Barry Herman, José Antonio Ocampo, and Shari Spiegel. Oxford University Press.

Hernandez, Christian. 2020. "IMF Flexibility or Neoliberal Adaptation: A Discursive Content Analysis of Article IV Policy Biases in Argentina." *Governance* 33 (1): 135–54.

Herring, Cedric. 2009. "Does Diversity Pay?: Race, Gender, and the Business Case for Diversity." *American Sociological Review* 74 (2): 208–24.

Hironaka, Ann. 2014. *Greening the Globe: World Society and Environmental Change*. Cambridge University Press.

Hobson, John M. 1997. *The Wealth of States: A Comparative Sociology of International Economic and Political Change*. Cambridge University Press.

Hofmann, Stephanie C., and Patryk Pawlak. 2023. "Governing Cyberspace: Policy Boundary Politics Across Organizations." *Review of International Political Economy* 30 (6): 2122–49.

Holmes, Marcus. 2013. "The Force of Face-to-Face Diplomacy: Mirror Neurons and the Problem of Intentions." *International Organization* 67 (4): 829–61.

Honig, Dan, and Catherine Weaver. 2019. "A Race to the Top? The Aid Transparency Index and the Social Power of Global Performance Indicators." *International Organization* 73 (3): 579–610.

Hooghe, Liesbet, and Gary Marks. 2015. "Delegation and Pooling in International Organizations." *Review of International Organizations* 10 (3): 305–28.

Hopgood, Stephen. 2006. *Keepers of the Flame: Understanding Amnesty International*. Cornell University Press.

Horne, Christine, and Stefanie Mollborn. 2020. "Norms: An Integrated Framework." *Annual Review of Sociology* 46 (1): 467–87.

Hovy, Dirk. 2020. *Text Analysis in Python for Social Scientists: Discovery and Exploration*. Cambridge University Press.

Hurd, Ian. 2019. "Legitimacy and Contestation in Global Governance: Revisiting the Folk Theory of International Institutions." *The Review of International Organizations* 14 (4): 717–29.

Hwang, Hokyu. 2006. "Planning Development: Globalization and the Shifting Locus of Planning." In *Globalization and Organization: World Society and Organizational Change*, edited by Gili S. Drori, John W. Meyer, and Hokyu Hwang. Oxford University Press.

Ikenberry, G. John. 1992. "A World Economy Restored: Expert Consensus and the Anglo-American Postwar Settlement. *International Organization* 46 (1): 289–321.

IMF. 1985. *Consensus of Cartagena, Declaration of Montevideo, "Emergency Proposals for Negotiations on Debt and Growth"* (December 16–17).

IMF. 1997. *World Economic Outlook, Interim Assessment—Crisis in Asia: Regional and Global Implications*. IMF.

IMF. 2009. *Creating Policy Space—Responsive Design and Streamlined Conditionality in Recent Low-Income Country Programs*. IMF Policy Paper. https://www.imf.org/external/np/pp/eng/2009/091009a.pdf.

IMF. 2011a. *Articles of Agreement of the International Monetary Fund*. IMF. https://www.imf.org/External/Pubs/FT/AA/pdf/aa.pdf.

IMF. 2011b. *By-Laws Rules and Regulations of the International Monetary Fund*. IMF. https://www.imf.org/external/pubs/ft/bl/blcon.htm.

IMF. 2012. "Liberalizing Capital Flows and Managing Outflows." IMF Policy Paper (13). https://elibrary.imf.org/openurl?genre=journal&issn=2663-3493&volume=2012&issue=013.

IMF, ed. 2013. *Fiscal Monitor, October 2013: Taxing Times* (World Economic and Financial Surveys). IMF.

IMF. 2017a. *Adequacy of the Global Financial Safety Net: Proposal for a New Policy Coordination Instrument.* IMF Policy Paper. https://www.imf.org/en/Publications/Policy-Papers/Issues/2017/07/26/pp072617-adequacy-of-the-global-financial-safety-net.

IMF. 2017b. *IMF Fiscal Monitor: Tackling Inequality, World Economic and Financial Surveys.* IMF.

IMF. 2017c. *IMF Staff Salary Structure.* IMF. https://www.imf.org/external/pubs/ft/ar/2017/eng/assets/ar17-web-table-3-4.pdf.

IMF. 2018. "How to Operationalize Gender Issues in Country Work." *IMF Policy Paper.* https://www.imf.org/en/Publications/Policy-Papers/Issues/2018/06/13/pp060118howto-note-on-gender.

IMF. 2019. *Diversity and Inclusion: 2019 Report Supplement.* IMF. https://www.imf.org/external/np/div/2019/index.pdf.

IMF. 2021a. "IMF Strategy to Help Members Address Climate Change Related Policy Challenges—Priorities, Modes of Delivery, and Budget Implications." *IMF Policy Paper* 2021/057. https://www.imf.org/en/Publications/Policy-Papers/Issues/2021/07/30/IMF-Strategy-to-Help-Members-Address-Climate-Change-Related-Policy-Challenges-Priorities-463093.

IMF. 2021b. "Comprehensive Surveillance Review—Background Paper on Integrating Climate Change into Article IV Consultations." *IMF Policy Paper* 2021/032. https://www.imf.org/en/Publications/Policy-Papers/Issues/2021/05/18/2021-Comprehensive-Surveillance-Review-Background-Paper-on-Integrating-Climate-Change-into-460303.

IMF. 2021c. "Resilience and Sustainability Trust, India, Lebanon." November 4, 2021. https://mediacenter.imf.org/news/all/imf—resilience-and-sustainability-trust—india—lebanon/s/80403be7-e13d-4d71-aede-bbe232ca1c8d.

IMF. 2022a. "A Guide to Committees, Groups, and Clubs." Accessed December 1, 2022. https://www.imf.org/en/About/Factsheets/A-Guide-to-Committees-Groups-and-Clubs.

IMF. 2022b. *Proposal to Establish a Resilience and Sustainability Trust.* IMF Policy Paper. https://www.imf.org/en/Publications/Policy-Papers/Issues/2022/04/15/Proposal-To-Establish-A-Resilience-and-Sustainability-Trust-516692.

IMF. 2022c. *Staff Guidance Note on the Sovereign Risk and Debt Sustainability Framework for Market Access Countries.* IMF Policy Paper. https://www.imf.org/en/Publications/Policy-Papers/Issues/2022/08/08/Staff-Guidance-Note-on-the-Sovereign-Risk-and-Debt-Sustainability-Framework-for-Market-521884.

IMF. 2022d. "Strategy Toward Mainstreaming Gender." IMF Policy Paper. https://www.imf.org/en/Publications/Policy-Papers/Issues/2022/07/28/IMF-Strategy-Toward-Mainstreaming-Gender-521344.

IMF. 2023. "Economist Program." Accessed August 19, 2023. https://www.imf.org/en/About/Recruitment/working-at-the-imf/economist-program.

Independent Evaluation Office of the International Monetary Fund, ed. 2013. *Research at the IMF: Relevance and Utilization.* IMF.

Jackson, Patrick Thaddeus, and Daniel H. Nexon. 1999. "Relations Before States: Substance, Process and the Study of World Politics." *European Journal of International Relations* 5 (3): 291–332.

James, Harold. 1996. *International Monetary Cooperation Since Bretton Woods.* IMF.

James, Kathryn. 2015. *The Rise of the Value-Added Tax.* Cambridge University Press.

James, Scott, Stefano Pagliari, and Kevin L. Young. 2021. "The Internationalization of European Financial Networks: A Quantitative Text Analysis of EU Consultation Responses." *Review of International Political Economy* 28 (4): 898–925.

James, Scott, and Lucia Quaglia. 2022. "Epistemic Contestation and Interagency Conflict: The Challenge of Regulating Investment Funds." *Regulation & Governance* 17 (2): 346–62.

Jelveh, Zubin, Bruce Kogut, and Suresh Naidu. 2014. "Political Language in Economics" (Columbia Business School Research Paper No. 14-57). *SSRN Electronic Journal*. https://www.ssrn.com/abstract=2535453.

Johnson, Juliet. 2016. *Priests of Prosperity: How Central Bankers Transformed the Postcommunist World*. Cornell University Press.

Johnson, Tana, and Johannes Urpelainen. 2014. "International Bureaucrats and the Formation of Intergovernmental Organizations: Institutional Design Discretion Sweetens the Pot." *International Organization* 68 (1): 177–209.

Jones, Calvert W. 2019. "Adviser to the King: Experts, Rationalization, and Legitimacy." *World Politics* 71 (1): 1–43.

Joshi, Anuradha, and Joseph Ayee. 2008. "Associational Taxation: A Pathway into the Informal Sector?" In *Taxation and State-Building in Developing Countries*, edited by D. Brautigam, O.-H. Fjeldstad, and M. Moore. Cambridge University Press.

Karell, Daniel, and Michael Freedman. 2019. "Rhetorics of Radicalism." *American Sociological Review* 84 (4): 726–53.

Kato, Junko. 1994. *The Problem of Bureaucratic Rationality: Tax Politics in Japan*. Princeton University Press.

Kaya, Ayse, and Mike Reay. 2019. "How Did the Washington Consensus Move Within the IMF? Fragmented Change from the 1980s to the Aftermath of the 2008 Crisis." *Review of International Political Economy* 26 (3): 384–409.

Keck, Margaret E., and Kathryn Sikkink. 1998. *Activists Beyond Borders: Advocacy Networks in International Politics*. Cornell University Press.

Keen, Michael. 2013. "The Anatomy of the VAT" (IMF Working Paper 13/111). International Monetary Fund.

Keen, Michael, and Ben Lockwood. 2010. "The Value Added Tax: Its Causes and Consequences. *Journal of Development Economics* 92 (2): 138–51.

Keen, Michael, and Joel Slemrod. 2022. *Rebellion, Rascals, and Revenue: Tax Follies and Wisdom Through the Ages*. Princeton University Press.

Kelley, Judith G., and Beth A. Simmons. 2019. "Introduction: The Power of Global Performance Indicators." *International Organization* 73 (3): 491–510.

Kennedy, David. 1986. "International Refugee Protection." *Human Rights Quarterly* 8 (1): 1–69.

Kentikelenis, Alexander E., and Sarah Babb. 2019. "The Making of Neoliberal Globalization: Norm Substitution and the Politics of Clandestine Institutional Change." *American Journal of Sociology* 124 (6): 1720–62.

Kentikelenis, Alexander E., and Sarah L. Babb. 2025. "International Financial Institutions: Forms, Functions, and Controversies." In *The Oxford Handbook of International Political Economy*, edited by Jon C. W. Pevehouse and Leonard Seabrooke. Oxford University Press.

Kentikelenis, Alexander E., and Leonard Seabrooke. 2017. "The Politics of World Polity: Script-Writing in International Organizations." *American Sociological Review* 82 (5): 1065–92.

Kentikelenis, Alexander E., and Leonard Seabrooke. 2021. "Organising Knowledge to Prevent Global Health Crises: A Comparative Analysis of Pandemic Preparedness Indicators." *BMJ Global Health* 6 (8): e006864.

Kentikelenis, Alexander E., and Leonard Seabrooke. 2022. "Governing and Measuring Health Security: The Global Push for Pandemic Preparedness Indicators." *Global Policy* 13 (4): 571–78.

Kentikelenis, Alexander E., Thomas H. Stubbs, and Lawrence P. King. 2016. "IMF Conditionality and Development Policy Space, 1985–2014." *Review of International Political Economy* 23 (4): 543–82.

Kentikelenis, Alexander, Thomas Stubbs, and Bernhard Reinsberg. 2022. *The IMF and the Road to a Green and Inclusive Recovery after Covid-19*. Cambridge Centre for Business Research (CBR) Special Report. University of Cambridge Repository. https://www.repository.cam.ac.uk/handle/1810/338625.

Kentikelenis, Alexander, and Erik Voeten. 2021. "Legitimacy Challenges to the Liberal World Order: Evidence from United Nations Speeches, 1970–2018." *Review of International Organizations* 16 (4): 721–54.

Kentikelenis, Alexandros, Leonard Seabrooke, and Ole Jacob Sending. 2023. "Global Health Expertise in the Shadow of Hegemony." *Studies in Comparative International Development* 58 (3): 347–68.

Kentikelenis, Alexandros, and Thomas Stubbs. 2023. *A Thousand Cuts: Social Protection in the Age of Austerity*. Oxford University Press.

Kentikelenis, Alexandros, and Thomas Stubbs. 2025. *Greening the International Monetary Fund*. Cambridge University Press.

Keohane, Robert Owen, and Joseph S. Nye. 1974. "Transgovernmental Relations and International Organizations." *World Politics* 27 (1): 39–62.

Keynes, John Maynard. 1943. "Proposals for an International Clearing Union." International Monetary Fund. https://www.elibrary.imf.org/display/book/9781451972511/ch001.xml.

Keynes, John Maynard. 1980. *The Collected Writings of John Maynard Keynes. 26: Activities 1941–1946. Shaping the Post-war World: Bretton Woods and Reparations*. Macmillan.

Kilby, Christopher. 2006. "Donor Influence in Multilateral Development Banks: The Case of the Asian Development Bank." *The Review of International Organizations* 1 (2): 173–95.

Kim, Hun Joon, and J. C. Sharman. 2014. "Accounts and Accountability: Corruption, Human Rights, and Individual Accountability Norms." *International Organization* 68 (2): 417–48.

Kindleberger, Charles P. 1951. "Bretton Woods Reappraised." *International Organization* 5 (1): 32–47.

Kindleberger, Charles P. 1955. "Economists in International Organizations." *International Organization* 9 (3): 338–52.

King, Lawrence P., and Aleksandra Sznajder. 2006. "The State-Led Transition to Liberal Capitalism: Neoliberal, Organizational, World-Systems, and Social Structural Explanations of Poland's Economic Success." *American Journal of Sociology* 112 (3): 751–801.

Kirshner, Jonathan. 1999. "Keynes, Capital Mobility and the Crisis of Embedded Liberalism." *Review of International Political Economy* 6 (3): 313–37.

Kohli, Atul. 2020. *Imperialism and the Developing World: How Britain and the United States Shaped the Global Periphery*. Oxford University Press.

Koremenos, Barbara, Charles Lipson, and Duncan W. Snidal. 2001. "The Rational Design of International Institutions." *International Organization* 55 (4): 761–99.

Kortendiek, Nele. 2021. "How to Govern Mixed Migration in Europe: Transnational Expert Networks and Knowledge Creation in International Organizations." *Global Networks* 21 (2): 320–38.

Kortendiek, Nele. 2024. *Global Governance on the Ground: Organizing International Migration and Asylum at the Border*. Oxford University Press.

Kozlowski, Austin C., Matt Taddy, and James A. Evans. 2019. "The Geometry of Culture: Analyzing the Meanings of Class Through Word Embeddings." *American Sociological Review* 84 (5): 905–49.

Kranke, Matthias. 2022. "Exclusive Expertise: The Boundary Work of International Organizations." *Review of International Political Economy* 29 (2): 453–76.

Krasner, Stephen D. 1981. "Power Structures and Regional Development Banks." *International Organization* 35 (2): 303–28.

Krugman, Paul R. 1990. "Debt Relief Is Cheap." *Foreign Policy* (80): 141–52.

Kupiec, Paul. 2005. "The IMF–World Bank Financial Sector Assessment Program: A View from the Inside." In *Systemic Financial Crises*, edited by Douglas D. Evanoff and George G. Kaufman. World Scientific.

Laffer, Arthur B. 2004. "The Laffer Curve: Past, Present, and Future." Heritage Foundation, June 1. https://www.heritage.org/taxes/report/the-laffer-curve-past-present-and-future.

Lagarde, Christine. 2015. "'Lifting the Small Boats,' Speech by IMF Managing Director." IMF, June 17. https://www.imf.org/en/News/Articles/2015/09/28/04/53/sp061715.

Lakatos, Imre. 1970. "Falsification and the Methodology of Scientific Research Programmes." In *Criticism and the Growth of Knowledge*, edited by Imre Lakatos and Alan Musgrave. Cambridge University Press.

Lake, David A. 2021. "The Organizational Ecology of Global Governance." *European Journal of International Relations* 27 (2): 345–68.

Lall, Ranjit. 2017. "Beyond Institutional Design: Explaining the Performance of International Organizations." *International Organization* 71 (2): 245–80.

Lall, Ranjit. 2023. *Making International Institutions Work: The Politics of Performance*. Cambridge University Press.

Lamba, Manika, and Margam Madhusudhan. 2022. *Text Mining for Information Professionals: An Uncharted Territory*. Springer.

Lang, Valentin, Lukas Wellner, and Alexandros Kentikelenis. 2024. Biased Bureaucrats and the Policies of International Organizations. *American Journal of Political Science*: 1–19. https://doi.org/10.1111/ajps.12921.

Latour, Bruno. 1986. "Visualisation and Cognition: Thinking with Eyes and Hands." In *Knowledge and Society: Studies in the Sociology of Culture Past and Present*. Vol. 6. JAI Press.

Lebaron, Frédéric. 2008. "Central Bankers in the Contemporary Global Field of Power: A 'Social Space' Approach." *The Sociological Review* 56 (Suppl. 1): 121–44.

Leaver, Richard and Leonard Seabrooke. 2000. "Can the IMF be Reformed?" In *Global Finance: New Thinking on Regulating Speculative Capital Markets*, edited by Walden Bello, Nicola Bullard, Kamal Malhotra. Zed Press.

Levitt, Peggy, and Sally Merry. 2009. "Vernacularization on the Ground: Local Uses of Global Women's Rights in Peru, China, India and the United States." *Global Networks* 9 (4): 441–61.

Lewis, Jeffrey. 2005. "The Janus Face of Brussels: Socialization and Everyday Decision Making in the European Union." *International Organization* 59 (4): 937–71.

Liese, Andrea, Jana Herold, Hauke Feil, and Per-Olof Busch. 2021. "The Heart of Bureaucratic Power: Explaining International Bureaucracies' Expert Authority." *Review of International Studies* 47 (3): 353–76.

Lim, Alwyn. 2021. "Global Fields, Institutional Emergence, and the Regulation of Transnational Corporations." *Social Forces* 99 (3): 1060–85.

Lipson, Charles. 1992. "International Debt and National Security: Comparing Victorian Britain and Postwar America." In *The International Debt Crisis in Historical Perspective*, edited by Barry Eichengreen and Peter H. Lindert. MIT Press.

Lissakers, Karin. 1991. *Banks, Borrowers, and the Establishment: A Revisionist Account of the International Debt Crisis*. New York: Basic Books.

Littoz-Monnet, Annabelle. 2020. *Governing Through Expertise: The Politics of Bioethics*. Cambridge University Press.

Littoz-Monnet, Annabelle. 2022. "Exclusivity and Circularity in the Production of Global Governance Expertise: The Making of 'Global Mental Health' Knowledge." *International Political Sociology* 16 (2): olab035.

Lombardi, Domenico, and Ngaire Woods. 2008. "The Politics of Influence: An Analysis of IMF Surveillance." *Review of International Political Economy* 15 (5): 711–39.

Lopez, Sophia Murillo. 2017. "Legal Legitimacy of Tax Recommendations Delivered by the IMF in the Context of Article IV Consultations." *Erasmus Law Review* 10 (2): 106–18.

Maaten, Laurens van der, and Geoffrey Hinton. 2008. "Visualizing Data Using t-SNE." *Journal of Machine Learning Research* 9 (86): 2579–2605.

Malik, Rabia, and Randall W. Stone. 2018. "Corporate Influence in World Bank Lending." *The Journal of Politics* 80 (1): 103–18.

Mann, M. 1986. *The Sources of Social Power: A History of Power from the Beginning to A.D. 1760*. Cambridge University Press.

Martin, Isaac William. 2015. *Rich People's Movements: Grassroots Campaigns to Untax the One Percent*. Oxford University Press.

Martin, Isaac William, and Nadav Gabay. 2018. "Tax Policy and Tax Protest in 20 Rich Democracies, 1980–2010." *The British Journal of Sociology* 69 (3): 647–69.

Martin, Jamie. 2022a. *The Meddlers: Sovereignty, Empire, and the Birth of Global Economic Governance*. Harvard University Press.

Martin, John Levi. 2011. *The Explanation of Social Action*. Oxford University Press.

Martin, John Levi. 2022b. "What Sociologists Should Get Out of Pragmatism." In *The New Pragmatist Sociology: Inquiry, Agency, and Democracy*, edited by Isaac Ariail Reed, Neil Gross, and Christopher Winship. Columbia University Press.

Martinez-Diaz, Leonardo. 2009. "Boards of Directors in International Organizations: A Framework for Understanding the Dilemmas of Institutional Design." *The Review of International Organizations* 4 (4): 383–406.

Mattli, Walter, and Tim Büthe. 2005. "Accountability in Accounting? The Politics of Private Rule-Making in the Public Interest." *Governance* 18 (3): 399–429.

Mauss, Marcel. 1985. "A Category of the Human Mind: the Notion of Person; the Notion of Self." In *The Category of the Person: Anthropology, Philosophy, History*, edited by Michael Carrithers, Steven Collins, and Stephen Lukes: Cambridge University Press.

McCourt, David M. 2016. "Practice Theory and Relationalism as the New Constructivism." *International Studies Quarterly* 60 (3): 475–85.

McLean, Paul. 2007. *The Art of the Network: Strategic Interaction and Patronage in Renaissance Florence*. Duke University Press.

McPherson, Miller, Lynn Smith-Lovin, and James M. Cook. 2001. "Birds of a Feather: Homophily in Social Networks." *Annual Review of Sociology* 27: 415–44.

Mehrpouya, Afshin, and Marie-Laure Salles-Djelic. 2019. "Seeing Like the Market; Exploring the Mutual Rise of Transparency and Accounting in Transnational Economic and Market Governance." *Accounting, Organizations and Society* 76: 12–31.

Menz, Georg. 2005. "Making Thatcher Look Timid: The Rise and Fall of the New Zealand Model." In *Internalizing Globalization: The Rise of Neoliberalism and the Decline of National Varieties of Capitalism*, edited by Susanne Soederberg, Georg Menz, and Philip G. Cerny. New York: Springer.

Merton, Robert K. 1959. "Notes on Problem-Finding in Sociology." In *Sociology Today: Problems and Prospects*, edited by Robert K. Merton, Leonard Broom, and Leonard S. Cottrell. New York: Harper & Row.

Merton, Robert K. 1973. *The Sociology of Science: Theoretical and Empirical Investigations*. University of Chicago Press.

Merton, Robert K. 1987. "Three Fragments from a Sociologist's Notebooks: Establishing the Phenomenon, Specified Ignorance, and Strategic Research Materials." *Annual Review of Sociology* 13: 1–28.

Meyer, John W. 1977. "The Effects of Education as an Institution." *American Journal of Sociology* 83 (1): 55–77.

Meyer, John W. 2010. "World Society, Institutional Theories, and the Actor." *Annual Review of Sociology* 36 (1): 1–20.

Meyer, John W., John Boli, George M. Thomas, and Francisco O. Ramirez. 1997. "World Society and the Nation-State." *American Journal of Sociology* 103 (1): 144–81.

Meyer, John W., and Patricia Bromley. 2013. "The Worldwide Expansion of 'Organization.'" *Sociological Theory* 31 (4): 366–89.

Meyer, John W., Gili S. Drori, and Hokyu Hwang. 2006. "World Society and the Proliferation of Formal Organization." In *Globalization and Organization: World Society and Organizational Change*, edited by Gili S. Drori, John W. Meyer, and Hokyu Hwang, 25–49. Oxford University Press.

Meyer, John W., David John Frank, Ann Hironaka, Evan Schofer, and Nancy Brandon Tuma. 1997. "The Structuring of a World Environmental Regime, 1870–1990." *International Organization* 51 (4): 623–51.

Meyer, John W., and Ronald L. Jepperson. 2000. "The 'Actors' of Modern Society: The Cultural Construction of Social Agency." *Sociological Theory* 18 (1): 100–120.

Meyer, John W., and Brian Rowan. 1977. "Institutionalized Organizations: Formal Structure as Myth and Ceremony." *American Journal of Sociology* 83 (2): 340–63.

Micah, Angela E., Ian E. Cogswell, Brandon Cunningham, Satoshi Ezoe, Anton C. Harle, Emilie R. Maddison, et al. 2021. "Tracking Development Assistance for Health and for COVID-19: A Review of Development Assistance, Government, Out-of-Pocket, and Other Private Spending on Health for 204 Countries and Territories, 1990–2050." *The Lancet* 398 (10308): 1317–43.

Mikesell, Raymond F. 1994. "The Bretton Woods Debates: A Memoir." *Princeton Essays in International Finance*, no. 192.

Mikolov, Tomas, Kai Chen, Greg Corrado, and Jeffrey Dean. 2013. "Efficient Estimation of Word Representations in Vector Space." (*arXiv* eprint 1301.3781). http://adsabs.harvard.edu/abs/2013arXiv1301.3781M.

Miller, George A., and Walter G. Charles. 1991. "Contextual Correlates of Semantic Similarity." *Language and Cognitive Processes* 6 (1): 1–28.

Miller, Toyah, and María Del Carmen Triana. 2009. "Demographic Diversity in the Boardroom: Mediators of the Board Diversity–Firm Performance Relationship." *Journal of Management Studies* 46 (5): 755–86.

Mirowski, Philip, and Dieter Plehwe. 2009. *The Road from Mont Pèlerin: The Making of the Neoliberal Thought Collective*. Cambridge University Press.

Mische, Ann. 2003. "Cross-Talk in Movements: Reconceiving the Culture-Network Link." In *Social Movements and Networks: Relational Approaches to Collective Action*, edited by Mario Diani and Doug McAdam. Oxford University Press.

Molho, Jérémie, Peggy Levitt, Nick Dines, and Anna Triandafyllidou. 2020. "Cultural Policies in Cities of the 'Global South': A Multi-scalar Approach." *International Journal of Cultural Policy* 26 (6): 711–21.

Moloney, Kim. 2022. *Who Matters at the World Bank? Bureaucrats, Policy Change, and Public Sector Governance*. Oxford University Press.

Momani, Bessma. 2004. "American Politicization of the International Monetary Fund." *Review of International Political Economy* 11 (5): 880–904.

Momani, Bessma. 2005. "Recruiting and Diversifying IMF Technocrats." *Global Society* 19 (2): 167–68.

Momani, Bessma. 2007. "IMF Staff: Missing Link in Fund Reform Proposals." *Review of International Organizations* 2 (1): 39–57.

Moretti, Franco, and Dominique Pestre. 2015. "Bankspeak." *New Left Review* 92 (March–April): 75–99.

Moschella, Manuela. 2009. When ideas fail to influence policy outcomes: Orderly liberalization and the International Monetary Fund. *Review of International Political Economy* 16 (5): 854–82.

Moschella, Manuela. 2010. *Governing Risk: The IMF and Global Financial Crises*. Palgrave Macmillan.

Moschella, Manuela. 2011. "Lagged Learning and the Response to Equilibrium Shock: The Global Financial Crisis and IMF Surveillance." *Journal of Public Policy* 31 (2): 121–41.

Moschella, Manuela. 2012. "IMF Surveillance in Crisis: The Past, Present and Future of the Reform Process." *Global Society* 26 (1): 43–60.

Moschella, Manuela. 2024. *Unexpected Revolutionaries: How Central Banks Made and Unmade Economic Orthodoxy*. Cornell University Press.

Mosley, Layna. 2003. "Attempting Global Standards: National Governments, International Finance, and the IMF's Data Regime." *Review of International Political Economy* 10 (2): 331–62.

Mudge, S. L., and A. Vauchez. 2012. "Building Europe on a Weak Field: Law, Economics, and Scholarly Avatars in Transnational Politics." *American Journal of Sociology* 118 (2): 449–92.

Mügge, Daniel. 2022. "Economic Statistics as Political Artefacts." *Review of International Political Economy* 29 (1): 1–22.

Mukherjee, Rohan. 2022. *Ascending Order: Rising Powers and the Politics of Status in International Relations*. Cambridge University Press.

Müller, Harald, and Carmen Wunderlich. 2018. "Not Lost in Contestation: How Norm Entrepreneurs Frame Norm Development in the Nuclear Nonproliferation Regime." *Contemporary Security Policy* 39 (3): 341–66.

Nelson, Stephen C. 2014. "Playing Favorites: How Shared Beliefs Shape the IMF's Lending Decisions." *International Organization* 68 (2): 297–328.

Nie, Mintao. 2023. IOs' selective adoption of NGO information: Evidence from the Universal Periodic Review. *The Review of International Organizations* 18 (1): 27–59.

Nilsson, Adriana. 2017. "Treating Market Failure: Access Professionals in Global Health." In *Professional Networks in Transnational Governance*, edited by Leonard Seabrooke and Lasse Folke Henriksen. Cambridge University Press.

Niskanen, William A. 1971. *Bureaucracy and Representative Government*. Transaction Publishers.

Nordquist, Sienna, David R. K. Adler, and Alexandros Kentikelenis. 2024. "The Globalization Backlash Revisited: Evidence from the United States." *Global Perspectives* 5 (1): 125070.

Noy, Shiri. 2017. *Banking on Health: The World Bank and Health Sector Reform in Latin America*. Palgrave Macmillan UK.

Ocampo, José Antonio. 2017. *Resetting the International Monetary (Non)System*. Oxford University Press.

Önder, Ali Sina, and Marko Terviö. 2015. "Is Economics a House Divided? Analysis of Citation Networks." *Economic Inquiry* 53 (3): 1491–1505.

Ota, Hiroshi. 2018. "Internationalization of Higher Education: Global Trends and Japan's Challenges." *Educational Studies in Japan* 12: 91–105.

Panitch, Leo, and Sam Gindin. 2013. *The Making of Global Capitalism: The Political Economy of American Empire*. London: Verso.

Pardo-Guerra, Juan Pablo, and Prithviraj Pahwa. 2022. "The Extended Computational Case Method: A Framework for Research Design." *Sociological Methods & Research* 51 (4): 1826–67.
Park, Susan. 2022. *The Good Hegemon: US Power, Accountability as Justice, and the Multilateral Development Banks*. Oxford University Press.
Park, Susan, and Jonathan R. Strand, eds. 2015. *Global Economic Governance and the Development Practices of the Multilateral Development Banks*. Routledge.
Paterson, Matthew. 2021. "Climate Change and International Political Economy: Between Collapse and Transformation." *Review of International Political Economy* 28 (2): 394–405.
Pauly, Louis W. 1997. *Who Elected the Bankers? Surveillance and Control in the World Economy*. Cornell University Press.
Payer, Cheryl. 1974. *The Debt Trap: The IMF and the Third World*. Monthly Review Press.
Peet, Richard. 2009. *Unholy Trinity: The IMF, World Bank and WTO*. Zed Books.
Peirce, Charles S. 1984. *Writings of Charles S. Peirce: A Chronological Edition. Volume 2, 1867–1871*. Indiana University Press.
Penati, Alessandro, and Michael Dooley. 1984. "Current Account Imbalances and Capital Formation in Industrial Countries, 1949-81." *IMF Staff Papers* 31 (1): 1–24.
Plehwe, Dieter, Moritz Neujeffski, and Werner Krämer. 2018. "Saving the Dangerous Idea: Austerity Think Tank Networks in the European Union." *Policy and Society* 37 (2): 188–205.
Polillo, Simone, and Mauro F Guillén. 2005. "Globalization Pressures and the State: The Worldwide Spread of Central Bank Independence." *American Journal of Sociology* 110 (6): 1764–1802.
Pollack, Mark A., and Gregory C. Shaffer. 2009. *When Cooperation Fails: The International Law and Politics of Genetically Modified Foods*. Oxford University Press.
Ponte, Stefano. 2014. "'Roundtabling' Sustainability: Lessons from the Biofuel Industry." *Geoforum* 54: 261–71.
Portugal, Murilo. 2005. "Improving IMF Governance and Increasing the Influence of Developing Countries in IMF Decision-Making." In *Reforming the Governance of the IMF and the World Bank*, edited by Ariel Buira. Anthem Press.
Pouliot, Vincent. 2021a. "Global Governance in the Age of Epistemic Authority." *International Theory* 13 (1): 144–56.
Pouliot, Vincent. 2021b. "The Gray Area of Institutional Change: How the Security Council Transforms Its Practices on the Fly." *Journal of Global Security Studies* 6 (3): ogaa043.
Prasad, M. 2006. *The Politics of Free Markets: The Rise of Neoliberal Economic Policies in Britain, France, Germany, and the United States*. University of Chicago Press.
Radelet, Steven, and Jeffrey D. Sachs. 1998. "The East Asian Financial Crisis: Diagnosis, Remedies, Prospects." *Brookings Papers on Economic Activity* (1): 1–90.
Ramos, Luma, Kevin P. Gallagher, Corinne Stephenson, and Irene Monasterolo. 2022. "Climate Risk and IMF Surveillance Policy: A Baseline Analysis." *Climate Policy* 22 (3): 371–88.
Rauh, Christian, and Michael Zürn. 2020. "Authority, Politicization, and Alternative Justifications: Endogenous Legitimation Dynamics in Global Economic Governance." *Review of International Political Economy* 27 (3): 583–611.
Reay, Michael J. 2012. "The Flexible Unity of Economics." *American Journal of Sociology* 118 (1): 45–87.
Reinhart, Carmen, Kenneth Rogoff, and Miguel A. Savastano. 2003. "Debt Intolerance." *Brookings Papers on Economic Activity* 34 (1): 1–74.

Reinsberg, Bernhard, Alexander E. Kentikelenis, Thomas H. Stubbs, and Lawrence P. King. 2019. "The World System and the Hollowing Out of State Capacity: How Structural Adjustment Programs Affect Bureaucratic Quality in Developing Countries." *American Journal of Sociology* 124 (4): 1222–57.

Reinsberg, Bernhard, Thomas Stubbs, and Alexander E. Kentikelenis. 2020. "Taxing the People, Not Trade: The International Monetary Fund and the Structure of Taxation in Developing Countries." *Studies in Comparative International Development* 55 (3): 278–304.

Reinsberg, Bernhard, and Oliver Westerwinter. 2021. "The Global Governance of International Development: Documenting the Rise of Multi-stakeholder Partnerships and Identifying Underlying Theoretical Explanations." *The Review of International Organizations* 16 (1): 59–94.

Reykers, Yf, John Karlsrud, Malte Brosig, Stephanie C. Hofmann, Cristiana Maglia, and Pernille Rieker. 2023. "Ad Hoc Coalitions in Global Governance: Short-Notice, Task- and Time-Specific Cooperation. *International Affairs* 99 (2): 727–45.

Rheault, Ludovic, and Christopher Cochrane. 2020. "Word Embeddings for the Analysis of Ideological Placement in Parliamentary Corpora." *Political Analysis* 28 (1): 112–33.

Rickard, Stephanie J., and Teri L. Caraway. 2014. "International Negotiations in the Shadow of National Elections." *International Organization* 68 (03): 701–20.

Rickard, Stephanie J., and Teri L. Caraway. 2018. "International Demands for Austerity: Examining the Impact of the IMF on the Public Sector." *The Review of International Organizations* 22 (4): 35–57.

Rodriguez, Pedro L., and Arthur Spirling. 2022. "Word Embeddings: What Works, What Doesn't, and How to Tell the Difference for Applied Research." *The Journal of Politics* 84 (1): 101–15.

Rodrik, Dani. 1998. "Who Needs Capital-Account Convertibility?" In *Should the IMF Pursue Capital-Account Convertibility?* (Princeton Essays in International Finance no. 207), edited by Stanley Fischer, Richard N. Cooper, Rudiger Dornbusch, Peter M. Garber, Carlos Massad, Jacques J. Polak, et al. International Finance Section, Department of Economics, Princeton University.

Rodrik, Dani. 2011. *The Globalization Paradox: Democracy and the Future of the World Economy.* W. W. Norton & Company.

Roos, Jerome. 2018. *Why Not Default? The Political Economy of Sovereign Debt.* Princeton University Press.

Rossier, Thierry, Christoph Houman Ellersgaard, Anton Grau Larsen, and Jacob Aagaard Lunding. 2022. "From Integrated to Fragmented Elites. The Core of Swiss Elite Networks 1910–2015." *The British Journal of Sociology* 73 (2): 315–35.

Rotem, Nir. 2022. "World Society and Field Theory: The Infiltration of Development into Humanitarianism." *The British Journal of Sociology* 73 (2): 402–20.

Rowden, Rick. 2013. "The Ghosts of User Fees Past: Exploring Accountability for Victims of a 30-Year Economic Policy Mistake. *Health and Human Rights Journal* 15 (1): 175–85.

Rudkowsky, Elena, Martin Haselmayer, Matthias Wastian, Marcelo Jenny, Štefan Emrich, and Michael Sedlmair. 2018. "More than Bags of Words: Sentiment Analysis with Word Embeddings." *Communication Methods and Measures* 12 (2–3): 140–57.

Ruggie, John Gerard. 1982. "International Regimes, Transactions, and Change: Embedded Liberalism in the Postwar Economic Order." *International Organization* 36 (2): 379–415.

Ruggie, John Gerard. 1998. *Constructing the World Polity: Essays on International Institutionalization.* Routledge.

Sachs, Jeffrey. 1989a. "Making the Brady Plan Work." *Foreign Affairs* 68 (3): 87–104.

Sachs, Jeffrey. 1989b. "The Debt Overhang of Developing Countries." In *Debt, Stabilization, and Development: Essays in Memory of Carlos Díaz-Alejandro*, edited by Guillermo A. Calvo, Ronald Findlay, Pentti J. K. Kouri, and Jorge Braga de Macedo. Blackwell.

Schäfer, Armin. 2006. "A New Form of Governance? Comparing the Open Method of Coordination to Multilateral Surveillance by the IMF and the OECD." *Journal of European Public Policy* 13 (1): 70–88.

Schlaufer, Caroline. 2019. "How Does Policy Advice of the International Monetary Fund Differ Along the Income of Advised Countries?" *Policy Studies* 40 (3–4): 287–302.

Schofer, Evan, Ann Hironaka, David John Frank, and Wesley Longhofer. 2012. "Sociological Institutionalism and World Society." In *The Wiley-Blackwell Companion to Political Sociology*, edited by Edwin Amenta, Kate Nash, and Alan Scott. Wiley-Blackwell.

Schofer, Evan, and John W. Meyer. 2005. "The Worldwide Expansion of Higher Education in the Twentieth Century." *American Sociological Review* 70 (6): 898–920.

Schofer, Evan, Francisco O. Ramirez, and John W. Meyer. 2000. "The Effects of Science on National Economic Development, 1970 to 1990." *American Sociological Review* 65 (6): 866–87.

Schwartz, Herman. 1994. "Small States in Big Trouble: State Reorganization in Australia, Denmark, New Zealand, and Sweden in the 1980s." *World Politics* 46 (4): 527–55.

Seabrooke, Leonard. 2001. *US Power in International Finance: The Victory of Dividends*. Palgrave.

Seabrooke, Leonard. 2007. "Legitimacy Gaps in the World Economy: Explaining the Sources of the IMF's Legitimacy Crisis." *International Politics* 44 (2/3): 250–68.

Seabrooke, Leonard. 2010. "Bitter Pills to Swallow: Legitimacy Gaps and Social Recognition of the IMF Tax Policy Norms in East Asia." In *Owning Development*, edited by Susan Park and Antje Vetterlein, 137–59. Cambridge University Press.

Seabrooke, Leonard. 2012. "Pragmatic Numbers: The IMF, Financial Reform, and Policy Learning in Least Likely Environments." *Journal of International Relations and Development* 15 (4): 486–505.

Seabrooke, Leonard. 2014. "Identity Switching and Transnational Professionals." *International Political Sociology* 8 (3): 335–37.

Seabrooke, Leonard, and Lasse Folke Henriksen, eds. 2017. *Professional Networks in Transnational Governance*. Cambridge University Press.

Seabrooke, Leonard, and Emelie Rebecca Nilsson. 2015. "Professional Skills in International Financial Surveillance: Assessing Change in IMF Policy Teams." *Governance* 28 (2): 237–54.

Seabrooke, Leonard, and Ole Jacob Sending. 2020. "Contracting Development: Managerialism and Consultants in Intergovernmental Oganizations." *Review of International Political Economy* 27 (4): 802–27.

Seabrooke, Leonard, and Ole Jacob Sending. 2022. "Consultancies in Public Administration." *Public Administration* 100 (3): 457–71.

Seabrooke, Leonard, and Annika Stenström. 2023. "Professional Ecologies in European Sustainable Finance. *Governance* 36 (4): 1009–1345.

Seabrooke, Leonard, and Eleni Tsingou. 2021. "Revolving Doors in International Financial Governance." *Global Networks* 21 (2): 294–319.

Seabrooke, Leonard, Eleni Tsingou, and Johann Ole Willers. 2020. "The Political Economy of Policy Vacuums: The European Commission on Demographic Change." *New Political Economy* 25 (6): 1007–21.

Seabrooke, Leonard, and Duncan Wigan. 2015. "How Activists Use Benchmarks: Reformist and Revolutionary Benchmarks for Global Economic Justice." *Review of International Studies* 41 (5): 887–904.

Seabrooke, Leonard, and Duncan Wigan. 2024. "Getting Action for Global Economic Justice: The Micro-foundations of Transnational Activism." *Socio-Economic Review* 22 (3): 1313–34.

Sendroiu, Ioana, and Ron Levi. 2023. "World Society Corridors: Partnership Patterns in the Spread of Human Rights." *Social Forces* 102 (1): 377–401.

Sending, Ole Jacob. 2002. "Constitution, Choice and Change: Problems with the 'Logic of Appropriateness' and Its Use in Constructivist Theory." *European Journal of International Relations* 8 (4): 443–70.

Shome, Parthasarathi. 1995. *Tax Policy Handbook*. IMF.

Shwed, Uri, and Peter S. Bearman. 2010. "The Temporal Structure of Scientific Consensus Formation." *American Sociological Review* 75 (6): 817–40.

Sikkink, Kathryn. 1998. "Transnational Politics, International Relations Theory, and Human Rights." *PS: Political Science & Politics* 31 (3): 517–23.

Simmons, Beth A., Frank Dobbin, and Geoffrey Garrett, eds. 2008. *The Global Diffusion of Markets and Democracy*. Cambridge University Press.

Singh, Ajit. 1990. "The State of Industry in the Third World in the 1980s: Analytical and Policy Issues" (Working Paper 137). *Kellogg Institute for International Studies*. https://kellogg.nd.edu/documents/1331.

Skidelsky, Robert. 1986. *John Maynard Keynes: Fighting for Freedom, 1937–1946*. Viking.

Skocpol, Theda. 1979. *States and Social Revolutions: A Comparative Analysis of France, Russia, and China*. Cambridge University Press.

Skovgaard, Jakob. 2021. *The Economisation of Climate Change: How the G20, the OECD and the IMF Address Fossil Fuel Subsidies and Climate Finance*. Cambridge University Press.

de Souza Leão, Luciana. 2020. "What's on Trial? The Making of Field Experiments in International Development." *The British Journal of Sociology* 71 (3): 444–59.

de Souza Leão, Luciana, and Gil Eyal. 2019. "The Rise of Randomized Controlled Trials (RCTs) in International Development in Historical Perspective." *Theory and Society* 48 (3): 383–418.

de Souza Leão, Luciana, and Gil Eyal. 2020. "Searching Under the Streetlight: A Historical Perspective on the Rise of Randomistas." *World Development* 127: 104781.

Spence, Crawford, and Chris Carter. 2014. "An Exploration of the Professional Habitus in the Big 4 Accounting Firms." *Work, Employment and Society* 28 (6): 946–62.

Squatrito, Theresa, and Thomas Sommerer. 2024. "Informal governance and transnational access in world politics". *Regulation & Governance*. https://doi.org/10.1111/rego.12636.

Stausholm, Saila, Richard Murphy, and Leonard Seabrooke. 2025. "Big Four Offshore: Transparency Arbitrage Across Legal and Geographical Boundaries." *Contemporary Accounting Research*, forthcoming.

Stedman Jones, Daniel. 2012. *Masters of the Universe: Hayek, Friedman, and the Birth of Neoliberal Politics*. Princeton: Princeton University Press.

Steffek, Jens. 2021. *International Organization as Technocratic Utopia*. Oxford University Press.

Steinmo, Sven. 1993. *Taxation and Democracy: Swedish, British, and American Approaches to Financing the Modern State*. Yale University Press.

Stephen, Matthew D., and David Skidmore. 2019. "The AIIB in the Liberal International Order." *The Chinese Journal of International Politics* 12 (1): 61–91.

Stern, Ithai, and James D. Westphal. 2010. "Stealthy Footsteps to the Boardroom: Executives' Backgrounds, Sophisticated Interpersonal Influence Behavior, and Board Appointments." *Administrative Science Quarterly* 55 (2): 278–319.

Stewart, Frances. 2016. "Changing Perspectives on Inequality and Development." *Studies in Comparative International Development* 51 (1): 60–80.

Stewart, Miranda. 2024. "International Institutions in Global Tax Governance." *Journal of International Economic Law* 27 (4): 618–23.

Stewart, Miranda, and Sunita Jogarajan. 2004. "The International Monetary Fund and Tax Reform." *British Tax Review* 146 (2): 146–75.

Stiglitz, Joseph E. 2000a. "Capital Market Liberalization, Economic Growth, and Instability." *World Development* 28 (6): 1075–1086.

Stiglitz, Joseph E. 2000b. "What I Learned at the World Economic Crisis." *New Republic*, April 17. https://business.columbia.edu/sites/default/files-efs/imce-uploads/Joseph_Stiglitz/What_I_Learned_at_the_World_Economic_Crisis.pdf.

Stiglitz, Joseph E. 2002. *Globalization and Its Discontents*. W. W. Norton & Company.

Stiglitz, Joseph E. 2010. "Development-Oriented Tax Policy." In *Taxation in Developing Countries: Six Case Studies and Policy Implications*, edited by Roger Gordon. Columbia University Press.

Stiglitz, Joseph E., and M. Shahe Emran. 2007. "Equity and Efficiency in Tax Reform in Developing Countries." *SSRN Electronic Journal*. http://www.ssrn.com/abstract=1001269.

Stiles, Kendall W. 1987. "Bargaining with Bureaucrats: Debt Negotiations in the International Monetary Fund." *International Journal of Public Administration* 9 (1): 1–43.

Stoltz, Dustin S., and Marshall A. Taylor. 2021. "Cultural Cartography with Word Embeddings." *Poetics* 88: 101567.

Stoltz, Dustin S., and Marshall A. Taylor. 2024. *Mapping Texts: Computational Text Analysis for the Social Sciences*. Oxford University Press.

Stone, Diane, Leslie A. Pal, and Osmany Porto de Oliveira. 2021. "Private Consultants and Policy Advisory Organizations: A Blind Spot on Policy Transfer Research." In *Handbook of Policy Transfer, Diffusion and Circulation*, edited by Osmany Porto de Oliveira. Edward Elgar Publishing.

Stone, Lawrence. 1971. "Prosopography." *Daedalus* 100 (1): 46–79.

Stone, Randall W. 2004. "The Political Economy of IMF Lending in Africa." *American Political Science Review* 98 (4): 577–92.

Stone, Randall W. 2008. "The Scope of IMF Conditionality." *International Organization* 62 (4): 589–620.

Stone, Randall W. 2011. *Controlling Institutions: International Organizations and the Global Economy*. Cambridge University Press.

Stone, Randall W. 2013. "Informal Governance in International Organizations: Introduction to the Special Issue." *The Review of International Organizations* 8 (2): 121–36.

Storeng, Katerini Tagmatarchi, Antoine de Bengy Puyvallée, and Felix Stein. 2021. "COVAX and the Rise of the 'Super Public Private Partnership' for Global Health." *Global Public Health* 18 (1): 1–17.

Stotsky, Janet, and Asegedech WoldeMariam. 2002. "Central American Tax Reform: Trends and Possibilities" (IMF Working Paper 02/227). International Monetary Fund.

Strange, Susan. 1990. "Finance, Information and Power." *Review of International Studies* 16 (3): 259–74.

Strange, Susan. 1996. *The Retreat of the State: The Diffusion of Power in the World Economy*. Cambridge University Press.

Strange, Susan. 1998. "The New World of Debt." *New Left Review* I/230 (July–August): 91–114.

Stroup, Sarah S., and Wendy H. Wong. 2017. *The Authority Trap: Strategic Choices of International NGOs*. Cornell University Press.

Stuenkel, Oliver. 2016. "Brazil and Responsibility to Protect: A Case of Agency and Norm Entrepreneurship in the Global South." *International Relations* 30 (3): 375–90.

Suddaby, Roy, David J. Cooper, and Royston Greenwood. 2007. "Transnational Regulation of Professional Services: Governance Dynamics of Field Level Organizational Change." *Accounting, Organizations and Society* 32 (4): 333–362.

Swedberg, Richard. 1986. "The Doctrine of Economic Neutrality of the IMF and the World Bank." *Journal of Peace Research* 23 (4): 377–90.

Swistak, Artur, and Nate Vernon. 2023. "Value Added Tax in the Extractive Industries." *IMF Working Papers* 23 (221).

Sytko, Yurii L., and Olga A. Kuzina. 2019. "Interpretation of Signs in the Conception of Ch.S. Pierce via Predicabilia and Categories of Aristotle. In *SHS Web of Conferences* 69: 00116.

Tait, Alan A. 1988. *Value Added Tax: International Practice and Problems.* International Monetary Fund.

Tait, Alan A. 1989. *IMF Advice on Fiscal Policy.* International Monetary Fund.

Tallberg, Jonas, Thomas Sommerer, Theresa Squatrito, and Christer Jönsson. 2013. *The Opening Up of International Organizations: Transnational Access in Global Governance.* Cambridge University Press.

Tan, Celine. 2007. "Debt and Conditionality: Multilateral Debt Relief Initiative and Opportunities for Expanding Policy Space. *TWN Global Economy Series.* Third World Network. http://www.twn.my/title2/ge/GE09.pdf.

Tan, Celine. 2014. "Reframing the Debate: The Debt Relief Initiative and New Normative Values in the Governance of Third World Debt." *International Journal of Law in Context* 10 (2): 249–72.

Tannenwald, Nina. 1999. "The Nuclear Taboo: The United States and the Normative Basis of Nuclear Non-Use." *International Organization* 53 (3): 433–68.

Tanzi, Vito. 1989. "The Impact of Macroeconomic Policies on the Level of Taxation and the Fiscal Balance in Developing Countries." *IMF Staff Papers* 36 (3): 633–57.

Tanzi, Vito. 1992. *Fiscal Policies in Economies in Transition.* International Monetary Fund.

Tanzi, Vito. 1994. "The IMF and Tax Reform." In *Tax Policy and Planning in Developing Countries*, edited by A. Bagchi and N. H. Stern. Oxford University Press.

Tanzi, Vito. 2014. "The Challenges of Taxing the Big." *Revista de Economía Mundial* 37: 23–40.

Tanzi, Vito, and Howell Zee. 2001. *Tax Policy for Developing Countries.* International Monetary Fund.

Tarrow, Sidney. 2019. "Comparison, Triangulation, and Embedding Research in History: A Methodological Self-Analysis." *Bulletin of Sociological Methodology* 141 (1): 7–29.

Tarrow, Sidney G. 2010. "Bridging the Quantitative-Qualitative Divide." In *Rethinking Social Inquiry: Diverse Tools, Shared Standards*, edited by Henry E Brady and David Collier. Rowman & Littlefield.

Tavory, Iddo, and Stefan Timmermans. 2013. "A Pragmatist Approach to Causality in Ethnography." *American Journal of Sociology* 119 (3): 682–714.

TCDIMF. 2021. *Toward Development-Centered Climate Change Policy at the International Monetary Fund.* Task Force on Climate, Development and the International Monetary Fund. https://www.bu.edu/gdp/files/2021/10/TF_Strategy-Report_FIN.pdf.

Terkper, Seth. 1996. *VAT in Ghana: Why It Failed.* Harvard Institute for International Development.

Thacker, Strom C. 1999. "The High Politics of IMF Lending." *World Politics* 52 (1): 38–75.

The Times of London. 2009. "Alan Tait: Economist Who Championed the Introduction of the VAT as a Representative of the International Monetary Fund." December 9. https://www.thetimes.co.uk/article/alan-tait-economist-who-championed-vat-hf3qvx00lq9.

Thiemann, Matthias, Carolina Raquel Melches, and Edin Ibrocevic. 2021. "Measuring and Mitigating Systemic Risks: How the Forging of New Alliances Between Central Bank and Academic Economists Legitimize the Transnational Macroprudential Agenda." *Review of International Political Economy* 28 (6): 1433–58.

Tilly, Charles. 1992. *Coercion, capital, and European states, AD 990–1992.* Blackwell.

Timmermans, Stefan, and Iddo Tavory. 2022. *Data Analysis in Qualitative Research: Theorizing with Abductive Analysis.* University of Chicago Press.

Tomsick, Emily, Julia Smith, and Clare Wenham. 2022. "A Gendered Content Analysis of the World Health Organization's COVID-19 Guidance and Policies." *PLOS Global Public Health* 2 (6): e0000640.

Tsingou, Eleni. 2015. "Club Governance and the Making of Global Financial Rules." *Review of International Political Economy* 22 (2): 225–56.

Tsingou, Eleni. 2022. "Effective Horizon Management in Transnational Administration: Bespoke and Box-Ticking Consultancies in Anti-money Laundering." *Public Administration* 100 (3): 522–37.

Ueda, Junji. 2017. "The Evolution of Potential VAT Revenues and C-Efficiency in Advanced Economies" (IMF Working Paper WP/17/158). International Monetary Fund.

UNCTAD. 2017. *Trade and Development Report—Beyond Austerity: Towards a Global New Deal.* United Nations Conference on Trade and Development.

UNHCR. 2010. "Guidance Note on Refugee Claims Relating to Victims of Organized Gangs." Accessed December 18, 2023. https://www.unhcr.org/us/media/unhcr-guidance-note.

UNHCR. 2012. "Guidelines on International Protection No. 9: Claims to Refugee Status Based on Sexual Orientation and/or Gender Identity." Accessed December 18, 2023. https://www.unhcr.org/fr-fr/en/media/unhcr-guidelines-international-protection-no-9-claims-refugee-status-based-sexual-orientation.

Union of International Associations. 2019. *Yearbook of International Organizations.* Union of International Associations.

Valdés, Juan Gabriel. 1995. *Pinochet's Economists: The Chicago School in Chile.* Cambridge University Press.

Van Gunten, Tod, John Levi Martin, and Misha Teplitskiy. 2016. "Consensus, Polarization, and Alignment in the Economics Profession." *Sociological Science* 3: 1028–52.

Van Gunten, Tod S. 2015a. "Cycles of Polarization and Settlement: Diffusion and Transformation in the Macroeconomic Policy Field." *Theory and Society* 44 (4): 321–54.

Van Gunten, Tod S. 2015b. "Washington Dissensus: Ambiguity and Conflict at the International Monetary Fund." *Socio-Economic Review* 15 (1): 65–84.

Van Houtven, Leo. 2002. *Governance of the IMF: Decision Making, Institutional Oversight, Transparency, and Accountability.* IMF Pamphlet Series 53. International Monetary Fund.

Van Houtven, Leo. 2004. "Rethinking IMF Governance." *Finance and Development* (September): 18–20.

Van Loon, Austin, and Jeremy Freese. 2023. "Word Embeddings Reveal How Fundamental Sentiments Structure Natural Language." *American Behavioral Scientist* 67 (2): 175–200.

Van Waeyenberge, Elisa, Hannah Bargawi, and Terry McKinley. 2013. "The IMF, Crises and Low-Income Countries: Evidence of Change?" *Review of Political Economy* 25 (1). Routledge: 69–90.

Vaubel, Roland. 1983. "The Moral Hazard of IMF Lending." *The World Economy* 6 (3): 291–304.

Velasco, Kristopher. 2023. "Transnational Backlash and the Deinstitutionalization of Liberal Norms: LGBT+ Rights in a Contested World." *American Journal of Sociology* 128 (5): 1381–1429.

Verdun, Amy. 1999. "The Role of the Delors Committee in the Creation of EMU: An Epistemic Community? *Journal of European Public Policy* 6 (2): 308–28.

Vestergaard, Jakob, and Robert Hunter Wade. 2013. Protecting Power: How Western States Retain the Dominant Voice in the World Bank's Governance. *World Development* 46: 153–64.

Vestergaard, Jakob, and Robert Hunter Wade. 2015. "Still in the Woods: Gridlock in the IMF and the World Bank Puts Multilateralism at Risk." *Global Policy* 6 (1): 1–12.
Vetterlein, Antje, and Manuela Moschella. 2014. "International Organizations and Organizational Fields: Explaining Policy Change in the IMF." *European Political Science Review* 6 (1): 143–65.
Vreeland, James Raymond. 2003. *The IMF and Economic Development*. Cambridge University Press.
Vreeland, James Raymond. 2007. *The International Monetary Fund: Politics of Conditional Lending*. Routledge.
de Vries, Margaret Garritsen. 1985. *The International Monetary Fund, 1972–1978: Cooperation on Trial; Vol. II: Narrative and Analysis*. International Monetary Fund.
de Vries, Margaret Garritsen. 1986. *The IMF in a Changing World, 1945–85*. International Monetary Fund.
Wade, Robert Hunter. 1996. "Japan, the World Bank, and the Art of Paradigm Maintenance: The East Asian Miracle in Political Perspective." *New Left Review* I/217: 3–36.
Wade, Robert Hunter. 1997. "Greening the Bank: The Struggle over the Environment, 1970–1995." In *The World Bank: Its First Half Century, Vol. II*, edited by John Prior Lewis, Devesh Kapur, and Richard Charles Webb. Brookings Institution Press.
Wade, Robert Hunter. 1998. "The Coming Fight over Capital Flows." *Foreign Policy* (113): 41–54.
Wade, Robert Hunter. 2003. "What Strategies Are Viable for Developing Countries Today? The World Trade Organization and the Shrinking of 'Development space.'" *Review of International Political Economy* 10 (4): 621–44.
Wade, Robert Hunter. 2009. "Accountability Gone Wrong: The World Bank, Non-governmental Organisations and the US Government in a Fight over China." *New Political Economy* 14 (1): 25–48.
Wade, Robert Hunter. 2013. "Protecting Power: Western States in Global Organizations." In *Global Governance at Risk*, edited by David Held and Charles Roger. Polity.
Wade, Robert Hunter, and Frank Veneroso. 1998. "The Asian Crisis: The High Debt Model Versus the Wall Street-Treasury-IMF Complex." *New Left Review* I/288: 3–24.
Wade, Robert Hunter, and Jakob Vestergaard. 2015. "Why Is the IMF at an Impasse, and What Can Be Done About It?" *Global Policy* 6 (3): 290–96.
Walder, Andrew, Andrew Isaacson, and Qinglian Lu. 2015. "After State Socialism." *American Sociological Review* 80 (2): 444–68.
Walter, Stefanie. 2021. "The Backlash Against Globalization." *Annual Review of Political Science* 24: 421–42.
Waltz, Kenneth N. 2000. "Structural Realism After the Cold War." *International Security* 25 (1): 5–41.
Watson, Maxwell, and Claus Regling. 1992. "History of the Debt Crisis." In *Current Legal Issues Affecting Central Banks, Volume I*, edited by Robert C. Effros. International Monetary Fund.
Weaver, Catherine. 2008. *Hypocrisy Trap: The World Bank and the Poverty of Reform*. Princeton University Press.
Weaver, Catherine, Mirko Heinzel, Samantha Jorgensen, and Joseph Flores. 2022. "Bureaucratic Representation in the IMF and the World Bank." *Global Perspectives* 3 (1): 39684.
Weaver, Catherine, and Manuela Moschella. 2017. "Bounded Reform in Global Economic Governance at the International Monetary Fund and the World Bank." In *International Politics and Institutions in Time*, edited by Orfeo Fioretos. Oxford University Press.
Wenham, Clare. 2019. "The Oversecuritization of Global Health: Changing the Terms of Debate." *International Affairs* 95 (5): 1093–1110.

Wenham, Clare, Joshua W. Busby, Jeremy Youde, and Asha Herten-Crabb. 2023. "From Imperialism to the 'Golden Age' to the Great Lockdown: The Politics of Global Health Governance." *Annual Review of Political Science* 26 (1): 431–50.

Westerwinter, Oliver, Kenneth W. Abbott, and Thomas Biersteker. 2021. "Informal Governance in World Politics." *The Review of International Organizations* 16 (1): 1–27.

Westphal, James D., and Ithai Stern. 2006. "The Other Pathway to the Boardroom: Interpersonal Influence Behavior as a Substitute for Elite Credentials and Majority Status in Obtaining Board Appointments." *Administrative Science Quarterly* 51 (2): 169–204.

White, Alexandre I. R. 2020. "Historical Linkages: Epidemic Threat, Economic Risk, and Xenophobia." *The Lancet* 395 (10232): 1250–51.

White, Alexandre I. R. 2023. *Epidemic Orientalism: Race, Capital, and the Governance of Infectious Disease*. Stanford University Press.

White, Harrison C. 2008. *Identity and Control: How Social Formations Emerge*. Princeton University Press.

Widmaier, Wesley W. 2007. "Where You Stand Depends on How You Think: Economic Ideas, the Decline of the Council of Economic Advisers and the Rise of the Federal Reserve." *New Political Economy* 12 (1): 43–59.

Widmaier, Wesley W., Mark Blyth, and Leonard Seabrooke. 2007. "Exogenous Shocks or Endogenous Constructions? The Meanings of Wars and Crises." *International Studies Quarterly* 51 (4): 747–59.

Wilensky, Harold L. 2002. *Rich Democracies: Political Economy, Public Policy, and Performance*. University of California Press.

Wilkerson, John, and Andreu Casas. 2017. "Large-Scale Computerized Text Analysis in Political Science: Opportunities and Challenges." *Annual Review of Political Science* 20 (1): 529–44.

Wimmer, Andreas. 2021. "Domains of Diffusion: How Culture and Institutions Travel Around the World and with What Consequences." *American Journal of Sociology* 126 (6): 1389–1438.

Woods, Ngaire. 2000. "The Challenge of Good Governance for the IMF and the World Bank Themselves." *World Development* 28 (5): 823–41.

Woods, Ngaire. 2004. "Accountability, Governance and the Reform of the IMF." In *The IMF and Its Critics: Reform of Global Financial Architecture*, edited by David Vines and Christopher L. Gilbert. Cambridge University Press.

Woods, Ngaire. 2006. *The Globalizers: The IMF, the World Bank, and Their Borrowers*. Cornell University Press.

Woods, Ngaire, and Domenico Lombardi. 2006. "Uneven Patterns of Governance: How Developing Countries Are Represented in the IMF." *Review of International Political Economy* 13 (3): 480–515.

World Bank. 2004. "2004 Annual Meetings of the Boards of Governors—Summary Proceedings." World Bank, October 3, 2004. https://documents.worldbank.org/en/publication/documents-reports/documentdetail/888061468324278229/2004-Annual-Meetings-of-the-Boards-of-Governors-summary-proceedings.

World Bank. 2015. "Speech by World Bank Group President Jim Yong Kim: Shared Prosperity: Equal Opportunity for All." World Bank, October 1, 2015. https://www.worldbank.org/en/news/speech/2015/10/01/speech-world-bank-group-president-shared-prosperity-equal-opportunity.

World Bank. 2021. "June 25, 1946: The World Bank Opens Its Doors." Video, June 23, 2021, 2:09. https://www.worldbank.org/en/news/video/2021/06/23/june-25-1946-the-world-bank-opens-its-doors.

Young, Kevin L., Seth K. Goldman, Brendan O'Connor, and Tuugi Chuluun. 2021. "How White Is the Global Elite? An Analysis of Race, Gender and Network Structure." *Global Networks* 21 (2): 365–92.

Zapp, Mike. 2017. "The Scientization of the World Polity: International Organizations and the Production of Scientific Knowledge, 1950–2015." *International Sociology* 55 (4): 413–34.

Zee, Howard H. 2000. "Retarding Short-Term Capital Inflows Through Withholding Tax." (IMF Working Paper no. 40). International Monetary Fund.

Zhu, David H., Wei Shen, and Amy J. Hillman. 2014. "Recategorization into the In-Group: The Appointment of Demographically Different New Directors and Their Subsequent Positions on Corporate Boards." *Administrative Science Quarterly* 59 (2): 240–70.

Zucman, Gabriel. 2015. *The Hidden Wealth of Nations*. University of Chicago Press.

Index

For the benefit of digital users, indexed terms that span two pages (e.g., 52–53) may, on occasion, appear on only one of those pages.

Tables, figures, and boxes are indicated by an italic *t*, *f*, and *b*.

abduction, dataset, time, and intersituational variation, 48, 61–63
abductive logic/reasoning, 1–2, 15–16, 46–49, 68, 97, 134–135, 168–169, 192, 218–219, 223, 225–226
academics, 17–18, 37, 87–89, 92, 101–103, 115, 152, 188
 as contrarians, 152
accounting firms, 228, 232
actorhood, 1, 3, 67–68, 162–163
ad hocism, 42–43, 232
agency, 27, 61, 82, 109
Al-Jasser, Muhammad, 184–185, 198–199
Article IV consultations, 119–121, 123, 179, 204
Articles of Agreement, 20, 81, 179–183, 185–192, 219
Asia and Pacific Department, 107*f*, 204
Asian Development Bank, 31–32, 226
Asian Infrastructure Investment Bank, 21–22, 233–234
Australia, 204–205
Austria, 89, 123
authority, 8, 13–14, 31, 65, 100, 227
 cognitive/epistemic/expert, 13–14, 86, 113, 225–226

Baker, James, 129–131
Baker Plan, 129–130
Barnett, Michael, 29–30
Belgium, 74, 89
benchmarking, 85–86, 109–110, 115, 132, 208, 227–228
Best, Jacqueline, 108–109, 113
Bhagwati, Jagdish, 165–166
Block-Lieb, Susan, 227–228

Board members, 17, 19–20, 26, 35–36, 38–39, 72–73, 81, 84–86, 94–96, 135–136, 144–145, 152, 155, 217–219, 228–230
 composition of, 86–92, 96, 162
 positions from word embeddings, Global North *vs.* Global South, 138–145, 162, 168–171, 173–182
Bourdieu, Pierre, 50
Brady Plan, 130–131
Brazil, 101, 121, 123, 128, 222
Bretton Woods, 13, 71–72, 73–74, 100–101, 123, 167, 233–234
bureaucracy, 4, 29–30, 37, 41, 67, 80, 100–101, 103, 122–123, 167, 221–222
Business people, 149, 155

C-efficiency (consumption efficiency), 208–209, 211–213, 222–223
Canada, 89, 191
Capacity Development, *see* Technical Assistance
capital account liberalization, 20, 110, 165–167, 176–182, 185–186, 189–193, 229
capital flight, 164–165, 167, 176, 184
capital mobility, 94–95, 164, 170
central bankers
 consensus among, 146–149, 155, 160, 163, 176, 219
 prevalence of, 92–94
 socialization of, 30, 145, 161, 176
Chile, 90, 185–186
China, 27–28, 72, 74–75, 89–90, 92–94, 110, 123, 222, 233–234
Chwieroth, Jeffrey, 104
Clark, Richard, 32, 158–160
Clift, Ben, 109

268 Index

climate change, 4, 7, 13–14, 21–22, 48–49, 53–54, 119, 155–156, 221, 223–225, 234
Colbert, Jean-Baptiste, 194–195
colonialism, 45–46, 195, 229–230, 232
conditionality, 82–83, 104, 124, 158, 160, 163, 202–203, 207–208
consultancies, 8, 21–22, 37, 41, 115, 122, 227–228, 232
Copelovitch, Mark, 35–36, 80–81

Dallara, Charles, 184, 190
Debt Sustainability Analysis, 111–113, 115, 221–222
deliberation, 3, 17, 34–36, 40–41, 57–58, 63–65, 80–81, 83, 137, 157, 161–162, 170, 234
Denmark, 52–53, 204
diffusion, 3, 7–9, 12, 27–29, 119–120, 122–123, 209
diversity, 3, 17, 38, 66–67, 102–103
Dooley, Michael, 184, 186
dual loyalists, 2–3, 10–11, 13–15, 38, 40–41, 96, 158, 219

École Nationale d'Administration, 87, 89–90
economic crises, 100–101, 114, 121–122, 127–129, 164, 189–192, 205–206, 222
economics schools of thought, 18
    Freshwater *vs.* Saltwater, 105–108, 123
Egypt, Arab Republic of, 121, 191
Eichengreen, Barry, 116–119
Eilstrup-Sangiovanni, Mette, 230–231
El-Khouri, Samir, 57, 59f
elite education, 72–73, 87, 89–90, 107, 145, 157, 229–230
enactment, 12, 27–28, 44–45
Enhanced Structural Adjustment Facility, 129–130, 132, 158, 160
epistemic communities, 8–9, 12, 15, 30, 31, 145
European Union, 196, 211–212
expertise, 3, 10–11, 30–31, 37–38, 40, 42–43, 72, 80, 85–86, 96, 100–102, 113, 124, 162–163, 183, 217–218, 227, 229, 231
extended computational case, 65, 134, 162, 233

Financial Sector Assessment Program, 108, 121–122
Financiers, *see* Business people
Finnemore, Martha, 15–16
Firth, John Rupert, 54
Fiscal Affairs Department, 21, 116, 195, 198–199, 200–203, 208–209, 212–213, 219–220, 222–223
Fischer, Stanley, 189–190
France, 74–75, 79–82, 89–90, 94, 196
Fransen, Luc, 228
Frenkel, Jacob, 184–185
Friedman, Milton, 104–105, 106–107
Fujino, Hirotake, 57

Gallagher, Kevin, 222
gatekeeping, 9–10, 25–26, 226–227
Gates Foundation, 230–231
Gavi, the Vaccine Alliance, 230–231
Geithner, Timothy, 111–113
gender, 3, 6, 13–14, 16–17, 49, 103–104, 220–221
Germany, 74–75, 80–81, 94
Global Fund against AIDS, Tuberculosis and Malaria, 231
global public health, 41–42, 67–68, 229–232
globalization, 1, 12–15, 21, 27–29, 45, 56–57, 71, 86, 166–167, 194–197, 211, 218–220, 232–234
goods and services tax, *see* value-added tax
Graz, Jean-Christophe, 227
group dynamics, 8–10, 38, 49–50, 123, 155, 157, 158–160, 162–163, 209

Haas, Ernst, 114
Halliday, Terence, 227–228
Harvard University, 89–90, 95, 105–107
Heavily Indebted Poor Countries, 111–113, 131–132, 137, 157–158, 161, 221–222
hegemony, 229
Henriksen, Lasse Folke, 106–107
Hofmann, Stephanie, 231
human rights, 48–49, 226–227

identity switching, 38–39
imperialism, 39, 45–46, 232
India, 27–28, 89–90, 110, 123, 187, 188–189, 191, 222
Indonesia, 74, 89, 189
inflation, 164–165, 204–205

informal governance, 10, 82–83, 84–85
inscription, 113
Institute of International Finance, 190
Institutionalization, 8–9, 14–15, 20–21, 27–28, 30, 55–56, 80–82, 119–120, 166–167, 185–186, 188–189, 191–192
Inter-American Development Bank, 132, 226
International Committee of the Red Cross, 226–227
International Energy Agency, 34–35
International Standards Organization, 227
International Telecommunications Union, 227
issue control, 42–43, 226–227
Italy, 75, 79, 89

Jacklin, Nancy, 57
Japan, 31–32, 57, 74–75, 80–81, 95, 122–123, 191, 196
Johnson, Juliet, 30
Joint Vienna Institute, 123–124, 211–212

Kaeser, Daniel, 161, 186–187
Kaya, Ayse, 53–54, 119
Keen, Michael, 203, 209
Keynes, John Maynard, 71–72, 164–165, 167, 171
Keynesianism, 18, 52–53, 105–109
Khaldun, Ibn, 195
Kiekens, Willy, 160
Kindleberger, Charles, 101, 103
Koo, Yee Chun, 72
Korea, Republic of, 92–94, 185–186, 189

Laffer curve, 195–196, 200–201, 203
Lakatos, Imre, 14
LeBaron, Genevieve, 228
legitimacy, 1, 4–5, 8–10, 26, 30, 33–34, 36–37, 39, 41, 45, 114, 121–122, 124, 165, 171, 188, 217, 220–221, 229
Levitt, Peggy, 27–28
LGBTI, 6–7, 25–26
Lissakers, Karin, 158–161, 186–188, 190–191
Littoz-Monnet, Annabelle, 229
London School of Economics, 89

Malaysia, 95, 187, 189
Malik, Rabia, 32
Martin, John Levi, 33–34

Massachusetts Institute of Technology, 105–107
Mauss, Marcel, 14
Merry, Sally, 27–28
Merton, Robert, 13
Mexico, 114, 127
Mikesell, Raymond, 73–74
ministry of finance, 92–94, 145–146, 149, 152, 155, 176–179, 186–187, 188–189, 206–208, 219–220
Mische, Ann, 109
Momani, Bessma, 121
monetarism, 104, 108–109, 184
moral hazard, 45–46, 140–146, 149, 152, 157, 158, 160
Moschella, Manuela, 167
multistakeholder initiatives, 21–22, 41, 44, 228
Mussa, Michael, 185

Nelson, Stephen, 50, 104–105, 107
neoclassical economics, 164–166, 229
neoliberalism, 13, 18, 31–32, 50, 87–89, 104–109, 204–205
New Zealand, 204–205, 206–207
non-governmental organizations, 7–9, 12, 44, 48–49, 226–227

optimal matching, *see* sequence analysis
Organisation for Economic Co-operation and Development, 119, 211–212

Palmason, Axel, 190
Paris Club, 128–129, 130–132
Paterson, Mat, 234
Pawlak, Patryk, 231
Peirce, Charles, 46–47
Philippines, 189, 205–206
Polak, Jacques, 116
Poland, 89, 207
political backlash, 3, 198–199
political salience, 31, 83–84, 86, 134–135, 206
populism, 233–234
Poverty Reduction and Growth Facility, *see* Poverty Reduction Strategy Papers
Poverty Reduction Strategy Papers, 111–113, 131–132
power politics, 10–12, 44–45, 149–152, 170–171, 197–198, 233

Princeton University, 89, 105–107
principal-agent framework, 32, 80–81, 138
professional networks, 9–11, 30, 87–89, 100, 211–212
professionalization, 17–18, 162–163, 208, 226–227
propaganda, 115–116, 196

rationalization, 6–7, 17–18, 26–27, 45, 90–91, 115, 138, 211–212
Reay, Mike, 53–54, 119
recognition, 8, 28–29, 39, 103, 195, 233–234
regularity of interaction, 42–43, 226
Reinhart, Carmen, 116–119
Reinsberg, Bernhard, 201–202
Reports on the Observance of Standards and Codes, 114–115
reputation, 30, 103, 132, 152, 227–228
Research Department, 132–133, 184–186, 199–200
Rickard, Stephanie, 35–36
rituals, 26, 79–80, 220–221
Rogoff, Kenneth, 138–140
Romania, 89, 121, 199–200, 207–208
Ruggie, John, 15–16, 46–47
Russian Federation, 74–75, 89, 187, 191, 222

Sarney, José, 128
Saudi Arabia, 74–75, 191, 198–199
Schäfer, Armin, 120–121
Sciences Po, 87, 89–90
scientization, 26, 33, 39–40, 44–46, 138, 146–149, 161, 175–176, 211–213, 219–220
script, definition, 4–6, 44
sequence analysis, as method, 50–52
Sliper, Ian, 206–207
socialization, 12, 19–20, 27, 29–30, 33–34, 90–92, 103–105, 108, 120, 145, 161, 168–169
Special Data Dissemination Standard, 114
standard-setting, 21–22, 114–115, 122, 208–209, 218–219, 221–222, 227–228
state capacity, 113, 194–195
status, of Board Members and technocrats, 38–39, 45–46, 101–103, 199, 206–207, 213
Stiglitz, Joseph, 101, 190
Stone, Randall, 32, 82–84

Structural Adjustment Facility, 129–130, 158, 160
Szczuka, Wieslaw, 207

Tait, Alan, 209–211, 210f
Tanzania, 199–200, 203
Tanzi, Vito, 116, 198–200, 207–209, 211–212
tariffs, 21, 194, 196–197, 199–200, 202–204, 205–206, 211, 212–213, 219–220
taxation, corporate and income, 21, 199–200, 201–202, 205–207, 211, 212–213, 219–220, 222–223, 233
Technical Assistance, 21, 101–102, 114, 122–123, 173–175, 179–182, 185–186, 190, 195, 196–197, 202–205, 222–223
Technocracy, mechanisms of, 6–7, 12, 15, 17–18, 29–31, 36–37, 40, 100–101, 102–104, 108–109, 114, 119–120, 122–123, 219–220
technocratic identity ('mini-Keynes'), 17–18, 101–102, 105, 108–109, 115
Thailand, 189, 191, 205–207
Training networks, 123, 211–212
transnational advocacy networks, 25–26
transparency, 114–115, 142–144, 221
Tulin, Dmitri, 187

Ukraine, 89, 123
UNAIDS, 230–231
United Nations, 35–36, 48–49, 73, 227–228
United Nations Framework Convention on Climate Change, 53–54
United Nations General Assembly, 16–17
United Nations Security Council, 82, 84
United States, 27–28, 184
University College London, 191
University of California at Berkeley, 89
University of California at Los Angeles, 105
University of Cambridge, 89–90
University of Chicago, 18, 87–90, 105–108, 184–185
University of Oxford, 89, 105–106
US Federal Reserve, 57, 94, 111–113, 116–119, 127–129
US Treasury, 57, 71–72, 74–75, 100–101, 111–113, 128–130, 165–166

value-added taxation, as replacement for tariffs, 194, 196, 211, 212–213, 219–220
vernacularization, 27–29, 34–35, 95, 218
voting in the IMF, 35–36, 73–74, 75–79, 80–81, 187–188, 217–218

Wade, Robert, 42, 165–166
White, Harry Dexter, 72–74
White, William H., 103
word embeddings, as method, 16–17, 53–55
word frequency analysis, as method, 53–54, 136

World Bank, 5–7, 19, 21–22, 32, 34–35, 41–42, 66–67, 71–72, 86, 104, 114–116, 120, 122, 131–133, 137, 157–158, 187, 233–234
World Health Organization, 16–17, 21–22, 32, 41–42, 48–49, 226, 230–231
World Intellectual Property Organization, 16–17, 34–35
world society, 8–9, 26–27, 33, 138, 146–149
World Trade Organization, 16–17, 34–35

www.ingramcontent.com/pod-product-compliance
Ingram Content Group UK Ltd.
Pitfield, Milton Keynes, MK11 3LW, UK
UKHW041054270426
470302UK00036B/93